D1345062

NINETEENTH CENTURY
BRITAIN

Nineteenth Century Britain
1815–1914

ANTHONY WOOD

ASSISTANT MASTER
AT WINCHESTER COLLEGE

LONGMANS

LONGMANS, GREEN AND CO LTD
6 & 7 CLIFFORD STREET, LONDON W I
THIBAULT HOUSE, THIBAULT SQUARE, CAPE TOWN
605–611 LONSDALE STREET, MELBOURNE C I
443 LOCKHART ROAD, HONG KONG
ACCRA, AUCKLAND, IBADAN
KINGSTON (JAMAICA), KUALA LUMPUR
LAHORE, NAIROBI, SALISBURY (RHODESIA)

LONGMANS, GREEN AND CO INC
I 19 WEST 40TH STREET, NEW YORK 18

LONGMANS, GREEN AND CO
20 CRANFIELD ROAD, TORONTO 16

ORIENT LONGMANS PRIVATE LTD
CALCUTTA, BOMBAY, MADRAS
DELHI, HYDERABAD, DACCA

First Published 1960

*Printed in Great Britain by Richard Clay and Company, Ltd.,
Bungay, Suffolk*

PREFACE

GREAT BRITAIN in the nineteenth century is not merely a highly colourful period of history in itself; it is also the background from which our own times have emerged. Unique in character, it consequently presents its own peculiar difficulties to the teacher. The tempo of change is far greater than that of any other period of history, its development more complex and the amount of recorded evidence positively overwhelming. The purpose of this book is simply to sketch some sort of introduction which may be of use to the sixth-form student before he moves on in his reading to more detailed and specialized works.

'The leaves of a tree delight us more than the roots,' wrote Tolstoy—a good maxim for any school history book. But the student who is beginning to take a serious interest in history quickly becomes aware of the interaction of political, social, and economic factors. The leaves of a tree may attract us, but the roots are ultimately inescapable. Thus in history, as in drama, the fascination of the story often lies in the tension between the individual and the circumstances of the time in which he lives, and I have accordingly tried to preserve a balance between the many striking personalities in which the period is so rich and the social and political background against which they played their various parts.

Naturally, a book of this sort, which aims primarily at elucidation, is always in danger of over-simplifying the story, particularly if the writer attempts to lay down a definite pattern of development over a period of a hundred years. I have, however, taken the risk of treating the subject in five chronological sections. These periods seem to me to have their own particular identity and may help to give some kind of conspectus of the whole century. If, on the other hand, the student is only aggravated by them, they will still not have been entirely pointless; it is always useful to have a hypothesis to demolish.

There is a further problem. The general background of Victorian life has acquired a name for respectability and conformity. Yet the whole period was a time of fierce intellectual questioning. In this country, never entirely free from the restraining force of Evangelicalism, a belief in the individual's right to decide upon his own scale of values grew more slowly than on the Continent, but, despite that, revolutionary notes echoed through every decade of the century. Here elucidation would seem to demand the insertion of the occasional isolated section on intellectual and cultural movements, but I have been loath to do this, since such sections tend to degenerate into a long catalogue of books and pictures. Instead, I have simply treated some of the significant trends of thought as an integral part of the background, alluding to the more important works in the course of the narrative and including a short list among the original sources in the Reading List at the end.

I am most grateful to Mr. N. Blakiston and to Mr. A. W. Mabbs of the Public Record Office for their assistance in working out the statistical table of the registered electorate before and after each of the Reform Acts, given at the end of the book. For the other figures in the statistical section I wish to thank Constable & Co., who allowed me to quote both from *Commerce and Industry*, Vol. II, Tables of Statistics, edited by W. Page, F.S.A., and from *The Growth of Modern England*, by G. Slater. There are many others to whom I am indebted, not only my own teachers, but also my colleagues and pupils, who have contributed more to this book than they probably realized at the time. Lastly, I should like to thank my wife for her unfailing encouragement and her endurance in putting up with the seamy side of authorship.

A. C. W.

Winchester, 1958

CONTENTS

Part III

THE AGE OF PALMERSTON, 1851–68

Part IV

THE AGE OF VICTORIAN DEMOCRACY, 1868–1901

Part V

PRELUDE TO THE TWENTIETH CENTURY, 1902–14

MAPS

many of the harsher Penal Laws against the Roman Catholics were repealed; the fiscal administration of the state was reorganized, governmental corruption cleared up, and the system of rule in British India reconstructed.

Much of this had been long overdue and, except for Pitt's unsuccessful attempt at Parliamentary reform, showed little awareness of the new industrial and agrarian problems that were to be foremost among the questions of the next century. Nevertheless, reform was in the air, and but for the war with France the course of English social history might have been very different. As it was, the French Revolution so alarmed the English governing classes that even the mildest measures of reform appeared to them as an attack on the existing society. The cost of living rose sharply and the demands of war inevitably gave a great impetus to the new industries in the northern towns, where the working classes lived amid a growing squalor. Thus a process of change which might have been more gradual, and possibly tempered by measures of reform, was considerably accelerated, presenting the post-war government with the problem of a fundamental readjustment.

After 1815 the growing vehemence of the discontented only strengthened the government's determination to defend the position of their own class. Soldiers returning to England after the rapid demobilization added to the numbers of hungry labourers, factory hands, and unemployed, while the factory-owners, conscious of a governmental system still strongly weighted in favour of the territorial magnates, represented another aspect of social unrest. Small wonder that the Tory government should have watched these manifestations with hostility; lacking any police force, as they did, it is, perhaps, remarkable that their measures were not sterner. They were convinced that if they gave way an inch, there was no knowing where the changes might end. In this they were certainly proved correct. The deadlock lasted eight years; when it began to break in 1822, a new era of change ensued whose repercussions continue to this day and which, coupled with an astonishing prosperity and a growing Empire, makes the nineteenth century the most remarkable in the whole course of British history.

INTRODUCTION

O N a morning in July 1815 a French brig, flying a flag of truce, put out from an island close to Rochefort and approached *H.M.S. Bellerophon*, which had been blockading the entrance to the port. A small boat was rowed over from the brig to the British ship, one last cry of '*vive l'empereur*' echoed across the water, and a few minutes later Napoleon Bonaparte, standing on the quarter-deck of the *Bellerophon*, formally surrendered himself to the British government. The Hundred Days, the epilogue to an extraordinary career, were over and Great Britain had at last emerged the victor from one of the most severe wars of her history.

The contrast, however, between her prestige abroad and her internal situation was striking, for the years after 1815 were to be a time of desperate discontent and turmoil at home. Many of the reasons for this lie back in the previous century. A stage in a country's development can seldom be clearly marked off by a single date. There is an overlapping in all processes of social change, since various aspects of society alter at different speeds. In one sense, the eighteenth century stretches far into the nineteenth; in 1815 the landed aristocracy were still the head of society and the control of national and local government lay almost entirely in their hands. In another sense, the nineteenth century reaches back into the eighteenth; long before the Revolutionary war an agrarian revolution had produced a large class of landless labourers, and an industrial revolution in the northern towns had created the beginnings of a proletariat and a new wealthy class of factory-owners.

In the same way the year 1815 is virtually meaningless for purposes of defining the character of governmental legislation, for although the nineteenth century may rightly be depicted as an age of reform, a number of measures had already been passed or attempted in the last years of the eighteenth century. Pitt's Bill for Parliamentary reform in 1785 failed. On the other hand,

I

THE AFTERMATH OF WAR, 1815–22

I

THE STATE OF THE KINGDOM IN 1815 (1)

1. A time of change

Hours of travel are a more significant measure than geographical miles in reckoning the size of a country. Until the eighteenth century the length and breadth of Great Britain could only be covered by journeys lasting many days or even weeks; different regions had been as remote from each other as foreign lands, and throughout the winters, when the few roads had become impassable, towns had held out almost in a state of siege. In the eighteenth century, however, these conditions began to change so strikingly that to contemporaries it must have seemed as if the whole island were shrinking rapidly.

The main incentive for improving communications was economic. The transportation of goods by river or sea was expensive and inconvenient, and when, in the middle of the century, the construction of the Duke of Bridgewater's famous canal halved the price of coal in Manchester, the building of artificial waterways appeared to be such a good investment that by 1800 the north and the midlands were threaded with 3,000 miles of them. By the same date the country had been covered by a network of highroads, in the hands of over a thousand turnpike trusts; although the bulk of the merchants' goods continued to go by water until the railway age, wagons could now take the place of pack-horses on the roads, and the stage-coach, protected by its guard with his blunderbuss ready for highwaymen, had become a part of the English scene. In 1774 Parson Woodforde could travel the hundred miles from Oxford to Somerset in a single day, and by 1796 the run from London to Glasgow took no more than sixty-three hours.

Nevertheless, to our eyes today life in most parts of the country

4

would still have seemed utterly remote. Travel was expensive, and towns and villages off the main roads were as isolated as ever. When, in 1794, Sydney Smith became curate of Netheravon on Salisbury Plain, the most exciting event of the week was the arrival of the butcher's cart from Salisbury. 'Nothing can equal the profound, the immeasurable, the awful dullness of this place.' The bleak loneliness of Haworth parsonage on the Yorkshire moors to which Patrick Brontë took his family in 1820 is familiar to all readers of his daughter Emily's *Wuthering Heights*. Personal contact was still sufficiently rare for letter-writing to remain an art. The government had recently established a very limited system of semaphore, but in the main, news travelled at the speed of a horse and great events lacked that sense of closeness that we know today. It is not altogether surprising that in all the novels of Jane Austen, written at Chawton, some twenty-five miles from the south coast, there is virtually no mention of that titanic struggle with Napoleon which was raging as she wrote.

Another fundamental factor at this time was the astonishing change in population.[1] The first official census was not taken until 1801, and figures before this are unreliable. Very roughly it seems that between 1600 and 1750 the population of England and Wales rose from 5 to $6\frac{1}{2}$ million. But from 1750 to 1801 it rose from $6\frac{1}{2}$ to 9 million. By 1811 it was 10 million, by 1821 12 million. The reason for this extraordinary rise was not an increase in the birth-rate—or at least not primarily. The cause was a sharp drop in the death-rate of children. In the first half of the eighteenth century 75% of children born alive had died before their sixth year. By the beginning of the nineteenth century this mortality rate had dropped to about 40%. Improved medical science was partly responsible for this; inoculation against smallpox was now possible, and the devastating epidemics of earlier centuries were less frequent. Sounder methods of farming and the construction of new roads were another reason, since fresh meat and milk were becoming available in the towns during the winter and the inhabitants no longer lived in fear of scurvy.

[1] See Statistics, p. 449.

The increase in population was accompanied by a radical shift in its centre of gravity. At the beginning of the eighteenth century three-fifths of the people lived south of a line drawn from the Bristol Channel to the coast of Suffolk. By the beginning of the nineteenth century this distribution had altered beyond recognition. The increased trade of the Atlantic ports and the prospects of employment in the new industrial towns had brought about a great migration towards the west and the north, in addition to an influx of Irish. In the last years of the eighteenth century Manchester grew from 50,000 to well over 100,000 inhabitants, Oldham from a village of 400 to a town of 20,000, Bolton from 5,000 to 17,000, Leeds from 17,000 to 53,000. These were some of the textile towns. The iron towns developed more slowly, Glasgow, Sheffield, and Birmingham only doubling their population in the second half of the eighteenth century.

London was the one city of the south that continued to show any comparable increase. By 1801 its population had risen to just under a million. The metropolis reached out north of the river to include Paddington, Islington, and Bethnal Green. South of the river there was a smaller urban area around Southwark and Rotherhithe. The Thames was crossed by three bridges—Blackfriars, Westminster, from which Wordsworth had written his great sonnet, and old London bridge, which dated back to 1209, although now cleared of all its houses. To the west of this last, where its nineteen broad piers impeded the tidal flow, the river sometimes froze, and fairs were held on the ice. To some London's relentless sprawl seemed alarming—the 'great Wen' William Cobbett called it; yet the thirty years before the Revolutionary war had been a golden age of building. The Adam brothers, Sir William Chambers, George Dance, Henry Holland, and James Wyatt had each made their contribution to Georgian London. Some of their work, such as Chambers' Somerset House, still stands, and a colourful record of the sights of the time is preserved in Ackermann's *Microcosm*, published in 1808. Ackermann was a German bookseller who, from his shop in the Strand, engaged Thomas Rowlandson and Auguste Pugin, a French *émigré*, to produce a hundred illustrations of London, and from these pictures one may cover the whole span of society, from the decorous interiors of St. James's Palace and Carlton House to the madhouse of St. Luke's Hospital and the chapel of Newgate Prison.

If the cities were changing, so, too, was the face of the country-side. The English landscape that we know today, the patchwork quilt of fields enclosed by trees and hedges, is a piece of historical evidence as compelling as any document. In many parts of England the social unit in the countryside, dating back to the Middle Ages, had been the peasant village surrounded by its two or three great open fields and an area of waste land. The cultivator held a variety of strips scattered over each open field. These strips were farmed independently, but between harvest and sowing time the whole field was used communally for pasture. One year in three one open field was left fallow. The waste land was to some extent common property for wood-gathering and fishing, but the extent to which it could be used as pasture often depended on the number of strips of land that a man held in the open field. The whole system was thus far from being communist, but the village with its fields did make up a social entity in which every man had his place. 'Many of these humble sons of the hills', wrote Words-worth of the yeomen in the Lake District, 'had a consciousness that the lands which they walked over and tilled had for more than five hundred years been possessed by men of their name and blood.'

For three centuries this mediaeval system, which was to be found in many parts of Europe, had been succumbing to a gradual attack. So long as the purpose of farming was simply to provide enough food for a man's family and to make a little money by selling his surplus produce to the nearby town, the open field was an adequate arrangement. It was, however, wasteful and in-elastic, and with the development of greater commercial possibi-lities it was natural that the wealthier and more enterprising landlord should wish to reorganize it on a more profitable basis. In the sixteenth century the expansion of the cloth industry had resulted in strip-holders being bought out or evicted so that enclosed fields might be used for sheep-grazing. In the eighteenth century the landed nobility, conscious of the new wealth of the commercial classes, were seriously turning to the development of their estates as a source of income. There was by now a great scientific interest in the improvement of farming methods. In 1731 Jethro Tull published the results of some thirty years of research in his book *The New Horse Hoeing Husbandry*. His ideas were not always sound, but they inspired others to experiment, such as Lord Townshend, the Marquess of Rockingham, the Duke of Bedford, and others, and by the middle of the eighteenth century a new class of gentleman farmer was emerging. A well-known example is Coke of Holkham, who increased the annual worth of his estate from £2,000 to £20,000.

This improved agriculture, invaluable in one respect to the nation, could be carried out only at the expense of the open-field system. Throughout the eighteenth century a growing number of Enclosure Acts were passed in Parliament—2,921 between 1750 and 1810. The process was a simple one, entirely in the favour of the great landowner. A petition was prepared, whose signatories had to represent four-fifths of the land to be enclosed; thus the poorer peasants, whose lands together probably did not amount to more than one-fifth of the whole, could be ignored. The petition was then presented to Parliament, where a Bill was drafted and usually passed. After this a small group of commissioners, often nominated by the petitioners, made the detailed arrangements for the enclosure. Technically this should have meant that the strips were simply rearranged so that each man's holdings were put together to make one enclosed field. The waste land was also included in this calculation. The commissioners saw to it, however, that their patrons gained the richest land, and since the smaller stripholders could not afford to fence their new plot, they were usually bought out—or evicted, if they had difficulty in proving a legal right to their original holdings.

The consequences of this agrarian revolution were enormous. The yeoman with his tiny stake in the community was disappearing fast. He had become a landless labourer, dependent on wages, and, when these were insufficient, drifting to the towns for employment in the new factories, or sometimes emigrating to America. Peasant villages were vanishing from the land.

> Ill fares the land, to hastening ills a prey,
> Where wealth accumulates, and men decay,

wrote Oliver Goldsmith in his poem *The Deserted Village*. 'I look around and see no other house than mine,' said the Earl of Leicester. 'I am like the ogre in the tale, and have eaten up all my neighbours.'

The French war emphasized the advantages and disadvantages of these changes. The new farming gave Britain a greatly improved supply of food, but inevitable wartime shortages, combined with a succession of bad harvests, sent prices up to a level which threatened the dispossessed wage-earning peasantry with starvation. Rabbits, hares, and pheasants were abundant, but it was illegal to kill game without a licence and the landowner could set man-traps to catch the poacher. The Game Laws became increasingly severe during the war and by the Act of 1816 the poacher ran the risk of a sentence of seven years' transportation. By Gilbert's Act of 1782 the able-bodied poor were not to be sent to the workhouse, but were to be given work by the parish. The Roundsman system meant that the labourer went the round of the parish, where the farmers were forced to employ him, although the bulk of his wages was paid out of the poor rate. The consequence of this was that the farmer would never employ free labour if roundsmen were available, and a man was driven to become dependent upon the parish before he could gain employment. This naturally sent the poor rate up, an added burden to the poorer farmer, who was thus indirectly subsidizing his richer neighbour. The Speenhamland system, introduced in 1795, only served to intensify this process. The Berkshire magistrates, meeting at the Pelican Inn at Speenhamland to find some method of regulating wages, proposed a scale of assistance whereby a man's wages were to be supplemented out of the poor rate according to the price of bread and the size of his family. This system, humane as it might sound, had the effect of pauperizing most labourers and was a direct encouragement to the farmer not to increase the wages that he paid.

Thus to many the 'dark satanic mills' were preferable to hungry humiliation for themselves and their families in 'England's green and pleasant land'; yet, when they moved to the new towns, it seemed as if they had only exchanged one evil for another, for here they found themselves at the mercy of the most remarkable revolution of all.

2. The Industrial Revolution

The significance of the Industrial Revolution may be summed up as a momentous change from an agrarian to an industrial society. Its causes are far more difficult to put in a nutshell, and it would be wrong to be too precise about them. It is not enough to say that technical discoveries were the natural outcome of man's inventiveness. There had often been inventions before and, in any case, the devising of some new machine was not necessarily followed by its general adoption. It has also sometimes been suggested that the rapid increase in population at home meant a greater market and labour force; yet, while this may have been a necessary condition, it could hardly have been decisive as a cause. Indeed, the invention of machines would rather imply a shortage of workers. A rising population need not mean increased production, and the history of Ireland and of the Far East has shown that Nature has a short way with over-population.

At best, it is possible to suggest a number of factors which, taken together, help the historian to gain some understanding of this revolution, although the list can never be entirely closed. First among these was a new demand for marketable goods. The eighteenth century had seen a remarkable growth of commercial activity in England and France; this meant increasing competition for markets and trading connections in Europe, Africa, and Asia. The loss of the American colonies had forced British business men to look elsewhere, although it became apparent within a few years of American independence that the United States was vitally in need of British trade. Later still, Napoleon's Continental System had encouraged the opening up of South American markets. But markets were no use without sufficient goods to sell, and the British manufacturer was faced with an ever-increasing demand, which could hardly be met. The iron works were suffering from the rising cost of charcoal needed for smelting the ore, and cottage spinning was no longer economical. 'It was no uncommon thing', wrote a contemporary of the 1760s, 'for a weaver to walk three or four miles in the morning and call on five or six spinners before he could collect weft to serve him for the remainder of the day.'

The need for inventions followed naturally from this. Some of the expedients that were hit upon were little more than gadgets, but there was, too, a definite exploration of possibilities according to scientific principles. In this the change that had overcome scientific thought during the previous hundred and fifty years was an important factor. The new experimental methods of the 'pure scientists' and the efforts of local inventors and industrialists went hand in hand.

There were other circumstances that were particularly favourable to the development of industry in Great Britain. The country had known a long period of political and social stability. The business man enjoyed a system of government under which he had a good chance of feathering his own nest; in 1780 Burke had gone so far as to call the House of Commons 'a confused and scuffling bustle of local agency'. There were none of the internal customs barriers that hindered the Continental merchant, and during the eighteenth century governmental regulation of industrial employment had seldom been enforced and in some parts of the country —significantly in Lancashire and the West Riding of Yorkshire— was practically non-existent. The development of new techniques in banking and a greater experience in the handling of credit were other factors that gave the country an increasing advantage over its rivals. Most important of all, years of successful commerce had caused a considerable amount of capital to accumulate, and since rates of interest on loans had been slowly falling throughout the eighteenth century, the capital without which the most enterprising business man could have done little was not merely available, but was also cheap.

The revolution in the production of cotton goods illustrates most simply the general nature of the change. A series of inventions gradually began to take spinning out of the home into the factory. Hargreave's multiplied spinning-wheel, Arkwright's water-frame, and Crompton's mule were all steps in the direction of enormously increasing the amount and improving the quality of thread that one person could spin. It only needed the application of steam power to the machines, first attempted in 1785, for spinning to have passed almost entirely into the factory. This naturally greatly increased the demand for raw cotton, which would not have been forthcoming, had not Eli Whitney's invention of the cotton-gin completely revolutionized the output of the southern States in America.

The fear of new machines which would bring unemployment has often been stressed and was not unjustified, but it is impossible to generalize about the whole of the working population in this period. The vastly increased amount of thread spun opened up tremendous possibilities for hand-loom weavers, and at the beginning of the nineteenth century these were among the most prosperous of the working classes. A contemporary told of a soldier who, while at home on leave from the war, made enough money to buy his discharge from the Army. Muslin weavers took on all the airs of a new middle class and, it was said, swaggered about with five-pound notes stuck in their hat-bands. This was not to last. A satisfactory power-loom took longer to perfect, but by 1813 2,400 were in use and by 1829 55,000, and the later sufferings of the hand-loom weavers are among the most deplorable aspects of the early nineteenth century.

The discoveries affecting the production of iron meant not merely an enormous increase in output, but were also indirectly an essential factor in the development of many other industries involving the use of iron. At the beginning of the eighteenth century charcoal had been used both for smelting iron ore in the furnace to make pig-iron and for converting the pig-iron into bar iron in the forge. Production had been declining owing to the rising cost of charcoal, since in the past it had been found impracticable to use coal. Then Abraham Darby's discovery that coked coal might be used in the furnaces for producing pig-iron led rapidly to a great increase in iron output. The use of coal in the forges and new processes of puddling and rolling followed, and shortly afterwards the application of steam power to the bellows, hammers and rollers meant that iron-works were no longer tied to river sides for water-power and began to congregate in the area of the coalfields of the Black Country and between the Firth of Clyde and the Firth of Forth. Between 1788 and 1794 the annual output of pig-iron rose from 50,000 to 100,000 tons, and there seemed no limit to the number of commodities that could be made in iron; the ironmaster John Wilkinson was even buried in an iron coffin.

This remarkable development in industrialist capitalism, coupled with her naval supremacy, unchallenged after Trafalgar, established Great Britain's position in the world during the first half of the nineteenth century. Even during the period of the Revolutionary and Napoleonic wars her foreign export trade was trebled, and when peace was restored the British manufacturer stood half a century ahead of his Continental rivals. Raw materials, markets, and command of the sea routes all lay in Britain's grasp. By 1815 Amsterdam had given up the struggle and London was the banking centre of the world, and after 1819 the notes of the Bank of England enjoyed a unique position throughout Europe.

The hero in this victory was as much the business man as the inventor. The new industrialist had to turn his hand to every aspect of his business; he had to sense future requirements of the public, to coordinate all stages of production, to organize and train his labour force, and to handle his own finances. He was not always the ogre that has sometimes been suggested; firms were still sufficiently small for the owner to be in daily contact with his employees, and working conditions were not necessarily worse than those of cottage industry, over which historians have sometimes grown sentimental. Thrift and hard work were the most striking characteristics of these industrialists. Merchants, small property owners, and yeomen were all represented among them —particularly Scotsmen and Dissenters, aided perhaps by their excellent schools and, in the case of the Dissenters, spurred on by their exclusion from the professions.[1]

The process was cumulative—coal for the iron-works, iron for machinery and steam engines in the cotton-mills and the mines. Into the towns poured men with their families seeking employment, and so the towns expanded into great ugly agglomerations of buildings, back to back, with few windows and no drainage. Courtyards were often inches deep in sewage, cleared once or twice a year in carts and emptied into the river. Water had to be taken from an outside tap which might run for a few hours on certain days of the week. Improvement Commissioners, established by various Acts of Parliament during the eighteenth century, were quite unable to cope with the new conditions, and it was hardly surprising that typhus should be endemic and that there should be occasional outbreaks of typhoid. There had been nothing like it before. The growth of these towns was so rapid and the extent of government action that would have been needed to control it so far beyond the conception of the times that one has an appalling sense of inevitability when considering these frightful slums. It was private enterprise at its very worst.

From these airless, stinking hovels men, their wives, and their children set out to work as long as fourteen hours a day in the factories and the mines. Children often had to work from the age of five simply because even the tiny wage that they earned was needed to give the family enough to eat; sometimes the authorities would allow no poor relief until the children had been sent to work, and, once at the factory, parents and overseers beat them to keep them awake during the long hours. Women and children also worked in the damp and darkness of the coal-mines, where conditions were appalling and accidents frequent. Until 1815, in Northumberland and Durham, inquests were not normally held on the victims. In many collieries the miners worked under a 'butty', a contractor who, in agreement with the proprietor of the mine, hired the labour and supplied the equipment. Sometimes the butty organized his own 'truck' shop, where the miners re-

---

[1] See p. 20.

ceived part of their pay in goods; often he was also the local pub-
lican, which gave him an extra hold over his men.

As prices soared and wages lagged further and further behind,
so the position of families living in one squalid room became more
desperate. While the countrymen could only accept poor relief,
the factory workers might have hoped to gain an increase in wages
—or at least to reduce the hours of work—by organizing themselves in combinations and threatening to strike. But in 1799, in
response to a petition from the master millwrights, the House of
Commons passed a Combination Act which made this form of
negotiation illegal. It is indicative of the many different con-
ceptions of reform at this time that one of the statesmen mainly
responsible for this piece of legislation was William Wilberforce,
the passionate enemy of slavery and the Slave Trade. Under the
Act any workman combining with any other to get an increase of
wages was liable to be imprisoned for three months. Protests
were sent in from all parts of the country to Parliament; William
Cobbett wrote a scathing public letter to Wilberforce, but the
Combination Laws remained in force until 1824. The government had abandoned the factory workers to their employers, and
the masters, now in a position to threaten their workmen with
imprisonment if they objected to their rate of pay, were able even
to reduce their wages.

No simple sweeping statement of the condition of the poor in
the towns and the country can safely be made. There were factory-owners who treated their workmen decently. Conditions in
London, the largest city of all, were better than in many of the
towns of the north. The countryside was not one vast scene of
expropriation, and William Cobbett, that biting critic of the
times, could note, as he rode through the shires of England, that
labourers 'lived comfortably in Sussex' and that Gloucester, 'a
fine clean beautiful place', was largely a county of small independent farmers.

But the picture as a whole is a depressing one. The country was
in the grip of changes more fundamental than it had ever known
before in its history, and the fear of revolution encouraged the

ruling classes to retain an iniquitously harsh criminal code. A
man could be hanged for any one of over 200 offences, including
stealing five shillings from a shop, and it was only after the turn
of the century that the punishment for pick-pockets was changed
from death to transportation for life.

> Men of England, wherefore plough
> For the lords who lay ye low?
> Wherefore weave with toil and care
> The rich robes your tyrants wear?

So wrote Shelley in 1819, and it was only to be expected that the
men of England, reinforced by the returning demobilized soldiers,
should more and more insistently ask the same questions.

2

THE STATE OF THE KINGDOM IN 1815 (2)

1. The social classes: education and religion

A T the top of the social pyramid the aristocracy and wealthy
landed families continued to enjoy that pleasant round of
elegance and entertainment that had been the unquestioned
privilege of their class throughout the eighteenth century. Their
world was one of good talk, good food, and an easy intimacy with
the great men of their day. Spacious country houses and the Sea-
son in London were the background of their lives, their pastimes
Newmarket, the prize-ring, Brook's or White's club, and the
occasional visit to the fashionable resorts of Brighton or Bath. It
was a small society, assured, uninhibited, and with a natural good
taste in building and furniture.

Land and birth were the main qualifications of those within the
charmed circle, yet theirs was far from being a closed order.
Throughout the eighteenth century successful business men had
bought their country estates, sent their sons to Eton and on the
Grand Tour, acquired control of a seat in the Commons for their
family, or perhaps seen their children marry into the aristocracy.
The upper classes were constantly renewing themselves from the
stock of merchants, bankers, successful soldiers, and 'nabobs', who
had made their fortune in the East India Company. A man had to
be lucky to climb from small beginnings to the very top, but in
two or three generations it was often done. The story of the rise
of the Pitt family is well known. Lord Eldon, Lord Chancellor of
England until 1827, and his brother Lord Stowell, a prize-court
judge, were the sons of a coal-factor at Newcastle-on-Tyne. Sir
John Moore was the son of a Glasgow doctor, and Nelson was
by no means the only great sailor whose background was a
humble country parsonage. Sydney Smith was a man of simple

17

middle-class origin, endowing his wife on his marriage with all his worldly goods, 'six small silver teaspoons', but his wit and his active pen gave him the entrée to Holland House and the acquaintance of the social *élite*. Among the architects Sir John Soane, designer of the Bank of England, rose from poverty, and Henry Holland was a builder's son. Ability—and the luck to be able to demonstrate it—could take a man very far. To this fluidity was due England's fundamental stability; a society in which ambitious able men have a good chance to rise is not one that is likely to succumb to violent revolution.

Between the upper classes and the labourers and industrial workers lay all the varying degrees of 'middling folk'. In the counties the wealthier tenant farmers were beginning to ape the gentry, riding to hounds and bringing up their daughters in a new atmosphere of gentility. One of the most striking developments in English society at this time was the growth of government stock-holders. By 1829 they numbered as many as 275,000, and of those over 90% enjoyed an annual income of not more than £200, forming a class of slightly impecunious *rentier* brilliantly depicted in Mrs. Gaskell's *Cranford*. Work by now was hardly deemed lady-like, and a careful respectability had become an over-riding social consideration long before the accession of Queen Victoria.

The circulation of newspapers was mainly restricted to the upper and middle classes by their price—normally sevenpence a copy, owing to a tax of fourpence. There were also a variety of journals, such as the Whig *Edinburgh Review* and the Tory *Quarterly*. Cobbett's *Political Register* managed to escape the tax by concentrating on political commentaries, but otherwise the poor had to be content with cheap newspapers that circulated surreptitiously. No official censorship of the Press was enforced, but there were many prosecutions for seditious or blasphemous libel, as, for example, when Leigh Hunt suffered two years' imprisonment for a violent attack on the Prince Regent in the *Examiner*.

The education of children varied enormously according to class. There were no state institutions of any kind. Dame schools and charity schools gave instruction in the three R's, and schools of industry had been established, primarily to teach pauper children a trade. But despite a growing interest in education, illiteracy was widespread, and the possibility of state aid to educational societies was prevented for a long time by a deadlock between the Anglicans and Nonconformists over the kind of religious instruction to be given in the schools thus supported.

Secondary education was similarly incoherent. The endowed grammar schools took in a number of fee-paying pupils, but the details of curriculum, as well as the salaries of the teachers, laid down in their statutes, belonged to an earlier age. In the middle-class paradise of the later half of the nineteenth century a public-school education was to play an essential part in turning the sons of the new rich into gentlemen and was thus to become the basis of a great social cleavage. At the beginning of the century this was not so. Most of the places were free and quite a number of local tradesmen sent their sons to them. A boy at a public school would make contacts that, in an age of patronage, might be useful to him in later life, but the lack of a public school education was not in itself a handicap. The upper classes might make use of a public or a grammar school, or their children might be educated privately; it was all largely a question of convenience.

Indeed, public schools at this time were hardly attractive institutions. Living conditions for the boarders were appallingly hard, and the playing-fields of Eton were a very suitable prelude to the field of battle. 'Have you had a rebellion lately?' asked George III of a young Etonian. At Rugby the door of the headmaster's study was blown in and his books burnt. At Winchester, in 1793, the boys held the College for two days and the red flag flew from Middle Gate; in 1818 troops had to be called in to put them down. There were also the private schools, exclusive but less expensive. Dickens' *Nicholas Nickleby*, Thackeray's *Vanity Fair*, and Charlotte Brontë's *Jane Eyre* all include pictures of these depressing establishments. As for Oxford and Cambridge, these had both been virtually moribund, but an overhaul of the examination system at Oxford at the beginning of the nineteenth century included the setting up of two Honours Schools in Classics and Mathematics, in which Peel and Gladstone were each to gain double firsts.

On the whole, education was in a poor state throughout the

country. Only two bright spots can be seen. Scottish education at this time was far ahead of the English system. A statute of 1696 had provided for a schoolmaster to be set up in every parish, from whom boys might pass on to a number of good secondary day schools in the towns. From these they could move on to the Universities at Edinburgh, Glasgow, and St. Andrews and the two colleges at Aberdeen, at all of which they had the advantage of a much wider and more flexible range of subjects than existed at Oxford or Cambridge. The other bright spot was the Dissenter Academies, established owing to the statutory exclusion of Dissenter teachers from English secondary schools and Universities.[1] It was not uncommon, as a consequence, for English boys to be sent to Scottish schools and for Anglican parents to send their children to Dissenter Academies.

Religious disabilities by this time were greater in theory than in fact. The laws which prevented Roman Catholics from practising their religion had long ceased to be imposed, and in the 1780s and 90s a large number of these had been repealed. Many civil disabilities, however, remained; they were excluded from the higher posts of most professions, the services, and all governmental or local office, as well as from both Houses of Parliament. Similar disabilities hampered the Nonconformists, but they were allowed to sit in Parliament and, since 1727, annual Indemnity Acts had made it possible for them to hold office, so that their position was more tolerable.

The Anglican Church in England was headed by two archbishops and twenty-six bishops, all nominally appointed by the Crown—in fact, by the Prime Minister. Most of these were either of noble birth or had been tutors to the nobility. Of the lower clergy, about 1,500 livings were within the gift of the bishops—useful for providing for sons and sons-in-law—but the bulk of the patronage was in the hands of landowners and corporate bodies such as public schools and Oxford and Cambridge colleges, and this sometimes resulted in a living remaining within the same family for over a hundred years.

[1] Only Anglicans could enter Oxford as undergraduates. At Cambridge Nonconformists could study, but were excluded from taking degrees.

The income of the Church of England came from three main sources—rent from land, the tithe which all farmers in the parish had to pay, regardless of their own religious beliefs, and the Church rate, which was another local tax for the upkeep of the church building. Few of the bishops could complain of financial hardship, although there were great differences in their incomes. Canterbury and Durham were each worth £19,000 a year and London £15,000, while Rochester brought in as little as £1,500. In contrast to the bishops, the lower clergy were usually poorly paid, unless the living itself chanced to be well endowed. Curates were occasionally forced to become farmers as well. The consequence of this was pluralism. On Sundays the vicar would ride from church to church, but when the weather was wet it was said that Doctor Drop was taking the service, and in country parishes Holy Communion was often celebrated only three or four times a year. In all, out of 11,000 livings, there were 6,000 where the incumbent was non-resident.

The Anglican Church stood for the established order of things, its hierarchy being an integral part of the social and political framework. Such a body was hardly likely to encourage the emotionalism of religious revival. She was 'religious without enthusiasm', runs the eighteenth-century memorial of one worthy lady in a country church in Hampshire; there could have been no higher praise. But by the beginning of the nineteenth century a new feeling was beginning to stir within the Church. It was inspired by the violent force of Methodism, the great religious storm of the eighteenth century; the idea that a man's religion should govern his everyday life and should drive him to champion the humble and oppressed certainly smacked of enthusiasm. Gradually laymen and clergy of the Low Church were touched with this new spirit, and their energy lies behind much of the movement towards reform later in the century. The Evangelicals, with their centres at Clapham and Cambridge, brought the fire of eighteenth-century Methodism to the Anglican Church, and the cathedral closes of England could slumber no longer.

2. The system of government

The central point in the system of government was the legal concept of King-in-Parliament, whereby all legislation had to receive the consent of the King and of a majority in the House of Lords and the Commons. Both Houses met in the old Palace of Westminster. The Lords, about 360 in all, sat in the Court of Requests. Elevation to the peerage had become the normal way of rewarding supporters of the government as well as distinguished servants of the state. While Pitt had been Prime Minister as many as 109 new peers had been created, among whom were included generals, admirals, and manufacturers. Since 1707 sixteen had represented the aristocracy of Scotland, chosen at each general election by all the Scottish peers, while by the Irish Act of Union of 1800 twenty-eight Protestant Irish peers were elected for life.

Since the reign of Edward VI the Commons had met in the Chapel of St. Stephen, later panelled by Sir Christopher Wren. A picture in Ackermann's *Microcosm* shows the members facing each other on long, green-cushioned seats down the sides of the rectangular hall; the mace lies on the table in the middle in front of the wigged Speaker presiding in his chair. There were 658 members [1]—489 for England, twenty-four for Wales, forty-five for Scotland, and, since the Act of Union in 1800, 100 for Ireland. The advent of the Irish members necessitated certain structural changes which, however, still left the chamber very cramped.

> There we are, crammed into this little hole [wrote Cobbett] squeezing one another, treading upon each other's toes, running about to get a seat, going to the House at seven o'clock in the morning, as I do, to stick a bit of paper with my name on it on a bench to indicate that I mean to sit there for that day; then routed out of those places again after a division has taken place and running and scrambling for a seat in just the same manner as people do when they are let into a dining room at a public dinner at the Crown and Anchor or elsewhere.

[1] See Statistics, p. 452.

Holders of certain minor offices were excluded from sitting in
the House, but the major restrictions were concerned with religion and property. The machinery of the religious restrictions
consisted of a series of oaths that a member had to swear before
taking his seat. These included the oaths of supremacy and
allegiance, an oath of abjuration of any Pretender to the throne,
and, since 1678, a full declaration against transubstantiation. Practising Jews and Roman Catholics were thus naturally excluded
from sitting in either House. Quakers, however, who would not
swear an oath, were allowed to make an affirmation. A property
qualification had only been imposed since 1710, but the principle
that it involved had always been implicit in English Parliaments.
'There could be no truer maxim in our government than this,'
wrote Swift to Pope in 1721, 'that the possessors of the soil are the
best judges of what is to the advantage of the kingdom.' Representatives of the shire had to possess an income of £600 a year
from land, and burgesses £300 a year, but provided the member
had wealthy friends or relations, there were ways round this difficulty—as the careers of Burke, Pitt, Fox, and Wilkes all show. In
any case some private means would have been necessary, as constituencies had long since given up the practice of paying wages to
their members, and the expenses of election were sometimes ruinous.

A general election had to be held at least once every seven years;
a splendid series of pictures by Hogarth has captured the scenes of
riotous corruption on these occasions, but not even Hogarth
could portray all the extraordinary complexities of the electoral
system. In all parts of the kingdom the old mediaeval distinction
between shire and borough members had been maintained, but
in their respective Acts of Union Scotland and Ireland[1] had retained something of their own original systems.

Each of the forty English counties returned two members, the
Welsh counties only one. The franchise dated back to the Act of
1430, whereby the right to elect these was granted to all who occupied freehold land that was worth forty shillings a year; the term
'freehold' applied also to certain local offices and in some cases

[1] The system in Ireland will be described separately in the next section.

even to a pew in church; for example, the brewer, butler, bell-ringer, gardener, cook, and organ-blower of Westminster Abbey all voted in a Middlesex election. Since 1781 the worth of the elector's freehold had been established by the certificate of payment from the land-tax commissioners, which he brought with him to the hustings as proof of his right to vote. There had not been any serious statutory effort to disfranchise the Roman Catholic freeholder, but at the end of the seventeenth century an attempt to make electors take the oaths of supremacy, allegiance, and abjuration might have disfranchised some of the stricter ones. The business of administering the oaths, however, was found to be so lengthy that it was discontinued, except when the candidate demanded it, and in 1794 an Act had made this omission legal.

The considerable decline in the value of money since 1430 made the forty-shilling freehold franchise a fairly wide one. The elector was certainly wooed for his vote. He was given dinners and what Johnson called 'septennial ale'; his travelling expenses were paid. One of Hogarth's pictures shows him receiving bribes in each hand simultaneously from the rival sides. Two factors, however, considerably diminished his independence. The freeholder was also often a tenant farmer dependent on the local landlord; the voting was open, so that the squire had only to look at the poll-book to see how his tenants had voted. Consequently, in the majority of counties, the influence of great landowning families or the Crown was predominant; in some counties two families would agree to take one seat each, but no generalization is absolutely safe.

The English boroughs, on the other hand, present a scene of such chaos that generalization is not merely unsafe, but utterly impossible. The right of a town to return two members to Westminster had been awarded indiscriminately by the Crown during previous centuries, and the distribution of boroughs took no account whatever of the rapid growth of the great towns of the north and the decline of many others in the south. The county and borough representation of Cornwall alone amounted to forty-four seats, and the combined borough representation of Cornwall and Wiltshire equalled that of eight northern counties. More than half the English boroughs were to be found in the seaboard counties of the south and south-east of England, while Manchester, Birmingham, Leeds, and Sheffield had no representation at all.

The franchise within these boroughs varied enormously. In a few it was extraordinarily wide. In Preston all the inhabitants could vote—including, until 1782, anyone who spent the night there during the election. In some, anyone not on poor relief could vote—the pot-wallopers; in others, all who paid the local imposts, scot and lot. Burgage boroughs, corporation boroughs, freemen boroughs, all abounded with strange and illogical customs. It is not even possible to say that the system was entirely in the favour of the rich. In Liverpool the vote was enjoyed by the journeymen shipwrights and their apprentices, to the exclusion of wealthy taxpayers and public officials. In the City of London the vote was restricted to members of Livery Companies, and a small retailer might enjoy a vote while a rich merchant might not. The most notorious aspects of the whole system were, of course, the pocket boroughs, whose small electorates were entirely in the pocket of a great landlord, and the rotten boroughs, even smaller, and in some cases non-existent as towns, which were simply bought and sold. The Duke of Bedford controlled the nine electors of Camelford; Old Sarum is a byword; so is Gatton on the North Downs with its six houses and one elector.

In Scotland thirty out of the forty-five seats represented the counties. The electors consisted of freeholders whose land had been liable to a tax of forty-five shillings on lists dating back to the fourteenth century. The rolls of these freeholders were more carefully drawn up than in England and the county electorate remained extremely small—less than 3,000 for the whole of Scotland. Roman Catholics were excluded by statute from voting. The sixty-six royal burghs were organized in groups to return the other fifteen members, and since voting was indirect, the number of electors who played a direct part in a burgh election was very small indeed. Scotland, with a population of nearly 2 million, had a total electorate of about 4,000, and its smallness, combined with considerable government patronage, made control of the Scottish vote a fairly simple matter.

The mathematical anomalies of the whole system were endless. In 1793 307 members of the House of Commons were returned by 154 individuals; in 1827 it was reckoned that 276 seats were under the control of landed patrons. Eight members of the House of Lords had the disposal of fifty-one seats. In England and Wales, out of a population of about 10 million, there were roughly 435,000 electors.[1]

Three major criticisms of the system could be made—the corruption, the out-of-date distribution of seats, and the inequalities of the franchise. In defence, it was argued that in a haphazard way every significant element of the population had some form of representation. There was even a case for the rotten boroughs. It was claimed that they gave young men of talent a chance to enter Parliament early in their career. Rich merchants and Indian 'nabobs' could similarly find a seat without difficulty. In fact, the only explanation is historical. It had been the growth of the importance of the Commons since the struggle in the seventeenth century that had made it so vital for the Crown and the great magnates to have control over its composition, and King and magnates had thus entered upon a struggle in which there were many instances of electors playing one patron off against another. The electoral system was an integral part of the British Constitution.

This can best be understood when the position of the Crown is considered. The King, as head of the executive, chose his own ministers from either House of Parliament. Thus ministers were responsible to the Crown and to Parliament, but although in theory this was supposed to mean a constitutional balance between legislature and executive, Crown patronage at the time of an election, together with a great number of minor posts and sinecures with which the King could make sure of certain members' votes between elections, usually provided the Prime Minister with a working majority in the Commons. Had there been a highly disciplined party system, this would have perpetuated the rule of one party, until the King chose to have a change. There were, however, no organized parties; there was not even an organized

[1] See Statistics, p. 453.

opposition; both Houses of Parliament were still a preserve of individualism, and the existence of patronage and placemen never meant absolute control. Even those who held their seats through the patronage of the Crown or a Lord had considerable freedom to vote as they liked on most matters, and the Prime Minister could never know the strength of the opposition which he would have to meet. Nor could he demand a dissolution followed by a new election whenever he was defeated in the Commons, since the unwritten Septennial convention denied the right of the Crown to dissolve Parliament before the full seven years had elapsed. The convention was broken in 1784 by George III, when he wanted to secure an amenable House of Commons for William Pitt. But this greater use of Crown influence hardly compensated for the series of economic reforms towards the end of the century, which wiped out a good many of the places at the Crown's disposal and thereby definitely tipped the balance in favour of the independence of Parliament.

The central administration through which the ministers were expected to carry on the government of the country was extraordinarily slight. Clerks and customs officials at the ports were appointed mainly through patronage, although the economic reforms of the 1780s had abolished a certain number of sinecures and cleared up some of the corruption which, owing to the low rate of pay, had been a part of the system. During the Napoleonic war the service departments had been overhauled, yet even as late as 1821 the entire staff of the Foreign Office numbered no more than twenty-eight, and in most departments ministers were often burdened with an overwhelming quantity of clerical work. The actual forces at the disposal of the executive were equally limited, partly because the age-old prejudice against a standing army or an established police force was still strong. During the social unrest after the war the government was forced to depend on spies, but these did not represent any official organization and most of them were little more than self-appointed informers. After the demobilization, however, there did remain a standing army [1] of about 100,000, mostly scattered in small detachments throughout

[1] For the organization of the Army itself, see p. 193.

the country, and it was on these that the Home Secretary and the magistrates had to rely when disorder threatened.

The work of local government rested almost exclusively with the heads of provincial society. Squire and parson still ruled rural England. For several centuries the Justice of the Peace had been the unpaid factotum in English government. Appointed from among the prominent landowners of the district by the Lord Chancellor, on the recommendation of the Lord Lieutenant of the shire, the Justices were responsible for every form of local administration and justice, sometimes taking their decisions independently, sometimes conferring together in Quarter Sessions.

The administrative unit of local government was the parish, of which there were about 10,000. The parish council had originally been the most democratic element in English government, but by the beginning of the nineteenth century many of the parish vestries had become closed—tiny cliques whose members were co-opted. They chose the Churchwardens, fixed the Church rate, and levied fines on those who refused to accept local office. The position of the Churchwardens, however, was largely nominal. The other parish officials were selected by the J.P.s. The office of Constable—a highly unpopular one—was held for a year at a time. The Overseers of the Poor were responsible for the administration of relief, for which they could raise a rate; the Surveyors of the Highway were responsible for the maintenance of roads, on which they could set members of the parish to work.

The system was essentially patriarchal. It had long ceased to be self-government within the community. Even where the vestry was open, it had no control over the majority of local rates that had to be paid. Perhaps the most significant feature was the absence of any separation of powers. Legislature, executive, judiciary—within his district the J.P. virtually stood for all three, and continued to do so throughout most of the nineteenth century. In the rural areas it was not an ineffective system. Where it was beginning to fail was on the outskirts of the big towns, where the growing urban population had overflowed the old municipal boundaries. Here the greater administrative requirements were simply not met. Or, as in Bethnal Green, where the local franchise was made as wide as possible, a local demagogue, such as Joseph Merceron, arose, and corruption and embezzlement became far more rife than under the rule of the country Justices.

The administration of some of the towns was more complex. There were about 230 municipal corporations in England and Wales. A municipal borough was not necessarily a Parliamentary borough; it consisted of a township which at some time in the past had been granted a royal charter that conferred upon it special rights of local government, including taxation, the administration of justice, and the ownership of corporate property. The Corporation Act of 1661 still excluded from the municipal corporations anyone who would not take the sacrament according to the rites of the Church of England, and although annual Indemnity Acts made it possible for the less strict Dissenters to be elected,[1] the councils which governed these boroughs had long been in the hands of small groups of Anglican Tories.

It is almost impossible to sum up the governmental system of Britain at this time. There existed an uneasy balance between legislature and executive. The King and his ministers had wide powers of government, yet were held in check by a Parliament whose electoral system was so varied that it allowed considerable, but not absolute, control by the Crown and the great landlords. The system was not even remotely democratic, yet it answered ultimately to the pressure of public opinion. In the provinces it was an autocracy of the local landowners, yet an autocracy exercised almost entirely without the use of troops or police, one in which the individual enjoyed his right of freedom from arbitrary arrest and in which the law of the land was a higher authority than the whim of the local squire. The miseries suffered by the poor in this period hardly allow a panegyric of such a system. It deserved much of what its critics said. But, for all its inadequacies, it had a fundamental stability and elasticity that saved Britain from bloody revolution in the most revolutionary century of her history.

---

[1] An interesting example of the slackening of restrictions on Dissenters is to be seen in Portsmouth. In 1780 influence hitherto exercised by the Admiralty was thrown off when John Carter, a member of a prominent Unitarian family, became Mayor. From then until 1835 the Corporation, packed with Dissenters, remained under the control of the Carters and on Sundays even used to accompany their Mayor, headed by the mace, to chapel.

3. Ireland

In 1851 William Gladstone, protesting by letter to Schwarzen-berg at the state of the Neapolitan prisons, received a tart reply that the English might do well to consider first the living conditions of the Irish. The taunt has often been made and has usually been justified. On the whole, the English much preferred to forget the Irish; from time to time the English government had been forced to pay them some attention, but the outcome had seldom been more than despair. The legacy of unhappy centuries of English rule presented the most fair-minded statesmen in the nineteenth century with a social, religious, and political problem that seemed almost beyond solution.

Originally Ireland had been treated as a military conquest, and its lands, cut up into great estates, had been an easy way for the Sovereign to reward his followers. The majority of the population of 6 million had remained Roman Catholic, and this situation had been so played upon by Spain and France that the English had come to regard the Irish as potential traitors.

Ireland in 1815 was a land of vast estates divided up into myriads of tiny holdings. The reason for this was that the English landlord was usually absentee, leaving the management of the estate to an agent, who often acquired a position of great social significance in the district. Farmers who rented land on these estates found it profitable to sub-let sections of it to cotters who paid in money or, when they had none, in labour on the farmers' own land. Often these holdings were sub-divided again, so that the landlord's estate was soon transformed into hundreds of patches, some no bigger than a back garden. One landlord, during the famine of 1846, thinking that he had sixty tenants, discovered that he had, in fact, 600. Land which he had originally let at ten shillings an acre had been subdivided by middlemen so many times that the price was finally £1 10s. for a quarter of an acre. Such a system naturally made scientific farming utterly impossible, the peasant simply living on a diet of potatoes which he grew on his own plot.

A fundamental grievance was the landlord's right of eviction.

A farmer who farmed his land economically might well be evicted so that the landlord might get a higher rent for it. Nor was any allowance made for improvement in the form of buildings. The tenant rented only the land. Any building that he put up or any improvement that he made to existing buildings was his own responsibility, and he received no compensation when he gave up the tenancy. As a result, Irish tenants lived in squalor, and the thousands of little mud huts that housed the cotters on their potato patches were more primitive than almost anywhere else in Europe. The greatest enemy of the peasantry was the improving landlord. In England the labourer, expropriated through Enclosure Acts, could at least look for employment in the new industrial towns. In Ireland there was little industry and the immediate consequences of improvement were something very close to extermination. The landlord had no need of any parliamentary legislation. After 1816 he had only to apply to the county court, and the peasants, expelled from the land and with their homes destroyed, could choose between starvation and taking ship for England in the hope of casual employment. The only protection for the peasantry came from secret Ribbon societies—the Whitefeet, the Blackfeet, the Molly Maguires—who organized local reigns of terror. Evicting landlords went in danger of their lives, and since this first step in any improvement must also mean a loss of rent, it was hardly surprising that the majority of them were content to leave Ireland unimproved and to enjoy their income in England. Yet even here they could not entirely ignore the condition of their estates, for much of the rent often could not be paid and many estates were drifting into bankruptcy.

Religion was a further barrier between the native Irish and their landlords. At one time, particularly after 1690, the Penal Laws had been ruthlessly harsh in Ireland, but towards the end of the eighteenth century a series of Relief Acts had softened much of their severity. The restrictions on the owning and leasing of land had been removed; Roman Catholics were allowed freedom of education and worship; after 1793 they could vote and hold commissions in the Army below the rank of colonel. But the law still excluded them from posts of administration and from sitting in

Parliament and the government of the land remained under the control of an Anglican oligarchy.

In a country where three-quarters of the inhabitants were Roman Catholic, there was no endowment for the Roman Church. The Catholic clergy lived on the charity of their parishioners—£300 being the average income of a bishop, and £65 that of a priest. In contrast to this, the Anglican Irish Church, in order to minister to the needs of 850,000 Anglicans, was heavily endowed. There were four archbishops, twenty-seven bishops, and some 1,400 benefices. It was reckoned later in the century that the total income of the bishoprics alone was £150,000 a year. All the peasantry had to pay the cess, a church rate; all except the graziers, a small wealthier section of the community, who were exempt until 1823, had to pay tithe. The indignation that this last aroused was due not only to the fact that it had to be paid to what the majority of them regarded as a heretical Church, but also to the system of collection, since it was farmed out to tithe-proctors, who made their own profit in the process.

It had been Pitt's hope that if the Irish Parliament at Dublin, which represented the Anglican landlord interest, could be abolished by parliamentary union with Great Britain, and Roman Catholics be given the right to sit at Westminster, reform might be possible. He knew that the one without the other would be useless, but he failed to persuade George III, and the Union of 1800 came without Catholic emancipation. The Irish Parliament was bribed to consent to its own extinction with £1½ million of public money. By the Act of Union twenty-eight Irish peers were to be elected for life to sit in the House of Lords, together with four spiritual peers to represent the Anglican Church. One hundred seats for Ireland were added to the English House of Commons.

This change meant a considerable reduction in the number of Irish constituencies, since the old Dublin Commons had totalled 300 seats. Thus, in a sense, the Irish system of Parliamentary representation was the first to undergo some degree of reform in the nineteenth century. Out of the thirty-four boroughs that were now to return thirty-six members, only ten, however, could be

said to be relatively open, the rest being in the hands of the corporations or limited bodies of freemen. The other sixty-four
members were returned by thirty-two counties. Since 1793 the
forty-shilling freehold franchise had been extended to include
Roman Catholics. In Ireland the term 'freeholder' included those
who held land only for a term of years, and the landlords, knowing the market value of votes, had hastened to partition their
estates into forty-shilling freeholds, whose occupants would, they
believed, remain under their control. 'A new trade sprang up in
the country,' wrote Lord Cloncurry. 'Men speculated on the
multiplication of the forty-shilling freeholders as they ought to
have done on the breeding of sheep.' Not too much attention
was paid to whether a man's land did bring in as much as forty
shillings a year, and between 1795 and 1821 the number of
registered county electors rose from 40,000 to 184,000. By 1829
they amounted to 216,000.

There were two consequences of this rapid increase. One was
an acceleration in the process by which Ireland was cut up into
tiny holdings. The other—ultimately more significant—was that
the landlords were creating a large county electorate, predominantly Catholic, which, one day, if capably led, might vote contrary
to their interest. The seeds of Catholic emancipation were sown
by the Anglican landlords of Ireland.

This was the country whose affairs were to play an increasingly
large part in English political life in the nineteenth century. The
Irish peasant, living his animal-like existence, crude, violent,
quixotic, the figure whom John Synge depicted much later in his
plays of the west coast of Ireland, came to be the despair of English
statesmen and Irish national leaders. Coercion Act after Coercion
Act was to be passed in the English House of Commons. Landlords were threatened and attacked and no local jury would
convict. The only effective authority was that of the Catholic
priests; no movement could hope to succeed without their support. Yet absolute unity was bound to elude any Irish movement,
for the national parties that organized themselves in the course of
the century always had to face the possibility of their efforts
degenerating into a local war between the Catholics and the

c

Orangemen of the north—as in the great rising of 1798. No English government had been able to solve the problem of Ireland, and it seemed unlikely that any Irish government would be allowed to try.

4. Overseas possessions

In 1783 Great Britain had acknowledged the independence of her thirteen American colonies. This loss did not immediately affect her attitude towards her other possessions overseas, but it did automatically mean a profound change in the nature of her empire. These American settlements, which in the eighteenth century had formed the bulk of her colonial strength, had been offshoots from the mother country, a population of 2 million, predominantly British in origin, except for New York and New Jersey, which had been captured from the Dutch. After the American war the possessions which were still left to Great Britain were by no means inconsiderable, but were utterly different in character, for what was left of the empire consisted of a number of tiny strategic points scattered over the world, together with one or two larger areas, where small English communities controlled an alien or native population.

In the New World she held Canada, whose inhabited area amounted to no more than small settlements in Nova Scotia and Newfoundland, the line of the St. Lawrence occupied by the subject French colonists, and the trading points of the Hudson's Bay Company. Farther south she retained Bermuda, the Bahamas, Jamaica, and a few smaller islands, whose sugar interests had made them the most highly considered and influential of the British possessions. In the Mediterranean, Minorca had been lost and her only remaining naval base was Gibraltar. On the west coast of Africa she held a few trading stations, while in the south Atlantic the island of St. Helena was the last staging point on the route round the Cape. The East India Company, in the course of its struggle with the French in the eighteenth century, had acquired appreciable concessions around Bengal, as well as maintaining its trading establishments at Bombay and Madras, but until Pitt's India Act of 1784 all these were primarily the concern of the Company.

Between 1783 and 1815 considerable additions were made to this empire, but only two new areas were actually settled by people of British origin—Ontario, on the north side of the Great Lakes, where the American loyalists had emigrated after the War of Independence, and New South Wales, on the east coast of Australia, now used for the transportation of convicts.

Most of the new acquisitions were made during the Revolutionary and Napoleonic wars. Great Britain had command of the sea, and as Spain and the United Provinces came under Napoleon's wing, their colonies were legitimately open to conquest. In the West Indies Great Britain gained Trinidad, Tobago, St. Lucia, and Dominica. A part of Guiana, on the coast of South America, was taken from the Dutch, although Dutch possessions in the East Indies were given back after the war. In the Mediterranean, Malta and the Ionian Isles were retained for strategic purposes, while Heligoland, taken from Denmark, was thought to be useful for the Baltic trade. In Africa, Cape Colony was not returned to the Dutch; Mauritius and the Seychelles were taken from France, while Tristan da Cunha in the Atlantic was occupied in order to guard against any attempt by Napoleon to escape from St. Helena. All these gains, together with considerable acquisitions in India, did little to affect the changed character of the empire, which, with the exception of the growing provinces in Canada, remained primarily commercial and maritime.

The main lesson that the Tory government drew from American independence was that a tighter hold should be kept on their imperial possessions. In 1801 colonial administration was shifted from the Home Office and was made the responsibility of a Secretary of State for War and Colonies, an arrangement that was to last until 1854, but little attempt was made to revise fundamentally the system which had goaded the Americans into rebellion. In fact, the colonial question played no part in the political scene during the early years of the nineteenth century; governments seemed to have little interest in it, and the most active party of reform, the Radicals, regarded colonies as a nuisance of which the mother country should rid herself as soon as possible. Thus the central administration of the colonies remained almost the private concern of a few permanent officials in London. The colonies that had recently been captured were placed under the rule of a governor without any form of representative government—except in Guiana and Cape Colony, where the existing institutions were allowed to continue. In British colonies of longer standing the governmental pattern remained in accordance with the eighteenth-century system. A governor and executive council were appointed by the Crown; so also was the upper house of the legislature, while the lower house was elected by the colonists. Thus executive posts in the colonies were simply part of the patronage of the home government and were often used to get rid of individuals whose presence at home was thought to be undesirable.

The only major piece of governmental legislation carried through after the loss of the American colonies was the Canadian Constitutional Act of 1791. The terms of the Quebec Act, drawn up seventeen years earlier on the assumption that the population along the St. Lawrence would be almost entirely French, had established French civil law and complete freedom for the Roman Catholic Church. The liberal nature of the Act had had the effect of leaving the French unmoved by the Americans' appeals to join them, but within a few years the arrival of large numbers of loyalists of British origin had made the original plan almost unworkable. The Act of 1791 divided the whole area of the river and the land north of the Great Lakes into two provinces—Upper Canada or Ontario under English criminal and civil law, and Lower Canada, where civil law remained French and the Catholic clergy enjoyed something of the position of an established church. The actual system of government in each province was to be as in other British colonies, and no attempt was made to create any kind of union between the two new provinces or the maritime provinces of Nova Scotia and New Brunswick.

The economic restrictions imposed on the colonies—another

powerful factor in the American revolt—remained virtually unchanged. The establishment of colonies had always been something of a business enterprise. 'Planting of countries is like planting of woods,' Francis Bacon had written in the early days of the
American settlements, 'for you must make account to leese almost
twenty years' profit and expect your recompense in the end.' The
mother country had supplied the initial capital, it gave protection
through its navy and troops, and in return the enterprise had to
show some profit. As the Americans themselves soon discovered,
this colonial system, imposed through the Navigation Acts and
supplemented in the eighteenth century by other Trade Laws, was
by no means harsh and in some ways was distinctly advantageous
to the colonies, but it remained an unquestionable fact that the
fundamental motive was to create an economic system within
the empire which should operate in the interest of the mother
country.

In most British colonies occupation and possession had thus
been a means to an end. In India, however, the whole process had
been in reverse. Since the seventeenth century the merchants of
the East India Company, enjoying a monopoly of trade with the
mother country, had been concerned simply to establish agents
and depots with their headquarters at Madras, Calcutta, and Bombay, and had worked to gain agreements and concessions from
local Indian rulers. They resided as privileged foreign merchants,
except in Bombay, which had been a possession of the British
Crown since 1662, and there had never been any question of
government. By the eighteenth century, however, the empire of
the Great Mogul had become the Sick Man of Asia and the long
duel fought out between Great Britain and France had transformed the rough and tumble of commercial rivalry into a political and military struggle in which each side endeavoured to in-
stall favourably disposed Indian princes in Bengal and the Carna-
tic. In 1763 the French acknowledged British supremacy and the
directors of the East India Company found that in saving their trade
they had acquired an empire in Bengal and on the east coast of
India. This was only the beginning. The continuation of French
intrigues in India during the American War of Independence

and the Napoleonic War led to further campaigns, first under Warren Hastings, later under Lord Wellesley; and as the ragged, rambling frontier of British possessions moved haphazardly into the centre of the Indian continent, the power of the Maratha confederacy was eventually challenged and broken. By 1813 British rule ran through Bengal and Bihar and as far as the upper waters of the Ganges and the Jumna. The entire east coast, the west coast from Goa to Travancore, as well as much of the inland regions in the south, were in British possession. Oudh, Travancore, Mysore, and Hyderabad were under the Company's protection, and the Maratha princes and Ranjit Singh in the Punjab had signed treaties of alliance. Ceylon, valuable for its harbour at Trincomalee, had already been taken from the Dutch in 1795.

The problem of the government of these startling acquisitions was complicated by the wealth of India, since if the British government had taken over absolute control, the new revenue available to the Crown would have made the King independent of any Parliament. Pitt's Act of 1784 had found a way round the difficulty by establishing a Dual Control. Political and administrative rule was to be supervised by the government through a Board of Control, whose President was to have a seat in the Cabinet. This, however, left a good deal of local political control with the Company, which was to appoint all officials, including the Governor-General, the head of the executive in India, assisted by a council of three. Trading interests and patronage also remained the Company's concern. Thus the work of government was not entirely divorced from the profits of commerce by this Act. In the early years of the nineteenth century, however, the Company's monopolies were gradually whittled away. In 1813 independent British traders were allowed to send their ships round the Cape to India; ten years later the export trade to Europe from India was thrown open—except in tea—and in 1833 the Company's monopoly of the China trade was lost. The Dual Control lasted until 1858, but long before that the growing demand for free trade and the notion of trusteeship in British colonial development had brought about a change of attitude that made the position of the Company something of an anachronism in the government of India.

This, then, was the extent of Great Britain's overseas possessions in 1815. It is clear that the political and economic assumptions were still set in an eighteenth-century mould, yet it would be untrue to say that no new ideas were at work. Adam Smith's *Wealth of Nations*, published in 1776, had refuted much of the old theory of mercantilism, on which the colonial system was based, and the influence of his thought was already apparent during William Pitt's administration. The commercial treaty with France in 1786 had modified some of the duties on either side of the Channel. Jay's treaty of 1794—admittedly a hard bargain for the Americans—had given the United States a limited right of entry in the West Indian trade. In fact, the West Indies themselves were vitally dependent on American commodities, and the treaty is a good illustration of the way in which the secession of the American colonies had really disrupted the whole basis of the old system. The Irish Act of Union had established free trade between Ireland and the United Kingdom, and Pitt's attempt to bring in Catholic emancipation at the same time is consistent with the extremely reasonable terms that were granted to the French in the province of Lower Canada. Certainly these were only small beginnings, but they are another indication of the way in which the last decades of the eighteenth century foreshadowed the changes in the century to come.

3

TORY RULE, 1815–22

1. *The Tories and their opponents*

BY 1815 George III had long been mad; his son, the Prince Regent, selfish and indolent, although a man of wit and good taste, preferred a life of pleasure to the work of government. At the head of affairs stood Lord Liverpool, Prime Minister from 1812 until 1827. He was a modest man, amiable but shy, comfortably at home in the simplicity of George III's Court, but quite lost amid the frivolous gaiety of the Brighton Pavilion. His principal skill lay in the management of other politicians, a gift which accounts for the remarkable length of his career. He chose able men as his ministers, persuaded them to work together, and exercised a very gentle supervision over their activities. 'The misfortune of this government is that it is a government of departments,' wrote George IV in 1823. It was a valid criticism, for Liverpool was no autocrat; yet he succeeded where many others, more forceful, but less subtle, would have failed.

One reason for his comparative obscurity was the fact that he could not sit in the House of Commons. It was the Foreign Secretary, Robert Stewart, Viscount Castlereagh,[1] who led the Tories there. A reserved, aristocratic figure, he was seldom known to give way to temper or impatience; colleagues and opponents alike were met with an aloof unconcern that broke down only in the last weeks of his life. Most of the leading Tories, however, sat in the Lords. Henry Addington, Viscount Sidmouth, was Home Secretary, nominally responsible for home policy after the war, although Castlereagh, being in the Commons, suffered much of the blame for it; Lord Eldon was Lord Chancellor, a Tory of the

---

[1] As an Irish peer he could sit in the Commons.

least compromising kind. One of the most powerful figures of the time was the Duke of Wellington. Unskilful in the art of political manoeuvre, possessed of a soldierly straightforwardness that led him to expect politicians to take orders or resign, he was, nevertheless, the most significant influence behind the Tories in the House of Lords until his death in 1852. Two other members of the Tory group in the Commons were George Canning and Robert Peel. Canning had enjoyed high office during the Napoleonic war, but his ambitious nature and biting tongue had gained him too many enemies for the success that his undoubted brilliance might have won him. Peel had entered the House of Commons in 1809 after a distinguished career at Oxford. He was the son of a wealthy cotton manufacturer who had received a baronetcy from Pitt in 1800, and true to his upbringing, he remained a Tory all his life, although he was perpetually on the left wing of the group—a fact which accounts for the later triumphs and vicissitudes of his party.

What did the Tories stand for? It was an age in which politics had little to do with a party platform, and men's votes were decided more by temperament than by doctrine. As a whole, the Tories stood for the old patriarchal conception of government. Their duty was to prevent anarchy, to preserve the Anglican Church, to regulate trade, and to safeguard a society that had its roots in landed property. Ideally this should have meant mild government; they did, in fact, introduce humanitarian reforms— the repeal of many religious disabilities, the partial abolition of the pillory in 1816, and the abolition of the whipping of women in 1820.[1] In 1802 and 1819 Robert Peel's father had been responsible for the passing of Acts that restricted the number of hours a day that pauper children might work in the factories—although the lack of inspectors made this legislation practically useless. Tory government became harsh only when confronted with social developments that were really beyond its ken, and the Reign of

[1] The most famous reform of all, the abolition of the Slave Trade, was the work of the Ministry of All-the-Talents (1806-7), which, although a coalition government, was under the leadership of Grenville and Charles James Fox. This was, however, a non-party measure which many Tories supported, and the succeeding Tory governments enforced the Act vigorously.

Terror in France was still too recent for their reaction to be anything else.

The term 'Whig' implies the natural opponent of the Tory. The distinction had been virtually meaningless during the main part of the eighteenth century, and although the issues of the French Revolution had breathed some life into it for a time, the Whigs had shown long before 1815 that they had as little love for revolution as the Tories. Catholic emancipation, the reduction of Crown patronage, and an undefined reform of the electoral system were the changes for which they hoped. They had no fixed programme and little unity amongst themselves. They had nothing to say about the new problems of the age and, since most of them belonged to the same landed class as the Tories, hardly differed from them during the social turmoil that followed the war. Lord Grenville and Lord Grey were their leaders, neither of them men of political ambition. Lord Althorp was a simple, honest countryman; William Lamb, later Lord Melbourne, was too indolent to create a great party out of them, and Lord John Russell in 1815 was only twenty-three. Henry Brougham was, in many ways, their most striking personality. He was a man of humble background, a clever lawyer whose quick-wittedness in debate gave him a great advantage in the Commons. He had been an associate of Sydney Smith, with whom he had founded the *Edinburgh Review*, a Whig periodical, but although his Whig colleagues realized his ability, they mistrusted his lack of 'ballast', as Greville [1] put it. In English politics it does not always pay for a man's cleverness to be too apparent.

The Tories might look for support from some of the milder Whigs; the Whigs could only look to another group of more recent origin, the Radicals, although the likelihood of such an alliance was certainly remote in the early decades of the century. In 1830 Grey was able to bring it about for a few years, but it was not until 1859 that a union of Whig and Radical in Palmerston's second administration led to the emergence of the Liberal party.

The Radicals were one of the few political groups in English

---

[1] See Further Reading, p. 458.

history to take their stand on a doctrine. Utilitarianism was a body of ideas that had grown out of the teaching of Jeremy Bentham and David Ricardo. Bentham's standard of utility was 'the greatest happiness of the greatest number', and the means by which this was to be achieved were twofold. First, the administration of the country must be made more efficient, education must be provided for all by the state, and the electoral system reformed, although Radicals were divided over the precise details of this last. Second, apart from these essentials, the greatest happiness could only be attained by leaving the individual free to act as he wished, and it was this notion of *laissez faire*, demanding the removal of governmental restrictions, that dominated Radical thought in the first half of the century. Thus the doctrine was always in danger of including two contradictory arguments. Ultimately there was to be almost no limit to the degree of interference that efficiency in government might demand, and certain aspects of political supervision and economic freedom were clearly incompatible. This explains the changing character of the movement during the course of the century and points to the fundamental paradox of Radicalism, a creed of individualism that was later to contribute enormously to the development of the collective state.[1]

The basic principle over which they never wavered was Free Trade. This was more than a point in a programme: it was an article of faith passionately held in the belief that if commerce and manufacture were free from every kind of trade law, the prosperity—and hence the greatest happiness—of the greatest number would be assured. The natural working of economic laws would solve all problems by encouraging nations to concentrate on what they were best suited to produce. It was obvious why Free Trade should attract the industrialist of the north, conscious of the lead that he had over his counterpart on the Continent; and during the first half of the century Radicalism came close to being a sectional interest, concerned to gain better representation of the manufacturers in the House of Commons, where they might strengthen the

[1] For developments in Radicalism in the last half of the century see Chapter XVI, p. 325.

attack on import duties and attempt to block any measures that might interfere with the working of their factories.

These were the major political groups in 1815, but there were, in addition, two other movements in ideas which played a considerable part in the history of the century. The first was humanitarianism. This particular movement had already been active in the eighteenth century—especially among the *philosophes* in France. In England the motive force was religious rather than philosophical. The Evangelicals sought to ameliorate the appalling conditions of the poor, but since this kind of reform could only be carried out by restrictive legislation, most of the Radical industrialists opposed it, and it is no surprise to find that many of the leading Evangelicals were Tories. Wilberforce had been prepared to fight on behalf of the slaves, but ignored the English factory workers. Others did battle continually to improve conditions in the factories, the mines, and the towns. But of these Oastler was a firm Protectionist, Michael Sadler was opposed to Catholic emancipation and Parliamentary reform, and Anthony Ashley Cooper, Earl of Shaftesbury, the greatest of them, believed in Protection and stood out against Catholic emancipation.

One other figure, who stands quite alone, may be mentioned in this context—William Cobbett. He was a brilliant journalist who loved rural England and hated the financiers and industrialists whom he believed to be destroying it. His father had kept an inn outside Farnham, called 'The Jolly Farmer', and the name is applicable to the son: 'the pattern John Bull of his century,' Carlyle called him, 'strong as the rhinoceros, and with singular humanities and genialities shining through his thick skin.' He started his *Political Register* in 1802 and the *Parliamentary Debates* in 1804. In 1810 he was fined £1,000 and imprisoned for two years for attacking flogging in the Army. In the 1820s he began a series of rides through England, an account of which he published in 1830, commenting on the bad effects of enclosure and the absurdity of the rotten boroughs. He belonged to no party; he was certainly no revolutionary, wishing only to put the clock back; and he detested the Evangelicals. He never fully understood the political and economic questions with which he dealt, and he was fighting for a lost cause, but he remains one of the most striking and observant commentators of his day.

The second movement, Socialism, was very much in its infancy and can hardly be considered as an important factor in 1815. As has been seen, the Radicals were the very opposite of the Socialists; yet Ricardo, a Radical economist, produced a theory of value which was seized upon by Socialist writers such as Karl Marx. The theory was simply that the value of a commodity depended on the amount of labour that had been expended upon it. The first move in the direction of practical Socialism was made by a successful business man, Robert Owen. He intended that his mills at New Lanark should be an example to the world of how good living conditions for the workers would in fact produce the greatest profits. He sounds at first more of a benevolent capitalist than a Socialist, but later he took his ideas further; his scheme was for industry to be organized in small integrated communities in which the producers would own the means of production themselves and would exchange their products on the basis of the labour value of the commodity. In 1824 Owen went to America, lost £40,000 in endeavouring to set up his new communities there, and in the 1830s was back in England to play an important part in the early Trade Union movements.[1]

Clearly it would be utterly incorrect to imagine the nineteenth century as a simple conflict between reactionaries and reformers. Tories, Whigs, Radicals, humanitarians, and Socialists all believed in reform; it was the nature of that reform that divided them. Their standpoints differed, but their ideas on particular questions sometimes coincided. Even the names of the groups are an over-simplification; they stand very loosely for the opinions of individuals who often accepted only part of the ideas of the group. All this helps to explain the fluidity of party politics in the nineteenth century. The old conception of Whig and Tory no longer served any purpose, and out of the imbroglio of new ideas politicians had continually to create temporary coalitions of interests in order to secure a majority, until some new issue broke them up again.

[1] See p. 126.

2. Social distress and the maintenance of order

For the farmer and the manufacturer war had meant high prices for their commodities, and the immediate economic consequences of peace were disastrous for them both. The farmers' fears sprang from a growing abundance of wheat that naturally brought down the selling price. The harvests of 1813 and 1814 were good, and since 1813, as Napoleon's armies were being pushed back to the frontiers of France, corn had once more become available from the Continent. The average price in 1813 was one hundred and nine shillings and sixpence a quarter, in 1814 seventy-four shillings and fourpence, in 1815 sixty-five shillings and sevenpence, and by January 1816 it had fallen to fifty-two shillings and sixpence. This last figure does not seem particularly low when compared with price levels before the war, but the farmer's position had changed. War-time taxes, the considerable increase in the poor rate, and the interest on loans raised to cover the cost of enclosure placed a financial burden on him that made such a sharp drop in prices alarming—and in many cases disastrous. The number of bankruptcies among farmers rose enormously after 1814, and this naturally meant unemployment for the labourers. Farmers who survived could do so only by reducing the wages that they paid, and the wretchedness of the agricultural poor increased. 'I see scores of young men, formed by nature to be athletic, rosy-cheeked and bold,' wrote Cobbett in 1816, 'I see scores of young men formed by nature to exhibit this appearance; I see them as thin as herrings, dragging their feet after them, pale as a ceiling and sneaking about like beggars.'

In 1815 Parliament, a stronghold of the landed classes, attempted to produce a remedy. The Corn Law was worked out on the assumption that eighty shillings a quarter was the lowest selling price that would give the producer a reasonable remuneration. When the price fell below this, the ports would be closed to the importation of any foreign corn whatsoever; when it rose above eighty shillings, the ports would be open to free importation. Thus the new law would bring in no revenue. The ports would

simply be open or shut for three-monthly periods according to
the average selling price in the preceding six weeks. The system
was clearly cumbersome, lagging behind the fluctuations in price,
so that, in fact, the ports were sometimes open when the price was
below eighty shillings and shut when it was above. Quite apart
from its administrative inadequacies, it aroused considerable anger
among the Free Traders, the industrialists, and their workers, who
saw the measure simply as a means whereby the landlord could
keep the price of bread high. The Radicals, arguing from Ricardo's theory of rent, complained that by encouraging the cultivation of poor soil the Corn Law made rents higher than they would
be otherwise and kept labour on the land when it could be more
profitably employed in the factories. The landowners—Whigs
and Tories—retorted that cheaper bread would simply mean a
chance for the industrialist to pay his workers less wages.

The manufacturers had their own problems at this time. The
pattern of the post-war industrial crisis was slightly different from
that of the farmers'. Peace naturally meant the end of a considerable war-time market for the iron and textile industries, but the
opening of the Continent and the renewal of trade with America
—nominally closed during the 1812–14 war—seemed to offer
tremendous possibilities. The result was a short boom, the value
of British exports amounting to £51·6 million in 1815. The
bubble soon burst. Foreign markets became glutted with British
goods, prices dropped, and Continental manufacturers, frightened
by this overwhelming competition, persuaded their governments
to impose protective tariffs. Within two or three years British export figures had dropped by a third and the inevitable consequence
of the slump was unemployment. Another factor adding to the
general destitution at this time was the worsening plight of the
hand-loom weavers. As has been seen, the inventions affecting the
growth of machine-spinning had given them a short-lived prosperity. After the war, however, manufacturers could sell the spun
yarn overseas, for to have prohibited this would only have encouraged the establishing of spinning-mills abroad. As a result,
the British weaver had to compete with foreign weavers; a price
war at home also developed and this, combined with the gradual

adoption of power-looms, was to bring about the long-drawn-out destruction of the hand-loom weavers as a class.

This is the background that explains the rick-burning and machine-breaking that confronted the government in these unhappy post-war years. On the one side were starvation and despair; on the other a governing class lacking any police force, fearful of revolution, and dependent on the discretion of Lords Lieutenant of the counties and the magistrates. In 1816, in almost every county, local agitations, uncoordinated but often violent, were met by small forces of special constables, raised among the gentry, or by troops of yeomanry. At Littleport seventy rioters were captured and five hanged. In Leicester and Nottingham, where machine-breakers were at work, the leader, James Towle, was taken and executed. Many groups set off with the intention of presenting their case in London, but were turned back by troops.

The government's main fear was that these movements were part of a great conspiracy, but, in spite of the use of spies, evidence for this was never discovered. Some of the Radicals would have liked to make use of the social unrest, but the Seditious Societies Act of 1799 made it illegal for any society to organize branches. Major Cartwright had succeeded before the end of the war in encouraging clubs throughout the country, making it clear that they were independent and in no way branches of a central organization. Petitioning Parliament was still open to them, but since an old statute forbade any more than twenty signatures on a petition concerned with laws affecting Church and State, schemes had to be devised for each little group or club to send its 'Score Petition' to London. The law of the land thus made it extremely difficult for a concerted movement to be organized, but in any case an effective union between the middle-class Radicals and the poor was highly problematical, for social and political reasons. Their aims were utterly different and, however much the Radicals might wish to take advantage of the situation, most of them had as little love as the government for popular rule. This difference is illustrated by the Spa Fields meeting in December 1816, from which the political reformers withdrew. The meeting turned into a mob raiding the armourers' shops and marching towards the City of London, until they were stopped by a force collected by the Lord Mayor. In consequence of this riot the Habeas Corpus Act was suspended and a Seditious Meetings Act was passed.

In 1817 a group of petitioners, protesting against the suspension of Habeas Corpus, set out from Manchester carrying their own blankets and determined to march to London to present their case to the Prince Regent. But the Blanketeers, as they were called, were stopped at Stockport. A large number were at first detained in prison, but eventually only thirteen were reserved for trial. In the same year there was rioting in Huddersfield and Nottingham. The most famous episode in this period is the 'massacre of Peterloo'. In August 1819 a mass meeting of some 50,000–60,000 people was addressed by 'Orator' Hunt on St. Peter's Field at Manchester. The magistrates, alarmed at the size of the crowd and at the drilling which had taken place the previous evening, ordered the arrest of the speakers. Neither the Chief Constable nor the yeomanry could break through the crowd, and a troop of Hussars were ordered to clear the way. Their sabres flashed, panic ensued, and in the stampede eleven people were killed and 400 injured. Hunt and the other speakers were arrested and imprisoned, but the whole affair had been hopelessly bungled. The 'charge of Peterloo' was a gift for the cartoonists and the pamphleteers. Anger swept the country. Meetings in many towns demanded that the Prince Regent should dismiss the ministry, while in Italy, on hearing the news, Shelley wrote the bitter lines of his *Mask of Anarchy*:

> I met Murder on the way—
> He had a mask like Castlereagh—
> Very smooth he looked, yet grim;
> Seven bloodhounds followed him:
>
> All were fat; and well they might
> Be in admirable plight.
> For one by one, and two by two,
> He tossed them human hearts to chew
> Which from his wide cloak he drew.

Seldom in English history has a government been so hated by the people. Certainly this was not entirely without justification. If, for example, the taxes on food had been remitted, the situation of the poor might have been relieved a little; instead, the income tax, which weighed most heavily on the upper and middle classes, was dropped. Yet the removal of the taxes on food would barely have scraped the surface of the problem. Only a nation-wide system of economic control could have eased the birth-pangs of a new industrial society, and such measures of interference were beyond the power and knowledge of any government of this time. Indeed, the most coherent demand for reform pointed in precisely the opposite direction—the Radical cry for the removal of existing controls.

The government's answer to Peterloo was an attempt to define more precisely the powers of the local executive. Since there seemed to be uncertainty over the legality of the magistrates' action, they decided to pass six Acts which would put such matters beyond all doubt for the future. Unauthorized persons were prohibited from practising military exercises; the procedure in trials for treason was altered; magistrates were authorized to issue warrants for the search for arms; seditious and blasphemous libels were to be suppressed; the size of public meetings was restricted, and, lastly, all publications below a certain size were to be subject to the same duty as newspapers.

Viewed today, these six Acts, so often quoted, can hardly be termed severely repressive, yet they were the most strenuous measures so far taken by the government, and since economic conditions began slowly to improve, the disturbances which had caused the Acts subsided. The price of corn had fallen steadily since 1817; less money had to be spent on poor relief, and the numbers of emigrants began to drop.[1] The Cato Street conspiracy, a wild, foolish plot led by Arthur Thistlewood, to assassinate the Cabinet ministers, has little political importance beyond appearing to justify the six Acts, and the government had no difficulty in suppressing the minor disturbances that followed the arrest of the conspirators.

[1] See Statistics, pp. 453, 456.

In 1820 death at last released George III from his madness at Windsor. 'An old, mad, blind, despised, and dying King', Shelley had called him, and the deadly roll of monosyllables is like the knell of a whole epoch. Now, at last, the Prince Regent ascended the throne as George IV:

> Princes, the dregs of their dull race, who flow,
> Through public scorn, mud from a muddy spring—

Shelley's sonnet continued, and the new reign opened with a sordid farce that certainly confirmed his opinion.

George had been married twice; the first marriage with Mrs. Fitzherbert had been considered illegal, since she was a Catholic. His second marriage, in 1795, with Princess Caroline of Brunswick-Wolfenbüttel, had been disastrous; Princess Caroline had departed to indulge in a colourful Mediterranean existence, while George proceeded to enjoy the Regency. On hearing of George III's death, however, Caroline decided that she wanted to be a queen, and announced her intention of returning to England. This was too much for George, who demanded that his ministers should begin divorce proceedings on his behalf. Liverpool thought it wiser to offer Caroline a larger allowance, if she would agree to remain abroad. This plan was upset by Caroline's arrival in June at Dover, where she received a royal salute of guns from the Castle. Popular feeling saw her as a wronged woman and, in any case, warmly supported anyone who might embarrass the government. She made a majestic entry into London, where the sentries outside Carlton House saluted her as she passed. Now there was nothing for it but to introduce a Bill of Pains and Penalties which would enable George to divorce Caroline. The inquiry in the House of Lords dragged on from August until November, while a series of dubious Italian witnesses were questioned; the Bill passed by a narrow majority, and was then dropped, since there seemed little chance of getting it through the Commons. Caroline was still a popular heroine, but when she accepted an increased allowance of £50,000, the enthusiasm of the hungry poor waned. The last act of the farce was played out before Westminster Abbey, where she attempted to enter in order to take her part in the coronation. The doorkeeper refused to admit her, since she had no ticket. After this she gave up the struggle, and died a month later.

The government, already unpopular enough, had been further discredited by the scandal of the royal 'divorce'. The question for Lord Liverpool was whether he could reshape his Cabinet before Lord Grey could get together a working majority of Whigs and borderline Tories and Radicals. Liverpool proved the more astute political leader. Grey had offended George IV by his attitude during the proceedings over Caroline. He had fallen out with Grenville, who had supported the government's suspension of the Habeas Corpus Act in 1817, and he was unable to reconcile the rest of his group to joining the Radicals. Another nine years were to pass before the Whigs attained power, and in the meantime some of their thunder was to be stolen by a new Tory Cabinet under Liverpool, who set out to show that they, too, stood for reform.

4

CASTLEREAGH'S FOREIGN POLICY, 1815–22

IN the late summer of 1814 there came together at Vienna one of the most brilliant gatherings of diplomats and princes that Europe has ever seen. The Emperor Francis played host to nearly all the royal families of Europe. Forty tables were laid for dinner at the Hofburg every night; hunting parties were organized, and Beethoven, now stone deaf, conducted one of the gala concerts given at the Opera House. While the diplomats of the great Powers argued, the ruling families of the *ancien régime* celebrated their restoration in a succession of balls and banquets amidst sumptuous costumes and glittering candelabra.

Peace had already been concluded with France. Napoleon had abdicated and had by now sailed for Elba. Louis XVIII, brother of the guillotined Louis XVI, had been restored, a tired, elderly man, only thankful to sink on to his throne at last after long years of exile. The terms of the first Treaty of Paris had purposely been made mild, in the hope of discouraging latent Bonapartism. France had been allowed her frontiers of 1792, and although she did not recover all her lost colonies, she was to keep the art treasures that had been looted from the rest of Europe. Now that France had been defeated, the Allies had a further task: to root out the new order in Europe and to re-establish the old. For this reason the France of Louis XVIII was given a place in the Congress.

'The real purpose of the Congress', wrote Gentz, secretary to Metternich, 'was to divide among the conquerors the spoils taken from the vanquished.' Each of the victors thought in terms of a balance of power, but for each the perfect balance varied slightly. Each of them, too, still had an army in the field. At the beginning of the Congress Castlereagh had said: 'It was agreed that the

53

effective Cabinet was to be based not on the Treaty of Paris nor on any other public document, but on the distinction between great and small Powers'. No statement could have been more apt. The representatives of the five Powers—Britain, France, Austria, Prussia, and Russia—meeting at Metternich's house on the Ball-platz, decided how the frontiers of Europe were to be redrawn in accordance with their own requirements, regardless of the wishes of the smaller governments or of the resident populations. The second Treaty of Paris, after the Hundred Days and Napoleon's final defeat at Waterloo, added only one or two amendments, by which France lost small sections of Belgian territory and most of Savoy.

The British delegation consisted of four plenipotentiaries, headed by the Foreign Secretary. Castlereagh's aim on the Continent was to create a Central European *bloc* which might stand firm against either France or Russia. In this one may see the main thread of British diplomacy for the future. Great Britain was later to withdraw from Continental commitments, but throughout the nineteenth century France and Russia remained her most likely opponents. The Netherlands, too, had to be placed in friendly hands. Otherwise his main concern was to exclude from the scope of the Congress the question of colonies, and particularly Spanish America, where there were now considerable British interests.

The major difficulty was that the Russians, after pursuing Napoleon from Moscow to Paris, had no intention of giving up the Grand Duchy of Warsaw, through which they had passed on their way. 'His Imperial Majesty', wrote Castlereagh to Liverpool in October 1814, 'insinuated that the question could only end in one way, as he was in possession.' From this factor the rest developed. Austria feared this expansion of Russia, since Prussia's compensation for not regaining the whole of the Polish territory that she had previously held was to be all or most of Saxony. This fear could have meant ruin for Castlereagh's hope of a Central European *bloc*. It was also a great opportunity for Talleyrand to play upon the differences of the Allies. At one moment, in January 1815, a secret treaty was actually signed between Britain, France, and Austria against the other two Powers, but this was only a precaution, and a compromise was eventually reached.

Russia kept what had been the Grand Duchy of Warsaw, the Tsar styling himself King of Poland. Her possession of Finland, including the Åland Isles, was also confirmed, Sweden receiving Norway from Denmark in compensation, while giving up Swedish Pomerania. Prussia regained part of her Polish territories and received, in addition, about a third of Saxony, as well as a considerable section of the Lower Rhineland and Westphalia. Austria received back all her old dominions, except for the Netherlands, and added Venetia, which until the time of Napoleon's invasion had been an independent republic. Similarly, Genoa was incorporated in the kingdom of Sardinia, which included Piedmont and Savoy. The United Provinces and the old Austrian Netherlands were created into the kingdom of the Netherlands under the House of Orange.

Not merely was national sentiment ignored in these arrangements: in the territories that the Powers did not want for themselves measures were taken to ensure that neither German nor Italian national unity might be even partially achieved. In Germany a Confederation was established under the presidency of Austria. In Italy there was not even a confederation, but only a jumble of duchies in the north, whose ruling houses looked to Austria as their guardian, and in the south—after the Hundred Days—the kingdom of the two Sicilies, ruled by a Spanish Bourbon. Thus, while the territorial gains of Prussia in north Germany were considerable, Austria was to remain the dominant Power of Central Europe for the next half-century.

For Britain the essentials had been gained. Russia and France seemed safely held in check. The Low Countries were independent. The simple fact of British naval supremacy settled all other questions with which she was concerned; she had retained Heligoland, Malta, Mauritius, Trinidad, St. Lucia, Tobago, and the Cape of Good Hope, as well as gaining a protectorate over the Ionian Isles in the eastern Mediterranean.

The Congress was followed in the autumn of 1815 by two international treaties, both indicative of the underlying tensions

within the Concert of Powers. The first was the work of Tsar
Alexander; the second was shaped primarily by Castlereagh.
Each reflected clearly the mind of its creator.

On 26 September, 1815 the Sovereigns of Russia, Prussia, and
Austria signed the text of the Holy Alliance, drawn up by Alexander. The document opened with the phrase: 'In the Name of the
Holy and Undivided Trinity', and its first Article stated that 'in
accordance with the words of Holy Scripture, which command
all men to regard one another as brothers, the three contracting
monarchs will remain united by the bonds of a true and indis-
soluble brotherhood', and would lend each other mutual aid in all
future difficulties. The idea excited a certain ironical amusement in
Castlereagh and Metternich. Austria and Prussia had no objection
to signing, but when the invitation was extended to all the Christian Sovereigns of Europe, Castlereagh, mistrusting the whole
thing, was able to use the excuse of the constitutional position of
the Prince Regent to leave Britain outside the Alliance. Were
there, in fact, hidden motives behind the scheme? Alexander's
mind was a strange compound of mysticism and realism, and the
Alliance, including France but excluding Turkey, might well have
been an attempt to isolate the Turks, with whom Russia had been
at war in 1812, when the threat from Napoleon had interrupted
her. As it turned out, the Holy Alliance was never destined to be
a firm diplomatic *bloc*, but its name came to stand for the maintenance of autocratic government within the central and eastern
states of Europe.

In contrast to Alexander's scheme, the treaty of 20 November
was a straightforward renewal of the Quadruple Alliance that had
defeated Napoleon. It was primarily a guarantee by Britain,
Prussia, Austria, and Russia, making 'a European invasion the
inevitable and immediate consequence of Bonaparte's succession
or that of any of his race to power in France', as Castlereagh had
written earlier to Lord Liverpool. Alexander at once attempted
to enlarge the plan into a guarantee of all existing European frontiers, suggesting also that the signatories should have the right to
supervise the activity of all governments in Europe, so that any
revolutionary tendencies might be immediately suppressed.

Castlereagh avoided both these proposals. He had no wish to tie the hands of the British government for the future; as a minister of a Parliamentary government, he certainly did not wish to be bound indefinitely to a policy of supporting the autocratic monarchies. The closest that the treaty came to envisaging a *general* supervision was in the famous Article VI:

> to facilitate and to secure the execution of the present treaty and to consolidate the connections which at the present moment so closely unite the four Sovereigns for the happiness of the world, the High Contracting Parties have agreed to renew their meetings at fixed periods, either under the immediate auspices of the Sovereigns themselves or by their respective ministers for the purposes of consulting upon their common interests, and for the consideration of the measures which at each of these periods shall be considered the most salutary for the repose and prosperity of nations and for the maintenance of the peace of Europe.

Thus the only frontiers specifically guaranteed were those enclosing France. So, too, only in the eventuality of a Bonapartist rising in France were the Powers pledged to intervene. And even here no precise engagement had been drawn up. The notion of periodic congresses of the four Powers was an interesting one—something new in European diplomacy. They have sometimes been regarded as the forerunner of a League of Nations. It is, however, highly dangerous to read the twentieth century back into the nineteenth. The statesmen concerned had been schooled in eighteenth-century diplomacy, and the congresses now suggested were no more than a device for carrying on that diplomacy more effectively.

Only three congresses took place along the lines suggested in the treaty of 20 November—at Aix-la-Chapelle in 1818, at Troppau and Laibach in 1820 and 1821, and at Verona in 1822. Long before the last of these, revolutions in Spain, Portugal, and Naples had raised the question of intervention in a practical form and a growing rift had separated Britain from the Continental Powers.

The Congress of Aix-la-Chapelle was straightforward enough.

It was mainly concerned with France. The second Treaty of Paris had stipulated that the eastern departments of France should be occupied for five years by an army of 150,000 and that an indemnity of 700 million francs should be paid. Russia and Britain had reasons for wishing to relieve France of the burden of occupation earlier than this. Alexander was on good terms with the French minister, Richelieu, who had once been governor of Odessa, and hoped to make a useful ally of France. Castlereagh was anxious for the moderates to remain in power in France, and wanted, therefore, to make things as easy as possible for them. Wellington, who commanded the army of occupation, was in agreement, and by the spring of 1818 the four Powers had virtually decided that the army should be withdrawn.

The congress, which met in September, simply ratified this agreement. Negotiations that followed, however, again emphasized their differences in aim. Alexander at once proposed a general league of Powers, including France, whereby every Sovereign would be guaranteed his throne and his frontiers. It was simply a wider form of his earlier proposal of November 1815, and Castlereagh would not accept it. Nor would Austria and Prussia, who feared collaboration between France and Russia. On the other hand, the continued exclusion of France might drive her to make a private treaty with Russia. The outcome was a compromise. France was to be allowed a place at all future congresses, while Alexander agreed to stand by the continuation of the Quadruple Alliance as a safeguard against a revival of French ambitions. At the same time France, now free from further occupation and clear of her indemnity, had, by a law of 1818, made provision for increasing her own army to 240,000 men, based on conscription by ballot, and while this might reassure the Powers that the Bourbon government could successfully resist a Bonapartist rising, it meant also that France was now completely restored as an independent factor in European diplomacy.

For the moment the split between Britain and the autocratic Powers was postponed, but the events of the next two years turned it into an inescapable reality. In the German states the activity of a number of liberal and democratic movements culminated in the assassination of Kotzebue [1] in 1819, which was followed by Metternich's stern measures of repression, known as the Carlsbad decrees. In January 1820 a military rising at Cadiz imposed a liberal constitution on the Spanish King Ferdinand VII. In May there were further disturbances in Germany over the execution of Kotzebue's murderer. In July General Pepe marched on Naples and forced Ferdinand I to accept a constitution similar to the Spanish one, and the revolt spread rapidly to Sicily. In August army officers in Lisbon and Oporto demanded the convocation of the Cortes and the return of King John VI from Brazil.

Such a spate of revolution decided the rulers of the autocratic Powers that they must at once confer. The Congress of Troppau in October 1820 was continued at Laibach in January 1821. The time was clearly ripe for a renewal of Alexander's scheme for a general mutual guarantee of their thrones by the European sovereigns. Since no European frontiers were affected and there was no immediate question of a Bonapartist rising in France, it was natural that Castlereagh should continue to think differently. At Aix-la-Chapelle he had won the Austrians over, but now, with his own sphere of influence in Italy involved, Metternich swung round to Alexander's side. France at first remained non-committal, but the advent of the 'ultras' to power, in October 1821, with the ministry of Villèle, led her to press for intervention on Ferdinand's behalf in Spain.

Thus France and Austria had taken up the principles of the Holy Alliance, since it seemed at this moment to operate in their own interests. Alexander, however, was not entirely consistent in his views. At the Congress of Laibach he actually suggested that the kingdom of the Two Sicilies should be granted a liberal constitution, and it is clear that Alexander saw the scheme of a general power of interference simply as an opportunity to meddle in the territories or spheres of influence of other countries.

To Castlereagh it was evident by now that an open split with the Continental Powers could not long be avoided. He did not

[1] He was a writer who had attacked the liberal movement in the German Universities. He was stabbed to death by a young theological student named Sand.

attend either Troppau or Laibach, but sent his half-brother, Lord Stewart, as an observer. The British view had already been crystallized in the State paper of 5 May, 1820, drawn up for the Cabinet principally by Castlereagh. It put forward the earlier objections to any interference on the basis of a general guarantee. 'We shall be found in our place', it concluded, 'when actual danger menaces the system of Europe: but this country cannot and will not act upon abstract and speculative principles of precaution. The Alliance which exists had no such purpose in view in its original formation.' In the House of Commons, Castlereagh announced that he had no objection to the Austrians suppressing the Neapolitan rising, but he would not consider this as part of any collective action. He was adamant that there must be no French intervention in Spain.

The Austrians did suppress the revolution in Naples and another that broke out immediately afterwards in Piedmont. A rising of the Greeks against the Turks that followed in 1821 raised new issues with regard to Russia, and Metternich was hoping for some new basis of agreement with Castlereagh at the Congress of Verona in 1822, but before this met the British Foreign Secretary was dead.

For years Castlereagh had been appallingly overworked. Reserved and aloof, he had shared his anxieties with no one. Now suddenly, in the summer of 1822, his friends noticed an alarming change. He became wild and excited, filled with a strange persecution mania. The moving story of the end has often been told. The Duke of Wellington and Castlereagh had been comrades in war and in peace; in the darkest days of the Peninsular campaigns it had been Castlereagh's support at home on which Wellington had always been able to rely. Now at the end it was the Duke who had to tell his friend the awful truth: 'I am bound to warn you that you cannot be in your right mind.' And Castlereagh, covering his face with his hands, said: 'Since you say so, I fear it must be so.' A few days later, on 12 August, after his pistols and razors had been removed, he managed to get hold of a knife that had escaped the notice of his attendants, and he cut his throat.

Castlereagh was one of the greatest British Foreign Secretaries.

The settlement at Vienna and the uneasy years that followed are a tribute to his shrewd sense of restraint. He was concerned with what was possible and immediately relevant, but he never lost sight of the goal of lasting peace with security. His judgement was never unbalanced by the disputes of the moment or, more important, by the intoxication of military victory. He treated France with consummate tact, in spite of the long years of bitter war. The war of 1812–14 between Britain and the United States ended with a series of agreements that settled the problems of the Canadian frontier amicably and left it virtually demilitarized.[1] Even when Andrew Jackson executed a couple of adventurers who could claim the protection of the British government he saw the greater issues and abstained from action. It is a striking fact that whatever criticism may be made of the underlying principles of the Congress of Vienna, it did usher in the most peaceful century that Europe has ever known.

A new period of home government opens with his death. The contrast between his personality and Canning's has sometimes suggested a similar break in foreign policy. Canning often acted more forcefully and more rashly. But the break with the Holy Alliance had come before Castlereagh's death; it had been implicit since 1815, and it is another testimony to Castlereagh that the Concert of Powers had remained a Concert as long as it had.

[1] See p. 239.

II

THE GRADUAL REVOLUTION, 1822-50

5

LIBERAL TORYISM, 1822-30

1. Canning, Peel, and Huskisson, 1822-7

SINCE the beginning of 1820 Lord Liverpool had been aware that the government needed new blood, and had been hoping to give the Tory Cabinet a more liberal tone. This would win over the moderate reformers and would make a Whig government impossible, since Grey did not feel that he could bring his followers to come to terms with the Radicals. At the end of 1821 Peel was persuaded to accept the Home Office, and a little later the twelve votes of the Grenville group were brought over to the side of the government. By the summer of 1822 it seemed, however, that he would get no further, for George IV was obdurate over accepting Canning, who had resigned his post as President of the Board of Control in protest at the Queen's treatment.

Canning himself had given up hope and had accepted the Governor-Generalship of India, when Castlereagh's death changed the whole situation. With Castlereagh gone there was only one man who could lead the Commons, and although George held back for a month, trying to avoid the inevitable, he had eventually to agree to Canning taking over Castlereagh's position as Foreign Secretary and Leader of the House of Commons. Canning said that it was like being given a ticket of admission with the words 'Admit the rogue' written on the back, but after hesitating for three days he accepted. The reconstruction of the government was completed by January 1823, when William Huskisson accepted the position of President of the Board of Trade, with the promise of a place in the Cabinet after twelve months' service.

These three men—Canning, Peel, and Huskisson—were the main force in the new policy that is so striking in the last years of the Tory reign. In Europe, Canning finally broke with the Powers of the Holy Alliance;[1] Peel set about a fundamental remodelling of the criminal code; and Huskisson, with the support of Robinson, Chancellor of the Exchequer, began the great task of tidying up and rationalizing the Trade Laws. But Lord Liverpool remains the man who had made all this possible through the patient, tactful negotiation by which he had created this new Cabinet, and it was he who was fundamentally responsible for the new turn that governmental policy was to take.

At the Home Office, Peel turned at once to the reform of the criminal code. The existing laws were confused and harsh. A man could be hanged for innumerable offences, including stealing from a shop or on a navigable river, taking forty shillings from a dwelling-house, and even impersonating a Greenwich pensioner. The result was that the laws did not really protect the citizen. A man knew that he might as well be hanged for a sheep as a lamb, and juries would often acquit a prisoner on a trivial charge which happened to be a capital offence. The humanitarians had already fought a long campaign to end some of these laws. Romilly had struggled for years to repeal the statute that made hanging the penalty for stealing five shillings from a shop. He had failed, but on his death, in 1818, Mackintosh took up the cause, and after a committee of inquiry had been set up, succeeded in carrying three Bills abolishing the death penalty for a number of offences.

Now the humanitarians found that the new Home Secretary was on their side. The death penalty was abolished for over a hundred offences. The punishment for minor offences was also mitigated. One hundred and thirty statutes concerned with larceny were condensed into one Act, and Benefit of Clergy was abolished. Peel also concerned himself with the state of the prisons, which were appalling centres of corruption and disease. Here again the humanitarians had long been agitating, and Elizabeth Fry, a Quaker, following on the work of John Howard, had formed, in 1817, an association for the better treatment of female prisoners in Newgate. Peel's measures of prison reform compelled the Justices to inspect the prisons and to send quarterly reports to

[1] See p. 149.

D

the Home Secretary. Prisoners were to be visited by the chaplain and surgeon in their cells. They were to be given work, to receive religious instruction, and to be taught to read and write, while jailers were to be paid, instead of receiving fees.

Naturally all this only scratched the surface of the problem, and there remained much to be done in the way of improvement of living conditions and diet. In any case, Peel's measures applied only to the prisons of the county Justices—London, Westminster, and seventeen provincial towns—and did not affect the debtors' prison in London and the prisons in the smaller municipalities. Readers of *The Pickwick Papers* will remember Mr. Jingle's imprisonment for debt, an episode which Dickens could write with feeling, since he had twice seen his father suffer that fate. This penalty was not abolished until 1869, transportation continued until 1867, and executions were carried out in public until 1868.

A fairer criminal code was only one aspect of the problem. A more fundamental question was the prevention of crime, and in his careful, thoughtful way Peel gave this a great deal of attention during the whole time that he was in office. The existing police system was utterly inadequate. In London parishes were responsible for their own security, and there was little cooperation between them; in twelve of these parishes there was not a single policeman on duty at night. In Manchester the police were corrupt. Elsewhere there were almost none. In Carlisle, for example, the entire force consisted of two policemen. When a mob seemed dangerous, the magistrates could only resort to the military for aid.

After at first considering the creation of a police force for the whole kingdom, Peel eventually decided to set up an organization for a limited number of parishes in London. It was to be under two magistrates, later known as commissioners, with a headquarters at Scotland Yard, and to be directly responsible to the Home Office. He drew his recruits from retired Army N.C.O.s with certificates of good conduct, and within a year had extended the system to cover all districts of London.

The 'Bobby' or 'Peeler' has now become such an established institution, seeming to sum up the restraint and common sense of

English life, that we are inclined to forget that Peel's contemporaries regarded him at first with extreme hostility. 'Peel's police, raw lobsters, Blue Devils or by whatever other appropriate name they may be known . . .' one anonymous placard called them. 'Unity in Strength', ran a notice distributed by hand from door to door. 'Join your brother Londoners in one heart, one hand, for the abolition of the new police!' And when, in 1833, a policeman had been killed in a riot, the jury returned a verdict of justifiable homicide.

It was, perhaps, understandable that the new force should be seen as one more weapon in the hands of the Tory government. But the creation of a force whose object was to prevent crime, coupled with the repeal of much of the senselessly harsh criminal code, was a reform whose benefits were soon felt. The Metropolitan Police proved their worth a hundred times during the turbulence at the end of the decade, and the system was gradually adopted by local authorities throughout the whole country. The passing of the Municipal Corporations Act in 1835 led to a serious overhaul of local arrangements, and by 1840 108 boroughs had established their own police force. The strengthening of the police in the counties remained under discussion for some years, and although it has sometimes been maintained that the main motive was the exodus of criminal classes from London soon after the effectiveness of the Metropolitan Police had become apparent, it was ultimately the threat of the first Chartist outbreaks in 1839, at a time of acute economic depression, that led to the rapid passing of the County Police Act.

An important piece of legislation in 1824 was the repeal of the Combination Laws. The chief organizer of the movement to repeal them did not sit in Parliament at all. This was Francis Place, who kept a tailor's shop in Charing Cross Road. He was an arrogant, self-educated individualist, a man of great vigour, whose library behind his shop became a meeting-place for Radicals in London. With the help of Joseph Hume, a Radical M.P., he managed to get a committee of inquiry set up, packed it, and drilled the working men in the answers that they were to give. The outcome was a very liberal Act for Trade Unions,

passed before Liverpool or Huskisson, as they afterwards admitted, had fully realized its implications. Nor, for that matter,
had Francis Place. Imbued with the doctrine of free enterprise,
his main objection to the Combination Laws had been that their
very existence caused industrial unrest; once they were removed,
he believed, the natural working of economic laws would end the
necessity for negotiation and the Unions would disappear. In fact,
the new Act was followed by such a wave of strikes and intimida-
tion that a second Act was passed in 1825 re-establishing the com-
mon-law prohibition of combinations, with the exception of
associations formed to negotiate wages and hours of labour.
With the later development of Trade Unions this compromise
was found extremely unsatisfactory, since it left much unsettled,
and it was almost another fifty years before the questions of
striking, picketing, and the protection of Union funds were
cleared up.

Meanwhile, William Huskisson at the Board of Trade had embarked upon a policy that was to continue long after his death. A
tall, physically clumsy man, Huskisson had spent nine years in
France before the outbreak of the Revolutionary war. Like
Liverpool, he had witnessed the fall of the Bastille, and he had
been in Paris during the riotous days of June and August 1792.
These experiences made him a Tory for the rest of his life; on the
other hand, as a disciple of Adam Smith, he was conscious of the
need for considerable change in economic policy. Unrestricted
free enterprise for the commercial classes in all parts of the world
was for him the only sound theory, but such an attitude naturally
ran counter to a whole host of trade regulations, many of them
passed as war-time measures, and some simply a legacy from the
old days of Mercantilism.

Huskisson's legislation reduced innumerable import duties.
Cotton, linen, woollen goods, coffee, glass, books, paper, porce-
lain, china, copper, zinc, lead, iron, and rum were all affected.
This stimulated English manufacturers and brought prices down.
A general duty of 50% on manufactured goods was lowered to
20%. A Reciprocity of Duties Act in 1823 gave the government
power to conclude a treaty with any trading country whereby the

extra charges levied on goods imported into Great Britain in foreign ships would be lowered in return for equal concessions to British ships bringing goods into that country's ports. The freedom of colonial trade was increased, and large preferences were given in the home market for colonial goods to make up for the bounties which were being dropped. As yet, however, complete free trade was out of the question, since the government relied on import duties for a substantial portion of its revenue. Even a Free Trader had to realize that there must be a slight time lag between the removal of duties and the increased prosperity which he believed would follow as a natural consequence. This problem of the time lag was never solved satisfactorily. Some twenty years later Peel, when Prime Minister, hoped to bridge the gap by bringing back the unpopular income tax. He meant this to be only a temporary expedient, but Free Trade had run its course by the first World War, and income tax has been with us since 1842.

These few years in the 1820s had seen a remarkable achievement. Yet they only postponed the evil day for the Tories. At first the government was aided by a period of prosperity, which naturally led to great financial speculation. Then, in the autumn of 1825, over-production caused a sharp drop in prices. Panic ensued; there was a run on the banks, and seven London and eighty county banks failed. By January 1826, 10,000 Spitalfields silk-weavers were unemployed, and distress had soon spread throughout the north. Machinery was destroyed, shops were raided for food, and there were serious clashes between troops and the mob.

At the height of the crisis there came a further blow. In February 1827 Lord Liverpool had a stroke, and the man who had kept together so many discordant elements was removed from the political scene. For the Tories political disintegration was to follow on social turbulence, and within three and a half years the Whigs were to return to the power that had been denied them since the collapse of the Fox–North coalition in 1783.

2. The end of 'Church and State' and the break-up of the Tories

Lord Liverpool lingered on, a helpless invalid, until December 1828, but already in March 1827, a month after his stroke, it had become apparent that he could play no further part. Who was to succeed him? 'I think somehow', wrote Creevey [1] on 19 February, 'that it must be Canning and that he'll die of it.' George IV was determined to have a Tory government, and since a Tory Cabinet proved to be impossible without the Canningites, Canning kissed hands on 10 April. In the past Canning had often flared up at the stolid conservatism of Wellington and Eldon; he was known, moreover, to be in favour of Catholic emancipation, and his acceptance of office was followed by the resignation of Wellington, Peel, and Eldon and three others, while four Whigs accepted places in his government. This was the nearest that Liberal Toryism ever came to creating a centre party.

It was a short and unhappy ministry. Canning made several liberal pro-Catholic appointments, and the ejected placemen joined with the Old Tories in virulent attacks on him in the Commons. The Whigs feared that this liberal tendency on the part of the Tories would prolong their own exclusion from government, and in the Lords Grey, who personally detested Canning, poured invective upon him. A Bill to amend the Corn Laws was wrecked by the Lords and Canning could only promise to introduce a second Bill in the next Session. 'I can recall the lightning flash of that eye,' said Disraeli, who heard him on this occasion, 'and the tumult of that aethereal brow; still lingers in my ear the melody of that voice.'

But Canning was a dying man. His health had been failing for a long time, and he never fully recovered from a chill contracted at the funeral of the Duke of York in January that year. On 30 July, after a last audience with the King at Windsor, he was taken violently ill, and expired a week later in the little tapestried room in the house at Chiswick where Charles James Fox had died. Shortly before his death he said: 'I have laboured hard for the last few years to place the country in the high station which she now holds. Two years of the Duke of Wellington's government will undo all that I have done.'

His words were proved correct. There was, first, an unfortunate interlude. During Canning's ministry Robinson had been raised to the peerage with the title of Lord Goderich, so that he might look after the government's interests in the House of Lords. George IV now turned to him, believing him to be a weak man whom he could easily dominate. The difficulty was that Goderich could be dominated by almost anybody. For three months, bullied on all sides, he struggled to form a ministry, until at last he went to Windsor to tender his resignation, amid such a flood of tears that George had to offer him his own pocket handkerchief.

The Duke of Wellington was asked to form a ministry in January 1828. No Whigs would serve under him, but Huskisson and a few of the Canningites remained and Peel returned to the Home Office. It had only been with reluctance that the Duke had agreed to form a government, and he was not the man to deal with the situation. As Liverpool had realized, the main hope of the Tories was to win over the more conservative element of the Whigs, who would welcome a chance to avoid alliance with the Radicals. This called for consummate political skill, which the Duke simply lacked.

Parliamentary reform brought the first split in this new government. Corruption had been proved in two boroughs, East Retford and Penryn, and Lord John Russell introduced a measure for disfranchising them. A compromise was arranged within the government. Penryn's seats were to be transferred to Manchester, since Penryn was a Cornish borough and Cornwall was the most over-represented county in England. Nottinghamshire returned only eight members in all, and East Retford's seats were, therefore, not to go outside the county. The House of Lords, however, amended the Bill so that Penryn's seats should also remain within Cornwall, and Huskisson demanded in retaliation that East Retford's seats should be given to Birmingham. Accordingly he, Palmerston, and Lamb felt forced to vote against the government over the East Retford Bill. Huskisson had actually changed his mind over the distribution of the seats during the negotiations, and, feeling that his position was an uncomfortable one, wrote to Wellington offering to resign if the Duke thought that he should. He hardly expected to be taken at his word, but the Duke, who believed in a literal interpretation of such statements, accepted his resignation. Palmerston, Lamb, Charles Grant, and Lord Dudley resigned out of sympathy with Huskisson.

Before his departure Huskisson had been at work on an important amendment to the Corn Laws, and disagreements over this had already brought him into conflict with the Duke. Repeal was out of the question, but the system whereby ports were open or closed to duty-free corn during three-monthly periods had proved too rigid. Huskisson's plan was to leave the ports open, but to give the English farmer protection by means of a sliding scale. Sixty-six shillings a quarter was selected as the pivot point on this scale, at which price the duty on imported corn would be twenty shillings and eightpence. If the price dropped, the duty rose; if the price rose, the duty fell. A defective feature of the scheme, introduced after Huskisson's resignation, was that by the time the price reached seventy shillings, the duty was still ten shillings and eightpence, but since the duty was intended to be only a shilling when the price reached seventy-three shillings, the duty had to decrease very sharply between seventy and seventy-three shillings. Thus foreign importers were encouraged to hold their corn back until the price had risen well into the seventies, since every shilling increase in price meant a reduction of four shillings of duty. The British speculator, realizing that his foreign competitor would wait so long, could also reckon to hold his corn back until the price was fairly high, without fear of competition from abroad. This measure, known as the Duke of Wellington's Sliding Scale, was passed in 1828, and remained in force until 1842, when Peel revised the working of it.

The continued protection of English corn was naturally perfectly consistent with Tory principles. But the most remarkable measure passed by the Duke of Wellington's government makes utter nonsense of the careful distinctions implied in party labels. It is a striking feature of the nineteenth century that party politics continually broke down because politicians, very often with their careers at stake, insisted on speaking and voting according to what they felt was best for the country. The passing of Catholic emancipation by a Tory government is an interesting example of this.

One of the basic tenets of the Tory party was a deep respect for the established Church. This was not simply a question of religious belief. 'Westminster Abbey', Croker [1] had said, 'is part of the British constitution'; for the Tory, Church and State were inseparable and the responsible positions in the land should be the preserve of the Anglicans. In theory, the Corporation Act of 1661, the Test Act of 1673 and the oaths of supremacy made it impossible for anyone who was not an Anglican to occupy any of the higher executive or judicial posts. As has been seen, it was only the Catholics who were rigorously excluded, since an annual Indemnity Act was passed to cover Dissenters who broke the law.

In March 1828 Lord John Russell introduced a Bill for the repeal of the Test and Corporation Acts, and since by itself it did not directly affect the Catholics [2] and amounted to no more than a tidying up of the Statute Book, it was supported by a considerable majority in the Commons. Peel and Wellington did not care greatly for it, but decided not to oppose it, and the repeal was passed. This development was watched with keen interest by the Catholics and those who favoured Catholic emancipation, for it had been highly unlikely that relief from religious disabilities could be gained for the Catholics while the Dissenters were also still theoretically bound by them. In the same year a startling turn of events in Ireland presented the government with a challenge that brought about emancipation within a year.

In 1823 an Irish Catholic lawyer, Daniel O'Connell, had formed the Catholic Association, supported by the peasantry, who each contributed a penny a month. He was a vigorous, persuasive speaker, and by 1825 the Association had an income of £1,000 a

---

[1] See Further Reading, p. 458.

[2] Roman Catholics were excluded from the Houses of Parliament by a separate Test Act of 1678 and from executive and judicial posts by a mass of legislation dating back to the reign of Elizabeth.

week. His aims were to re-establish an Irish Parliament in Dublin in which Catholics would sit, and to bring about the disestablishment of the Anglican Church in Ireland. The first step in this plan was to get Catholic M.P.s into Westminster, and to achieve this the county electors had to be won over from subservience to their landlords. The Irish authorities, alarmed at its rapid growth, dissolved the Association, but O'Connell simply changed the name of the organization and continued to collect the contributions. The Catholic priests lent their support to the movement, and in 1826 the first victory was won when the Association successfully supported a Protestant candidate at Waterford during the general election, with the result that the Beresford family lost a seat which they had come to regard as their own property. The freeholders paid the penalty for their boldness; evictions followed by the hundred, but O'Connell maintained his hold.

Canning's death in 1827 was naturally a blow to O'Connell's hopes, and he viewed the appointment of the Duke of Wellington with despair. Then, in 1828, he saw his chance to force the issue before the government. Charles Grant's resignation in sympathy with Huskisson meant that Wellington had to find a new President of the Board of Trade. He chose Vesey-Fitzgerald, the member for Clare, who therefore had to resign his seat and fight a by-election.[1] Vesey-Fitzgerald was a popular landlord, known to be in favour of Catholic emancipation, but his new office would make him a member of a Cabinet whose policy was anti-Catholic, and his popularity waned. O'Connell himself stood as the opposing candidate; the electors, headed by their priests, flocked to the polls in support of him, and after five days Vesey-Fitzgerald gave up. The sheriff was in an unenviable position. Catholics were perfectly entitled to give their votes to a Catholic, if they wished—yet he could not announce O'Connell as the new member, since no Catholic might sit at Westminster. On the other hand, if he declared O'Connell's election void, the result would be rebellion, in which the opening shots would probably be fired at him. His way out of the difficulty was simply to an-

---

[1] The Place Act of 1707 required this from any M.P. who accepted an office of profit from the Crown.

nounce the figures of the polling, and the problem was transferred to London.

The Duke of Wellington's mind had, in fact, been moving towards an acceptance of emancipation. 'Bets have been laid', wrote Greville in June 1828, 'that Catholics will sit in Parliament next year.' The situation in Ireland convinced Wellington at last that it must come. The Irish peasantry were in a state of excitement, and if O'Connell were not allowed to take his seat, it was doubtful how long he could hold them in check. It was obvious that at the next general election Catholics would be returned in many parts of the country and the Union would have become a farce. It would be absurd to suggest that troops could not have put down an Irish rising, but the notion of open civil war was obnoxious to both Wellington and Peel. The only way out of the emergency was to pass Catholic emancipation, which would have to apply to the whole of the United Kingdom. This would betray the principles of the party, but there seemed to be little alternative. Dissolution was out of the question so soon after the previous general election. If, on the other hand, Wellington resigned, it was certain that no non-Tory government would succeed in getting such a Bill through the House of Lords and accepted by George IV.

The Duke spent the winter in negotiation with the King, the bishops, and Peel. George IV stormed, and threatened to abdicate. The Archbishop of Canterbury and the Bishops of London and Durham remained opposed to the idea. Peel felt that if he did announce his conversion to emancipation this must be followed by his resignation, but after seeing the Duke's desperate situation, agreed to remain. Peel has often since been accused of holding on to office regardless of his principles. Such a charge is inconsistent with his character. It was, in fact, his principles which, in a crisis, rose above party loyalty and led him to support measures that might have jeopardized his political career. As it turned out, he survived Catholic emancipation; the repeal of the Corn Laws, seventeen years later, he did not survive.

The Speech from the Throne in February 1829 spoke of reviewing religious disabilities, and the Old Tories knew that Wellington and Peel had won the battle with the King. There were bitter scenes. As soon as the preliminaries were over, Peel felt that he could quieten his conscience by resigning his seat for Oxford University and fighting a by-election, but the infuriated University Tories gave vent to their rage by throwing him out, and he had hastily to find a pocket borough. Wellington, inundated with insulting letters, eventually issued a challenge to Lord Winchelsea, and the two men fought a duel at Battersea.

On 6 March Peel introduced the Emancipation Bill in a four-hour speech. The struggle in the Commons lasted the rest of the month. For one day the country was without a government, when George changed his mind and the Cabinet resigned. Then he weakened, and sent a note that night to Wellington, recalling him. Peel himself was in high spirits, for this cold, aloof man loved a fight, once his mind was made up. His father followed the contest with delight in the newspapers. 'Robin's the lad, after all,' he would say. 'The Duke could do nothing without him.' Croker admitted as much to Vesey-Fitzgerald in May. 'His single speech has every night supported the whole debate upon our side.' The Emancipation Bill passed the Lords early in April and by the middle of the month had become law.

In one of her early writings Charlotte Brontë gave an account of how the news was followed in the remote parsonage at Haworth.

I remember the day when the *Intelligence Extraordinary* came with Mr Peel's speeches, containing the terms on which the Catholics were to be let in. With what eagerness Papa tore off the cover and how we all gathered round him and with what breathless anxiety we listened as one by one they were disclosed and explained and argued upon so ably and so well, and then when it was all out, how aunt said that she thought it was excellent and that the Catholics could do no harm with such good security. I remember also the doubts as to whether it would pass the House of Lords and the prophecies that it would not, and when the paper came which was to decide the question, the anxiety was almost dreadful with which we listened to the whole affair; the opening of the door; the hush; the royal dukes in their robes and the Great Duke in green sash and waistcoat; the

rising of all the peeresses when he rose; the reading of his speech—
Papa saying that his words were like precious gold; and lastly the
majority . . . in favour of the Bill.

Three Bills in all were involved. One suppressed the Catholic
Association—which had already dissolved itself. The principal
one repealed all penal laws that subjected Roman Catholics to civil
disabilities. From now on all offices in the United Kingdom and
seats in both Houses of Parliament were open to Catholics, except
the positions of Regent, Lord Chancellor, and Lord Lieutenant
and Lord Chancellor of Ireland. The only requirement was that
they should take an oath denying the power of the Pope to interfere in domestic affairs, recognizing the Protestant succession, and
repudiating any intention to upset the Anglican Church. A third
Bill raised the freehold qualification in Ireland for a vote in a parliamentary election from forty shillings to ten pounds.

The purpose of this last Bill was to prevent the Irish vote from
falling into the hands of demagogues, and one of the results was
that the landlords now got rid of their forty-shilling freeholders.
They had, in any case, shown the unreliability of their vote in the
O'Connell election, and now they had no vote at all. In fact, the
county electorate had dropped from over 200,000 to 19,000. It
had been calculated by the Duke that the outcome of emancipation would be about sixty Catholic M.P.s at Westminster. Apart
from this, the change was more theoretical than practical; the
hold of the Anglicans on most of the higher posts was too firm
to be shaken at once, and the University Tests still remained.
But the essential had been achieved. From now on the Irish
vote in the Commons was to be a vital factor in English political
life, particularly at times when parties lacked an absolute
majority.

Catholic emancipation was one more nail in the Tories' coffin.
Wellington and Peel had acted according to their sense of duty to
the Crown, but the right-wing Tories did not intend to forgive
them, and Churchmen, squires, and Oxford dons fulminated at
the betrayal of 'Church and State'. Yet the government had not
succeeded in winning back the Canningites, and only the divisions

among the Whigs preserved Wellington's administration for a few more months.

In 1829 the harvest was poor, and the social distress which had been serious in the north for the last two years spread to the south. Unions among the working classes were formed, and in January 1830 Thomas Attwood started the Birmingham Political Union of the Lower and Middle Classes, demanding 'manhood suffrage and paper money'. It was a highly significant alliance; the Radicals were succeeding in harnessing the social unrest to their demand for electoral reform and it did not seem that the question could be postponed much longer.

Events moved quickly after this. On 26 June, 1830 George IV died and a general election automatically followed. While the polling was going on, news from France began to filter through. Revolution had broken out in Paris. Charles X had been driven from the throne and Louis Philippe had been set up in his place. The news of a revolution, so quick and virtually bloodless, spread like wild-fire, and it has often been assumed that this had the effect of enormously strengthening the anti-Tory vote. In fact, owing to the nature of the electoral system, only about seventy constituencies in England and Wales were seriously contested in 1830. A full report of events in Paris first appeared in English newspapers on 3 August, and by this date the polling for about thirty-six of these constituencies had already been completed. Naturally, newspapers were not the only means of communication, and it is impossible to assess the influence of the French revolution of 1830 in so intangible a matter as public opinion. Nevertheless, it seems likely that the major factors in the British elections of that year were the growing demands for Parliamentary reform and cheap bread, and that the activities in France were considered as a belated imitation of the English revolution of 1688 rather than as a guide for the electorate of 1830.

The atmosphere was, none the less, revolutionary. In the countryside, as soon as the harvest was in, labourers, driven at last to desperate action, attacked the wealthier farmers, demanding higher wages and destroying the new threshing machines that threatened to rob them of their employment, and throughout the southern counties the hayricks blazed.

In October the new Parliament reassembled. What would the Duke of Wellington make of it? Even now there was no formed opposition against the government. If the Duke had cut his losses with the Old Tories and proposed a moderate measure of parliamentary reform, he might have saved his government. He might have won back the Canningites and even gained some of the borderline Whigs. As it was, Parliament gained the worst possible impression. The Speech from the Throne made no mention of any relief measures for the economic distress; there was a hint that the government might assist the Dutch in putting down the Belgians who had revolted against Dutch rule. It was left to the Duke himself to say the last word. In a speech in the House of Lords he stated that 'the system of representation possessed the full and entire confidence of the country'. Sitting down at the end he whispered to Lord Aberdeen: 'I have not said too much, have I?' 'You'll hear of it,' replied Aberdeen, and when a friend asked him afterwards what the Duke had said, he remarked briefly: 'He said that we're going out.'

He was right. A wave of fury swept the whole country and ministers were bombarded with threatening letters. The party finally disintegrated. The Old Tories were still in high dudgeon over Catholic emancipation; the Canningites would compromise no longer, and joined the Whigs. On 15 November the government was defeated over a motion on the civil list and on the next day Peel was happy to announce their resignation to the Commons. The new King, William IV, turned to Lord Grey, who stood now on the right wing of the Whig group. Grey was still not comfortable about an alliance with the Radicals, but the revolutions in Europe had strengthened his belief in the possibility of Parliamentary reform, and having made a Reform Bill a condition of acceptance, he agreed to form a government.

6

LORD GREY'S REFORM MINISTRY, 1830–4

1. The struggle over the Reform Bill

THE men whom Lord Grey chose for his Cabinet in November 1830 could hardly have been less like the earnest reformers of the Victorian age, of whom they were the immediate forerunners. Their world was of the eighteenth century. Grey himself, glad at first to be in power, soon tired of the responsibility and frustration of office and longed for the peace of his library at Howick Hall. Lord Althorp, his Chancellor of the Exchequer, was happiest when managing his estates, and even at the height of the Reform Bill crisis read his bailiff's letters before the rest of his mail. William Lamb, now Lord Melbourne, Home Secretary, regarded the whole world of politics with the same amused, leisurely air as he did everything else in life, while the cocksure, gallant spirit of the Foreign Secretary, Lord Palmerston, stamped him as a man of the Regency. All but four of the Cabinet were members of the House of Lords, and of those four Althorp was heir to an earldom and Palmerston an Irish peer. This body of eighteenth-century aristocrats, who had wished so long to bring about some measure of constitutional reform, knew that they were living in an England that had changed out of all recognition since the days of their youth, and they were uneasily aware of new social forces that might well take reform into unknown channels.

The moment was certainly tense. In the month when Grey took office labourers were still rioting in Hampshire, Wiltshire, and Berkshire. There was, however, very little that was coordinated among these movements that sprang from the threat of unemployment and hunger. The danger of organized conspiracy came mainly from the political unions, organized by middle-class

Radicals, who saw no chance of passing legislation in their own interest through the House of Commons as at present constituted. It had been a similar group of bourgeois, joining forces with the mob in Paris, that had knocked Charles X from his throne. Grey's belief now was that a reform of the representative system was no longer an abstract question of political justice. It was vitally necessary if a revolution, led by the middle classes, was to be averted. Constitutional reform would have two main aims: to redistribute the constituencies in accordance with the present population, wiping out the old pocket and rotten boroughs; [1] and to extend the franchise in the counties and, more particularly, the boroughs, so that it might include the new industrialist classes. It is doubtful whether Grey had any greater love for the middle class than the Duke of Wellington. He simply interpreted the present crisis differently. In May 1831 he told King William IV that 'it was the spirit of the age which was triumphing; that to resist it was certain destruction'. Whereas the Duke stated with typical vigour: 'I see in thirty members for the rotten boroughs thirty men, I don't care of what party, who would preserve the state of property as it is.' This difference of attitude was now to culminate in one of the greatest Parliamentary battles of the century.

The Cabinet had to bear in mind three major considerations. First, they needed the support of the King. The royal veto had not been used since 1707, but this had been partly because legislation had been dropped or ministers had resigned if the King was known to be opposed to it, as Pitt had done over Catholic emancipation in 1801. Second, if the conservative outlook and personal interest of the territorial magnates caused the Bill to be rejected in the House of Lords, would William agree to create sufficient peers to overcome this resistance? And, if he did, what would be the reaction to this drastic step among the peers who, up till then, had favoured reform? Third, in the Commons, Grey's supporters included many whose notions of reform were only lukewarm and who might easily turn to the Tories through fear of the violent forces of revolution at work in the country.

The last of these was dealt with at once. Lord Melbourne, the

[1] See p. 25.

new Home Secretary, gave orders for the existing laws to be strictly enforced. All rioting was rigorously suppressed by troops, and special commissioners were appointed with full powers, so that the trials might begin at once. Hundreds were sentenced to death by the courts sitting at Salisbury and Winchester, and although only a few sentences were carried out, 457 were transported to Australia. Disorder was by no means quelled. Political unions and radical journalists continued to organize resistance, and in December a mob of workmen marched to St. James's Palace bearing with them the tricolour. But the government, by its action, had at least made it clear to its more doubtful followers that it meant to stand firm against revolution.

The other difficulties could be met at first only by the terms of the Bill itself. In January 1831 Lord Grey gained William's approval of a Bill of reform that had been drawn up by a committee consisting of Sir James Graham, Lord Durham, Lord Duncannon, and Lord John Russell. Throughout February the country waited and on 1 March Lord John Russell presented the Bill to the Commons. The House listened in eager excitement that changed gradually to astonishment and then anger, and the speech was increasingly interrupted by the jeers and shouts of the Tories as the names of the disfranchised boroughs were read out. Even many of the Whigs listened in consternation, and Peel, who, although a Tory, had hoped that he might be able to come to terms with a moderate measure of reform, sat with his head in his hands, knowing that he could only oppose such a Bill.

The government had certainly been bold. Sixty boroughs of less than 2,000 inhabitants were to be disfranchised (Schedule A). Forty-seven boroughs of between 2,000 and 4,000 inhabitants were to lose one member (Schedule B). These seats had been redistributed mostly among the new manufacturing towns and the counties. The franchise had been made uniform—in the boroughs householders rated at £10 or over, in the counties £10 copyholders and £50 leaseholders for a term of years as well as the forty-shilling freeholders. The government had hoped, however, that certain aspects of the Bill might win over some of the Tory waverers. There was no suggestion of manhood suffrage; the absence of ballot meant that the landlords would still be able to check up on their tenants' votes, and the county representation had been considerably increased to compensate for the enfranchisement of the industrial towns. Yet the initial reception of the Bill proved that they were to be disappointed; nor were they likely to gain any support from the extreme Radicals, who regarded the Bill as 'a damnable delusion, giving us as many tyrants as there are shopkeepers'.

On 23 March the Bill passed its second reading by one vote and shortly afterwards was defeated in committee. Two courses were open to the government—to resign, or to ask the King to dissolve Parliament and then fight a general election. Now that the terms of the Bill were known to the country, there was a good chance that an election would result in Grey's group being returned with a large majority. The Tories thus strongly opposed dissolution, but William IV, at last convinced that only Grey could save his throne, set off from St. James's Palace for Westminster. A furious debate was in progress in the Commons, and as the firing of cannon announced the King's approach, government members cheered derisively. Peel was in the middle of an impassioned speech when Black Rod came to summon the Commons to the Lords' Chamber. Here some of the peers had almost come to blows, when William at last arrived and Parliament was dissolved.

Not all the rotten and pocket boroughs and the power of the landlords could prevent the government's return with a much greater majority. A second Reform Bill was introduced, extending the vote to £50 tenants-at-will in the counties, an amendment suggested by Lord Chandos, which might win over some of the Tory waverers, since it increased the power of the landlord. The Bill passed the Commons, and on 22 September received its first reading in the Lords. A fortnight later the second reading began, and on the night of 7 October the Lords rejected it by a majority of forty-one.

October 1831 was the month when England came closest to violent revolution. The reform Press spread the news in blackedged editions, and a wave of outbreaks swept the country. At Nottingham the castle belonging to the Duke of Newcastle was

burnt; in Derby the jail was broken into and the prisoners released; at Bristol the mob set fire to the jails, the town hall, and
the bishop's palace. Detached, outwardly unperturbed, Melbourne repeated his measures of the previous year to keep the
capital under control and to quell the disorder in the provinces.
'Damn reform! I wish I had never touched it!' said Grey at this
time, but it was clear that lasting peace depended on the successful
passage of the Bill, and he did not give up.

On 12 December Lord John Russell introduced the Reform
Bill for the third time in the Commons. A few more concessions
had been made. Five of the fifty-six disfranchised boroughs were
changed; eleven boroughs were withdrawn from Schedule B. On
18 March, 1832 the Bill passed its third reading in the Commons
with a majority of 162. In the Lords the second reading was
passed by a narrow majority of nine, but when Lord Grey refused
to accept an amendment, which would have allowed the Tories
to prevent the abolition of the nomination boroughs, he was
defeated. Grey now turned to the King, demanded the creation
of fifty peers, and when William would not agree to more than
twenty, resigned on 8 May.

William could only look to the Tories. Yet he knew that if they
formed a government the state of the country demanded that they
should pass some measure involving Parliamentary reform. What
could the Tories do? The Duke of Wellington was prepared to
make the attempt, believing this to be the duty of a loyal subject
of the King. It was Peel who stopped him. At a meeting at Lord
Stormont's house he made it plain that he would have nothing to
do with it. 'It is *not* a repetition of the Catholic question,' he said
in a written reply to Croker. 'I was then in office. I had advised
the concession as a Minister. I should now assume office for the
purpose of carrying the measure to which up to the last moment
I have been inveterately opposed.' When Harrowby, too, had
refused the premiership, Wellington attempted to form a government himself. 'To stop the Duke go for the gold', read Francis
Place's placards, and a run on the bank actually began. But it was
a Tory in the Commons, Sir Robert Inglis, who finally stopped
the Duke, by condemning his attempt as ignoble, and a little later

the Duke took Peel's advice and informed the King that he could not form a government.

It was thus that revolution was averted. The Whigs returned to power. William consented to create fifty peers, if they were needed, and the Tory lords, under Wellington's leadership, withdrew their opposition to the Bill. On 4 June the Bill passed its third reading, the royal consent was given, and the Reform Bill became law.

What was the practical extent of the reform? There had been no increase in the 658 seats of the House of Commons. They had simply been redistributed. After separate Bills for Scotland and Ireland had been passed, the total electorate of the United Kingdom had risen from 478,000 to 814,000.[1]

Of the English constituencies fifty-six boroughs had been entirely disfranchised, Weymouth reduced from four members to two, and thirty boroughs left with one member each. There had been created in their place twenty-two new two-member boroughs and twenty returning one member each. Seven counties received a third member and twenty-six counties were divided in half, each division returning two members. The Isle of Wight received one member and Yorkshire was raised from four to six. In the counties the franchise was retained by the forty-shilling freeholder and extended to the copyholders and long leaseholders whose land was of the clear yearly value of £10, as well as to the £50 short leaseholders and to the tenant farmer paying not less than £50 a year in rent. In the boroughs the new qualification was the occupation of property rated at £10 or more a year. Existing qualifications in the boroughs mostly remained untouched, provided that the voter was resident. These ancient rights, however, were to terminate with the lives of the present holders, with the exception of the freeman franchise.

For Scotland the forty-five seats in the Commons were raised to fifty-three, the extra eight being given to the burghs. The transformation of the Scottish franchise was revolutionary, since the previous situation had been far more corrupt and unrepresentative than in England. Out of a population of 2,300,000 there had

---

[1] See Statistics, pp. 452-3.

been an electorate of 4,000. This was now increased to 64,000, the vote in the counties going to those who held land of the annual value of £10 or other property of £20, and in the burghs to those who occupied houses of the annual value of £10. In the Irish Bill less change was brought about, since many anomalies had already been removed by legislation in 1800 and 1829. Representation in the House of Commons was increased only from 100 to 105 seats. The forty-shilling freeholder, who had lost his vote in 1829, remained disfranchised, and in the counties the property qualification was still a £10 freehold and certain leaseholds. In the boroughs a £10 rate-payer franchise was introduced. The total electorate in Ireland now numbered about 93,000.

In spite of the emotional fervour which the Bill had inspired, however, its immediate significance must not be over-estimated. The counties' representation had risen from 186 seats to 253, while the boroughs, main hope of the new industrialist class, had dropped from 472 seats to 405. In addition to this, a Boundaries Commission was set up, after the Act had been passed, in order to enlarge some of the boroughs whose population had only just been great enough to justify survival, and its findings, which affected all but twenty boroughs, resulted in the inclusion of many disfranchised boroughs within new boundaries. This rearrangement was usually in the interest of the landed class. The Act had not destroyed all nomination boroughs, and it has been reckoned that after 1832 there were still about fifty boroughs in England and Wales returning sixty members who depended on some territorial magnate.

The increase in the electorate had not brought the system much closer to anything resembling democracy. The 814,000 voters were no more than one-thirtieth of the total population. The power of the landlord was still considerable, first, because of the inclusion of the tenant farmers, who were particularly in his power—between a quarter and a fifth of the county electorate—and, second, because voting was still open. The introduction of the ballot had been considered and then dropped at the very beginning of the negotiations, since the exercise of a man's vote was considered a responsibility that could be safeguarded only by publicity. 'What pitiful figures we should cut,' wrote Lord William Russell in 1838, 'sneaking up to the ballot box, looking with fear to the right and the left and dropping in our paper, the contents of which we are afraid or ashamed to acknowledge.' The poor had gained little, since the £10 householder was usually middle class, although in a few boroughs this qualification did include a section of the working classes.

The social level of the M.P.s themselves changed even less, since the property qualification remained untouched, county members needing a landed estate worth £600 annually and borough members £300. An election was still an expensive matter after the Act. His election at Nottingham cost John Hobhouse £2,000 in 1834 and £4,000 in 1837, while at Sudbury, in 1841, two votes cost as much as £30. Electors were given dinners, made drunk, promised contracts and loans, and sometimes kidnapped by the opposing candidate. The election at Eatanswill, which Charles Dickens described in the *Pickwick Papers*, was hardly an exaggeration of such scenes, and the corruption and violence at elections remained a striking feature of English political life.

Yet the significance of 1832 is undeniable. The system might still be far from democratic, but the old assumptions and prerogatives in society and government were no longer operative, for it seemed hardly possible that the new electorate might be organized and disciplined as the old had been. Neither the Crown nor the Lords would be able to enjoy their former control over the composition of the Commons. 'You return me to Parliament', said young William Gladstone to the electors of Newark in December 1832, 'not merely because I am the Duke of Newcastle's man, but because the man whom the Duke has sent, and the Duke himself, are *your* men.' His remark was not entirely appropriate, since Newark was one of the pocket boroughs that had escaped the reform, and Gladstone himself had spoken against the Bill in the Oxford Union; yet it summed up the general form of the change. The effects would only gradually make themselves felt, but the ultimate consequences were to be immense. As Peel had seen, the Act had opened a door, and through that door there was to come a whole mass of social and administrative reform, which was to bring in its wake the succeeding Parliamentary Reform Acts of the nineteenth century.

2. The Whig reforms

The new Parliament that met in 1833 gave Grey a very considerable majority, and the next two years were remarkable for the measures of reform that were passed. But the victory of the industrialists was bound to weaken the alliance that they had formed with their workers, and behind much of this legislation it is possible to see the growing divergence between the purely humanitarian and the Benthamite outlook.

Some issues were relatively simple. In 1833 £20,000 was voted by Parliament 'for the purposes of education' to be shared between the Anglican National Society and the British and Foreign School Society, whose teaching was undenominational. Much of the money was spent on the building of schools, and although the education of the children of the poor remained wretchedly inadequate, the government grant was an acknowledgement of responsibility that was later to have tremendous repercussions.

The abolition of slavery in the British colonies was also fairly straightforward. It was a question that had troubled the minds of humanitarians and Evangelicals like Wilberforce and Clarkson for many years. England had been the first nation to prohibit the Slave Trade in 1807, and by 1820 most European countries had passed similar legislation. But the suppression of the trade, unaccompanied by the abolition of slavery itself, had made slave-smuggling a highly profitable enterprise, and the conditions under which blacks were smuggled across the Atlantic had become even more terrible than when the trade had been legitimate. In the 1820s Wilberforce had led petitions in favour of abolition with compensation for the owners, but although Canning's government had favoured some measure of reform, the planters had usually been able to avoid any change. In 1833 Lord Stanley, the Colonial Secretary, introduced a scheme of emancipation. All slaves were to be freed within twelve months; planters were to be granted a total of £20 million in compensation by the mother country. Wilberforce died a few weeks later, conscious that his life-work had been accomplished. It had been a great altruistic measure, but for some years afterwards European countries and certain sections of England watched the West Indies critically for any unfavourable economic repercussions.[1]

If middle-class Radicals and humanitarians had joined hands over the slavery issue, they were not so united over industrial and social legislation within England. The conditions in the factories in the north of England at this time were deplorable. Men, women, and children worked fifteen or sixteen hours at a stretch and, allowing for the time required to reach the mill, a child would be lucky to enjoy more than four hours' sleep. In 1830 an Evangelical, Richard Oastler, published a letter on 'Child Slavery' in the Leeds Mercury and opened a new campaign of agitation for a legal regulation of the working day. After getting little support from the Radicals, among whom the mill-owners were strongly represented, he turned to the Tories, many of whom responded to the opportunity of scoring a point off the industrialists. At Westminster Michael Sadler, a Tory Evangelical, succeeded in having a Select Committee on Child Labour set up. When Sadler was defeated in the 1832 election, Lord Ashley took up the cause and proposed a Bill by which children between nine and eighteen should work only ten hours a day, and no one under twenty-one should work at night. The cunning of the suggestion lay in the fact that child and adult labour were so interlocked in the organization of the mills that if this regulation were accepted the mills themselves would not be able to work for longer than ten hours out of every twenty-four. Thus, under the guise of protecting the children, the adult working day would have been made more tolerable.

The manufacturers were at once up in arms, and succeeded in passing a measure by one vote that a Royal Commission should re-examine the whole question. Ashley warned Althorp that if there were much further delay the masses in the north would break out. Melbourne acted quickly and decided that a government Bill

[1] See p. 206.

must forestall Ashley's, which was due for its second reading on
17 July. Edwin Chadwick, a lawyer and a confirmed Benthamite,
was appointed to preside over the Commission—'a set of briefless
barristers and fee-less doctors,' sneered Oastler. Regarded as a tool
of the manufacturers, they were severely mistrusted by the working classes and the humanitarians, as they made their rapid tour of
the north.

> 'We will have the Ten Hours Bill
> That we will, that we will,'

sang the children at Leeds in an organized demonstration. And
this mistrust was justified, for the Commission discovered a neat
way of protecting the children without interfering with the running of the mills.

Chadwick's report was in by the end of June, and the government at once announced legislation based on his findings. It was
to apply to almost all textile factories. Children under nine were
not to be employed. Those under thirteen were to work only
forty-eight hours a week or nine hours a day, and those under
eighteen only sixty-nine hours a week or twelve hours a day—
none of these hours to be at night. But the hours of daytime were
defined as being between 5.30 a.m. and 8.30 p.m., and a relay system of child labour was permitted so that the mills might run for
the whole of this time and there would thus be no restriction on
the adult working day. Boards of inspectors were to be set up to
see that the law was obeyed and to superintend the two hours'
schooling that the children were to have every day. Amendments
by the House of Lords later made these educational clauses almost
ineffective. On 18 July the government Bill beat Ashley's Ten
Hours Bill and in August 1833 it became law.

The Poor Law Amendment of 1834 was also largely Edwin
Chadwick's work and was an even purer example of Benthamism
in practice. The whole system had long been in need of overhaul.
Elizabethan measures whereby the parish was made responsible
for the relief of 'impotent, aged, and needy persons' had ceased to
be effective during the period of economic revolution in the
second half of the eighteenth century, and the Speenhamland

scheme, which had granted a man a dole as a supplement to his wages, according to the size of his family, had pauperized the English labourer and had sent the cost of poor-law administration rocketing from £619,000 in 1750 to almost £8 million in 1818.

Grey's government determined to settle the question and set up a commission of inquiry in whose report the ruthless, vigorous mind of Edwin Chadwick is everywhere in evidence. Reform there was to be, but not as a humanitarian would have wished it. The Speenhamland system must go. It was expensive and, furthermore, it interfered with the natural operation of economic laws. The answer was to discourage men from becoming paupers. 'Nothing is necessary to arrest the progress of pauperism,' ran the Report, 'except that all who receive relief from the parish should work for the parish exclusively, as hard and for less wages than independent labourers work for individual employers.' By the Act of 1834 parishes were to be grouped into unions, in which workhouses would be set up, where the level of life would be so low that only the genuinely destitute would allow themselves to become a burden on the parish rates. It was the pleasure–pain principle translated neatly into an efficient administrative machine. A central authority of three Commissioners was to control the whole system, while local Boards of Guardians were to be elected by the ratepayers of the parishes to superintend the work of the paid officials in the workhouses. The Act strongly discouraged the granting of outdoor relief, which was to be strictly controlled by the Commissioners.

At first a couple of good harvests and a higher level of employment through the building of railways kept the workhouse population down. In any case, it took the parishes a few years to organize their union workhouse, and in the meanwhile outdoor relief was continued. The great depression in 1837 came just when the houses were ready in most parts of the country to receive their unhappy occupants, and as the numbers of paupers rose, so, too, did popular hatred of the 'three Bashaws' of Somerset House and of their new 'Bastilles'. The same type of work was demanded from every kind of pauper over the age of seven. They were allowed little exercise and few visitors; married couples were separated; parents could not see their children; and over-crowding led to outbreaks of disease. Again, Charles Dickens had no need to exaggerate when he depicted the wretched childhood of Oliver Twist. Certainly, in one respect Chadwick had suc-ceeded; no one who could avoid it went to the workhouse and the consequent drop in the poor rates was most marked—from an annual average of £6,750,590 for 1830-4 to an average of £4,567,988 for 1835-9. Yet the results were not entirely as he had hoped. 'First', he had said, 'the labourer becomes more diligent; next, the more efficient labour makes the return to the farmer's capital larger and the consequent increase of the fund for the em-ployment of labour enables and induces the capitalist to give better wages.' In this last point he was wrong. Wages did not rise. With the threat of the workhouse the employer did not have to offer higher wages; if anything, they went down, and the labourer, now deprived of Speenhamland relief, had to see his wife and family go out to work in the fields in the hated gang system. Thus the years following the Poor Law Amendment brought no immediate end to the destitution and starvation in the countryside, which was only relieved in the course of time by mounting prosperity in the 1850s.

3. The end of Grey's ministry

It was Irish affairs that eventually brought the ministry to grief. Catholic emancipation had not ended the turbulence in Ireland. Lord Grey maintained early in 1833 that 9,000 acts of crime had been committed during 1832; no local jury could be relied upon to convict, and accordingly, early in 1833, a Coercion Bill was introduced by Stanley, the Irish Secretary,[1] and duly be-came law. This was to be followed by remedial legislation which it was hoped would go to the root of the trouble.

O'Connell's group held firm to its two main objectives—repeal of the Union and the disestablishment of the Anglican Church in Ireland. The government had no intention of touching the Act of Union, but the position of the established Church was being

---

[1] Stanley became Secretary for War and Colonies in March 1833.

seriously questioned at this time—in England as well as Ireland.[1] In 1833 an Irish Church Bill was introduced proposing the suppression of ten sees, as well as the parishes where there was no Protestant congregation. The income of the remaining bishoprics and benefices was to be taxed by the state; it was reckoned that this should bring in £69,000 a year, which would be spent within the Church, thereby making it possible to abolish the unpopular Church rate. The opposition to the Bill was based on an objection to the whole conception of income tax—'a principle', Peel called it, 'dangerous to the security of all property, whether lay or ecclesiastical, corporate or individual'. The government had also suggested that any surplus might be spent as Parliament should choose. This last clause had to be dropped, and the Bill eventually became law.

The Church rate had gone, but tithe remained a deeper cause of Irish anger. In 1833 the government had already advanced £1 million to tithe-owners to make up for arrears that could not be collected. In 1834 Littleton proposed that tithe should be commuted into a land tax payable not by the cultivator, but by the landlord, and that the whole of this income should be handed over to a body of commissioners who would distribute it among the Irish clergy. It was Lord John Russell who objected to the last part of this proposal. He suggested that some of the revenue should be diverted to other purposes. This was tantamount to a partial disendowment, which would not be countenanced by many of the government. 'Johnny Russell has upset the coach,' wrote Stanley in a scribbled note to Graham, and after the resolution had been introduced, Stanley, Graham, Ripon, and Richmond resigned from the Cabinet.

One further episode over Ireland finally brought Grey's government down. The Coercion Act of 1833 was about to expire, and Littleton, now Irish Secretary, negotiated with O'Connell on the understanding that public meetings would in future no longer be prohibited, believing that he had Althorp's support in this. In return, O'Connell agreed not to oppose a Whig candidate standing at a by-election at Wexford. But Littleton had been too hasty.

[1] See p. 106.

The Cabinet refused to grant the concession, acting on the advice of Lord Wellesley, the Lord Lieutenant. An exactly similar Coercion Bill was introduced into the House, and O'Connell rose to denounce the government, making the whole of Littleton's offer public. 'The pig's killed,' said Althorp to Russell, and he was right. A government minister had been shown to have been in league with the opposition over a matter of policy; Althorp, conscious of some responsibility in this, felt bound to resign, and since he was leader in the Commons, Grey declared that he would be unable to carry on without him.

In fact, Grey was only too glad to resign. The King, feeling that there had been quite enough reform for the time being, hoped to engineer a coalition between Melbourne and Peel, and when this proved impossible, asked Melbourne to form a government. 'I think it's a damned bore,' said Melbourne to his secretary. 'I am in many minds as to what to do.' He decided, however, to attempt the task, provided that Althorp would continue to serve as the government's leader in the Commons. To this Althorp agreed, but, on Lord Spencer's death in November 1834, Althorp, his heir, moved to the House of Lords. A new leader in the Commons had to be found, after all, and when William violently refused to accept Lord John Russell in this capacity, Melbourne made no objection to the King's dismissal of the entire ministry.

William turned to the Duke of Wellington, who said that Peel must be Prime Minister. Peel hurried back from Italy, where he had been on holiday, and formed a ministry in which William Gladstone occupied a junior Lordship at the Treasury. Having no majority in the Commons, Peel decided to fight an election at once. The Tories made a gain of about a hundred seats, but this was useless from the point of view of the government. Peel tried to carry on, but after a succession of inevitable defeats he resigned in April 1835, and Melbourne formed his second ministry.

Two major points of significance emerge from this political imbroglio. First, in his election address to his own constituents at Tamworth, Peel had stated that he was prepared to accept the Reform Act of 1832 and to follow a policy of moderate reform.

This Tamworth Manifesto, which was to be the basis of the new Conservative party, illustrates Peel's determination to build a new party out of the wreckage of 1830. Second, the short life of Peel's first ministry throws an interesting light on the full significance of the constitutional change. William had technically been perfectly within his rights in dismissing Melbourne and appointing Peel with only a minority in the Commons. But in the days of the unreformed constitution the King's minister who fought an election could be certain of returning with a majority to the Commons, owing to the immense powers of patronage and influence at the King's disposal. The hundred seats, which were all that Peel could gain when campaigning as the King's minister, showed the extent of the change that Grey's Reform Act had brought. The old system had gone, and to many the destruction of the Houses of Parliament by fire in October 1834 must have seemed symbolic of the end of an era that could never return.

7

RAILWAYS AND RELIGION

1. The dawn of Victorianism

THE railway embankment, Thackeray once suggested, symbolized the great dividing line in the lives of his contemporaries, and he added that those who could remember the pre-railway age now lived on, severed from the world of their youth, like Noah and his family after the deluge. But the 1830s saw another change that was of even greater significance in dividing the eighteenth from the nineteenth century—a new seriousness of mood, a growing concern for social respectability that was to shatter the easy-going gaiety of Regency days. The time had passed when Lord Chesterfield's *Letters to his Son* could be an effective guide to the young, or when Hogarth's *Marriage à la Mode* could have much social relevance.

Many factors combined to bring about this remarkable transformation. The activity of the Evangelicals, the tremendous force of Methodism among the poor, the growth of a middle class whose wealth derived from thrift and hard work, the reforming zeal of Dr. Arnold at Rugby, who was to bring a new spirit of Puritanism into English education, all had a profound influence that it is impossible to analyse beyond a certain point. Victorianism, in some ways, preceded Victoria. Ladies such as Hannah More and Harriet Martineau had already pointed the way to a recognizable nineteenth-century type—the blue stocking of devastatingly high principles. In 1818 Thomas Bowdler added a word to the English language by publishing an edition of the works of Shakespeare gutted of every phrase that might cause offence in a decent household, and the Family Shakespeare stands as the natural comment of nineteenth-century England on the full-blooded imagination of the Tudor age. But the instinct to name a period after the reigning sovereign is not an entirely unjust one. The Court was a strong guiding force in social life, and of all individuals who played some part in the forming of this new spirit, the young Queen Victoria, who ascended the throne in 1837, and the serious-minded, well-intentioned German prince whom she married in 1840 together exercised the greatest influence on the society of their time.

The change is also reflected in the nineteenth-century Englishman's attitude towards the Continent. Despite intermittent wars with France, his forbears had seen the Paris *salons* as the height of civilization; now they seemed to the early Victorian only a symbol of a way of life that combined moral laxness with political instability. Hogarth, it is true, had hated Frenchmen, but there had been nothing priggish about his patriotism. The Victorian, on the other hand, did not hate foreigners; he simply regarded them with a sense of moral superiority that the eighteenth-century Englishman had reserved only for Scots. Mr. Podsnap in Dickens' *Our Mutual Friend* was the personification of this trait. '. . . although his business was sustained upon commerce with other countries, he considered other countries, with that important reservation, a mistake, and of their manners and customs would conclusively observe, "Not English!" when presto! with a flourish of the arm, and a flush of the face, they were swept away!' But Dickens relied essentially upon exaggeration. An instance, more telling because it was unconscious, is to be found in a remark in a letter of Walter Bagehot to his father, after he had witnessed the street-fighting in Paris during Louis Napoleon's *coup d'état* of 1851. 'If you go calmly and look English, there is no particular danger.' A whole book could be written on the assumptions that lie behind those few words, for they sum up the spirit of an entire generation.

Yet, while the Victorian seemed outwardly to know so few doubts, he had, none the less, his own peculiar nostalgia. The Gothic revival, which had already been in evidence before the end of the previous century, was not simply a movement in architecture; it was a symbol of a growing veneration for the mediaeval past. This yearning appeared in a number of forms—in the

E

historical novels of Walter Scott, in the social philosophy of Carlyle's *Past and Present*, in the paintings of the Pre-Raphaelites, and in the art criticism of their great protagonist John Ruskin. It finds its simplest and most direct statement in *Contrasts*, a book published in 1836 by Augustus Pugin, the son of Rowlandson's collaborator in Ackermann's *Microcosm of London*. Pugin was a Roman Catholic, and it was natural that he should delight in producing pictures of the mediaeval town, set in the mould of Catholic unity, side by side with the nineteenth-century city, sprawling, ugly, centreless, and soulless, littered with a diversity of churches and humanitarian institutions. But the contrast was not absolute. The Victorian was far from being soulless; he may have been obsessed with the thought of material progress, but a minority, at least, were aware of its dangers, and the love of the mediaeval which on the Continent remained purely romantic, had in England powerful religious overtones. Thackeray's symbol of the railway embankment is only one half of the picture. The Gothic windows of the station-master's office are a more apt expression of the duality of Victorian aspirations.

2. *Railways and communications*

In the last years of his life the English artist Turner painted a picture of a train driving across a bridge over the Thames. The uncanny effect of rain, steam, and speed against the misty outlines of the bridge and the river fired the imagination of French artists in London, and Turner's work is now recognized as one of the great formative influences on the French Impressionists. Yet the subject of his picture was a symbol of an even greater revolution in the history of the world. If a Tory squire of 1800 could have returned to England 100 years later, the vast network of railways and the lines of trains rushing along them to every corner of the country would have been the sight that would have amazed and doubtless horrified him the most.

Like most revolutions, the railways took the government unawares and grew rapidly into a force whose full implications could never have been foreseen. In the early decades of the century there was little faith in the new experiment and no question arose of its being developed under government sponsorship; independent companies simply acquired authorization to lay a length of track by a private Act of Parliament. It was only in the 1840s that English governments were aware that railway transport was becoming a national phenomenon, and it was not until the 1890s that a firm governmental hold had been gained over the major companies.

Railways of a kind had already long been in existence in England. In the seventeenth century wooden rails had been used for running tracks from collieries to the rivers, and in the later part of the eighteenth century iron rails had been laid to take goods down to the loading points on the canals. In 1801 a line for public hire between Croydon and Wandsworth was built, and between 1801 and 1821 nineteen Railway Acts were passed by Parliament authorizing the opening of similar lines. Normally horses were used to draw the trucks, but experiments had also been made with stationary machines at the side of the line, which would draw the trucks over a length of track by means of a cable.

The essence of the revolution lies in the development of steam locomotion. By 1815 George Stephenson, a civil engineer of genius, had shown the practical possibilities of steam traction, but it was several years before any company was prepared to take up his invention. In 1821 the Stockton and Darlington Railway Company, promoted by the Quakers of Darlington, was authorized by Act of Parliament to open a line for transporting coal from the Darlington collieries to Stockton-on-Tees. A great decision was taken two years later when an amending Act was passed allowing the company to run locomotives and to carry passengers. It is a sign of the general caution, however, that when the line was finally opened in 1825, only goods were carried by locomotive, while passengers were drawn by horse. 'What can be more palpably absurd', commented a writer in the *Quarterly Review* that year, 'than the prospect held out of locomotives travelling twice as fast as stage coaches?'

In 1826 the Liverpool and Manchester Railway Act was passed, but for the next two years the promoters remained doubtful

whether to use locomotives, until an independent opinion by two
outside engineers encouraged them to take the risk. A competition for the best design of locomotive was held in 1829 at Rainhill,
where Stephenson's Rocket won the prize of £500. Tragedy
crowned this success. At the opening ceremony, in 1830, Huskisson, stepping out of the train to greet the Duke of Wellington,
was knocked down and fatally injured by a passing engine. Not
even the death of a former Cabinet minister could diminish
Stephenson's triumph, and Huskisson's obituary was overshadowed by the staggering news that the Rocket had attained
the speed of thirty-six miles an hour.

There were, however, many powerful opponents to the railway
companies. Stage-coach proprietors, innkeepers, and horse-
dealers all saw their livelihood threatened; the canal companies
became aware of a powerful competitor. The most potent force
of resistance lay simply in the natural conservatism of the country.
Trains were considered to be 'dangerous and a nuisance'. It was
claimed that they frightened cows and hens, killed birds with
their smoke, and set houses on fire with their sparks. The Duke
of Cleveland had succeeded in holding up the Stockton and Darlington Railway Bill for three years, since the new line would dis-
turb his foxes, while on the line from Newcastle to Carlisle no
locomotives were to be allowed at all and not even stationary
engines 'within view of the Castle of Naworth or Corby Castle'.
Oxford University was able for a long time to prevent the Great
Western Railway from coming any nearer than Didcot, and
when the line was eventually laid as far as Oxford the proctors
retained the right to arrest any undergraduate found at the
station. Creevey summed up the general attitude when he spoke
of 'the locomotive monster carrying eighty tons of goods and
navigated by a tail of smoke and sulphur coming through
every man's grounds between Manchester and Liverpool'. It
is easy to make fun of these objections; we now know that railways were made safe and became a vital part of the national
economy. But these fears were genuine and not always unrealistic.
Problems of danger and inconvenience are bound to accompany
every revolution in transport, and the modern jet plane passing

through the sound barrier is only Stephenson's Rocket in another guise.

This resistance to railways added enormously to the expense of starting new lines. It has been reckoned that the cost of surveying the ground and the legal expenses involved in getting a Bill through Parliament amounted to an average of £4,000 per mile of route. Once the Bill had been passed, the land still had to be bought from landowners, most of whom were strongly opposed to the laying of the track and were prepared to sell only at an exorbitant price. The purchase of land for the London–Birmingham line cost £6,300 per mile, the Great Western line £6,696, and the London–Brighton line £8,000. In fairness, it should be stated that many of these landowners believed quite seriously that their land would be ruined; the Duke of Bedford gave back £150,000 and Lord Taunton £15,000 when they discovered that the results were not as bad as they had feared. Another factor involving expense was the nature of the ground in the west and the north, where many tunnels, viaducts, bridges, and gradients were needed. No Continental railway system cost as much as the British, and it is a remarkable comment on the wealth of the country that so much private capital should have been available. By 1855 no less than £300 million had been invested in the railways.

The initial boom was followed by a financial crisis in 1837, but by 1844 capital was again available and an even greater boom began. The little isolated lengths of track were gradually linked up; by 1837 it was possible to reach Manchester from London via Birmingham, and by the end of 1850 6,621 miles of track were open. The lack of any coordinating authority, however, produced several complications. The companies were still thought of as owners of a special type of road on which anyone could run his own trucks, providing that he paid a toll, and this gave rise to a great deal of private traffic. Another more serious factor was the difference in gauges that often made through-traffic an impossibility.

Inevitably this anarchy was succeeded by a process of amalgamation. A Clearing House was set up in 1842 as a central agency

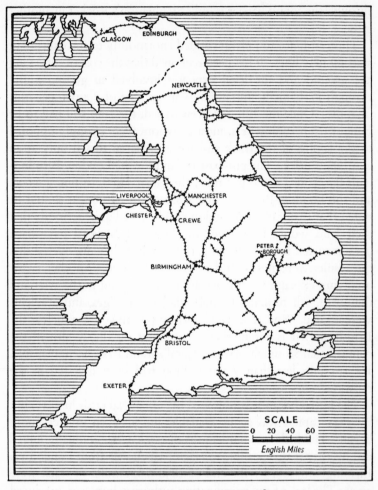

I. THE BRITISH RAILWAY SYSTEM, 1847

whereby through-rates might be assessed over lengths of track
owned by a variety of companies. George Hudson, a leading
citizen of York, was responsible for much of this simplification.
He had seen the financial possibilities of organizing through-
traffic, and set about the task with prodigious energy and business
acumen, on one occasion persuading sufficient shareholders in two
days to promote forty Railway Bills, involving a capital of

£10 million. Most important of all was the government's growing
interest in this new power in the land. In 1842 an Act of Parliament ruled that no new railways were to be opened without the
Board of Trade's permission, and although inspectors could do
little once the line had been opened, they could at least withhold
this permission until the company had complied with certain
conditions of safety. In 1844 an Act of much greater significance
was passed. Parliament now assumed the right to revise all tolls,
fares, and charges of any railway company whose dividend was
more than 10%, and the Treasury would be able to purchase, if it
wished, all railways opened after 1844. This second clause was
not acted upon and was no more than a precautionary measure.
Another clause, which did become operative, ruled that there
should be at least one train daily on every passenger line, stopping
at every station, if required, and carrying third-class passengers
for a penny a mile. These Acts of 1842 and 1844 were the work
of William Gladstone and, as a mark of his concern for the third-
class passenger, he often insisted on travelling third class himself.
In 1846 Parliament came to grips with the problem of the different
gauges and limited the broad gauge of seven feet to certain districts. Although this helped the organization of through-traffic,
the two gauges remained in operation for many years and the
Great Western did not reconstruct its line with the four foot eight
and a half inches gauge until 1892.

Even at this early stage the effects of railway development were
manifold. Canals could soon hardly compete, since agglomerations of buildings made it impossible to widen them so that they
might take the greater volume of goods proceeding to and from
the factories; in many cases they were bought up by railway companies. The laying of track provided employment for thousands
during the boom years. Factories could get their raw materials
more easily and cheaply and draw on a greater number of workers,
who could travel to the factory by train. Distribution of the
finished goods became simple—the final blow to local industries.
In 1838 the trains were entrusted with the mails, and speedier
communications proved to be a great asset to the various movements for reform, enabling them to organize themselves on a

nation-wide basis. Travel by rail was becoming a common factor in everybody's life. Once on the train, the rich and the poor were divided only by the difference between a third- and a first-class ticket. 'I fear it has a very dangerous tendency to equality,' remarked Lord de Mowbray in Disraeli's *Sybil*, and his Lordship's fears were by no means entirely unfounded.

A new method of communication was directly encouraged by the growth of railways—the electric telegraph. A system of semaphore poles had been invented in France during the Revolutionary war for sending military information rapidly to Paris, and the British Admiralty had copied this idea with lines of poles to the ports. Naturally an electric wire would be a vast improvement on this. In 1833 two German professors succeeded in establishing communication over a wire 1,000 yards in length, and in 1836 Morse invented his system in America. In 1839 experiments were being made in England in running wire in iron tubes along the Great Western line from Paddington to West Drayton. Progress was slow, since the system proved expensive; but in 1846 the Electric Telegraph Company was formed, and since it had a monopoly prospered so well that within eight years it had seventeen metropolitan offices, of which eight were at the great railway termini.

The penny post, established in 1840 by Rowland Hill, was another minor revolution in communications at this time. Since the days of the younger Pitt mail had been carried in stage-coaches. It was liable to government censorship; the writer of a letter paid a tax instituted during the Napoleonic war and the recipient paid for the cost of postage according to the distance. The whole system was clumsy and not particularly lucrative, since there was widespread smuggling. Rowland Hill's plan was to maintain a government monopoly, but to charge a uniform rate of only a penny, regardless of distance, for any letter in the United Kingdom, the penny to be pre-paid by the sender. The scheme was regarded as ruinous in some governmental quarters, and it did at first result in a loss of £1,000,000 a year to the revenue. Hill was later dismissed and became chairman of the London–Brighton railway. The new postal service, however, was rapidly organized throughout the kingdom. 'Never, perhaps,' said Gladstone in typical phraseology, 'was a local invention (for such it was) and improvement applied in the lifetime of its author to the advantage of such multitudes of his fellow creatures.' It would obviously be impossible to enumerate the indirect consequences of this development. Two, at least, could hardly have been anticipated. Rowland Hill's scheme started a new hobby; and it was while planning postal deliveries in the West Country that Anthony Trollope, a Post Office official who aspired to write, came to know the setting of the imaginary county of Barsetshire, which is his particular contribution to nineteenth-century literature.

3. Iron and coal

The natural concomitant of the development of railways was a remarkable increase in the production of iron and coal. The making of rails ate up thousands of tons of iron; for instance, the 2,000 miles of track laid in 1847–8 required in all approximately 400,000 tons. There was a similar market abroad, where railways were beginning to be built. This increasing demand naturally stimulated ironmasters to find more efficient and cheaper methods of production. It was the Scots who led the way in this later period of technical improvement. Neilson's hot-air blast, coupled with the discovery that Lanarkshire coal could be used in the furnaces without being coked, enabled the Scottish works so to increase their output of pig-iron that the English ironmasters became seriously worried. The hot-air blast was less effective with English coal, but other refinements, such as improved processes of puddling and Nasmyth's steam hammer, helped to swell the output of the United Kingdom as a whole. In the first two decades of the century the output of iron had risen from only 250,000 tons to 400,000 tons a year, but by 1847 the annual figure had reached 2 million tons.

Naturally an enormous quantity of coal was needed for the smelting of all this iron; for instance, the smelting of 2 million tons of iron already quoted must have required about 8 million

E 2

tons of coal. British locomotives consumed more and more—
750,000 tons in the year ending 30 June, 1849—and after the repeal
of the general export duty in 1834 there was a growing market for
British coal on the Continent. France, Russia, Germany, Denmark, and Italy were all large buyers, and the annual export
figure rose from 1 million to 3 million tons between 1837 and
1849. Before 1854 the figures for the mines are only approximate,
but the following statistics have been calculated for the first half
of the century: 1816, 16 million tons; 1826, 21 million; 1836, 30
million; 1846, 44 million; 1856, 65 million. These figures represent only one aspect of the economy of Great Britain at this time,
but they do help to explain the extraordinary prosperity that the
country was to enjoy in the mid-century decades.

4. The attack on the Church:
the Oxford Movement and the Ecclesiastical Commission

At the same time as the country entered upon the railway age,
a controversy was raging within and about the Church of England
that reflected every aspect of the Victorian conscience. The assault on the Church took a variety of forms. The liberal churchmen attacked the maladministration of the wealth in the Church
and the abuses of pluralism and patronage. The *Extraordinary
Black Book* of 1831 had thrown a glaring light on many anomalies.[1] Within the gift of the bishops there existed many posts that
were little more than sinecures. The endowments of Bishop
Sparke of Ely, his son, and his son-in-law had amounted to
£30,000 a year. One archbishop had given sixteen benefices to
seven of his relations and another was able to provide his elder
son with £12,000 a year. The twelve canonries of the Chapter at
Durham were said to be each worth about £3,000 a year. This is
not to suggest that the money was spent unworthily; John Fisher,
nephew and chaplain to the Bishop of Salisbury, for example, had
been one of the earliest patrons of the painter Constable. Yet
many of the lower clergy were wretchedly underpaid and in an

[1] See p. 21.

era of reform it was not surprising that both Whigs and new Conservatives should wish to take this situation in hand.

A second body of critics was to be found among the clergy
themselves. This was the result of several generations of Evangelical activity among the Anglicans and the Nonconformists.
Their concentration on individual example and their unashamed
enthusiasm had made them the spearhead of many of the humanitarian movements and of the missionary societies, but their lack
of interest in the dignity and authority of the Church as part of
the established order of society gained them many enemies among
the High Churchmen—a feud brilliantly depicted a few years later
by Anthony Trollope in his novel *Barchester Towers*.

The most startling attack, also from within the Church, came
from a totally different direction. The Oxford Movement stood
for the defence of the Church as the sacred guardian of the Apos-
tolic Succession, a trust handed down from the Fathers of the early
Christian Church, which must be protected against Romanism
and Protestantism. In July 1833 John Keble, Professor of Poetry
at Oxford, preached a sermon denouncing the government's recent action in radically revising the organization of the Anglican
Church in Ireland.[1] The Church, he claimed, was an instrument
of divine will and no secular government had the right to touch it.
That summer a group of his supporters met with him at Hadleigh,
where they decided to publish a series of *Tracts for the Times*, most
of them written by Keble, Richard Froude, Edward Pusey, and
John Newman, all of whom were Fellows of Oriel College. Newman at this time was also Vicar of St. Mary's, Oxford, a man of
Evangelical upbringing, who had recently returned from a journey to the Mediterranean which had awoken in him a new sense
of mission, and his passionate sincerity and powerful personality
soon made him the most exciting figure in the Oxford Movement.

The continued publication of the Tracts in the following years
stirred up a storm of protest from the orthodox Anglicans and the
Evangelicals. To them the Movement's stress on the Catholic
Church and the peculiar significance of the priesthood, and its

[1] See p. 93.

tendency to dally with notions of fasting and purgatory smacked
of Rome. Yet the Tractarians were, in many ways, in tune with
the times. The Romantic Movement had turned a warm, mystical
light on many forms of mediaevalism. Men who were never
likely to become Papist were, nevertheless, growing aware of the
strength derived from an unbroken historical tradition. On the
first occasion that he entered St. Peter's at Rome, Gladstone was
suddenly conscious of the Church as a historic institution, 'its
unending line of teachers joining from the Head'. 'I was deeply
moved', wrote Macaulay during a visit to Rome in 1838, 'by
reflecting on the immense antiquity of the Papal dignity, which
can certainly boast of a far longer, clear, known and uninterrupted
succession than any dignity in the world; linking together, as it
does, the two great ages of human civilization.'

To many it seemed in the early years of the Whig ministry that
these simultaneous attacks on so many fronts must lead to disendowment and disestablishment. 'No human means are likely to
avert the threatened overthrow of the Establishment', wrote
Southey. In fact, the threat was illusory. The enemies of the
Church were too divided. The liberals were bound to note the
Oxford Movement's defence of the University Tests, and the
Movement could hardly ally itself with Evangelicals and Nonconformists. The Anglican church-goers in the parishes had
no liking for Irish Catholics now joining in the attack. The
Tracts, too, led something of a counter-attack against the secular
enemies of the established Church. 'Do not be compelled, by the
world's forsaking you,' wrote Newman to the clergy in the first
of the Tracts, 'to recur, as if unwillingly, to the high source of
your authority. Speak out now, before you are forced, both as
glorifying in your privilege, and to ensure your rightful honour
from your people.'

The danger passed. To some extent, the Church saved itself by
cooperating with the suggested measures of reform, and the Oxford Movement lost much of its force when its more extreme
members were converted to the Roman Church.

Ecclesiastical questions were prominent in the Commons' debates, and in Durham the Dean and Chapter anticipated the

government, when in 1831 they hastily decided to create a University from the income that was surplus to the requirements of the Cathedral church. It was eventually Peel who, during his short ministry (1834–5), adopted a Whig proposal and set up a Commission on the state of the established Church. This Commission issued four reports in 1835 and 1836 and its recommendations formed the basis of three important Acts.

By the Act of 1836 diocesan boundaries were revised; two new sees, Ripon and Manchester, were created, and the incomes of the bishops were redistributed, so that in future the Archbishop of Canterbury received £15,000, the Bishop of London £10,000, Durham £8,000, and Winchester £7,000, while no other bishop received less than £4,500. A permanent body, the Ecclesiastical Commission, consisting of the two Archbishops, the Bishop of London, and a number of laymen, was set up to administer Church finances, its regulations needing only the consent of the Crown before coming into force. A second Act in 1838 dealt with the question of pluralism, forbidding members of chapters to hold more than one benefice. No clergyman was to hold two benefices if they were more than two miles apart, if either benefice had a population of more than 3,000, or if the additional stipend was more than £1,000. The Act of 1840 restricted the number of canons in every Cathedral chapter, and the income thus saved was used to increase the stipends of the poorer clergy.

Other legislation in this period affected the laity. London University was thrown open to all, without any religious distinction. A civil register of births, deaths, and marriages was opened, so that from henceforth Dissenters were freed from the necessity of being married in Anglican churches. The tithe question was partly settled by a commutation of tithe into a money payment. The Church rate, levied on men of every religious persuasion for the upkeep of the parish church, presented a more difficult question and no solution was found for the time being.

How significant was all this ecclesiastical legislation? Extremists in the Church complained that such Parliamentary action implied that the Church was now under the control of the government. Yet the need for reform was undeniable and the measures imposed had been moderate. The Church had lost none of its land or income, and the clearing up of the abuses banished the immediate likelihood of disestablishment. The reforms were not always carried through with great speed; it was not until 1851, for example, that the misuse of the income of the Hospital of St. Cross at Winchester was brought before the Court of Chancery, when the case probably supplied Trollope with the theme of his novel *The Warden*. The Hospital's finances were reconstituted in 1857, and St. Cross still performs the function originally intended by its founders.

The Liberals had gained their objective. Oxford, on the other hand, remained a centre of controversy for some years. Forty years later Matthew Arnold wrote an account of Newman's four o'clock sermons at St. Mary's. 'He seemed about to renew what was for us the most national and natural institution in the world, the Church of England. Who could resist the charm of that spiritual apparition, gliding in the dim afternoon light through the aisles of St. Mary's, rising into the pulpit, and then, in the most entrancing of voices, breaking the silence with words and thoughts which were a religious music—subtle, sweet, mournful?' In 1841 Newman produced *Tract 90*, the most explosive of them all, in which he attempted to show that the Thirty-Nine Articles, the doctrinal basis of the Anglican Church, were not incompatible with the main lines of Catholic thought. 1845 marked the last stage in Newman's mental conflict. In that year he was received into the Church of Rome, and a shiver of horror ran through the homes of Protestant England.

Another group in the Oxford Movement, under the leadership of Pusey, remained High Churchmen and were to have a considerable influence on the forms of Church service in the later half of the century. Due to them was the reappearance of candles, surpliced choirs, and turning to the east for the Creed. Many of the laity continued to regard the Movement with suspicion. 'Please, Mr. Bishop,' asked *Punch* in a cartoon, 'which is Popery and which is Puseyism?' The suspicion was not quietened by the establishment, in 1850, of a regular Roman Catholic diocesan hierarchy in England, instituted by Pius IX.

This ferment had seriously affected only the middle and upper classes. Ritual and the hierarchy of the Church were not important matters for the hungry poor. It was the Christian Socialists who tried to bring the attention of the Church back to the social question. The leaders of the group were Frederick Maurice, Professor of Divinity at King's College, London, Charles Kingsley, a country parson, and Thomas Hughes, the author of *Tom Brown's Schooldays*. In a sense, their concern with practical reform gave them many points in common with the Evangelical humanitarians, but there was one great difference. The humanitarians had given help from above to those socially below them; their aim had been charity, not egalitarianism. The Christian Socialists embraced egalitarianism; they envisaged a new classless world under the rule of Christ. They made contact with the Chartists, the Co-operative Movement, and the Trade Unions, and Kingsley spread their ideas in his novels *Yeast* and *Alton Locke*. They were naturally mistrusted by most of the upper and middle classes, but they stood firmly by the name that they had chosen. 'It will commit us at once,' said Maurice, 'to the conflict we must engage in sooner or later with the unsocial Christians and the unchristian Socialists.' Christian Socialism never developed as an independent political force of its own, yet the revolutionary sentiment that sounds in Maurice's words was an appropriate comment on the spirit of the age. Middle-class liberalism had not yet entirely defeated the old conservatism, and already beyond that struggle there was opening up a prospect of change whose possibilities were to run far on into the twentieth century.

8

THE TWO NATIONS, 1830–50

1. *The condition of the poor*

IN 1845 there were published two books, both inspired in different ways by social conditions in England. One was a novel, *Sybil, or The Two Nations*, in which the following passage occurs:

> 'Well, society may be in its infancy,' said Egremont, slightly smiling; 'but, say what you like, our Queen reigns over the greatest nation that ever existed.'
>
> 'Which nation?' asked the stranger, 'for she reigns over two.'
>
> The stranger paused; Egremont was silent, but looked inquiringly.
>
> 'Yes,' resumed the younger stranger after a moment's interval. 'Two nations; between whom there is no intercourse and no sympathy; who are as ignorant of each other's habits, thoughts and feelings, as if they were dwellers in different zones, or inhabitants of different planets; who are formed by a different breeding, are fed by a different food, are ordered by different manners and are not governed by the same laws.'
>
> 'You speak of——' said Egremont, hesitatingly.
>
> 'THE RICH AND THE POOR.'

The other, *The Condition of the Working Class in England in 1844*, was published in Germany and not translated into English until 1885. The writer comments:

> . . . it is not surprising that the working class has gradually become a race wholly apart from the English bourgeoisie. The bourgeoisie has more in common with every other nation of the earth than with the workers in whose midst it lives. The workers speak other dialects, have other thoughts and ideals, other customs and moral principles, a different religion and other politics than those of the

bourgeoisie. Thus they are two radically dissimilar nations, as unlike as difference of race could make them, of whom we on the Continent have known but one, the bourgeoisie.

The author of the novel was Benjamin Disraeli, later to be the leader of the Conservative party and twice Prime Minister of England; the author of the second book was Frederick Engels, the close associate of Karl Marx. That two men who stood poles apart in political outlook should write at the same moment in such remarkable agreement is a sufficient comment on the condition of the poor in the 1830s and 1840s. Whatever the political remedy might be, the facts of squalor and near-starvation that divided them from the upper classes were inescapable.

The harvest was the basic factor in the life of the poor. The periods of intense distress in these two decades—1829-30, 1838-41, and 1846-7—were all preceded and to some extent explained by bad harvests. The intervening years saw excellent harvests, and this rhythm is naturally reflected in the fluctuations in the price of corn—in 1829 sixty-six shillings and threepence a quarter, in 1834 forty-six shillings and threepence, in 1839 seventy shillings and eightpence, and in 1845 fifty shillings and tenpence. Another factor peculiar to these years was the erratic development of railways, offering employment to thousands in the booms and throwing them out of work in the depressions.

The 1840s have always had a bad name, due partly to the writings of the Anti-Corn Law League, and partly to Engels' book. In fact, neither of these is a very reliable guide, since each was a form of propaganda. The phrase 'the hungry 'forties' does not seem to have been current at that time at all and was first widely in use at the beginning of the twentieth century, when the Free Traders saw the likelihood of a return to Protection. Engels' book certainly gives an appalling picture of industrial conditions in England, but recent research has shown that much of what he wrote did not really refer to the 1840s at all. During his twenty months' stay in England he had first-hand experience only of the textile factories in Manchester and Salford. His information on the coal-mines, iron works, and housing conditions was drawn to a certain extent from newspaper articles or official reports, some of them more than twenty years out of date, and thus he has little to say about the improvements that were beginning to be made in the 1830s, particularly after the passing of the Municipal Corporations Act of 1835.[1] No one could deny that conditions were still very bad. It would, however, be untrue to suggest that they had never been worse.

In general, the time was one of falling prices, and although wages fell too, it seems, as far as it is possible to generalize, that they dropped less than prices. In the years of good harvests, then, the condition of the poor was slowly changing for the better; yet the rate of progress was so gradual and the level of life from which they were emerging so low that, although the '40s were in no way as hungry as some of the early years of the century, any depression was bound to lead to serious unrest.

This economic pattern is of tremendous significance in the political and social events of these years. Good harvests after the Reform Act and the first boom in railway building meant, on the whole, a peaceful countryside. A bank crisis in 1837 curtailed the amount of capital available for railway enterprises, and the consequent unemployment, coupled with bad harvests in 1837 and 1838, produced the most acute period of economic distress in these decades. Now the hatred of the Corn Laws and of the workhouses of the new Poor Law became violent. The torches of the Chartists [2] burned, and in 1839 and 1842 their riots had to be put down by the military; the demands for further factory reform grew fierce again; the Anti-Corn Law League was formed. Then after 1842 the harvests improved and prices dropped; capital was again available and a second prodigious railway boom followed. In these happier years Chartism ceased to be violent and the Anti-Corn Law League entered upon the most uphill part of its struggle. Another bank crisis in 1847 ended the second railway boom, and bad harvests in the two preceding years brought another period of depression, during which the Corn Laws were repealed and the government faced the last desperate convulsion of Chartism.

Yet, despite this periodic turbulence, the '40s form something of an epilogue to a time of economic and social readjustment. Out of that readjustment emerged stability and comparative prosperity in the middle decades of the nineteenth century. Some of the causes for which men had fought had been won; others could temporarily be forgotten. Two contrary movements in Parliamentary legislation—towards free trade in commerce and towards governmental regulation of the conditions of work in the factories and mines—played their part in producing this mid-century calm, together with the slow development of Trade Unions among the skilled workers, and it was not until the '70s and '80s that a new period of economic uncertainty reawoke the old antagonism between the Two Nations.

2. State interference and laissez faire

During the two decades following the passing of the Reform Act a great conflict ensued between the manufacturers and the landlords. There were two major issues. One was the demand for free trade, concentrating in particular on the repeal of the Corn Laws. This was the cry of the manufacturing classes, who had little to fear from foreign competition and who complained that the Corn Laws kept the price of bread high for their workers and interfered with the expansion of their markets. The landed class, all too afraid of the competition of corn from the Continent, looked to the Tories for continued Protection and, wanting a stick with which to beat the manufacturers, joined forces with the humanitarians in pointing out the appalling conditions of the workers in the factories, which could be alleviated only by some form of governmental regulation. Thus two antagonistic sections of the rich claimed to speak on behalf of the poor. Naturally there existed many shades of opinion, and the divisions between Whig, Tory, and Radical became hopelessly confused, culminating in the conversion of Peel himself to the repeal of the Corn Laws—a conversion that ended the existence of the Tories as a coherent party for more than twenty years.

A. MINES, FACTORIES, AND PUBLIC HEALTH

The Factory Act of 1833 had been the first effective piece of governmental restriction. But, like most English industrial legislation, it had been limited in its application, since adults were still to work from 5.30 a.m. to 8.30 p.m. It had also had the effect of aggravating the evil in other forms. As the textile factories were now closed to children under nine, parents tended to send their children into other types of factory or to the mines, where no regulations hindered them. With the great demand for coal, the mines were particularly in need of labour, and in 1842 it was reported that there were hardly any boys left in the union workhouses of Walsall, Wolverhampton, Dudley, and Stourbridge.

> 'Do ye hear the children weeping, O my brothers,
>   Ere the sorrow comes with years?'

wrote Elizabeth Barrett Browning in *Blackwood's Magazine* in 1838. Ashley demanded further investigations, and since the depression at the end of the 1830s and the Chartist riots lent an urgency to the whole question of the poor, a series of commissions were set up, and in the early 1840s published their findings, which, in some cases, were so frightful that Parliamentary action resulted almost at once.

The most sensational of these was a report on the conditions of employment in the coal-mines, published in 1842. From the age of five or six children were kept over twelve hours in the pits, often sitting in pitch darkness to operate a trap-door. Women and boys were harnessed to the trucks of coal and made to draw them along through the wet, narrow tunnels on their hands and knees. 'I went into the pit at seven years of age,' said one witness, quoted by Ashley in the Commons, 'where I drew by the girdle and chain. The skin was broken and the blood ran down. I have seen many draw at six.' Such working conditions produced physical deformity and ill health and, in the words of the report, the adult miner 'slips into the grave at a comparatively early period, with perfect willingness on his part, and with no surprise on that of his family and friends'.

The Mines Act of 1842 stated that no women or girls were to be employed underground and no boys under the age of ten. The Act also established inspectors who could enforce these regulations, but, important as it was, it left untouched the hours and conditions of work for adult labour. In 1850, however, the Coal Mines Inspection Act, prompted by a series of disasters in the mines, ruled that inspectors were to look after the safety of the miners, and in the following year the Royal School of Mines was set up to train these officials.

The 1840s also saw a renewal of the Ten Hours Movement under the leadership of Ashley. Textile-factory owners, deprived of child labour by the Act of 1833, began to recruit girls and women, who were still unprotected. The struggle over the 1833 Act had shown that it was possible for the government to make concessions to the humanitarians over the employment of children without altering the length of the adult working day. Ashley now took up the cause of the women in the factories, in the hope that this might shorten working hours. The significance of the campaign was grasped by all sides. 'To enact that no young persons or women of any age should work more than ten hours,' said Milner Gibson in the House in 1844, 'was, in point of fact, to enact that no factory engines should be kept in operation more than ten hours.'

The struggle was bitter. The manufacturers took their stand on the sanctity of *laissez faire*, and Nassau Senior, the first Professor of Political Economy at Oxford, claimed in his *Letters on the Factory Acts* that the whole profit of industry was derived from the last hour of labour each day. The Tories, who had come into power under Peel in 1841, were less favourably inclined towards factory legislation than when they had been in opposition, and, as in 1833, the government attempted to forestall the extremists by launching a compromise measure. The debate grew extremely confused; at one point the Commons actually passed an amendment that was tantamount to establishing a ten-hour day, and then reversed the decision. 'The discussions and divisions on the Factory Bill have been of the most confused and ludicrous kind,' commented the *Leeds Times*. 'Whigs, Tories and Radicals are jumbled together in inextricable disorder.' The Act that was finally passed in 1844 laid down a six-and-a-half hour day for children between eight and thirteen, but a twelve-hour day for all women above the age of thirteen. Regulations were also included for the fencing of machinery. This meant that, for the moment, the ten-hours men had failed, but at least the evident fluidity of opinion in the Commons could give them hope for the future.

They were not disappointed. Within three years it did seem that the battle was virtually won, when an Act of 1847 laid down a ten-hour day and a fifty-eight-hour week for all women and young persons. Three factors explain this success. First, in the general election of that year the ten-hours men campaigned independently of any party allegiance. Second, the landed interest smarting from the repeal of the Corn Laws in 1846, were all the more ready to vote for a measure which the manufacturers disliked. Third, a short trade depression had spoilt the manufacturers' argument that they could not stand a reduction in hours, since very few mills were open longer than ten hours a day at this time.

Yet the victory was not complete. Mill-owners found a loophole in the Act and fell back on the relay system, so that their mills might still operate from 5.30 a.m. until 8.30 p.m., but eventually Ashley was able to arrange a compromise. By the Act of 1850 it was settled that the factories should be open for only twelve hours, with an hour and a half for meals, while on Saturdays they would close at 2 p.m. Thus, in return for extending the working week to sixty hours, Ashley was able to achieve something close to the working day that he sought.

State regulation produced none of the bad results that its critics had predicted. Accidents in the mines became fewer. Nor did the shorter working day bring about a marked decrease in output in the mills. Workers became healthier and less tired, so that the machines could be operated faster, and it seemed as if the nineteenth century had learnt its first lesson in industrial fatigue.

There was another side of English social life that cried aloud for reform. The foul insanitary condition of the towns was, perhaps, no worse than anywhere on the Continent, but to our eyes it is almost inconceivable that such dangerous filth and squalor could have been tolerated. Yet it was not merely tolerated; the effort to bring in some elementary measure of sanitary reform was ardently resisted in the Commons and by local authorities. For here was an issue that touched private property in every city in the country, and the vast body of affected interests stood firm against the handful of reformers.

In the eighteenth century Commissioners, appointed for the larger cities, had been able to clean up some of the main streets. But they could do little with the side streets where the bulk of the population lived, and the rapid growth of the industrial towns had simply defeated them. Conditions had grown far worse since the beginning of the century. In these tightly packed, filthy slums there was little air or light; there was still virtually no drainage and no pure water supply. Improved medical science averted some of the worst consequences. Quarantine laws were imposed on ships suspected of carrying plague. In 1798 Dr. Jenner had published his discovery of vaccination against small-pox. But typhus and typhoid often raged, and such statistics as are available show that the situation was sharply deteriorating. In Glasgow, for example, there was a death rate of twenty-eight per thousand in 1821, of thirty-eight per thousand in 1838, and of forty per thousand in 1843.

Now a new terror appeared—cholera, against which medical science was almost helpless. It came from the East and first struck England in 1832. The victim was seized with violent stomach pains and vomiting; his body became cold and his skin blue. Sometimes it killed within two hours. There was, for example, the Earl of Clarendon's maid-servant, who sat down to gooseberry fool in the evening and was brought out in a coffin in the morning. The germ could be carried in water or by contact with excrement; thus in slums without drainage or pure water supply cholera could spread like wild fire, and in 1832 it claimed 18,000 victims.

The problem of public health was taken up by Edwin Chadwick. He had been interested in the establishment of central health departments since 1820, and while Secretary to the Poor

Law Commissioners he made use of his contact with Lord John Russell to propose investigations into sanitary conditions as part of the problem of destitution. Several doctors helped him with information, and in 1842 Chadwick published his *Report on the Sanitary Condition of the Labouring Classes of Great Britain*. A Health of Towns Committee had reported two years earlier and had made several recommendations, including a General Sewage Act and the creation of a Board of Health in every town. For several years the struggle went on to set up machinery whereby conditions might be improved, but there was always powerful resistance to any kind of centralized authority or interference in the towns. Then Chadwick was aided by a cruel and uncompromising ally. The news came that a fresh wave of cholera was sweeping into Europe from the East and in 1848 a Public Health Act was finally passed.

The Act laid down much less than Chadwick had hoped. A Board, consisting of a chairman and two Commissioners, was set up to advise Parliament and to encourage urban authorities to organize their own local Boards. The Board, however, only had the power to compel local authorities to take action if the average death rate over the previous seven years was more than twenty-three per thousand. London was to be excluded from its jurisdiction and the life of the Board itself was limited to five years. To achieve this the reformers had had to face heated opposition. 'Even in Constantinople or in Grand Cairo,' said a correspondent in the *Morning Chronicle*, 'where plague and cholera are decimating the population, it is doubtful whether such a Bill would be desirable.' His readers were soon to be able to make up their minds for themselves. The cholera epidemic had already reached Berlin, and in the summer months of 1848 and 1849 it raged in the cities of England.

It seemed extraordinary that at such a time of crisis there should not have been an end to resistance to the recommendations of the Board—the flushing of public sewers, inspection, evacuation of children, attempts to find pure drinking water, and measures to prevent the overcrowding of graveyards. The ravages of the second summer were particularly frightful. 'I was yesterday with

W. and M. over the cholera districts of Bermondsey,' wrote Charles Kingsley to his wife; 'and, oh, God! what I saw! people having no water to drink—hundreds of them—but the water of the common sewer which stagnated full of dead fish, cats, and dogs under their windows.' Ashley and Chadwick, the two Commissioners of the Board, toiled to overcome the resistance. The epidemic died out; their work went on, and by 1853 182 local Boards had been set up and 123 surveys had been undertaken. In 1853 the cholera returned, and the figures are a testimony to the Board's work. Outside London only 12,895 died, compared with the 40,412 in 1848-9: in London, where the Board had had no power, the drop was only from 14,789 to 11,621. But this could not save the Board. 'The Board of Health is to be destroyed,' wrote Ashley, now Lord Shaftesbury, bitterly in his diary. 'Its sin is its unpardonable activity.' In 1854 the Board of Health was abolished in the Commons by 74 votes to 65, and its place was taken by a Board of Ministers, who were likely to take reform at a more leisurely pace.

It had been a gallant attempt. It failed mainly because of the hatred of any kind of interference with private property and the deep mistrust of state control, but also, to some extent, because of Chadwick's uncompromising and sometimes tactless methods. Like most reformers, he could argue that this was no time for compromise. There are interesting points of similarity between Chadwick and Florence Nightingale, whose own work was just about to begin. Both were autocratic; both fought long and often fruitless campaigns against vested interests and lethargy; both were obsessed with the thought that deaths were not due to medical ignorance, but to bad conditions that could be altered. This was Chadwick's final major effort in public administration, but it is gratifying to know that, at last, in 1889, a year before he died at the age of ninety, he received a knighthood in recognition of his services against such hopeless odds.

B. THE ANTI-CORN LAW LEAGUE

State interference on behalf of factory reform and public health had been in utter opposition to the doctrine of free enterprise.

Such success as had been won had been possible only through the shocking revelations of the Commissions of Inquiry and the feud between the manufacturer and the landlord.

The movement towards free trade, however, ran not against but with the tide; in the period 1822-50 duties on import and export were continually reduced, many of them by Tory governments, as has been seen in the period of Liberal Toryism. The removal of duties on many raw materials, and even the repeal of the Navigation Laws in 1849, brought no great national outcry. Thus the issue was not Protection in general, but the continued protection of the English farmer by the Corn Laws.

For a long time opposition to the Corn Laws had been considerable, although unorganized. An Anti-Corn Law Association, formed in London in 1836, was followed in 1838 by a new Association in Manchester, prompted by the rising price of wheat and the prospect of a bad harvest. £6,000 was raised by subscription within a month, and when, in March 1839, a motion was once more brought before the Commons for a reconsideration of the Corn Laws, the debate continued over five nights, but ended in a rejection of the motion by a large majority. As a consequence of this defeat, the delegates decided that the local Association must be transformed into an Anti-Corn League which should lead a nation-wide agitation directed from the central offices at Manchester.

Two great figures emerge as the leaders of this movement, Richard Cobden and John Bright. Cobden was a Sussex man who had set up in business and become a leading figure in Manchester municipal politics. Bright, seven years younger, came from Rochdale and ran his father's textile business. Cobden was an ideal leader for the Anti-Corn Law movement. About his plain, kindly features there was the simple sincerity of the countryman, and his energy and intelligence made him a winning speaker whose strength lay in his clear, logical argument and his integrity. 'Your conversation, evidence, and letters', wrote Rowland Hill to him, 'have created a feeling in my mind so like that which one entertains towards an old friend that I am apt to forget that I have met you but once.' Bright, a more austere man of

Quaker background, was one of the greatest orators of the century, and before his audiences his arguments would thunder in a wrathful passion of indignation. Cobden won men with the charm and clarity of his eloquence; Bright dominated them with the fire of a Puritan preacher.

The two men had met in Manchester in the middle of the 1830s and each had been impressed by the other's qualities. Cobden had been one of the leading figures in the Anti-Corn Law Association, but it was not until 1841 that Bright joined the League. Cobden had called upon his friend that year three days after Bright's wife had died. 'After a time', said Bright describing the scene later, 'he looked up and said: "There are thousands of houses in England at this moment where wives, mothers, and children are dying of hunger. Now," he said, "when the first paroxysm of your grief is past, I would advise you to come with me and we will never rest till the Corn Law is repealed." '

The arguments put forward by the Anti-Corn Law League were economic and moral. They pointed out that corn was the major commodity which European countries could offer in order to buy English industrial goods. Through English protection these countries were now encouraged, almost forced, to build up their own industries. Thus a great market for English goods was being lost and potential competitors abroad enabled to develop. They argued that cheaper bread would ease the lot of the English workers, and, anticipating the reply that manufacturers might then reduce their wages, denied that wages would follow a falling cost of living, and retorted that, on the other hand, the growing population of the country would make it impossible for wages to remain as high as they were, unless more markets could be opened up.

The landlords' opposition was never so united, although the show of local resistance was often considerable. They denounced the repealers as disloyal and self-interested. 'If nothing will serve you but to eat foreign corn,' wrote the *Morning Post*, 'away with you, you and your goods, and let us never see you more!' The horrors of increasing industrialization were stressed, together with the depopulation of the country districts. 'Tell not to me any more', said Sir James Graham in the Commons, 'of the cruelties of the conveyance of Poles to the wintry wastes of Siberia; talk not to me of the transportation of the Hill Coolies from Coromandel to the Mauritius; a change is contemplated by some members of this House, far more cruel, far more heartrending in the bosom of our native land.' Indeed many of the working classes suspected the whole movement as a plot on the part of the employers, and the most violent opposition came from the Chartists.

But the League was irrepressible in its activities. 'For five years or more [1841-46] we devoted ourselves without stint,' said John Bright; 'every working hour almost was given up to the discussion and to the movement in connexion with this question.' By 1842 £100,000 had been spent, and by 1844 expenditure amounted to £1,000 a week. Lecturers and pamphlets were despatched to every part of the country, and the recent developments of the railways and the penny post were a godsend for the movement. Three hundred thousand electors were circularized. Later in the West Riding and Lancashire forty-shilling freeholds were being bought up by business men through an office of the League, so that even the county seats in the Commons were threatened.

In 1846 the battle was won.[1] The Corn Laws were repealed. 'Hurrah! Hurrah!' wrote Cobden to his wife, 'the Corn Bill is law and now my work is done.' Indeed it had been his work, as Peel said in his speech of resignation three days later.

> 'The name which ought to be, and will be associated with the success of these measures is the name of a man who, acting, I believe, from pure and disinterested motives, has advocated their cause with un- tiring energy, and by appeals to reason, expressed by an eloquence, the more to be admired because it was unaffected and unadorned— the name which ought to be and will be associated with the success of these measures is the name of Richard Cobden. Without scruple, Sir, I attribute the success of these measures to him.'

It is not difficult to suggest the general reasons for the success of the Anti-Corn Law League. Its leaders had been resourceful men of the middle class. They had been able to raise a great deal

---

[1] The Parliamentary aspect of the struggle is given in the next chapter.

of money by which public opinion might be mobilized. Their programme, simple to understand, had united large sections of the rich and the poor, and thus stood for a sectional rather than a class conflict. Although the Commons still strongly represented the agrarian interest, there was a group of M.P.s who never ceased to lead the attack. Cobden himself entered the House in 1841 as member for Stockport, and was joined there by Bright in 1843. Lastly, their case was respectable; this was no revolutionary party with a new social and political programme. They wished merely to repeal constitutionally an Act of Parliament at a time when the tide of economic legislation was moving in the direction of free trade.

It is less easy to assess the economic significance of the Corn Laws and their repeal. In the years of good harvests in England the price of corn was low, the country was almost self-sufficient, and there was little market for foreign corn. In the bad years the harvest on the Continent was also often poor and the price was consequently high. On the whole, judging from the availability of foreign corn before 1846, it seems unlikely that the price of corn would have been very much lower if there had been no Corn Laws.

After repeal there were considerable imports from France, Italy, Turkey, Egypt, and North America, but the price of corn did not drop greatly. The average price in 1840–6 was fifty-six shillings and eightpence a quarter. In 1847 it was as high as sixty-nine shillings and ninepence, but dropped to an average of forty-three shillings between 1848 and 1852. It was high again during the abnormal conditions of the Crimean war, but from 1858 to 1877 the average figure was fifty-one shillings and fourpence. This does not mean that the Free Traders were wrong. The mid-century period was a time of rising prices in the world, owing to the discovery of gold in Australia and California, and thus these figures do represent a relative drop in the price of corn. Had the Corn Laws not been repealed, the price would undoubtedly have been much higher. Disaster for the English farmer came later, not from the plains of Europe, but from across the Atlantic in the 1870s and 1880s, when new machines enabled the North American farmer to develop the wide prairies, and railways and fast steamships could bring his wheat in vast quantities to the United Kingdom at a price with which the English farmer could not compete.

3. Socialism and Chartism

Factory reform and cheap bread had been battle-cries in the feud between landlord and manufacturer. Since both were achieved, the working class naturally benefited. But the underlying attitude was paternal and there had never been any suggestion of a political or social reorganization that would bridge the gulf between the Two Nations. At the same time, however, the poor themselves were struggling for self-expression. The movements that they developed varied greatly in form and implication, but since they sprang from a sense of social indignation, all of them tended inevitably to be intensely class conscious and to veer towards revolutionary action. Equally naturally, the middle classes took their stand with the established society and refused to become involved.

One of these movements developed shortly after the poor realized that they had gained nothing from the Reform Act of 1832. The Grand National Consolidated Trades Union was formed in 1834, a direct outcome of the ideas of Robert Owen. His belief that society should be organized in small groups of producers owning the means of production themselves was simply an elementary type of Socialism, and it was not surprising that it found little or no support among the middle classes. The setting up of the Union, which very soon had half a million members, led to a series of strikes, and the government had no hesitation in putting down the movement. In the course of this repression six labourers of Tolpuddle in Dorset were found guilty of administering illegal oaths and were sentenced to transportation for seven years. Two years later, in 1836, the men were pardoned and brought home, and five of them were given farms through subscriptions raised among working men.

The Grand National Union did not survive, and it was followed by two other types of enterprise which made no attempt to alter the general economic relationship of employer and employee. One of these, the Co-operative movement, first appeared when a general store was opened in Rochdale in 1844 with a capital of £28. The significant feature of the scheme was that all profits were to be shared among the members of the society in proportion to their purchases. Since the organization was geared to the consumer and not to the producer of the goods, it excited no alarm as a revolutionary body and was able to expand enormously throughout the nineteenth century. The second movement was the development of small Trade Unions of skilled workers, who now fought shy of any grandiose nation-wide scheme of Socialism and put their faith in direct local bargaining between themselves and their employer. Each Union restricted itself to the skilled workers of one particular craft in a locality, and set about organizing its funds for the assistance of its members when they were sick or unemployed or when the Union called a strike.

Both these developments had economic and social implications; neither of them involved any political programme. It was the peculiar feature of the Chartist movement that the Charter, from which it took its name, was entirely concerned with political aims and that there was never any vestige of agreement over social and economic policy. In 1836 a group of working-class men, of whom William Lovett was the leader, disappointed at the collapse of the Grand National Union, founded the London Working Men's Association. In May 1838 this body published the 'People's Charter'. It made six demands: annual parliaments, universal male suffrage, equal electoral districts, the end of a property qualification for membership of Parliament, the payment of members, and a secret ballot. The purpose was thus to change the existing constitution in such a way that the working classes, who formed the bulk of the population, should have a controlling influence over the government of the country.

The Chartist riots, which form the background of Disraeli's *Sybil*, were centred round three petitions to Parliament, each launched at a time of great economic distress—1839, 1842, and 1848. When the first petition was ready in May 1839, the government gave the military command of the northern district of

England to Sir Charles Napier, who invited Chartist leaders to a demonstration of artillery fire. The Chartists, despairing of insurrection if the petition were rejected, turned to planning a general strike and a refusal to pay rent, rates, or taxes. On 12 July the Commons refused to discuss the petition by 235 to 46 votes. The bluff had been called. The country did not rise; there was no general strike. Rioting in Birmingham was put down, and in November an attack in Newport under John Frost, which aimed at the release of one of their leaders, was driven off by troops after the Riot Act had been read. Frost and two others were condemned to death, but the sentences were afterwards commuted to transportation for life.

Lovett now began to feel that it was hopeless to continue without some alliance with the middle classes and joined forces with Joseph Sturge, a corn-miller of Birmingham, who published, in 1841, some articles on the 'Reconciliation between the Middle and Working Classes'. Over this the Chartists inevitably became divided. The extremists regarded such a move as treason to the cause, and they had a leader in Feargus O'Connor, a remarkable individual of Protestant Irish stock, whose uncle had gained the rank of general in Napoleon's army and had married the daughter of Condorcet. He was a tough, heavily built man, a good orator, skilled in the give and take of public meetings. His popularity among the rank and file of the movement derived from the *Northern Star*, a weekly newspaper printed at Leeds. It had been started in 1837 by a small group of Radicals who had intended that it should put forward their general programme, but in a very short time Feargus O'Connor had turned it into a vehicle for his own ideas. 'Upon my word,' remarked O'Connell, 'this paper of Feargus's is a literary curiosity. The first page is filled with praise of Feargus: second page, praise of Feargus; third page, ditto: fourth page, ditto: and so on all through till we come to the printer's name.' O'Connor broke with Lovett and went ahead with the second petition, which concentrated mainly on the iniquities of the Poor Law and the demand for universal suffrage. In May 1842 the Commons again refused to hear the petitioners.

This refusal was followed by sporadic outbreaks of rioting and striking, many of them the result of the hard times rather than the organization of the Chartists; but within six months order had been restored and the leaders had been imprisoned or transported, O'Connor himself managing to escape punishment.

The third petition, in 1848, was inspired by events on the Continent, but turned out to be the feeblest of all the Chartists' efforts. This time the disturbances were centred on London. The Duke of Wellington took elaborate precautions, over 150,000 special constables were sworn in—including Louis Napoleon Bonaparte— and when a large body of petitioners reached Kennington Common, they were warned by the police that they would not be allowed to cross the Thames from the south to the north side. O'Connor decided to tell his followers to disperse, while the petition, which weighed over 5 cwt., was taken to Westminster in three cabs; but when it was discovered that it contained many bogus signatures, such as 'Victoria Rex', Sir Robert Peel, and 'Mr. Punch', this last manifestation of Chartism was virtually laughed out of existence.

Why did Chartism fail? It had lacked effective support in the Commons and effective leaders among its organizers, but there were deeper reasons than these. It had been essentially a working-class movement and had never succeeded in making that alliance between sections of the middle and lower classes which characterized the more successful efforts of the Anti-Corn Law League and the factory reformers. Friendship with the Anti-Corn Law League itself might have given it a better chance, but the League had met its most violent opposition from the Chartists. To the middle and upper classes it appeared simply as a militant working-class movement, and that seemed tantamount to insurrection. Thus Chartism is hardly the equivalent of an English 1848 revolution. On the Continent the revolutions took the form of a momentary alliance between the lower and middle classes against the government. In most cases the governments were able to play off one class against the other and to defeat both; in France the middle classes were victorious and then put down the working classes. But everywhere the middle classes were an essential

F

element in the outbreak. In England they did not stir because they already had what they wanted. The Revolution of 1688 and the Reform Act of 1832 together ensured that the year 1848 was to be almost without significance in English history.

Division among the Chartist leaders was another fundamental reason for failure. They never agreed over their social policy and eventually two entirely opposing views emerged—O'Connor's, which stood for a return to a society of small landholders and which resulted in the formation of a Cooperative Land Society in May 1845, and Lovett's which was prepared to come to terms with the new world of industrialism.

A further reason for the Chartists' lack of success was the use that the government was able to make of the railways and the electric telegraph. Troops were rushed quickly from town to town, magistrates requisitioning railway carriages at the time when they applied for troops from the nearest military centre. Such an assistance gave the authorities greater confidence and enabled them to hold back from direct military action until the last moment. The attacks made by the mob on the railway track show that the Chartists were well aware of their value to the government. And while the telegraph and postal services were a great assistance to any wide-scale movement, the government was similarly aided. The Act of Parliament setting up the Electric Telegraph Company had stipulated that the government might take over entire control in times of emergency, and during the 1848 riots they acted on this. The effect was two-fold. Chartists were prevented from communicating by telegraph, and the government could take decisions affecting distant localities and exercise a closeness of control over the provinces that had never before been possible. After the disturbances were over, a bill for £500 was sent in by the Electric Telegraph Company.

There are two comments that must be added. The danger of insurrection was averted with very few repressive measures. In 1848 a Bill was accepted that made transportation for life the punishment for seditious language. Apart from this, little legislative action was taken. Chartist newspapers and pamphlets were freely published. The majority of sentences of imprisonment were mild and troops were used with considerable restraint. It is the measure of the weakness of Chartism that so little was needed to put it down. Secondly, with the exception of annual Parliaments, every political demand in the Charter was later to be granted. It had never been these that had alarmed the upper and middle classes, but only the revolutionary violence of class war with which they had been presented.

9

THE PARLIAMENTARY SCENE, 1835-50

1. Lord Melbourne's administration, 1835-41

NOTHING would have pleased William IV more than for Peel to have remained in office in 1835. 'I would rather have the devil than a Whig in the House,' he said, but if he had to have a Whig, Melbourne was clearly the least likely to launch out on fresh reforms. 'I am for holding the ground already taken,' the new Prime Minister told his Cabinet, 'but not for occupying new ground rashly.' Peel, in his Tamworth Manifesto, had said no less.

Melbourne was as good as his word. During his ministry he showed that he was personally opposed to most measures of reform under discussion. He had no wish to take energetic action to enforce the suppression of the Slave Trade. He had no liking for plans for popular education. He was opposed to the secret ballot, which might have ended much electoral corruption, had no intention of repealing the Corn Laws, and later objected to the penny post. He had no interest in the ecclesiastical controversy and hated his task of recommending new bishops. A quiet life was all that Melbourne wanted.

But it was hardly the time for a quiet life for a Prime Minister. The government's need to keep the Irish members in alliance with them resulted in long-drawn-out struggles over the Irish corporations, the Irish Poor Law, and tithe. There was serious unrest in Canada.[1] The railway boom was soon to be followed by the slump of 1838–41, bringing in its wake unemployment, Chartist riots, and the organization of the Anti-Corn Law League. Yet Melbourne hardly set his mark on any of these problems.

The Municipal Corporations Act of 1835 was the major work

[1] See p. 209.

of reform passed during his ministry. It was hardly surprising that the government which had carried the Reform Act of 1832 should turn its attention to the reform of the corporations. A commission set up in 1833 had revealed many anomalies. In Portsmouth, with a population of 46,000, there were 102 freemen, while in Leicester, with a population of 40,512, the freemen numbered 4,500. There were a great number of ways in which the freedom of the borough might be acquired, many of them involving purchase or gift. But the freemen themselves often played little part in local elections; out of 237 boroughs 186 had self-elected councils, and in twenty-six there were no councils at all. The corporations' source of income was mainly borough property, but a rate was also levied, if this was insufficient. 'It is not often', ran the report, 'that much of the corporate property is expended on police or public improvements.' The commissioners had been prejudiced, but it was certainly high time for reform, and Peel's support of the proposals brought Wellington round and enabled the government to get the major part of the Bill through the Lords.

The Municipal Corporations Act of 1835 swept away the old system, gave the local vote to all rate-payers, and provided that one-third of the council should be elected annually. The corporations retained their income, which was to be applied to various forms of municipal administration. The judiciary was separated from the municipal government, and magistrates were still to be appointed by the Crown—not elected, as the Radicals would have liked. Some concessions were made to the conservatives. Rate-payers had to have resided three years; there was to be an income qualification for members of the council; a body of aldermen was to be created, equal in number to one-third of the council and elected by the council for six years. Thus the Act laid down the lines along which municipal government has developed to this day.

The significance of the Act was ultimately to be enormous. The change in the condition of the towns is one of the most striking aspects of nineteenth-century Britain, and much of this was to be the result of local activity, barely supervised by the central government. The Municipal Corporations Act provided the machinery whereby this transformation was made possible. The effect was at first only gradually felt and the movement did not reach its heyday until the 1870s, when development was so fast that it acquired the slightly erroneous name of 'municipal socialism'.[1] Nevertheless, the starting-point had been in 1835, one more instance of how a single piece of legislation had opened the door to profound and unforeseeable changes.

The one aspect of his ministry that held Melbourne's interest was his quiet, tactful tuition of the young Queen Victoria during the first three years of her reign. William IV died in 1837, to be succeeded by an eighteen-year-old girl whose name now sums up a whole epoch in English history. Her father, Edward, Duke of Kent, the fourth son of George III, had died seventeen years before, and his daughter had been brought up by her German-born mother and her governess, Fräulein Lehzen. There was little that was remarkable about her. She was an unaffected girl, fond of riding and the open air. Court life had forced her to keep her views to herself. Her mother had fallen out with William IV and hoped to gain a position of ascendancy on his death, but William lived just too long for this hope to be realized.

At six o'clock in the morning on 20 June, 1837 Victoria was awoken by her mother and told that the Archbishop of Canterbury and Lord Conyngham wished to see her. 'I got out of bed,' she wrote in her Journal, 'and went into my sitting-room (only in my dressing-gown) and alone and saw them. Lord Conyngham then acquainted me that my poor Uncle, the King, was no more and had expired at 12 minutes past 2 this morning, and consequently I am Queen.' She had time at half past eight to write to her uncle Leopold, King of the Belgians: 'I expect Lord Melbourne almost immediately, and hold a Council at eleven.' 'At 9 came Lord Melbourne,' runs her Journal, 'whom I saw in my room, and of course quite alone, as I shall always do all my Ministers. He kissed my hand, and I then acquainted him that it had long been my intention to retain him and the rest of the present Ministry at the head of affairs, and that it could not be in

[1] See p. 329.

better hands than his.' Later that evening she had 'a very important and a very comfortable conversation with him'.

So began for Melbourne a delightful epilogue to the unhappiness of his personal life. His wife, Lady Caroline Lamb, had become the mistress of Lord Byron; his only son, to whom he was devoted, was mentally defective. His worldly cynicism was, to some extent, the façade of a man who longed for affection, and during the next three years, until Victoria's marriage, he found a deep contentment in giving fatherly guidance to the young Queen. For Victoria such a tutor was a blessing; she was determined to rule free from the influence of her mother, and the quiet, worldly-wise advice of her Prime Minister gave her support and courage. 'Try to do your best,' he told her, 'and leave the rest to fate. . . . It never does when people think of what they ought to do and of what they do do.' But she had a mind of her own. It was no coincidence that her reign should now be regarded as the epitome of high-mindedness and respectability. She spoke with horror of the free, gay days of the Regency. 'But they were jolly fellows . . .', rejoined Melbourne wistfully; 'times have changed, but I do not know if they have improved.' Such a divergence of outlook did little to upset the harmony of their relations. 'As for the confidence of the Crown,' she wrote, 'God knows! No Minister, no friend, EVER possessed it so entirely as this truly excellent Lord Melbourne possesses mine.'

The election of 1837 left the Whigs still dependent on the support of the Irish members. It is possible that they would not have got back at all, if a story had not been spread around that the Conservatives intended to put the unpopular Duke of Cumberland on the throne, since the Salic Law prevented Victoria from succeeding to the Electorate of Hanover. Among the Conservatives Benjamin Disraeli was at last, after several unsuccessful attempts, able to win a seat in the Commons. This young novelist, a Jew—although of Christian upbringing, and hence able to take his seat —is one of the most colourful personalities of the nineteenth century. His background was not as exotic as he liked to make out. The son of a literary man, he had been educated at a Unitarian seminary and had worked for a few years in a London solicitor's office before making his name as a novelist. But it was the thought of his Italian grandfather that fired the young Disraeli's imagination with the romance of history, the Jews of Spain, and the mystery of the East. This romantic strain is apparent in many of his political utterances and his books. It was not a trait that always endeared him to the Anglican Tories, whom he was later to lead. An enigmatic Jew, Sidonia, who appears in his novel *Coningsby*, was referred to by Trollope in his *Barchester Towers* as 'a dirty little old man'. Nor was the beginning of his political life particularly auspicious. He had told Melbourne three years before that he intended to become Prime Minister; yet his maiden speech, carefully prepared and rich in classical allusions, was hooted and shouted down in the Commons, until they wrung from him a cry better known now than almost anything that he said later: 'I sit down now, but the time will come when you will hear me.'

The Whig ministry dragged on. Irish tithes were commuted into a charge payable by the landlord, without the government appropriating any of this revenue. Irish municipal corporations were reformed, the franchise being extended to £10 rate-payers. The new Poor Law was introduced into Ireland. But by now the government were as much in need of Peel's support as they were of the Irish members. 'The Whigs govern nothing but Downing Street,' jeered a Radical. Lord Durham's visit to Canada did not bring an immediate pacification, although his report in 1839 was to be of the highest significance.[1] The country was in the throes of economic depression and the government had to face the first of the Chartist outbreaks. In 1839 the ministry, reduced to a majority of five, decided to resign. Peel, who through his own efforts and the lassitude of the Whigs had managed to construct a new Conservative group, should have taken office then; but when he asked the Queen to change a few of her Ladies of the Bed-chamber, Victoria, insisting to Melbourne that he had demanded that they should *all* be changed, refused. In fact, she was simply anxious to retain Melbourne, and Peel, outwardly cold and re-served, was not the man to win her over. Without some sign of the Queen's confidence, he declared, he was unable to take office.

---

[1] See p. 210.

This unexpected and undeserved reprieve for Melbourne's ministry produced no fresh measures. The government had become involved in a war with China over the illicit importing of opium and there were angry scenes in the Commons in 1840.[1] The Whigs had little resistance to offer. 'A government of departments,' Charles Buller called them in 1841, 'absolutely without a chief, hating, distrusting, despising one another, having no principles and no plans, living from hand to mouth, able to do nothing, and indifferent whether they did anything or not, proposing measures without the hope or the expectation of carrying them, and clinging to their places for no other reason than that they felt themselves bound to the Queen.' But since 1840 the Queen had found a new councillor, her beloved husband, Prince Albert of Saxe-Coburg, and although Victoria's relations with Peel were hardly improved when he brought about the reduction of the Prince Consort's annual allowance from £50,000 to £30,000, she was now no longer entirely dependent upon Melbourne for guidance.

In the end a financial crisis was the government's undoing. The annual deficit was now well over £2 million, partly due to the introduction of the penny post in 1840.[2] The debate roused Peel to make a joke. 'Can there be a more lamentable picture than that of a Chancellor of the Exchequer seated on an empty chest—by the pool of a bottomless deficiency—fishing for a budget.' 'And then', commented Sir John Hobhouse, 'he giggled, as if he had said something exceedingly funny.' The government decided to dissolve.

Economic depression, the ferment over the Corn Laws, and the Chartist movement were all considerable factors in the electoral battle of 1841. The most significant change of sides was the Radicals' loss of confidence in their alliance with the Whigs. 'If Peel were in', Lord Sydenham had written in 1839, 'he could muzzle or keep away his Tory allies and we should support him. If he got in, and had courage, what a field he would have.' The Whig proposal at the election to end the sliding scale of duties on imported corn and to introduce in its place a fixed duty of 8s.

[1] See p. 227.   [2] See p. 104.

was an attempt to break up this possible Tory–Radical alliance, but it won little favour. Feargus O'Connor, banking on Tory criticism of the Poor Law and of the conditions in the industrial towns, told Chartists to support the Tory candidates. The alignments that had brought the Whigs into power eleven years before had broken down and had been reshaped against them. The outcome of the election was an overwhelming Conservative majority. Only now did Melbourne resign, and after a compromise had been reached with Victoria over the Ladies of the Bedchamber, Peel took office at the head of a Conservative government.

2. Peel's administration, 1841-6

At fifty-three Robert Peel had lost little of his air of frigidity. As with William Pitt, it vanished only when he was in the company of younger men with whom he was well acquainted. Indeed, as his Cabinets showed, he had a gift for selecting young men of ability—Gladstone, Sidney Herbert, Edward Cardwell, and Lord Canning were all of his choosing. Among them he was a changed man, affectionate, charming, and fond of a bawdy story, which he would tell with shouts of laughter. Unlike Pitt, he was married, enjoyed a very happy family life, and was devoted to his five sons. But outside this small circle Peel was difficult to know. 'His smile', said O'Connell, 'was like the silver plate on a coffin.' Some of his shyness was defensive. He was a little sensitive of his Lancashire accent and the knowledge that he was the son of a self-made man made him ill at ease as leader of the landed classes. He had a temper which he had to keep carefully under control. His intellectual powers were considerable and Gladstone called him 'the best man of business who was ever Prime Minister'. He took time to make up his mind, but he was impossible to shift on a point of principle, once he believed that he was right. This dispassionate determination laid him open to the charge of arrogance and disregard for his party's future, but his integrity was unquestionable, and it is striking that Victoria, who found him hard to like at first, developed a very deep respect for him.

With one or two changes Peel's Cabinet in 1841 was almost exactly as in 1834. Two Whigs who had earlier left Grey's government joined him, Sir James Graham becoming Home Secretary and Lord Stanley Colonial Secretary. Gladstone, as Vice-President of the Board of Trade, had no seat in the Cabinet until 1843, when he succeeded Lord Ripon as President. Disraeli found no place in spite of his letter of protest, a fact which may have added virulence to his attacks on Peel five years later.

During the course of the ministry the humanitarians succeeded in passing the Mines Act and the 1844 Factory Act, while Gladstone was responsible for establishing the Parliamentary train with its third-class railway fare of a penny a mile.[1] But the major efforts of the government were directed towards economic reform and the pacification of Ireland.

A. FREE TRADE AND IRISH AFFAIRS, 1841-5

The immediate economic problem was to get rid of the deficit. Peel believed that the answer lay fundamentally in the stimulation of trade through a further reduction of import duties. The officials at the Board of Trade were almost unanimously of the same opinion. They knew, of course, that this was a long-term view and that a reduction would probably mean, at first, a decrease in revenue. To cover this and to end the deficit at once, Peel proposed in his Budget of 1842 to reintroduce the income tax for three years at a rate of 7d. in £1 on all incomes over £150 a year. At the same time he reduced duties to a possible maximum of 5% on all raw materials, 12% on all articles partly manufactured, and 20% on all articles completely manufactured. More reductions followed with each succeeding Budget, and in 1845 he asked for a renewal of the income tax for a further three years, so that he might 'repeal other taxes pressing on industrial and commercial enterprise'. These Budgets form a coherent financial policy and represent Peel's greatest achievement during his ministry. They also made it clear that the Radicals had been right to shift their allegiance to his party.

In 1842 he revised the Corn Law, altering the sliding scale

[1] See p. 103.

adopted in 1828. Now the duty was only to fall at exactly the same rate as the price rose, shilling for shilling, so that there would be less encouragement for the foreign dealer to hold corn back until the high price of the corn had made the duty disproportionately low.

His most important financial measure was the Bank Charter Act of 1844. In the past, an economic slump usually followed upon a boom during which more and more enterprises had been floated on credit until confidence failed, credit collapsed, and there ensued a commercial crisis and industrial distress. Peel decided that it was essential in future to restrict the issue of paper money by the banks. The Act aimed at gradually concentrating the right of issue into the Bank of England, where, except for a fiduciary issue of £14 million, all notes were to have a 100% gold backing. No new bank was to issue notes at all, and existing banks were not to increase their issue beyond their average during the twelve weeks preceding the passing of the Act. Peel was aware that the scheme was not foolproof. It was now less likely that credit would get out of control, but if it did happen again and a slump followed upon a boom, then the immediate need would be easily available money—the very thing that the Act prevented. In fact, there was a slump in 1847, and the government's answer was to suspend the Act, so that the Bank of England might issue notes without gold backing. There were further crises in 1857 and 1866, by which time the Bank of England was learning to avoid some of the more unpleasant features of the trade cycle. Peel's Act was certainly a great measure, an essential element in Britain's economic supremacy in the nineteenth century.

Over Ireland it was obviously much more difficult to lay down a general policy. Peel was fortunate in that Thomas Drummond had been Under-Secretary for Ireland from 1835 until his death in 1840. Drummond had refused to use Coercion Acts, repressed the Orangemen as well as the Ribbon societies, and encouraged the entry of Catholics into the police and juries. His administration is one of the happier periods of Anglo-Irish relations, but the work that it involved virtually killed him.

Meanwhile, O'Connell was still hoping to gain the repeal of

the Act of Union by constitutional means. He had, however, never gained the support of more than about forty of the Irish members, and after the movement had lost ground in the 1841 election the younger Irish nationalists broke with their old leader and began to resort to violence, imitating Mazzini's Italian movements with the title of 'Young Ireland'. An outbreak seemed likely in 1843, but after passing an Arms Act and drafting troops to Ireland, Peel remained master of the situation. O'Connell was arrested and condemned by a packed jury, but on appeal to Westminster this verdict was quashed by the law lords.

The more constructive side of Peel's policy was to conciliate the Irish by various measures to assist education and the Irish Catholic clergy. Among these was the increase of the annual Parliamentary grant to the Catholic Maynooth College in Dublin from £9,000 to £26,000. It was over this that Gladstone felt compelled to resign in January 1845, since he had condemned the original grant in his book on *Church and State*. Gladstone did his best to explain the precise moral distinction between £9,000 and £26,000 in a speech lasting an hour in the Commons, but at the end Peel, Cobden, and Disraeli all confessed themselves mystified. His feelings, however, were not entirely incomprehensible. Catholic emancipation and the Oxford Movement had awoken a storm among the Anglicans. 1845 was to be the year of Newman's entry into the Roman Catholic Church, and, as a High Churchman, Gladstone was bound to feel that this was hardly the moment for the government to add so heavily to its subsidizing of the Catholic clergy.

In an attempt to get to the heart of the agrarian problem, Peel also set up, in 1843, a Commission under Lord Devon. On reading its findings he put forward a Bill for limited compensation for tenants who carried out improvements in fencing, draining, and building, but the strength of the opposition caused its withdrawal for amendment. This had, at least, been a constructive attempt, although, even if it had succeeded, the fundamental problems of Ireland would still have been left untouched. Before the Bill got any further, the Irish potato crop failed and the resultant famine in a country whose population had now reached 8 million reduced all governmental action to desperate expedient, bringing Peel to the supreme crisis of his career.

B. THE REPEAL OF THE CORN LAWS, 1845-6

Up to the summer of 1845 Peel's Conservative government could claim to have followed a far more positive and energetic policy than its Whig predecessor. It seemed as if this new Toryism could not merely survive in an age of reform, but had a definite contribution of its own to make. 'Tory men and Whig measures,' commented Taper, a character in Disraeli's *Coningsby*. But one step it dared not take. The landed class was the mainstay of the party, and although Peel might tinker with the Corn Laws, as in 1842, their repeal was absolutely out of the question.

The crucial factor in the story of the repeal is not the Irish famine, nor the failure of the English harvest. It is the gradual change in Peel's own attitude towards the Corn Laws. It was clear that he was no supporter of Protection in general, and during his ministry he had come to see the soundness of many of the arguments of the Anti-Corn Law League. England was not self-supporting. Protection did not encourage efficient farming. Cheap food since 1843 had not brought wages down. Already, by 1844, his colleague Gladstone had decided that the Corn Laws must go. Peel's own mental turmoil may be judged from an incident in the Commons in March 1845. Cobden was delivering another of his great onslaughts on the Laws, when Peel crumpled up his notes, turned to Sidney Herbert next to him, and whispered, 'You must answer this, for I cannot.'

Peel's dilemma was that if he brought in an Act of Repeal he would be betraying the interest of his electors. He knew, too, that such a move would split the Cabinet and the government supporters in the House. For the moment the plan was to hold on in the hope that no agricultural crisis would face the government before the next general election, when Peel could announce his change of mind to his constituents. It all rested on the intervening harvests. 'It is a high probability', Gladstone had written in 1844, 'that one bad harvest, or at all events, two, would break up the

Corn Law and with it the Party. Hitherto it has worked better than could have been hoped, but I cannot deny that it is a law mainly dependent upon the weather.' Thus the summer of 1845 found Peel and Cobden both anxiously watching the barometer. May was wet. June was fine. And then, when it seemed that the harvest was safe, a downpour of rain lasted throughout August. The price of corn rose to sixty shillings; then, in September, it dropped to fifty-four shillings, and the hopes of the Anti-Corn Law League fell with it.

But now news of a far greater disaster arrived from Ireland. Potato blight, which had appeared the previous year in America, spread to Europe, and the second Irish potato crop of the year was ruined. In England, where the potato was cultivated to some extent, this meant hunger. For the Irish peasant, who lived entirely on potatoes, it meant death. Peel summoned his Cabinet and proposed relief measures in Ireland. The expenditure of £600,000 was authorized. Public works were to be organized to give employment. £160,000 worth of maize was purchased from the United States to be sold at a penny a pound to the Irish—later known among them as 'Peel's brimstone'.

The Irish famine has always loomed large in the discussion of the repeal, since the poor English harvest made it impossible to send corn to Ireland. 'Rotten potatoes have done it all,' said the Duke of Wellington; 'they have put Peel in his damned fright.' Yet the connection between the two was more emotional than rational. The majority of Irish peasants had little interest in cheap or dear corn, since they never ate bread. The arguments of the Anti-Corn Law League did not apply in Ireland, since, except for a little in Ulster, there was no industry that might benefit; on the other hand, the Irish farmers who did grow corn—the most desirable feature of Irish economy—might suffer considerably from foreign competition. This had been another of the considerations that had held Peel back earlier in 1845.

His critics claimed that he could have found some solution avoiding repeal, and it is conceivable that he could have done. But for Peel the Irish famine was not simply a tragedy; it was a lesson of what might happen in England if the poorer classes were encouraged through dear bread to turn more and more to the cultivation of potatoes. The good of the community, decided Peel, demanded repeal, and political considerations did not justify any further delay. On 6 November he proposed to his Cabinet that the corn duties should be reduced at once by Order in Council and that the government should introduce a Bill to reform the Corn Laws. Only three would support him in this—Lord Aberdeen, Sidney Herbert, and Sir James Graham—and this split in the Cabinet foreshadowed the destruction of the Conservative party. On 22 November Lord John Russell sent a letter from Edinburgh to his constituents in London declaring his conversion to repeal. Peel made a last effort to bring his Cabinet round, and when he failed, went to Windsor on 5 December to place his resignation before the Queen. It seemed as if repeal would be left to Russell's Whigs.

But it was not to be. Russell, when asked by Victoria to form a government, did not relish the situation. He would have a minority in the Commons. The Lords would be uncompromisingly hostile. The rank and file of the Whigs were still confused over the question. Russell attempted half-heartedly to form a Cabinet and then, encountering difficulties over including both Lord Palmerston and Lord Grey, son of the Reform Act premier, was glad to give up the task.

On 20 December Peel was recalled by the Queen, and, having now won most of them round, formed his Cabinet as before, with the exception of Lord Stanley, whose place at the Colonial Office was taken by Gladstone. At the beginning of 1846 Peel introduced a Customs Bill and a Corn Bill, which made repeal part of a general programme of tariff reform. The duties on many manufactured articles were reduced; those on maize were abolished at once; those on wheat, oats, barley, and rye were to be reduced to a shilling a quarter by 1849. In the meanwhile, a much lower sliding scale replaced the existing one.

The Corn Bill had passed the Commons by 15 May, due to the support of the Whigs and Peel's followers. While it lasted, the battle was fierce and revealed a new leader among the Protectionist Tories—Benjamin Disraeli, who rose again and again to denounce Peel's betrayal of his supporters. 'Let men stand by the principle by which they rise—right or wrong . . . it is not a legitimate trial of the principles of free trade against the principle of protection, if a Parliament, the majority of which are elected to support protection, be gained over to free trade by the arts of the very individual whom they were elected to support in an opposite career. It is not fair to the people of England.' At first Peel had been more jovial than usual, as he often was when the fight was hard. But gradually, as the attacks on both sides became more personal and vindictive, the strain told on him. At one point the Speaker thought he was about to burst into tears. On another occasion he remained sitting alone in the empty House, lost in thought, long after the end of the session, until the attendants came to put out the lights.

In the Lords Wellington supported Peel, and on 26 June the Corn Bill passed its third reading there. At the same time, after an all-night debate, Peel's government was defeated over an Irish Coercion Bill, when Whigs and Protectionists combined against him, and on the next day Peel resigned.

It had been a successful ministry in many ways. The American–Canadian frontier [1] had been successfully negotiated; Irish policy had been imaginative and humane; the Budget of 1846 had demonstrated the success of Peel's financial schemes. Yet the end had been disaster. Constitutionally the issue had been a simple one; assuming that it was too soon for a general election and that, as seems probable, Peel's government was the only one that could have got repeal through the Commons and the Lords, was he justified in reversing his policy over the Corn Laws? For Peel the answer was simple. 'When I fall,' he had said in the course of the debate, 'I shall have the satisfaction of reflecting that I do not fall because I have shown subservience to a party. I shall not fall because I preferred the interests of party to the general interests of the community.' He had changed his mind and, in the circumstances, had felt compelled to act. He had done the same in 1829 over Catholic emancipation, but there had been no Disraeli then to rally the dissentients of his own party. His was the attitude of

[1] See p. 240.

the detached statesman, respecting the electorate up to a point, but ultimately in an emergency listening only to his own conscience. In his voice there was still an echo of Burke's sentiments addressed to the electors of Bristol in 1774: 'Parliament is not a congress of ambassadors from different and hostile interests; which interests each must maintain as an agent and advocate against other agents and advocates. . . . If the local constituent should have an interest, or form an hasty opinion, evidently opposite to the real good of the rest of the community, the member for that place ought to be as far, as any other, from any endeavour to give it effect.' In Disraeli's voice, perhaps, one can hear something closer to the twentieth century, although it is possible that the speaker was more conscious of some of the characters in his own novels. For both of them the results were bad. For Peel his career was at an end; for Disraeli the party through which he was to become Prime Minister was split in two and the premiership was still over twenty years distant.

3. After repeal

The government that succeeded Peel's really belongs to that unstable period of English politics that lasted from the repeal until the passing of the second Reform Act in 1867. Russell became Prime Minister, and Peel and Disraeli found themselves sitting on the same Opposition Front Bench. A general election in 1847 brought back 325 Whigs or Liberals, 226 Tory Protectionists and 105 Peelites. For the time Russell was safe, since Peelites had no intention of voting with Protectionists. In any case, the leadership of the Protectionists was very uncertain. Stanley had moved to the House of Lords in 1844, and in the Commons Disraeli was not yet accepted by a number of the Protectionists, since Tory prejudice against a Jewish leader still had to be overcome, and for a while he had to share the leadership with Lord George Bentinck. A further difficulty for Disraeli at this time was that Protection was a lost cause. The general prosperity in the last years of the '40s made that undeniable, but Disraeli accepted this rather sooner than the rest of his party. It did not heal the rift. Disraeli's attack on Peel had not simply been against Free Trade; it had been against what he claimed was Peel's betrayal of his electors. And the Peelites had not forgiven the man who had led the attack.

The misery in Ireland lasted until 1848. The potato crop of 1846 failed utterly. 'The whole face of the country was changed,' wrote Captain Mann of what he had seen in County Clare. 'The stalk remained bright green, but the leaves were all scorched black. It was the work of a night.' The starving and dying roamed the countryside aimlessly. 'I recollect', wrote Josephine Butler of her childhood in Ireland, 'when walking through the lanes and villages, the strange morbid famine smell in the air, the sign of approaching death, even in those who were still dragging out a wretched existence.' By December 1846 cholera had broken out. By March 1847, 734,000 were being employed on relief works and 3 million in all were being supported by the public funds. In that month Russell gave up the attempt to organize public work and authorized the general distribution of food to the destitute. No one who held as much as a quarter of an acre of land was to qualify for relief, and the consequence of this was that thousands of families gave up their holdings in order not to starve. Thousands more scraped together the £4 or £5 that was the cost of a passage to America—usually undertaken in unseaworthy ships crammed with starving cholera-ridden peasants. Out of 89,000 who crossed to Canada in 1847, over 15,000 died.

The famine ended in 1848, when the harvest was good. In two and a half terrible years Nature, assisted by the more enthusiastic of the evicting landlords, had done what no Parliament at Westminster or Dublin could have achieved. More than half of all the holdings under fifteen acres had gone and some of the great estates lay virtually untenanted. Well over half a million had died. Hundreds of thousands continued to emigrate during the following years, and by 1851 the population of a country which, ten years earlier, had numbered over 8 million, had been reduced to 6½ million. Relief measures had cost the government £7,132,268, of which slightly less than half was a free grant. The remainder was considered to be a loan, but in 1853 this was cancelled against the extension of the income tax in Ireland. The cost in human suffering cannot be assessed; the minds of a whole people were scarred by the memory of it, and although the government had done its best at the time, the famine to the Irish was simply one more horror for which they could thank the English. A jury at an inquest at Connaught on a woman who had died of starvation brought in a verdict of wilful murder against the Prime Minister, Lord John Russell. The suffering might be over, but the hatred lived on, and among the survivors in Ireland and in America that hatred was to be nursed to the third and fourth generation.

10

THE TWILIGHT OF THE HOLY ALLIANCE, 1822–51

MEANWHILE, there had taken place on the continent of Europe a series of upheavals that had radically affected the alignments of 1815. The maintenance of the Holy Alliance had depended principally on two conditions—the desire on the part of all the great Powers to uphold the existing social and political order, and their willingness to forgo any national advantage that might be gained by fostering the revolutionary elements in their neighbours' countries. Canning's direction of British foreign policy after Castlereagh's death in 1822, the accession of Tsar Nicholas I of Russia in 1825, and the setting up of the July monarchy in the French revolution of 1830 were all factors in the destruction of this system; the Holy Alliance was afterwards to linger on for a couple of decades in the form of an uneasy friendship between Austria, Prussia, and Russia, until, in 1854, Austria's treaties with England and France against Russia in the Crimean war made it clear that the phrase had no further significance.

1. Canning: Spain, Portugal, and the New World

Canning's policy over Spain and Portugal at once established the new outlook of the British government. When Canning took office, Ferdinand VII was still appealing to the Powers for help in putting down the rising of the Spanish constitutionalists. At the Congress of Verona in 1822 Great Britain had already shown that she was not prepared to act alongside the other Powers in this, and when, in January 1823, Louis XVIII stated in his speech to the French Chamber that France was prepared to intervene on Ferdinand's behalf, Canning went a step further. He was by no means an advocate of revolution in Europe, much as he disliked autocracy. 'Let us not, in the foolish spirit of romance, suppose that we alone could regenerate Europe.' But the likelihood of French intervention forced him to warn France that the British government would strongly object to a permanent military occupation of Spain, the violation of Portugal's frontiers, or any French interference in the Spanish American colonies.

The French forces, completely remodelled since the passing of the Army Law of 1818, entered Spain, and by September 1823 the revolt had been suppressed. It was the question of the American colonies that immediately concerned the British government; French control over Spain might lead to French arms restoring Spain's New World possessions to her. This was unthinkable; Spain without her American colonies mattered less. At this point Canning turned to the United States, who had already recognized the new republican governments in South America, and suggested to Richard Rush, the American minister in London, that an Anglo-American protest should be made to the Powers of the Holy Alliance, warning them off any interference in the New World. He proposed also that each of them should give a pledge not to take any of the territories themselves. To John Quincy Adams it seemed that this second proposal was an attempt to ensure that the United States would never take possession of Cuba; the Americans parried with a counter-suggestion that Britain should at once recognize the new republics. This Canning would not do. In October, however, the main purpose of his diplomacy was gained when, after a conference with Polignac, the French ambassador, a memorandum was issued in which the French government denied any intention of taking action in Spanish America.

It was the Americans who made the most capital out of this situation. They had already been disturbed by Tsar Alexander's ukase in September 1821, in which he claimed that the coastline of Russian Alaska extended as far south as the 51st parallel. 'The ground that I wish to take', wrote Adams in his diary, 'is that of earnest remonstrance against the interference of the European Powers by force with South America, but to disclaim all interference on our part with Europe; to make an American cause, and adhere inflexibly to that.' He worked hard to persuade President Monroe, and a statement on foreign relations was included in the President's annual message to Congress in December 1823, which has come to be known as the Monroe doctrine. The American continents were not to be considered as 'subjects for future colonization by any European Power', nor were any colonies that had declared their independence to be interfered with; the United States would not interfere with any existing colonies of any European Power and had no intention of taking part in wars between European Powers.

The Monroe doctrine was an independent statement on the part of the American government. As has often been pointed out, it rested for its application mainly on the strength of the British Navy, but considerable British commercial interests made it unlikely that the United States would look in vain for this support—as the negotiations with Canning had suggested. Within another year Canning had decided that if the South American republics remained unrecognized they would be driven to reliance on the United States, and in December 1824 Great Britain recognized the republics of Buenos Aires, Mexico, and Columbia. George IV loathed the idea of recognition and refused to read the royal speech announcing these measures to the reassembled Parliament, protesting that he was suffering from gout and had lost his false teeth. Eldon read it instead, and the news was greeted with joy by the merchants and the representatives of the new states. Some two years later Canning put his case in one of his most famous speeches. 'If France occupied Spain, was it necessary in order to avoid the consequences of that occupation—that we should blockade Cadiz? No! I looked another way. I sought materials of compensation in another hemisphere. Contemplating Spain, such as our ancestors had known her, I resolved that if France had Spain, it should not be Spain with the Indies. I called the New World into existence to redress the balance of the old.' It was a fine phrase, but the danger from France had long been settled by the Polignac memorandum, and the main aim of this recognition was in fact to ensure that the

Americans did not gain too much through their own adroit diplomacy.

One further episode in the Iberian peninsula confirmed the Holy Alliance's hatred of Canning. Civil war broke out in Portugal in 1826 between two claimants to the throne. Don Pedro, the elder son of the late King John VI, had promised the Portuguese a constitution, and when the Spanish government gave assistance to the other brother, Don Miguel, the constitutionalists appealed to the British government. Canning responded at once. 'We go to Portugal', he said in the Commons, 'not to rule, not to dictate, not to prescribe constitutions, but to defend and to preserve the independence of an ally. We go to plant the standard of England on the well known heights of Lisbon. Where that standard is planted, foreign dominion shall not come.' A fleet with 4,000 troops was sent to Lisbon, and in a short time the constitutionalist party had been established in power.

So far in all these issues Canning had been able to speak and act with resolution in defiance of the Holy Alliance, since the command of the sea gave him a trump card. In handling the Eastern Question, however, this gave him little advantage, and the complexity of the interests involved demanded a more tentative, less spectacular type of diplomacy.

2. The Eastern Question

Ever since the emergence of Russia as a European Power the keynote of her foreign policy had been to push her frontiers further to the north-west, to the south, and south-east. The establishment of the new capital, St. Petersburg, together with its island naval base of Cronstadt, in 1704, and the annexation of Finland in 1808, had given Russia what she needed in the north-west. The main obstacle to Russian expansion southwards was Turkey, but Turkey was, as Nicholas I said later, 'the Sick Man of Europe', and Russia had been engaged in pushing south, when the threat from Napoleon had forced Tsar Alexander to make terms with the Turks by the Treaty of Bucharest in 1812. In 1821, when the Greeks revolted against their Turkish overlords, it had been a great temptation to Alexander to take advantage of Turkey's difficulties and to renew the attack southward, but Metternich was able to restrain him in the interest of the principles of the Holy Alliance. In 1825 Tsar Nicholas I ascended the Russian throne, and it was soon clear that no Holy Alliance would hold him back from what he regarded as the natural direction of Russian foreign policy.

Russia's problem was that, although she might wage war successfully against Turkey, the Powers of Europe would object to Russian annexation of Turkish territory. While Metternich clung to the hope of the Holy Alliance, the most forceful resistance would probably come from Great Britain, but, owing to her very small army, this resistance could be effective only if Britain had a Continental ally. The British government hoped mainly for support from France in this theatre, and Russian policy consequently had much to fear from Anglo-French friendship. For Russia the fact that direct annexation of Turkish territory might lead to a major war or—at best—a partition of Turkish possessions in Europe among the Powers, called for a diplomatic rather than a military approach to the problem. Thus Russia's policy was aimed mainly at preserving the *status quo* while gradually establishing a general influence over the Turkish government.

For Britain there were two dangers to be watched. Russia was now a naval as well as a military force. The Ionian Isles served as a useful naval base for the British fleet, but if British naval supremacy in the eastern Mediterranean was not to be seriously challenged, Russia must be prevented from gaining control of the Straits of the Bosphorus and the Dardanelles. The second danger lay in Russian interests east of the Black Sea, on the Persian and Afghan borders. One British route to India lay via Egypt and the Red Sea, but a second route under consideration ran overland along the line of the Euphrates. Concern for the security of these two routes was inevitably to play a great part in British policy in the following decades.

Two lines of policy were open to the British government. One was to bolster up Turkey against Russia and to maintain the existing situation in the Near East. The other policy rested on the assumption that Turkey's hold over her European possessions was doomed. In that case, some alternative had to be found to absorption by Russia, and this could only mean some form of agreement with Russia over the establishment of various independent national states in the Balkans. This second policy was hardly a final solution, since it would transform the struggle into one in which the neighbouring Powers, Austria and Russia, intrigued to gain political and economic control over the new states.

This complex of conflicting interests consequent on the decaying might of the Turkish Empire constituted the Eastern Question, and it was to bedevil international relations throughout the nineteenth century and in a slightly changed form has continued to do so throughout the twentieth.

3. British policy in the Near East, 1822-31

The revolt of the Greeks against their Turkish overlords in 1821 had caused a great stir of sympathy among the upper classes in England. Memories of the classics in the schoolroom combined with the emotional force of the Romantic movement to create a frame of mind that made it seem imperative to lend assistance to the Greeks. Byron, who left Italy to join their forces and who died at Missolonghi in 1824, seemed to them a martyr in the cause of national freedom. But the problem for the British government was that the Greek revolt could be Russia's opportunity, and by 1824 Tsar Alexander was near enough to considering intervention to suggest establishing three separate semi-independent Greek principalities.

Until now the Greek forces had been able to hold their own against the Turks, but in 1824 they became divided amongst themselves and civil war broke out. The hope of achieving Greek independence looked even more remote when the Sultan appealed to the Pasha of Egypt, Mehemet Ali, who was nominally his vassal. Mehemet Ali, encouraged by the French, who reckoned that an Arab empire in Greece would forestall the Russians, sent his son Ibrahim to subdue the islands and to make a

landing in the Morea. This was followed, in 1825, by the accession of Tsar Nicholas, which made it certain that the Russians
would not stay out of the conflict much longer.

For Canning the moment had come to act. He had to make his
decision whether to uphold Turkey and thus run the danger of
war with Russia, while facing intensely hostile opinion at home,
or to act alongside Russia and to find some solution which might
at least keep Russia out of Greece. He chose the second. Wellington went to St. Petersburg, and on 4 April, 1826 a secret protocol was signed with Nesselrode, the Russian minister. Russia
and Great Britain agreed to intervene together in Greece, where a
semi-independent state was to be set up, paying tribute to Turkey,
but managing her own affairs and enjoying liberty of conscience.
Austria and Prussia were invited to join this agreement, but refused. For Metternich the whole thing represented one more
blow at the Holy Alliance. 'The Continental alliance, on which
our peace and prosperity rests, has ceased to exist,' he said. That
September Canning was in Paris and by a major stroke of diplomacy persuaded the French government to join the agreement,
and in July 1827 the treaty between Britain, France, and Russia
was formally signed in London.

By this time the position of the Greeks[1] was almost hopeless.
Ibrahim's troops had cleared the Morea and a systematic colonization by Turks and Egyptians had begun. In the circumstances it
was only to be expected that the Sultan would refuse the armistice
proposed by the three European Powers. In September French
and English naval squadrons discovered the Turkish and Egyptian
fleets in Navarino Bay, and in October they were joined by a
Russian squadron from the Baltic. Vice-Admiral Codrington,
who strongly favoured the Greek cause, had received extremely
imprecise instructions which allowed him to use force, 'if
necessary', and on 20 October an attempt to send the fleets back to
Egypt led to a battle in which more than fifty of Ibrahim's ships
were sunk by the squadrons of the three Powers.

In England the news of Navarino was heard with mixed feelings
among the government circles. The destruction of the Turkish

[1] See map, p. 196.

fleet seemed to play into Russia's hands, and Canning, who might have been able to handle this unexpected development of his daring policy had died two months earlier. The Duke of Wellington's government was wavering, undecided over its foreign policy, when worse followed. In 1828 peace was signed between Russia and Persia, whereby Russia made certain gains to the east of Asia Minor. Then, in April 1828, the Russian government complained that the Turks had broken the terms of a private agreement, the Convention of Akkerman of 1826, by which the Turks had agreed to greater independence for Serbia and the Danubian principalities Moldavia and Wallachia. War followed, but Nicholas was careful to point out to Metternich that this was not as a consequence of the Treaty of London. 'I detest, I abhor the Greeks,' he told him. 'I consider them as revolted subjects and I do not desire their independence. . . . My grievance is against the Turk's conduct to Russia.' Thus Canning's Treaty of London had not entirely succeeded in forcing the Russian thrust southwards to run in harness with the western Powers.

The British government did nothing. Adrianople fell to the Russians, and Wellington thought frantically of some buffer state which could be created to take Turkey's place. 'We must reconstruct a Greek Empire,' he said to Aberdeen, 'and give it to Prince Frederick of Orange or Charles of Prussia.' Actually the Sultan came to terms shortly afterwards with the Russians. The Treaty of Adrianople was signed in September 1829, whereby he gave up the delta of the Danube to Russia, and a Russian garrison was to remain for five years in the Danubian principalities.

In the British Cabinet Canning's policy was viewed with more and more doubt. 'It does not appear to me to be possible', wrote Wellington to Aberdeen, 'to make out of the Greek affair any substitute for the Turkish power; or anything of which use could be made hereafter in case of its entire annihilation and extinction. All I wish is to get out of the Greek affair without loss of honour and without inconvenient risk for the safety of the Ionian islands.' By now, however, French troops had cleared the Egyptians out of the Morea and it was obviously impossible for Greece to be given back to Turkey. The main difficulty was to define a northern boundary for a new independent kingdom of Greece. This was finally settled in February 1830, and in the following year the Greeks chose Prince Otho of Bavaria to be their King.

So far as Britain was concerned, it had been an inglorious epilogue to Navarino. Canning's policy had been bold and vigorous, but on his death British diplomacy had lost the initiative, mainly because the Duke of Wellington was himself unhappy about the risks involved. From now on the British government reverted to its other policy in the Near East—that of supporting Turkey against Russian advance.

4. Lord Palmerston at the Foreign Office, 1830–41

In November 1830 Lord Palmerston became Foreign Secretary in Lord Grey's government. Of all the statesmen of the nineteenth century he is, perhaps, the most colourful personality. Gay, jaunty, intensely patriotic, a lover of horses, he acquired during his lifetime a remarkable list of nicknames. 'Cupid' suggests the measure of his success in society; 'Lord Pumicestone' sums up the rough arrogance with which he often treated his staff at the Foreign Office and foreign diplomats. 'Goose, goose, goose', he wrote on one incoming dispatch; another dispatch from a British representative at Washington was returned to him with the comment 'to be rewritten in blacker ink'; he disliked the use of French terms—difficult to avoid in nineteenth-century diplomacy—and Sir William Ouseley was even forbidden to use the expression *corps diplomatique*. He hated caution and sham. He had the careless assurance of the aristocrat, which might make him on one occasion devastatingly rude and on another boisterously good-humoured—rather more positive reactions than Lord Melbourne's, who simply talked to himself or went to sleep in his chair when the company was dull.

Palmerston's political record is remarkable. As an Irish peer he could sit in the House of Commons and during his life was returned by five different constituencies. He was Lord of the Admiralty as early as 1807, and from 1809 until 1828 was Secretary at

War. He identified himself with Canning's policy and shortly after Canning's death the break-up of the groups led him to turn to the Whigs. Except for the interval of Peel's administration of 1834–35 he remained Foreign Secretary until 1841; he returned to the same post in 1846, holding it until 1851, became Home Secretary in 1852, and Prime Minister in 1855. This last post he held until his death ten years later, except for the interlude of Derby's ministry 1858–59.

His policy, on the whole, led him to favour those states with constitutional governments.

> Hat der Teufel einen Sohn,
> So ist er sicher Palmerston.

This was Metternich's comment. There was no permanent system or alliance underlying his policy. 'We have no eternal allies,' he said in 1848, 'and we have no perpetual enemies. Our interests are eternal and those interests it is our duty to follow.' And follow them he did, with a patriotic gusto and a general contempt for foreigners that were soon made apparent to all the chancelleries of Europe.

A. THE BELGIAN CRISIS, 1830–1

A delicate situation faced Palmerston at once. The revolution of 1830 in France had passed almost without serious international repercussions, but the revolt of the Belgians against the government of the Netherlands led to a crisis that might have brought about conflict between France and Great Britain. Such a conflict would have delighted Tsar Nicholas, but Palmerston's handling of the situation almost as soon as he took office averted the danger and facilitated the creation of an independent kingdom of Belgium without great damage to Anglo-French relations.

The frontiers of the kingdom of the Netherlands, decided at the settlement of 1815, had been a typical example of the way in which the statesmen at the Congress of Vienna had redrawn the map of Europe. What had once been the Austrian Netherlands had been joined to the United Provinces of the Dutch and the whole area placed under a government that was predominantly

Dutch. Differences of language and religion and the possibility of any Belgian national feeling had been ignored. 'Il n'y a pas de Belges,' Talleyrand had said; 'il y a des Wallons et des Flamands,' and indeed local differences—particularly those between Catholics and anti-clerical liberals—had hindered for some time the development of any united resistance to Dutch rule.

Gradually, however, unity among the Belgian patriots did grow, and the July revolution of 1830 in France was a clarion call. On 25 August the Belgians drove the Dutch garrison out of Brussels and a month later successfully resisted a counter-attack. In November a Belgian Constituent Assembly voted in favour of national independence and declared that their new state should be a monarchy. Louis Philippe, the newly created King of the French, was aware that considerable public feeling in France supported the Belgians and would welcome their being placed under French protection. On the other hand, he knew that French military intervention in Belgium would lead to war with the Powers. Palmerston, too, was quite clear on this point. He favoured the idea of Belgian independence, but he set his face against any form of territorial concession to France. Meanwhile, King William I of the Netherlands had sent an appeal to Great Britain, Prussia, Austria, and Russia to assist him in maintaining the settlement of 1815. The Belgian revolt had become an international question.

For the moment no one moved. Metternich was concerned with unrest in Italy. Prussia and Russia were held back from intervening on the side of the Dutch by the fear of provoking Louis Philippe to send an army to the Belgians. Louis Philippe held back, not simply because of the Powers of the Holy Alliance, but because he knew that Great Britain could not be indifferent to the entry of French arms into the Low Countries. To him this last factor seemed the major difficulty, and accordingly that autumn he dispatched to London the cunning old ex-bishop of the *ancien régime*, Talleyrand, who had not merely survived, but played a leading part in almost every government during the previous forty hectic years of French history.

An international conference of the five great Powers was held at London in January 1831, and it was agreed that Belgian independence and neutrality should be recognized, while Dutch Flanders, Limburg, and Luxemburg were left in King William's possession. Thus far the agreement was a victory for Palmerston, who successfully resisted Talleyrand's attempts to gain two border fortresses, Philippeville and Marienbourg, which had been lost by France to the Netherlands in 1815. 'At last we brought him to terms,' said Palmerston afterwards, 'by the same means by which juries become unanimous—by starving. Between nine and ten at night he agreed to what we proposed, being, I have no doubt, secretly delighted to have got the neutrality of Belgium established.'

But the crisis was not over. The Belgians refused to accept the frontiers laid down at London and on 3 February elected the Duke of Nemours, the second son of Louis Philippe, as their king. There were rumours of French military preparations; and Talleyrand was continuing to bargain for concessions. Palmerston's reaction to this was immediate. 'Generally, when Lord Palmerston talks of diplomacy', Bulwer once said of him, 'he talks also of ships of war.' 'Pray take care in all your conversations with Sebastiani [the French Foreign Minister]', he wrote to Lord Granville, the British ambassador at Paris, 'to make him understand that our desire for peace will never lead us to submit to affront either in language or in act.' Louis Philippe had the good sense to retreat. Almost at once he had refused the Belgian crown on behalf of his son. On 13 March a more conservative French Cabinet was set up under Casimir Périer, and in April the French government announced that it was in entire agreement with the January protocol. For a couple of months there was a calm while the Belgians were talked into accepting Leopold of Saxe-Coburg-Gotha as their king and into giving up Dutch Flanders.

Then, in August, European war seemed dangerously near. This time it was King William of the Netherlands who refused to accept the terms on which the Powers had agreed. He marched into Belgium again, Leopold sent urgent messages to London and Paris, and at once a French expeditionary force entered Belgium and drove the Dutch out. With the French army in occupation of part of the Low Countries, it seemed as though the worst had happened.

'One thing is certain,' wrote Palmerston to Granville at Paris; 'the French must go out of Belgium or we have a general war, and war in a given number of days.' Indeed he was so suspicious of France that he thought it possible that the Dutch invasion had been instigated by the French. It was not difficult for him to take a strong line, since Prussia and Russia were now in a position to assist the Dutch. Louis Philippe chose the lesser of two evils, and the French withdrew their forces from Belgium. By November 1831 the five great Powers had concluded a treaty with Belgium recognizing her national independence.

The crisis was almost over, but the affair lingered on throughout 1832. The details of the destruction of the fortresses had still to be settled, and the King of Holland still refused to give up Antwerp, until a combined Anglo-French force brought about its surrender in December 1832, after which the French troops returned once more to France. Negotiations over other details continued until 1839, when the final treaty was signed defining Belgium's frontiers and establishing an international guarantee of her neutrality.

B. SPAIN AND PORTUGAL

Peace with France had been preserved, but Anglo-French relations remained uneasy throughout the 1830s until the second of two Egyptian crises again brought the two countries almost to the point of war. While the main focal point of tension remained in the Near East, a couple of dynastic disputes in the Iberian Peninsula were also a potential threat to their relations during this period. The constitutional Queens of Spain and Portugal were threatened by absolutist relatives, and Palmerston's concern was to ensure that the French did not take advantage of this situation. His plan was to set aside the straightforward proposal of an Anglo-French military alliance and to create a Quadruple Alliance of Great Britain, France, Spain, and Portugal. The constitutional parties in Spain and Portugal agreed, and France could not stay out. 'A capital hit and all my own doing', boasted Palmerston,

G

but although he could regard it as a minor diplomatic success, military activity lasted too long in Spain for Anglo-French relations to remain untroubled. The constitutional Sovereigns were restored, but France had withdrawn her troops in 1836 before the fighting was over and the British government had ceased to regard the French as allies in this venture.

C. THE TWO EGYPTIAN CRISES AND THE QUARREL WITH FRANCE, 1831–41

The events of 1827–30 had shown Tsar Nicholas that a policy of open hostility towards Turkey was bound to involve most of the Powers of Europe; a commission of experts pointed out that a partition of Turkish territories among the Powers could only be disadvantageous to Russia, and that a Turkey reduced to holding Asia Minor might be capable of reforms that would increase her capacity to resist and possibly to attack Russia. Another danger lay in the ambitions of Mehemet Ali, whose reforming activity in Egypt suggested that if he were ever to get control of the whole of the Turkish dominions, Russia would find herself confronted by a far more powerful opponent.

Accordingly, Nicholas turned to the other line of action open to him and began to consider the possibility of a treaty of alliance with Turkey against her enemies. As it turned out, this policy did not bring much in the way of direct territorial advantage, and after 1841 Nicholas abandoned the plan, but an indirect result was a considerable worsening of relations between Britain and France, which naturally suited Nicholas well and encouraged him in the 1850s to believe that Anglo-French hostility would make a successful military alliance against Russia impossible.

The occasion of the Russo-Turkish treaty was a war between the Sultan Mahmud and his vassal Mehemet Ali of Egypt. Mehemet's grievance was that he had not been rewarded for his help to the Sultan during the Greek rising; in 1831 he declared war and within a year had taken possession of Palestine and Syria. Mahmud, in despair, appealed to Russia, and Nicholas at once sent assistance, since this accorded well with his new policy. Mehemet Ali was bought off with territorial concessions, and the

Russians followed this up at once with the Treaty of Unkiar Skelessi with Turkey in July 1833. It was an agreement of mutual alliance and assistance, in which the Russians inserted a secret clause that the only assistance that Russia would require from Turkey in the event of war would be the closing of the Straits on the demand of the Russian government. This was an important modification of the Anglo-Turkish arrangement of 1809, whereby in time of peace the Straits were open to all merchant shipping and closed to all ships of war, and in time of war open to all ships of the Sultan's friends and closed to those of his enemies. Although Unkiar Skelessi did not allow Russian warships to sail through the Straits, it pointed to considerable Russian influence over Turkish policy.

The secret clause was soon known in all the chancelleries of Europe, and the British government might have been expected to react strongly against it. In fact, Palmerston contented himself with a protest. He could not rely on France, whose intrigues with Spain he mistrusted at this time; nor could he turn to Austria, since in September 1833 the Austrians and Russians had agreed at the Convention of Münchengrätz to maintain the political existence of Turkey against Egypt. This was not the moment to take a strong line. 'It must not be forgotten', said Palmerston, 'that the greatest danger for Europe is an eventual entente between France and Russia.' Nicholas, however, simply could not stomach Louis Philippe, a king who owed his throne to revolution, and for the next five years, while peace lasted between Turkey and Egypt, no further developments arose from the situation in the Near East.

The lull ended in 1839, when the Sultan Mahmud decided to take the bull by the horns and to reduce Mehemet Ali to the position of a real rather than a theoretical vassal. On his staff he had the services of a German captain, Moltke, but even he was unable to prevent the Turkish generals from losing the battle of Nezib in June 1839. The Turkish *coup* had failed and Mehemet had a legitimate right to carry the war into the Sultan's dominions.

The international reaction to this new war was different to what existing alignments suggested. This should have been

Nicholas' opportunity to take advantage of Unkiar Skelessi and to have come forcefully to the assistance of the Turks. Instead he played safe and announced that he was prepared to discuss the question with the other Powers. This was partly because he was already tiring of the new policy and was thinking of returning to Russia's earlier hostility towards Turkey; another reason was that he saw in this situation a chance to damage relations between France and Britain, at the same time as checking Mehemet Ali's advance.

There were two particular reasons why Palmerston should favour the Turks against the Egyptians at this time. In 1838 a commercial treaty had been signed between Britain and Turkey, whereby the Sultan had agreed to abolish the monopolies which had hitherto obstructed the activities of British merchants and which had operated mainly in the interest of the Egyptians. In the next year the Sultan of Aden, fearful of an attack by Mehemet Ali, had agreed to accept a British protectorate. Aden was a particularly important point in British routes to India, partly because it made an excellent coaling station for the new steamships and also because British hopes for establishing an overland route via Mesopotamia had been disappointed.

The French government, however, supported Mehemet Ali. Their interest in Algeria suggested that an ally in Egypt would be helpful, and certain business groups wished to import Egyptian cotton. British concern over new routes to India had already caused French jealousy, and one of the reasons why the scheme for an overland route had been abandoned had been the obstruction of the French consul at Basra. Louis Philippe's decision to stand firmly on Mehemet's side was demonstrated by his appointment of Thiers in February 1840.

This was a simple situation for Nicholas to work on, and in July he was only too prepared to join with Britain, Austria, and Prussia in presenting an ultimatum to Mehemet, leaving France unconsulted. The terms were hardly severe. Mehemet was to hold Egypt as a hereditary possession, and the south of Syria for his lifetime. The question was whether France would join with the Powers in persuading Mehemet to accept. Thiers was determined to stand out for better terms for Egypt, and throughout the rest of the summer Anglo-French relations grew steadily worse. Neither Thiers nor Palmerston seemed likely to climb down. French crowds attacked the carriage of Lord Granville, the British ambassador, and surged down the boulevards, singing the Marseillaise. 'If Thiers should again hold to you the language of menace', wrote Palmerston to Granville, 'convey to him in the most friendly and unoffensive manner possible that if France . . . begins a war, she will to a certainty lose her ships, colonies and commerce before she sees the end of it; that her army of Algiers will cease to give her anxiety and that Mehemet Ali will just be chucked into the Nile.' French fury reached new heights when British and Austrian marines assisted in the taking of Acre and Beirut, after Mehemet had rejected the terms offered in July.

It was Louis Philippe who pulled back. Palmerston had sensed that the French government had been bluffing. As soon as the French Press had taken up the idea of war and a revision of the treaties of 1815, the German states took up the same cry, but from a different point of view. The King of Bavaria had expressed the hope that Strasbourg might become a German city again. In Trier a newspaper published Becker's song: 'sie sollen ihn nicht haben, den freien deutschen Rhein'. Clearly war would be a foolish step. Thiers had to resign. France joined forces with the other Powers, and Mehemet Ali had to be content with Egypt, restoring Syria, Crete, and Arabia to Turkey. In July 1841 the Powers agreed to return to the original ruling of 1809 with regard to the Straits.

The breakdown of good relations between France and Britain had naturally suited Tsar Nicholas, but the course that the negotiations had taken really represented a triumph for Palmerston. He had realized that Russia dared not allow Mehemet Ali to gain control over the Turkish empire; he had reckoned correctly that fear of German ambitions would hold the French back from going to war. Thus he had been able to maintain the diplomatic initiative throughout the crisis. Unkiar Skelessi had served no purpose, and Tsar Nicholas now turned back to Russia's original policy and set about extending and fortifying Russian coastal fortresses—

Cronstadt in the Gulf of Finland, Bomarsund in the Åland Isles, in the Baltic, and, most important of all, Sebastopol in the Crimea.

5. Lord Aberdeen, 1841-6. *The troubled friendship with France*

In Paris Guizot had taken Thiers' place; in London Peel's new ministry of 1841 had brought Lord Aberdeen to the Foreign Office. It was the moment for a reconciliation between the two countries. The two men got on well together. Victoria paid two visits to France, in 1843 and 1845, and it looked as though the situation might mend. Yet the task was not easy; methods of suppressing the Slave Trade, rivalry in the Pacific, and the projected marriage alliances of the Spanish royal family, all presented both statesmen with difficulties that made continued disagreement only too likely.

The question of policing the Atlantic was settled more or less amicably. It was really only British and French cruisers that were involved in this, and Palmerston's suggestion that all cruisers should have a general right of search had roused French suspicion that this was a move to increase Britain's command of the sea. Guizot would have been prepared to grant a reciprocal right of search, but was unable to satisfy opposition in the French Chamber, and in 1845 Aberdeen agreed to a compromise. In future the patrolling vessels would have the right to assure themselves of the nationality of any merchant ship that they stopped, but would still only search ships of their own nationals.

The question of Tahiti was less easy to solve. In 1826 an English missionary, George Pritchard, had persuaded Pomare, Queen of Tahiti, to place her realm under the protection of the British Crown. Ten years later, after two Catholic missionaries had been refused permission to establish their mission on the island, a French naval officer, Captain Dupetit-Thouars, demanded an apology and an indemnity, to which Pomare gave way; this was followed by a treaty of friendship between Tahiti and France. On the departure of the French, Queen Pomare appealed to the British government, but in spite of Victoria's sympathy for the Queen in her predicament, the government would not consider anything more than a treaty of friendship. In 1842 Dupetit-Thouars, now an admiral, returned to Tahiti and suggested to Pomare that she should place her realm under the protection of the French Crown. He reckoned, however, without the redoubtable Mr. Pritchard, who in 1843 returned from leave in England, bringing with him a set of Victorian drawing-room furniture and a carriage as presents from Queen Victoria. In the following year Dupetit-Thouars formally annexed the island to France, arrested Pritchard and later had him deported.

It was not entirely absurd that a squabble over a Pacific island should lead to diplomatic tension. The maritime Powers were at this time highly interested in opening up the Pacific; in 1840 the annexation of the two islands of New Zealand had been authorized by the British government, mainly with an eye to forestalling annexation by France. In 1842 French influence had been established in the Marquesas, to the north-east. Between them Guizot and Aberdeen patched up a compromise. The French government disavowed the annexation, but the island remained under French protection, and Pritchard received £1,000 in compensation from Louis Philippe.

There was no such happy solution to the third difficulty. It arose over the prospective marriage of the ten-year-old Queen Isabella of Spain. The wrangling is reminiscent of earlier centuries, when European diplomacy was really dynastic. The French plan was originally that Isabella should marry one of Louis Philippe's sons. The French occupation of Algeria and the consequent threat to Gibraltar made the British government suspicious of French designs in Spain; they therefore insisted on another candidate—a Coburg prince or one of Isabella's Spanish cousins—and the negotiations dragged on interminably, complicated by personal hostility between the French and British ambassadors at Madrid.

6. Lord Palmerston, 1846-51

The issue was still undecided when Peel's government fell and Palmerston returned to the Foreign Office. With a typically uninhibited approach to the problem he took up the Coburg candidature, on which Aberdeen had been holding back. Guizot's reaction was immediate. Two betrothals were announced. Isabella was to marry her cousin; Louis Philippe's son was to marry her sister. In fact, the French had gained nothing, for earlier history had shown that the Powers would never allow the chance of inheritance to wipe out the Pyrenees. The only consequence was the shattering of the friendship that both Guizot and Aberdeen had been at such pains to preserve. British public opinion was disgusted at what was regarded as a breach of faith on the part of the French, and Queen Victoria wrote what Palmerston called 'a tickler' to Louis Philippe. The only gainers in this trivial squabble were Austria and Russia, who were delighted to see the two western constitutional Powers once again at loggerheads.

At first, Palmerston's major anxiety was the possibility of war with France. Then within eighteen months revolution blazed up in every part of Europe and a host of new diplomatic issues occupied his mind. 1848 is known as the year of revolutions, but the first hostilities were opened in 1847. Seven conservative Catholic cantons, the Sonderbund, left the Swiss Diet at Berne and prepared for war against the remaining liberal Protestant cantons. The Continental Powers favoured the Catholic group, but Palmerston was able to hold them back from intervention in 'Swizzerland'—which was how he preferred to spell it—until the Protestant cantons had succeeded in putting down the seceding group. 'The bankruptcy of the Metternich system', commented an Austrian minister much later, 'took place neither in Vienna in the days of March, nor in Paris, but in Switzerland in the previous year.'

The revolutions that followed in 1848 involved groups of every possible political opinion and social ambition. In Paris, Vienna and Berlin, in Poland, the German states, and North and South Italy, the old order, carefully reinstated at the Congress of Vienna in 1815, found its world threatened and crumbling. Louis Philippe and Guizot fled to England, and the Second Republic was proclaimed in France. They were followed a little later by Prince and Princess Metternich. Palmerston received them cordially, but public opinion in England was on the side of the revolutionaries. The main aim was the preservation of peace. The two dangerous areas were Denmark and North Italy. Prussian troops had invaded Schleswig-Holstein, since German liberal opinion was more interested in the national frontier than in any programme of social reform. Before the end of the year, however, Frederick William IV had changed his mind and recalled his troops, and the Parliament at Frankfurt was left without an effective striking force. North Italy was more dangerous. King Charles Albert of Sardinia had gone to the assistance of the Italians who had revolted in Lombardy against Austrian rule, and Palmerston was all too conscious that the new French government might join forces with Charles Albert. For this reason he and Russell urged the Austrians to grant Lombardy and Venetia full independence, hoping that some sort of kingdom might be created out of North Italy before the French could intervene. In Italy the defeat of the Sardinians at Custozza increased the appeals of the Italian nationalists to the French, and to Palmerston it seemed that the most dangerous moment had arrived. The situation was saved by the hesitancy of the French. For the rest of the year, as the Austrian government gradually regained control, they temporized until, in December 1848, Louis Napoleon was elected President of the Second Republic.

Palmerston was now approaching a crisis in his own affairs. The Queen and the Prince Consort sympathized with the exiled royalty and ministers and were irritated by Palmerston's support of the new liberal force abroad. When an Austrian general, Haynau, was mobbed by English workmen, because he had ordered the flogging of women in Italy and Hungary, Palmerston gave him and his government scant sympathy; a little later he welcomed Kossuth, the Hungarian rebel. In 1850 the Don Pacifico incident—so typical of Palmerston—added to the displeasure of the Court. The Greek government had failed to honour certain debts to British subjects, and when Don Pacifico, a Portuguese money-lender, who could claim British citizenship since he had been born in Gibraltar, had his house raided in Athens, Palmerston decided to make an issue of it and ordered a blockade of the Greek coast. Since this had been done without consulting either Russia or France, who were also guarantors of Greek independence, it was hardly a popular action and the French withdrew their ambassador from London. To Victoria and Albert this seemed a chance to get rid of their boisterous Foreign Secretary, but Palmerston won the day with one of his greatest speeches in the Commons, in which he claimed for all British subjects the same security as had once been enjoyed by the Roman who could say: 'Civis Romanus sum'.

The resentment of Victoria and her husband at Palmerston's arrogance might well have led to a constitutional crisis. The Revolution of 1688 and the Act of Settlement of 1701 had left the British Sovereign considerable influence over foreign policy. Only during the previous fifty years had this department of state affairs fallen more and more under the control of the ministers. It is never easy to define the term 'constitutional' in British government, yet it would clearly have been unfortunate if the Crown had now made an attempt to put the clock back to the eighteenth century. The Prince Consort had the sense not to push the issue too far, but the dispute made him unpopular with the British public, who were fully behind Palmerston. The Queen had gone so far as to lay down certain rules by which Palmerston was to be bound by the policy to which she had given her assent, but although Palmerston agreed to this, he showed in his handling of the Haynau incident that he was quite prepared to act without consulting the Queen at all.

His fall came at the end of 1851. On 2 December—that fateful day in the Napoleonic calendar—Louis Napoleon destroyed the constitution of the Second Republic, when in a quietly effective *coup d'état*—far neater than his uncle's in 1799—he proclaimed himself President for ten years. Palmerston at once told the

French ambassador that he entirely approved of this act, without any consultation of the Cabinet. For Russell, who had been more and more embarrassed by Palmerston's activity, this was the last straw. He demanded a resignation from Palmerston, who was naturally exceedingly angry and told Disraeli later that he had been 'kicked out'. The Court, many of the Tories, and the governments of the Central Powers were naturally delighted, and in Vienna Schwarzenberg gave a ball in celebration of the event. But they cheered too soon; it was not long before Palmerston was back in the Cabinet—and in little more than three years he was to take up his residence at No. 10 Downing Street.

MID-CENTURY: THE GREAT EXHIBITION
OF 1851

LONDON 1851. A city of fog and gaslights, an untidy metropolis that extended over the fields and meadows once within easy reach from Oxford Street or the Strand. The stately terraces and crescents of Regency London were now encased in a swelling, amorphous suburbia, for in fifty years the population had risen from 850,000 to $2\frac{1}{2}$ million inhabitants, most of them living out their lives amidst rambling alleyways, taverns, and dubious lodging-houses. In 1852 the first instalments of Charles Dickens' *Bleak House* began to appear in print, opening with a graphic description of the City in winter—the mud, the gas-lit shop windows, the 'smoke lowering down from chimney pots making a soft black drizzle with flakes of soot in it as big as full grown snowflakes'. In the previous year Henry Mayhew published his *London Labour and the London Poor*, a detailed piece of observation of every form of human life in the poorer quarters—the costermongers, the street musicians, the cabmen, the dock labourers, and the Thames watermen—analysing their way of life and recording their strange dialects. London had become a world of its own.

This was the backcloth to the Great Exhibition held in Hyde Park in 1851. Many exhibitions of manufactures had already taken place in France, and in the 1840s the Prince Consort, who was President of the Royal Society of Arts, began to foster the idea of organizing a similar exhibition in London. The announcement that it would be held was made by the Prince himself in 1849, and a Royal Commission was appointed for the purpose. The difficulties were innumerable. An Exhibition in which all nations would be able to display their goods would be a great advertisement for Free Trade, and this naturally aroused opposition from the Protectionists. The provinces were suspicious of the tendency towards centralization. The proposed site in Hyde Park had to be sanctioned by Parliament. Worst of all, the design for the building which would house the exhibits had to be settled. Discussion over the erection of any public building always seems to lead to something close to war. The new Houses of Parliament, for example, designed by Sir Charles Barry, and by this time nearing completion, had given rise to a series of violent disputes which were to be carried on from one generation to the next. *The Times* was highly critical of the projected Exhibition. *Punch* produced a picture of one gentleman putting up an Exhibition notice which ran: 'ici on ne parle pas français!' In the Commons Colonel Sibthorp fought a long battle against the whole idea, leaping to the defence of trees that might have to be cut down in Hyde Park and conjuring up terrible pictures of an invasion of foreigners, criminals, and Socialists.

Gradually the opposition was worn down, but the problem of the building remained unanswered. The final solution, which was, in fact, one of the greatest triumphs of the Exhibition, came from an unexpected quarter. Over 240 suggested designs had been turned down by the Commission, and the Building Committee had decided to draw up a design of their own—a vast, unlovely structure of brick with an enormous cupola. It happened that the Duke of Devonshire employed on his estate at Chatsworth a chief gardener by the name of Joseph Paxton, a man of remarkable originality, who had already developed great business interests in railways and various engineering enterprises. Paxton had come to London to see Mr. Ellis, an M.P., on matters concerning the Midland Railway, and the two men met in the newly constructed House of Commons, where the acoustics were being tested. 'Sir Charles Wood was addressing the House,' wrote Paxton, later, of the occasion; 'but not a word of what he said could be heard in the Speaker's gallery.' Whereupon Paxton remarked that the building for the Great Exhibition looked like being a similar disaster. On hearing one or two of Paxton's ideas, Ellis rushed him round to Lord Granville, and the upshot of the conversation was that Paxton was given ten days in which to submit a design. A few days later, during a committee meeting of the Midland Railway Company at Derby, he made out a rough sketch on a piece of blotting-paper and within a week had returned to London with full plans that the Building Committee soon accepted.

What Paxton had designed was nothing more than a gigantic greenhouse, 1,848 feet in length, 408 feet in breadth. The Crystal Palace—as *Punch* called it—was in many ways astonishingly ahead of its time. The skeleton of the building was to be composed of cast-iron columns and girders, the walls and roofing being of glass. Not merely did this make use of the most modern materials available; it was possible for all the thousands of parts to be mass-produced elsewhere and then to be rapidly assembled on the site. The Crystal Palace was one of the earliest examples of pre-fabrication, and the highly functional simplicity of the building was like a glimpse of twentieth-century architecture in the middle of the nineteenth.

The work of construction went ahead rapidly and the goods of 14,000 exhibitors began to be moved in. Then one further difficulty had to be overcome. It had been found possible to spare some of the elms by enclosing them in the building. Unfortunately, with the spring, countless sparrows, attracted by the greater warmth beneath the glass, established themselves within the Crystal Palace, and the consequences for the exhibits were disastrous. A story—unfortunately untrue—tells how the Prime Minister and the Cabinet were urgently consulted and how the Duke of Wellington, having first of all protested that he was not a bird-catcher, repented and gave one of his last pieces of advice to his Sovereign: 'Sparrow-hawks, ma'am.'

And so, on 1 May, Queen Victoria came down for the opening of the Exhibition to hear the report of the Royal Commission read by Prince Albert. There followed a prayer by the Archbishop of Canterbury, and then the Queen moved down the long aisles of the Crystal Palace. The sights before her were like a hymn of praise to the infinite resourcefulness of the human mind. Raw materials, machinery, manufactures, and fine arts all had their place. The British and Colonial section, one half of the whole exhibition, included Nasmyth's steam hammer, the hydraulic press used for the construction of the Britannia bridge over the Menai Straits, manufacturing machines and railway equipment, the Ross telescope and photographic apparatus. Then came every variety of textiles, precious metals, Wedgwood pottery, and even a mediaeval court designed by Pugin. Seven whole sections were given up to produce from the Empire. Then there were the foreign displays from almost every country in Europe—as well as from the United States, whose exhibits included the first trays from the Californian gold-fields, Colt's revolver, and Mc-Cormick's reaping machine. One exhibit not within the Crystal Palace was Prince Albert's Model Lodging-house, built near the Knightsbridge Barracks, designed to accommodate two working-class families.[1]

The Exhibition was an overwhelming success. Between May and October there were more than 6 million visitors—among them Colonel Sibthorp, who came to view it with a strong sense of disapproval. It has been calculated that about 17% of the entire population of Great Britain were able to see the Exhibition—another testimony to the revolution brought about by the railways. At the end of the Exhibition it was agreed, after considerable debate, that the Crystal Palace should be purchased by a company for £70,000, dismantled and re-erected as a Winter Garden at Sydenham, on the London–Brighton railway, where it remained until it was destroyed by fire in 1936.

The total profit realised was £186,000, and Prince Albert's wish was to buy some fifty acres in Kensington Gore and to found four great institutions, devoted to the encouragement of industrial education. The Prince did not live to see the fulfillment of his scheme. The planners ran up against all the difficulties that confront reformers, but eventually the South Kensington estate, as we know it today, came close to what Albert had had in mind. The Imperial College of Science and the Royal College of Art, Organists, and Music are congregated there, together with the Physical Society, the Royal Geographical Society, and the four

---

[1] Afterwards moved to Kennington Park, where it still stands.

great Museums: Science, Natural History, Geological, and the Victoria and Albert.

1851 remains a significant date in English nineteenth century history. The country was at last emerging from a troublesome period of social readjustment shot through with fear of revolution. The Exhibition was a symbol of a staggering prosperity and of a still greater prosperity to come. The fruits of Free Trade, the thought of constitutional reform achieved without violent revolution, nearly forty years of peace, and a growing Empire overseas, all combined to give the Victorian a sense of optimism and a certain self-satisfaction. Thrift, hard work, and high moral endeavour paid dividends and he saw it as a simple tale of Virtue Rewarded.

It was the Free Traders who felt most gratified by it all. Here was a living demonstration of how freedom to buy and sell without government interference would lead to the brotherhood of man engaged in peaceful trade; with the consequent rise in the standard of living the likelihood of war would fade, less money would be spent on armaments, and taxation would sink lower and lower. It seemed a spiral of ever-increasing prosperity. As we know today, they were utterly wrong. Great Britain, as the workshop of the world, was bound to be extraordinarily prosperous at this time. 'Free Trade is the weapon of the strongest nation,' wrote Bismarck some thirty years later. But prosperity and industrial advance cannot be enjoyed by one country alone. The development of machinery abroad was soon to bring a new threat from larger, potentially richer countries, hampered until now by other factors—under-population in America, lack of political unity in Germany, or general backwardness in Japan. The newly developed corn-lands of the United States and the refrigerator ships that could bring meat from the Argentine and New Zealand were later to mean ruin for the English farmer under a free-trade economy; similarly the growth of German and American industry was eventually to drive Great Britain back to Protection. At home the result of low taxes was military weakness, and this left Great Britain unable to intervene forcefully in the events that led to the creation of the German Empire and shattered the old balance on the Continent. At the same time un-limited economic expansion was bound to mean the growth of an enormous factory-worker class, whose political and social de-mands were to play a large part in the development of the col-lective state. This last was the most significant feature of all, for it illustrates the peculiar irony of Radicalism, that its realization in-volved its own destruction. The Radicals had made the mistake, common to many political theorists, that there was an immediate and final goal for the whole of human society, and they had yet to learn that all stages in history are but transitory.

III

THE AGE OF PALMERSTON, 1851–68

II

THE CRIMEAN WAR

1. *Russell, Derby, and Aberdeen*

AT no time in the nineteenth century did the two-party system operate in the government of Great Britain with the regularity to which we have become accustomed since the first World War. The predominant feature was the continual readjustment of groups out of which a momentary unity might be created, sometimes assisted, sometimes hindered by the force of individual personalities. Between 1830 and 1846 an apparent stability had begun to emerge, but the swing of the pendulum from a Whig to a Conservative government was as much due to changes of allegiance among the groups at Westminster as it was to the wishes of the electorate. After 1867 the consequences of the second Reform Act and the great duel between Gladstone and Disraeli, coupled with differences over foreign policy and Ireland, reimposed the appearance of the two-party system; yet this division of opinion was also short-lived, and it was not to be until the rapid rise of the Labour party that electors were confronted with a simple choice between two parties deeply divided over the question of a Socialist society.

In the middle years of the century there was nothing even remotely resembling the swing of the pendulum, since the Conservatives were only in office in 1852, 1858-9, and 1866-8—each time without an absolute majority. This was partly due to Stanley's negative leadership of the party, but there were other factors as well. Ever since the emergence of Liberal Toryism in the 1820s the Tories had been in danger of breaking up. The passing of Catholic emancipation had almost smashed them. Peel with his Tamworth Manifesto had managed to create a new Conservative party, but this more daring form of Liberal Toryism, during the 1841-6 administration, had reawakened the old doubts of the right-wing element, and the repeal of the Corn Laws had simply been the last straw. This was a deeper rift than Stanley could hope to close.

The Peelites now sided with the Whigs, but although this meant that their combined vote could usually command a majority in the Commons during the following twenty years, the coalition was an uneasy one, often at the mercy of personal differences. Paradoxically the Peelites were more actively concerned with reform than many of their Whig allies. 'When out of office, they were demagogues,' wrote John Roebuck of the Whigs; 'in power, they became exclusive oligarchs.' The Whigs stood, in fact, for the landed class, while the Manchester Radicals, headed by Cobden and Bright, were the spokesmen of the middle-class manufacturers. Thus Anglican landlords and chapel-going business men formed an uneasy partnership, confronting a Conservative opposition that was too weak to displace them.

Measures tending towards Free Trade and moderate reform were the natural outcome of this situation, but beyond that it was personality rather than party that counted. Peel was a key figure in this situation, but by 1850 he was finding it difficult to prevent many of his followers from joining either the Whigs or the Protectionists. In any case, Peel died in 1850 as a result of a fall from his horse, and it was Palmerston who captured the popular imagination in these mid-century decades. Possible questions of reform abounded, but there was no great outcry from the country. The middle classes felt themselves to be comfortably in the saddle, and Pam's rollicking patriotism was a pleasing emotion to the new rich, who had secured most of what they wanted. The Radicals' old supporters had moved over to the right, and John Bright was once more in the wilderness in his denunciation of the Crimean war and his demands for a further extension of the franchise.

In the election of 1847 Russell's Whig government had gained a slight majority, and the split between Protectionists and Peelites removed, for the moment, most of the danger from the opposition. It was by no means an unsuccessful ministry. The Public

Health Act of 1848 and the Factory Acts of 1847 and 1850 were passed and the storm of the third Chartist outbreak was weathered. Gradually, however, Peelite support grew less reliable, and it was in an attempt to win the allegiance of Protestant England that Russell embarked upon an attack on the Pope's decision to set up Roman Catholic dioceses with territorial titles in England. The Ecclesiastical Titles Bill prohibited Catholic clergy from taking titles already in use among the Anglican clergy. Whigs and Protectionists united momentarily over the measure, but the government naturally lost the support of the Irish members, and the leaders of the Peelites voted against the Bill.

The struggles over Ecclesiastical Titles was still undecided, when Sir Charles Wood's Budget produced further dissension. The financial position of the country was so good that there was a surplus of revenue over expenditure amounting to £2,521,000. The problem was to make the best political use of this, and in attempting to please everyone the Chancellor only succeeded in antagonizing most of the groups. He proposed to reduce duties on imported chicory, timber, and seed, and to abolish the window tax. The Radicals had hoped for the abolition of income tax—now at sevenpence in the £—while the agricultural interest were disappointed at the concessions granted to them. The final blow was the question of franchise reform. Russell had claimed to be in favour of reform, but when a private member, Locke King, brought in a measure for a uniform county and borough franchise, Russell felt unable to support it, since this would only increase the number of county voters dependent on the great landowners. As a result, the Radicals began to mistrust Russell's promises of constitutional reform and voted in favour of Locke King's motion, which was passed by 100 votes to 52. Nothing could have been more expressive of the anarchy of alignments, for of the 52 who voted with the Prime Minister 25 were Conservatives. Another indication of instability was Russell's own view that if Palmerston had chosen to be present and had spoken in the debate, the vote might have gone the other way. Russell decided that he could not go on and tendered his resignation.

The Queen had to find a political leader who might master

the situation. 'This is very bad,' she wrote to the King of the Belgians, 'because there is no chance of any other good Government, poor Peel being no longer alive.' Thus only two months before the opening of the Great Exhibition, which, among other things, was supposed to demonstrate to foreigners the virtues of constitutional monarchy, the country found itself without any government at all. Negotiations continued for ten days. Lord Stanley was approached on two separate occasions; a Conservative–Peelite coalition was suggested, but Stanley did not feel that he could yet officially abandon the policy of Protection, over which the Peelites were naturally adamant. If coalition was impossible, then perhaps Lord Stanley could form a purely Conservative government. Disraeli hoped earnestly that he might try, but few of Stanley's colleagues liked the idea, and it was abandoned. The eventual outcome was that Russell was restored to an office that no one else seemed to want.

His ministry lasted for another inglorious year. The Ecclesiastical Titles Act was passed, although considerably modified. It established fines for Catholic priests who assumed ecclesiastical titles which had already been adopted by the clergy of the Church of England, but since the new Catholic dioceses in England had different names to those of the Anglican Church, no fines were ever imposed, and the Act was repealed in 1871. Its significance lies mainly in demonstrating the strength of anti-papal feelings, now at their height, roused by Catholic emancipation and the growth of the Oxford Movement. The income tax had been due to expire, but a government proposal to continue it for a further three years met with great opposition, and the government was defeated once again when a Radical motion was passed in favour of the tax being imposed for only one year. The Cabinet decided to give way. It was apparent by this time that it was far easier to destroy a government than to create a new one, and so Russell lingered on.

At the end of the year came Palmerston's fall,[1] but only a few weeks passed before he had his 'tit for tat'—not difficult to achieve in the circumstances. In February 1852 Russell introduced a Bill

[1] See p. 170.

for a reform of the franchise which appeared to leave the House unmoved. In the same month he proposed that a local militia should be organized as a reserve for home defence. The new powers assumed by Napoleon in France had created something of a panic, and Russell's measure would have been a revival of the militia created during the Napoleonic war for the purpose of defending its own locality. Palmerston, however, had long held a different view, wanting instead a revival of the old national militia, which had been under the control of the central government and had become liable for service overseas. Consequently he moved an amendment, demanding the dropping of the word 'local', and carried it by a majority of eleven. Russell had already announced the measure as a question of confidence in the government and decided to resign a second time.

On this occasion Stanley, who had now assumed the title of Lord Derby, did attempt to form an administration, encouraged by growing rifts between the Whigs and the Peelites and the prospect of a general election. Palmerston was offered the Exchequer and the leadership of the Commons, but he would not accept, and it was Disraeli who took office in spite of his doubts about his abilities in this direction. 'You know as much as Mr. Canning did,' said Derby. 'They give you the figures.' But most of the other members of the Cabinet were unknown. 'Who? Who?' barked the Duke of Wellington, as the list was read out, and from then on the new government had a name.

Protection remained as an awkward question politically. Derby, as well as Disraeli, had by this time lost all faith in it, but despite this they still could not commit their party to Free Trade. At the general election in the summer of 1852 Conservative candidates simply tried to ignore the question—far the simplest course of action, since the prosperity of the country made it clear that the matter was closed. The government won about 300 seats, the Radicals 100, the Whigs about 200, while the Peelites and the Irish each kept about 40. The most striking change was the drop in the number of Peelites, many of whom had by now joined one of the two major groups. For the moment it appeared to be the Conservatives, and not the Peelites, who had survived

the tacit acceptance of Free Trade, and it was the falling off in the
number of Peelites that at last led Aberdeen to give up his position
of political neutrality. 'Union with Lord Derby is impossible,'
Newcastle wrote to him in August. 'Isolation is pleasant but not
patriotic. Cooperation with the Liberals is requisite.'

Lacking any serious issues to divide them, all groups were now
beginning to veer towards some form of Liberalism. Whigs and
Peelites were drawing together again, and in December Disraeli's Budget pointed to a Conservative change of front. 'I am
convinced', wrote Gladstone to his wife, 'that Disraeli's is the
least conservative Budget I have ever known.' Duties on malt
and hops were halved; the ship-owners were relieved of the payment of certain dues, and the sugar-growers were allowed
facilities for refining which would enable them to compete more
easily with foreign producers. All this was to be financed by extending the income tax to earned incomes of £100 a year and
unearned incomes of £50 a year. On 16 December, while a
thunderstorm raged outside, Disraeli made his final speech in
support of his Budget. After he had sat down at one o'clock in
the morning, William Gladstone rose to reply with an oration
that tore Disraeli's argument to shreds and poured scorn on the
oratorical devices that the Chancellor had employed. 'My great
object,' wrote Gladstone afterwards, 'was to show the Conservative party how their Leader was hoodwinking and bewildering them and this I have the happiness of believing that in some
degree I effected.' Gladstone was certainly the victor in the first
round of the long contest between these two personalities. The
House divided at four o'clock in the morning, and Disraeli's
Budget, opposed by a combination of Whigs, Radicals, and
Peelites, was defeated by nineteen votes. Sir Robert Peel was
avenged. Derby at once resigned and the country was once more
without a government.

The only possible outcome was some sort of coalition between
Whigs and Peelites, but a great deal of negotiation was necessary
before all the various personalities involved were satisfied. The
premiership was given to Lord Aberdeen, who was popular at
Court and under whom the Peelites were prepared to serve, since

he had been Peel's Foreign Secretary. Gladstone became Chancellor of the Exchequer, Sidney Herbert Secretary at War; Newcastle went to the Colonial Office and Sir James Graham to the Admiralty. In all, the Peelites gained six seats in the Cabinet. The Whigs were also given six, including Russell as Foreign Secretary and Palmerston as Home Secretary. The Radicals had only one: Sir William Molesworth as First Commissioner of Works. In spite of the variety of opinions held by the different members of this Cabinet, it was hoped that some sort of stability would now emerge; it was, perhaps, the kind of government that Peel, had he lived, would have tried to create. Queen Victoria was certainly optimistic. 'Our new Government', she wrote to the King of the Belgians, 'will really, I think, command a large support and, I trust, be of duration, which is a great object. Their only difficulty will be the Budget.'

Gladstone's first Budget was a very positive measure, marked by the continuation of the policy towards Free Trade. Most remaining duties on partially manufactured goods and foodstuffs were removed; duties on wholly manufactured goods were halved. He had one other aim, and that was to bring about the end of income tax. Peel had been forced to reintroduce the tax as a temporary measure to cover the immediate loss from reducing import duties, and Gladstone, having now reduced them still further, saw that the abolition of income tax could not come immediately. He reckoned, however, that by extending the legacy duty it should be possible to end it by 1859. Queen Victoria's immediate fears proved groundless. The government survived the Budget. It was the Crimean war that not only wrecked Gladstone's hopes by sending income tax up to one shilling and twopence, but also brought about the collapse of the Aberdeen administration.

2. The approach of war

If political instability failed to dim the optimism of the country, the Crimean war, which Great Britain and France entered in 1854, certainly did so. At first the country was in a mood of patriotic exultation, reflected in Tennyson's *Maud*, a hymn to the nobility of war, but long before its end the appalling conditions endured by British troops during the winter of 1854-5 had swung public opinion round to a fierce questioning both of the military machine and of the diplomacy that had led up to the outbreak of hostilities.

Since the Straits settlement of 1841 Russia had abandoned her policy of a positive alliance with Turkey. She still coveted some of the outlying Turkish provinces in Europe, but the old dilemma of gaining them without at the same time destroying Turkey remained. The collapse and dissolution of the Turkish Empire was a continual possibility in the nineteenth century, but since this could only result in a partition among the Powers of Europe, it never became Russia's immediate aim.[1] The Powers naturally had to be ready for such a collapse, but although schemes for the eventual partition were a constant feature of nineteenth-century diplomacy, the disintegration of Turkey was the last thing that any of the Powers desired. Thus, during the months immediately preceding the Crimean war two entirely separate strands of diplomacy are discernible in Russian negotiations—first, an occasional reference to the old grandiose schemes of partition, and second, a much more particular and immediate object: an attempt to bolster up Russian influence in Turkey.

There were two reasons why Tsar Nicholas should launch a diplomatic offensive at the beginning of 1853. In the first place, Napoleon, with an eye to gaining support from French clericals, had recently taken up the claims of the Latin monks over the control of the Holy Places in the Near East. The Turks had made certain concessions to the Latins and had then gone back on these in a secret agreement with the Greeks. In retaliation, the French ambassador coming to Constantinople in April 1852 had insisted on his ninety-gun screw-driven ship, the *Charlemagne*, sailing through the Dardanelles. In July a further demonstration of power—a threatened bombardment of Tripoli by a French squadron—convinced the Turks that the Latins must be given what they wanted over the Holy Places. Such a victory of prestige for the

[1] See p. 153.

French was naturally a direct challenge to the Tsar. The second factor that influenced Nicholas was a decisive diplomatic action by the Austrians. A Turkish army had been about to invade Montenegro, but a ten-day ultimatum presented to the Sultan by Count Leiningen caused the Turks to give way. Nicholas drew his own conclusions from these events. His prestige in Turkey was too important a matter to allow the recent French action to pass unanswered. The Turks must be brought to heel, and the success of the Leiningen mission suggested that strong diplomatic pressure would be sufficient to give him what he wanted. The moment certainly seemed propitious. Austria was indebted to Russia for the help that she had received in putting down the Hungarian rising in 1849; in Great Britain Palmerston's dismissal from the Foreign Office in 1851 removed one danger, and the new Cabinet of December 1852 under Aberdeen seemed unlikely to take positive action.

The first move was a series of conversations in January 1853 with Seymour, the British ambassador at St. Petersburg, in which the old gambit of Turkish partition was put forward. This was simply to encourage the British government in the belief that Russian action against Turkey would not necessarily be contrary to British interests, and the rejection of the suggestions did not matter greatly.

The second step was to dispatch Prince Menschikov, in February, to Constantinople with the object of impressing the Turks with the importance of their Russian neighbour. From now on the battle for prestige, fought out amid bewildering Oriental intrigue, led on gradually to the war which none of the nations involved had originally desired. Menschikov's visit was a fine piece of theatre. On his way he reviewed Russian troops in Bessarabia and the Black Sea fleet at Sebastopol. On his arrival in a man-of-war at Constantinople he was greeted by a carefully arranged crowd of Greek Christians; he paid an official visit to the Grand Vizier in ordinary civilian clothes and completely ignored Fuad, the Foreign Minister—two calculated insults. Menschikov's task was, first, to reverse the decisions taken over the Holy Places and, second, to enable the Russian government to enforce a protectorate over all the Orthodox Christians in Turkey. His initial success was to bring about the resignation of Fuad. On learning this, Rose, the British *chargé d'affaires*, sent a message to Malta asking for the fleet to be dispatched to Constantinople, but even in the age of Palmerston there was a limit to what a *chargé d'affaires* could undertake on his own initiative and the Cabinet countermanded the request. Napoleon, however, ordered the French fleet to Salamis.

One significant action that the British government did now take was to send Stratford Canning, Viscount Stratford de Redcliffe, back to Constantinople as ambassador. Stratford was a man of unrivalled experience of the Turkish problem; he had already had four periods of duty at the British embassy at Constantinople, and during the last (1842–52) he had acquired a remarkable personal influence over the Sultan Abdul Medjid and had been responsible for many of the reforms which he believed would alone preserve the Turkish Empire. He had a considerable hand in drawing up his own instructions in February 1853, and it is noticeable that, although he was authorized to ask the Admiral at Malta 'to hold himself in readiness', he was not allowed to summon the British fleet to Constantinople without instructions from the Cabinet. His principal object was to settle the dispute over the Holy Places. These details are important, since Stratford was afterwards blamed for the outbreak of hostilities, and it is only recent research that has done something to clear his name.[1]

Stratford's first achievement on his arrival was to distinguish between the two demands made by Menschikov and to persuade the Turks to give way over the Holy Places. The demand for a protectorate was turned down. This was partly due to Stratford's support, but in giving it he was being perfectly consistent with British policy, since such a protectorate coupled with Russian naval power in the Black Sea, based on Sebastopol, would have meant the end of Turkish independence. He did not promise naval aid, however, if Russia invaded the Principalities of Moldavia and Wallachia, and he encouraged the Turks not to break off negotiations.

[1] Harold Temperley: *England and the Near East: the Crimea.*

The outcome was Menschikov's departure in a rage on 21 May. Nicholas at once threatened to occupy the Principalities. This had the effect of stiffening the attitude of the British Cabinet, whom Aberdeen had been trying to hold in check, and on 2 June the fleet was ordered to sail to Besika Bay, outside the Dardanelles. They were supported in this by Napoleon, who, although he had no wish for war with Russia, was determined on an Anglo-French alliance, without which a revision of the treaties of 1815 would be impossible. A few days after the arrival of the British fleet at Besika Bay on 13 June, they were joined by the French. This apparent cooperation could hardly please the Tsar, but he did not consider the development decisive. 'The four of you could dictate to me,' he said to the French ambassador; 'but that will never happen. I can count on Vienna and Berlin.' On 2 July the Russian army crossed the Pruth, and by 6 July had entered Bucharest.

Fortunately the Turks were prepared to abstain from declaring war for the moment. No country can remain poised on the brink of war for long, however, and the story of the next three months is a maze of last-minute attempts at mediation, while Mohammedan agitators stirred up anti-Russian war fever in the narrow streets of Constantinople. Speed was an essential element, but the advent of the months of Ramadan and Bairam in the Mohammedan calendar slowed down all business, and since the electric telegraph reached only as far east as Belgrade, there was an inevitable time lag between the decisions of governments and new events in Constantinople.

The Turks under Stratford's guidance submitted a note for consideration by the four Powers, Britain, France, Prussia, and Austria, conferring at Vienna in July. The Powers at Vienna, however, had already drawn up their own Note, which included a clause whereby Turkey would not change the conditions of the Christians 'without previous understanding with the Governments of France and Russia'. To this Russia agreed, but although Stratford officially advised the Turks to accept, they refused on the grounds that this would mean a loss of national independence. It was suggested afterwards by Kinglake [1] that Stratford secretly

---

[1] A. W. Kinglake, *History of the Invasion of the Crimea.*

advised them to reject it, but there is no evidence for this. Had he wished to do so, it would not have been difficult for him to cover his tracks in this city of palace intrigue, but the question must remain unsolved. In any case, the Turks appeared to be justified in their rejection of the Vienna Note, since in September Nesselrode sent a 'violent interpretation' of the Note to the Russian minister in Vienna, claiming that it placed all Orthodox Christians in Turkey under the protection of Russia, and his interpretation was actually published in a Prussian newspaper.

This new turn in diplomacy stimulated fresh action. On 22 September the French suggested to the British Cabinet that their combined fleets should sail through the Dardanelles. On the following day Aberdeen and Clarendon, without consulting their colleagues, authorized Stratford to order the fleet to Constantinople. Such a move would be in direct contravention of the Straits settlement of 1841, and when Stratford received this order on 4 October, he regarded it as so serious that he did not act for another fortnight. Unfortunately diplomatic moves after the British government's decision only heightened international tension. The Tsar hoped to win Prussia and Austria over to his side. At the end of September he met Francis Joseph at Olmütz, where he repudiated Nesselrode's 'violent interpretation' of the Vienna Note, and later the two of them conferred with Frederick William IV at Warsaw. Nicholas failed to win either of them over; both were determined on neutrality. But the British government was convinced that a new plot for partitioning Turkey was being hatched and on 8 October decided, as Palmerston said, 'to play old Gooseberry with the would-be Partitionists'. A last attempt at mediation by the Austrians was turned down and Napoleon, a little doubtful by now, agreed to act alongside the British. Sharp orders were sent to Stratford to order the fleet to Constantinople at once.

The chances of peace were dwindling rapidly. On 4 October the Sultan, feeling unable to ignore the war fever in Constantinople any longer, had declared war on Russia, but Stratford had been able to restrain him from ordering an advance against the Russians in the Principalities. He could not, however, continue to ignore his own government; the French ambassador had been urging him to act for days, and at last on 20 October he sent the Cabinet's order to the British admiral at Besika Bay. Stratford was, in fact, in the middle of one last desperate effort to avert war. Negotiations were to be reopened, but before that the Turkish government must be persuaded to continue to suspend hostilities. The Turkish government did actually agree to this, but the long delays proved fatal. Before the necessary instructions could reach the responsible officers, Omar Pasha had crossed the Danube on 23 October, and with that raid the Russo-Turkish war had begun.

There were still hopes that a general European conflict might be avoided, since Stratford did persuade the Turks not to send their fleet into the Black Sea. They did, however, dispatch a light flotilla as far as Sinope, and on 30 November this was destroyed by the Russian fleet. This naval action—perfectly legitimate, since the two countries were at war—aroused a storm of public feeling in Great Britain. Large anti-Russian meetings had been held in the northern cities and the 'massacre of Sinope' was decisive. Aberdeen tried to hold back, but Palmerston left the Cabinet—although only for ten days—and Russell threatened to do likewise. Napoleon declared that if the British fleet would not enter the Black Sea with his, then he would act alone. On 3 January, 1854 Stratford was ordered to send the fleet into the Black Sea, and on 12 January Russia was informed that it was the intention of the Allies to confine the Russian fleet to its port at Sebastopol. In February the Russian ambassadors were recalled by Nicholas from London and Paris, and in March an ultimatum was sent by Great Britain and France to Russia, who gave no reply. On 12 March a formal alliance was made with Turkey, and two weeks later Great Britain and France were at war with Russia.

None of the combatants had wanted this war and there is little doubt that it could have been avoided. A series of misconceptions on all sides had brought about a situation from which nobody could withdraw. Nicholas had imagined that Aberdeen would make all necessary concessions, and the hesitancy of the British Cabinet in the first half of 1853 had strengthened his conviction that it was safe to occupy the Principalities. The fatal step of ordering the British fleet to Constantinople would not have been taken if the meeting of the Emperors at Olmütz and Warsaw had not been misconstrued by the British government as a preliminary to Turkish partition by the Powers of the Holy Alliance. The order to enter the Black Sea would not have been given if Napoleon's bluff that he was prepared to act alone had not been believed. Public opinion in Great Britain and Constantinople as well as the Russian Pan-Slavists played some part in forcing the hands of the rulers at times when it was least appropriate. Diplomats are usually blamed for an outbreak of war, but in this case it had been the diplomats who had struggled for peace and the populace who had demanded war.

But although the situation need not have reached this point, the issues over which the war was fought were certainly real. The Russian demand for a protectorate would have been a serious blow at Turkish independence, and, if it could have been achieved, would have been the consummation of Russia's policy of undermining Turkey without destroying her. For that very reason Great Britain was bound to resist it. Napoleon badly needed success for the sake of his position at home and also an alliance with Great Britain for the sake of his hopes of revising the treaties of 1815. Over these fundamental factors there had been no misconception, but if the particular crisis to which they had given rise had been handled differently, they would not have led to war.

3. *The war (1854–6) and its consequences*

It had been the Duke of Wellington's belief that there could be nothing wrong with an army that had won the battle of Waterloo. It has often been a failing among the military to fight a war along the lines of the previous one, and the greater the intervening period of peace, the more disastrous the consequences may be. In 1854 the rank and file of the Army were still considered 'the scum of the earth enlisted for drink'. Their living conditions were abominable at home and worse still abroad. In Jamaica the mortality rate was 121 per thousand and in Sierra Leone it

H

reached 75%. Discipline had, therefore, to be brutally harsh. The system whereby the Army was administered and supplied was confused and inefficient. Promotion for cavalry and infantry officers depended upon purchase, and since prices were high, none but the rich and usually aristocratic officers could hope to get very far. By this time almost the only officers who had seen any war service were those who had served in India, but these professionals were not rich and seldom had any chance of gaining high rank. The Navy was in a slightly better state. Ships were still built of wood, but experiments had been made with paddle-wheels driven by steam and by 1854 a certain number of screw steamers had been constructed.

As *The Times* pointed out, the most striking characteristic of the majority of officers who were given command in the British expeditionary force was their elderliness. Lord Raglan, the Commander-in-chief, was sixty-six, brave, popular, but not a brilliant soldier. He had fought at Waterloo, a formative experience that caused him usually to refer to the enemy as 'the French', even though they happened to be his allies. Lord Lucan, at the age of fifty-four, was given command of the Cavalry Division, which consisted of the Heavy Brigade under James Scarlett, who had been about to retire, and the Light Brigade under Lord Cardigan, aged fifty-seven. Cardigan and Lucan were related by marriage, and the difficulties of command were increased by the fact that they loathed the sight of each other. Another elderly appointment was Sir Charles Napier, who was given the task of taking a naval expedition into the Baltic to bombard the coastal fortresses in the Gulf of Finland. 'Lads, sharpen your cutlasses and the day is your own', ran his signal on the outbreak of war. Trafalgar and Waterloo were powerful factors in British service life.

In one respect, however, the Crimean war heralded the future. The war correspondent made his appearance for the first time, and since the military authorities refused to recognize such an innovation, the dispatches which appeared in the Press were unhampered by any form of censorship. Thus the Russian command had only to read an English newspaper to discover the Allied dispositions and the effect of their own artillery fire. Delane, the editor of *The Times*, made sure that he had an adequate number of correspondents in every theatre. William Henry Stowe, a Fellow of Oriel, was at Balaclava. General Eber, who had fought with the Hungarians in 1848, joined the Turks in Thessaly and actually became Omar Pasha's chief of staff. The most famous of them was William Howard Russell, an Irishman of overwhelming charm and resource, whose denunciation of the early horrors of the Crimean campaign was mainly responsible for Florence Nightingale's mission to Scutari.

The aim of the British government was to protect Constantinople, and accordingly Varna, a Bulgarian town on the coast of the Black Sea, was chosen as a base for operations against the Russians in the Principalities. By the beginning of June the first British and French contingents began to land there. Within a week most means of sanitation had broken down; the heat was overwhelming and the troops became stricken with dysentery and cholera. Meanwhile, to the north-west, Silistria, a Turkish fortress on the Danube, had been successfully defended against the Russians, and towards the end of June news reached the Allied forces at Varna that the siege had been raised.

Then a most remarkable thing happened. The Allies suddenly found themselves without an enemy to fight. On 20 April Buol, the Austrian minister, had succeeded in bringing about a treaty of alliance between Austria and Prussia by which Prussia would support Austria in demanding a Russian withdrawal from the Principalities. On 3 June the demand was made, and the Tsar, not wishing to add to his enemies, agreed to do so. At the beginning of August the Russians began to pull back to the line of the Pruth, and the Allies were left wondering what to do with their army.

The Times had already suggested an answer. 'The grand political and military objects of the war could not be attained as long as Sebastopol and the Russian fleet were in existence.' Palmerston had circulated a memorandum to the Cabinet on the same day putting the same point, and on 28 June the government sent an order to Raglan for an attack on Sebastopol. Raglan's staff, however, were extremely doubtful about the undertaking,

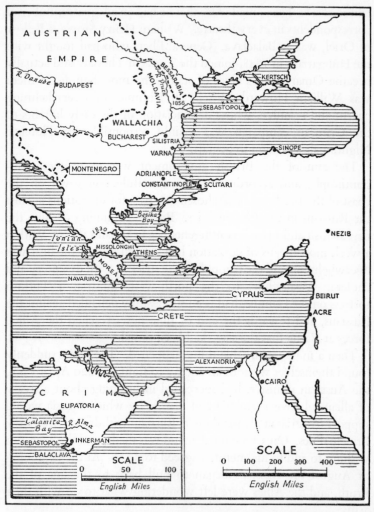

2. THE BALKANS AND THE EASTERN MEDITERRANEAN, 1830–56
The crosses show the Route of the Allied Expeditionary Force, 1854

since Sebastopol could not be taken from the sea, and an attack from the land side might require more troops and certainly more artillery than they possessed, if they were to take the fortress before winter.

On 24 August the embarkation from Varna began. Un-

fortunately, although the Allies' intentions had been announced
to the world during the previous two months, the supply departments had never been officially informed and there were insufficient transports for the army and its equipment. The solution
to this problem was to leave the equipment behind. On 7 September 30,000 men, with a total of twenty-one wagons for their
maintenance, sailed up the coast to the mouth of the Danube,
where they were to meet the French fleet. There they dropped
anchor for four days, while Lord Raglan, who had not yet made
up his mind where he would land, set off on his steamer, the
Caradoc, to inspect the Crimean coast. He came so close to
Sebastopol that Russian officers could be clearly picked out and
salutes were exchanged. He then selected what looked like a
suitable landing point to the north of Sebastopol and returned to
his fleet, which crossed the Black Sea to Calamita Bay, where the
troops were thankful to disembark.

Meanwhile the diplomats were trying to agree amongst themselves on the war aims. The Allies had been hoping to get the
Austrians on to their side, but dared not bring too much pressure
to bear for fear of driving them over to join the Russians. The
French and Austrian Foreign Ministers, Drouyn and Buol, did,
however, succeed in reaching agreement over four points that
were to be presented to Russia. They demanded that:

1. A European guarantee of the Principalities should replace a
   Russian protectorate.
2. The navigation of the Danube should be freed.
3. The Straits Convention of 1841 should be revised 'in the
   interests of the Balance of Power in Europe.'
4. The Russian claim to a protectorate over the Christian subjects of Turkey should be dropped.

The first two had been virtually settled by the Russian withdrawal from the Principalities and the last had ceased to be resisted by the Tsar. It was around the third point that the diplomats
skirmished. The question had never been broached before the
outbreak of the war, veiled by the struggle over prestige. Now it
emerged as the only issue over which the war was fought. Was

Russian naval power in the Black Sea, with its base at Sebastopol, to be limited or not?

By the middle of September the Allied forces in the Crimea were ready for action. In all they numbered over 50,000, the British with 66 guns, the French with 70, while available Russian regular troops were slightly less than 50,000. St. Arnaud, the French commander, had originally wished to postpone the advance until the following spring, but Raglan insisted on his orders, and the Allies began their advance southwards on Sebastopol on 19 September. The first battle was fought on the following day, when they encountered Prince Menschikoff's army of about 40,000, holding the heights on the southern side of the river Alma. The honours in the fighting rest with the private soldiers, who advanced with a courage and tenacity that their commanders did not deserve. Little or no reconnaissance had been made, but Menschikoff had been equally negligent in leaving some of the paths up the cliffs unguarded. A major feature of the defence, the Great Redoubt, was taken by a frontal assault under withering fire, but since Raglan had shifted his headquarters to a position well to the right, out of touch with his army and actually behind the Russian lines, the confusion among the British forces was so great that they could not hold their objective and the attack had to be put in a second time. The outcome of the whole murderous tangle was a British victory—a justifiable claim, since Raglan's troops had certainly borne the brunt of the fighting.

At this point a fateful decision was taken. Raglan wished to press on and to attempt to capture Sebastopol, which lay immediately ahead of them. Had he done so, there seems little doubt that the fortress would have fallen that autumn. St. Arnaud, however, thought the fortifications too strong and when a new Russian battery was discovered in front of them it was decided, on 24 September, that the armies should turn inland and march round Sebastopol to the south side of it. This hazardous operation was carried out successfully. Neither the Russians nor the Allies made use of scouts, so that although minor collisions took place, neither side had a definite idea of the whereabouts of the enemy. Once the manoeuvre had been completed, Canrobert, who had taken over the French command on St. Arnaud's death, offered Raglan the choice of siege positions. Raglan selected the inlet of Balaclava as his harbour, which meant that the British forces would occupy the eastern half of the line and would have to defend an exposed right flank, while the French were placed between the British and the sea. Here they all settled down for a winter siege, for which the British army in particular was quite unprepared.

There followed one of the most appalling winters in the history of military campaigning. The Russians made two attempts to dislodge their besiegers, both aimed at the British right flank. The first was a thrust at Balaclava harbour on 25 October, which was repulsed with heavy British losses. The second, the battle of Inkerman, on 5 November, was a direct attack at the British forces on the plateau—again repulsed, this time with heavier losses for the Russians. Both were confused soldiers' battles of the kind later depicted by Leo Tolstoy, who was serving with the Russian forces in this war. The most memorable incident in all this fighting was during the Balaclava battle, the charge of the Light Brigade, which seems to sum up both the superb gallantry of the soldiers and the criminal incompetence of their officers. The wrong guns were charged and the Light Brigade was utterly shattered. If Raglan's orders had been clearer, if Nolan, his aide-de-camp, who brought them to Lucan, the Commander of the Cavalry Division, had made sure that he understood them; if Lucan and Cardigan had been capable of friendly discussion, the tragedy might never have happened.

> 'When can their glory fade?
> O the wild charge they made!
> All the world wonder'd,'

wrote Tennyson, but the comment of the French general Bosquet was nearer the truth: 'c'est magnifique, mais ce n'est pas la guerre'. The only wonder is that the Crimean war was won at all.

Meanwhile a grim battle of a different kind was being fought out at Scutari, on the opposite shore to Constantinople, where a base hospital had been established for the sick and wounded from the Crimea. Cholera and dysentery rather than battle-wounds were the chief features of this hell, and the men lay on the bare floor, unwashed and unfed, amid mounting filth. It was William Howard Russell who first exposed the frightfulness of Scutari and his dispatches to *The Times* in October aroused a wave of public indignation at home. One immediate consequence of this was that Sidney Herbert, Secretary at War, requested Florence Nightingale to go to Scutari to superintend the nursing. Miss Nightingale selected thirty-eight nurses to accompany her and reached the Barrack Hospital at Scutari on 5 November. Throughout that dreadful winter, while the British army froze in the snow and piercing winds before Sebastopol and the transports crossed the Black Sea packed with troops suffering from exposure and near-starvation, she struggled with the material difficulties and the obstruction and incompetence of the authorities. She lived amidst the stench, the lice, and the appalling scenes of amputations performed without anaesthetics, but gradually, as the numbers of sick mounted and the despairing authorities turned more and more to her, she was able to use the money, which various funds had put at her disposal, to bring about some measure of improvement. She worked ceaselessly. She made enemies. She undermined her health. She would never give up. Indeed she could not give up. 'I can never forget,' she wrote afterwards, and for the rest of her life, a haunted woman, she was to fight for the improvement of the lot of the British soldier.

The revelation of these conditions did much to weaken the government's position. It was true that in December the Austrians had at last signed a treaty with the Allies promising armed aid if the Russians rejected the Four Points, but since the Russians had by now accepted them this amounted to very little. Otherwise the record of Aberdeen's ministry was depressing. The chance of taking Sebastopol in the autumn of 1854 had been lost. Sir Charles Napier had returned from the Baltic after having only taken Bomarsund, a half-constructed fortress in the Åland Isles. The confusion over the supply and administration of the troops in the Crimea seemed inexcusable, and a Radical M.P., John Roebuck, put forward a motion for a committee of inquiry into the condition of the army and the conduct of the war. The Cabinet rejected the motion, although Russell resigned in protest at this, but the motion was passed in January 1855 by a considerable majority. Aberdeen resigned and the customary negotiations ensued for the creation of a new government. The Queen turned to Derby, as the leader of the Conservatives. Derby, however, was unable to win over Palmerston, whom he regarded as indispensable, and to Disraeli's great disgust declined the invitation. Russell was then asked, but he found it impossible to form a government, since his recent resignation was regarded as a desertion of his side.

The Queen now turned to Palmerston. As he said himself: 'I am, for the moment, l'inévitable.' Disraeli did not think so— 'only ginger beer and not champagne, and now an old painted pantaloon, very deaf, very blind, and with false teeth which would fall out of his mouth when speaking, if he did not hesitate and halt so in his talk'. Palmerston was, in fact, by now a very spry seventy-one. The doorkeeper of the House of Commons commented that he looked about fifty-five—'walks upright as a dart and steps out like a soldier'. The Queen had hoped that the inclusion of several Peelites—Graham, Gladstone, and Herbert—in his Cabinet would hold the old man in check. But the ministry soon ceased to be a coalition, when Palmerston agreed to allow the motion for the committee of inquiry to go forward and the Peelites, out of loyalty to Aberdeen, resigned.

The Radicals' censure of the government had been over its mismanagement; their cry was not for peace, but for speedy victory. Yet one voice, that of their erstwhile leader, never ceased to denounce the government for prosecuting the war at all. John Bright fought a lonely battle in the Commons throughout these years. He was not exactly a pacifist, but his Quaker background and his economic instinct combined to make the outbreak of hostilities utterly repellent to him. War was usually wrong and always shockingly wasteful. 'If Turkey has been in danger from the side of Russia heretofore, will she not be in far greater danger when the war is over? Russia is always there. You do not propose

to dismember Russia or to blot out her name from the map, and
her history from the records of Europe.' And as the casualties
mounted, so his oratory scourged the House. 'The Angel of
Death has been abroad in the land; you may almost hear the beat-
ing of his wings. . . . He takes his victims from the castle of the
noble, the mansion of the wealthy, and the cottage of the poor,
and it is on behalf of all these classes that I make this solemn
appeal.'

But it was the country, and not John Bright, that had its way.
Under Palmerston the events of 1855 were certainly more
favourable to the Allied cause. A second Baltic expedition under
Dundas penetrated the Gulf of Finland in force and bombarded
Sveaborg, outside Helsinki, although the whole enterprise showed
that only a combined operation by the army and navy could be
effective in this area—as the Swedes and Russians had learnt many
years before. Lord Panmure combined the two offices of Secretary for War and Secretary at War and in February sent out a
Sanitary Commission to Scutari and the Crimea—a Commission
which, Florence Nightingale maintained, saved the British Army.
In the Crimea General Pélissier replaced Canrobert, and in May
the Allies took Kertsch. In June the first phase of an attack on
Sebastopol was opened, but Raglan, often at loggerheads with his
French allies, did not live to see the end. He was by now a
broken man, after having watched his army literally freeze to
death in the Russian winter. 'I could never return to England
now,' he said, and a few days after the failure of an assault to
which he had been opposed, he died of fever. He was replaced by
General Simpson, and in September the final assault on the fortress
was made. The French distinguished themselves in taking the
Malakoff Redoubt, and by the morning of 9 September Sebastopol
was in Allied hands.

The rest of the war was mainly fought by the diplomats. The
French, suspicious that they were acting as a cat's-paw for the
British, wished to come to terms with the Russians, and in view
of the far greater number of French troops in the field by this
time, Palmerston had to get the best terms possible as things stood.
The situation in Russia had also changed, since Tsar Nicholas had

died of a chill in February 1855, struck down by his own General *Février*, and the Allies were able to treat with his successor, Alexander II, who was anxious for peace.

A Congress opened at Paris in February 1856. By the treaty, which was signed in March, the Principalities were placed under a European guarantee and were to be given a constitution, although remaining nominally under the suzerainty of the Sultan. Russia surrendered southern Bessarabia, and the navigation of the Danube was put under international control. The terms of the Straits settlement of 1841 were reaffirmed. Most important of all for Great Britain, the Black Sea was to be neutralized, which meant that no Russian fleet or arsenal might be maintained there. The Åland Isles were given back to Russia, but Bomarsund was not to be refortified.

Thus, despite the diplomatic and military confusion that had led up to it, the Crimean settlement did produce some highly significant results. The neutralization of the Black Sea lasted only until 1870, when the Russians took advantage of the Franco-Prussian war to repudiate it, but at least during the fourteen years following 1856 Russia was unable to bring great pressure to bear on Turkey, and the loss of Bessarabia prevented any Russian interference with the mouth of the Danube. The settlement over the Principalities eventually involved the creation of Rumania, the second state to be carved out of Turkey-in-Europe, while Turkey herself had been preserved. The Eastern Question had not been solved, but at least it had been postponed, and Great Britain and France both had some reason to be satisfied with the outcome. It was Austria who suffered the worst consequences, since, owing to her attempt throughout the whole period to play the part of a rather aggressive mediator, she had failed to win the friendship of any of the belligerents and was now condemned to a fateful isolation. The Crimean war marks the end of the Holy Alliance.

Both Russia and Great Britain drew lessons from the war. Alexander II, aware of Russia's backwardness, embarked on a series of social reforms, including the emancipation of the serfs in 1861. In Great Britain the reforms were mostly administrative, involving the overhaul of the system of supply in the Army.

Permanent camps were established. Model military hospitals were set up and a school was established for the study of the treatment of wounds and diseases. The Victoria Cross, instituted in 1856, was to be open to all ranks—another indication of a greater concern for the private soldier. In 1864 a decision was taken to introduce a breech-loading rifle into the infantry. If it is true that experience can never be bought at too dear a price, the thousands who suffered and died so unnecessarily in the Crimea and at Scutari had not perished entirely in vain. The country had learnt at last that the memory of Waterloo was not enough.

12

THE COLONIES AND INDIA

1. The achievement of the Radical Imperialists

IT was only gradually that the many changes in the colonies since 1815 became a matter of some interest to the governing classes in Great Britain. During the first decades of the nineteenth century colonial administration was in the hands of a small group of permanent officials who were left comparatively undisturbed. Even amongst the reformers the idea of a future for the colonies played little part; the Radicals simply regarded them as a nuisance. 'Emancipate your colonies', ran the title of a pamphlet by Jeremy Bentham addressed to the National Convention in France in 1793, and he really believed that he was giving them good advice. Quite apart from the question of emancipation, the Free Traders naturally objected to the colonial system with all its restrictions on commercial intercourse. Huskisson's Reciprocity of Duties Act had struck them as far too cautious and niggling, but by the middle of the century they had gained most of what they wanted. The Navigation Acts were repealed in 1849, and although they had by this time been shot through with modifications and exceptions, the date none the less marks the end of an epoch. The colonial system, whose writ had run in all colonial affairs for more than 250 years, was at last officially at an end.

Only one other type of reform was seriously advocated during the early years of the century—the humanitarians' cry for the abolition of slavery. In 1807 the Slave Trade had been declared illegal by Great Britain, in the following year by the United States, and before 1820 most western European countries had agreed to enforce the same prohibition. This may have done something to improve the lot of the slaves in the West Indies, since the owners could no longer replace them so easily, but to the Evangelical the very existence of 670,000 slaves in the British West Indies seemed a sin. Gradually feeling against slavery was organized. In 1823 the Anti-Slavery Society, with Clarkson and Wilberforce among its vice-presidents, was founded in London. Missionaries were dispatched to Guiana and the West Indies, where they naturally came up against the slave owners; in Guiana a clergyman was found guilty, by a local court-martial, of encouraging a slave insurrection, was condemned to death, and died in prison before he could be reprieved.

Emancipation came at last with the Act of 1833, introduced by Stanley, when Colonial Secretary during Lord Grey's administration. Slavery was to end within twelve months, although the former slaves were to remain as unpaid apprentices for varying terms of years according to their form of work. By 1838 all local colonial legislatures had opted for ending the apprenticeship system and had changed over to wage labour. It was natural that a Parliament wedded to the notion of property should make provision for compensating the owners. Specially appointed commissioners were allowed to disburse up to a total of £20 million—at the rate of £37 10s. a slave—and, in all, £18½ million of this was actually distributed.

No measure could have been more indicative of the fundamental changes that the whole social and economic structure of the country was undergoing. The West Indian planter interest had been the darling of the eighteenth-century Parliaments; yet now they had been unable to prevent the passing of an Act which they claimed would be disastrous for them. Other countries watched the experiment very critically for the next few decades, since although most of the northern States of the U.S.A. had abolished slavery shortly after Independence, Stanley's Act was the first instance of abolition in communities whose whole economy had rested on slavery. The main argument against abolition had been that wage labour would be more expensive for the planter than slave labour, and that sugar would consequently rise in price. In fact, this fear proved unfounded. In many of the smaller islands over-population created competition for employment among the blacks and wages remained fairly low. Only on a larger island, such as Jamaica, or on the mainland in Guiana did the blacks move away and settle in villages of their own in the interior. Here the labour problem was greater for the planter, and was eventually solved by the appearance of free African and Indian coolies, whose arrival throughout the rest of the century was to have a marked effect on the racial make-up of the population in the West Indies.

At about this time there began to emerge a small group of Radicals whose views on colonies in general were in marked contrast to the apathetic pessimism of the government. Charles Buller, Gibbon Wakefield, and Lord Durham were among those who criticized the negative and crippling system, whereby a few anonymous permanent officials at the Colonial Office controlled the far-flung possessions of the Crown. 'In some back room,' wrote Charles Buller, '—whether in the attic, or in what storey we know not—you will find all the mother country which really exercises supremacy, and really maintains connexion with the vast and widely scattered colonies of Britain.'

In place of this stagnant rule they hoped for some rather more carefully planned and constructive policy. They wanted the form of government in the colonies to grow, through a fairly rapid process of evolution, into something resembling the English constitution—in other words, the development of a colonial legislature to which local ministers chosen by the Governor would be responsible. There was one great obstacle to this plan, summed up by Russell in a letter, in 1839, to a future Governor of Canada. 'It may happen, therefore, that the Governor receives at one and the same time instructions from the Queen and advice from his executive council totally at variance with each other. If he is to obey his instructions from England, the parallel of constitutional responsibility entirely fails; if, on the other hand, he is to follow the advice of his council, he is no longer a subordinate officer but an independent sovereign.' One attempted solution to this problem, put forward by Lord Durham in his Report on Canada in 1839, was to divide the spheres of government between the mother country and the colony, but this was hardly likely to be a satisfactory answer for long. The only sound solution, which did, in fact, emerge in the course of time, was for the personal power of the Sovereign to dwindle, while retaining an emotional hold on the subjects of the Crown.

Other parts of the Radical Imperialists' programme concerned the organization of emigration and the distribution of public land. This was the particular interest of Gibbon Wakefield, an enterprising and forthright individual who might have enjoyed a distinguished public career, if in his early years he had been able to resist the temptation to abduct an industrialist's daughter, an offence that resulted in a spell at Newgate. Wakefield was struck by the possibility of creating new healthy societies in the uninhabited lands that were attracting so many emigrants. In accordance with contemporary thought he regarded land, capital, and labour as the three major constituents of wealth. In the new countries, Australia and New Zealand, there was plenty of land, and since, by the 1830s, capitalists were seeing new possibilities of investment in the Empire, there was no great shortage of capital. It was labour that was lacking. Once in their new country, the emigrants,[1] whom unemployment or poor working and living conditions had driven to take this step, were determined not to become employees again. They seized on large tracts of land for themselves, and there soon developed a scattered community of farmers, none of whom had enough labour to work their lands. A good example of this was the Swan river settlement in Western Australia in 1829. Land was sold by the Crown for the extraordinarily low figure of one shilling and sixpence an acre, and for some years there was considerable doubt whether the settlement would survive at all.

Wakefield had a neat answer to the whole problem. A 'sufficient' price for land should be fixed by the Crown. This price should be high enough to prevent the majority of emigrants from buying land immediately on their arrival; Wakefield's idea of 'sufficient' was such that, in order to buy his own farm, a man would have to save for five years, while working in another colonist's employ. This would create a more closely knit society

[1] For figures of emigration throughout the century see Statistics, p. 451.

of farmers and labourers, gradually expanding at a rate which it could afford. The money which the Crown gained from these sales would be put into a fund, so that by means of subsidized emigration the scheme might attract young men of every class. This ingenious plan, which it was hoped would ultimately pay for itself, was a far cry from the notion of using outlying lands as dumping grounds for transported convicts. Wakefield complained that it was never put into practice as he wished, but his ideas were certainly partly responsible for a fundamental change of attitude towards the colonies in the later half of the century.

The first major document in which Gibbon Wakefield had any hand was the Durham Report on Canada. British North America had developed considerably in population and wealth since the turn of the century,[1] but this in itself had led to problems that could not be entirely solved by the arrangements of 1791.[2] Upper Canada's economic life-line ran down the St. Lawrence through Lower Canada, and with a growing commerce there were frequent quarrels between the provinces. In Lower Canada there was the particular problem of the French, who watched the growth of British immigration with apprehension, while in Upper Canada there was antagonism between the United Empire Loyalist families and the later arrivals. The climax of this unrest was an outbreak of rebellion in each province in 1837. Neither became a serious threat to the government, but even Lord Melbourne, who normally preferred to take refuge in inactivity, was bound to admit that all was not well, and, partly through Russell's persuasion, Lord Durham, who was known to be a supporter of the new Radical views on colonies, was sent over to Canada, accompanied by Gibbon Wakefield and Charles Buller.

The mission itself was not a great success. Durham had been allowed a wide power of discretion, but when he acted on this and sent eight of the leading rebels to Bermuda, while pardoning the rest, his political enemies at home saw a chance to strike at him. Brougham led the attack; Melbourne wavered and then weakly disallowed Durham's action. 'The time-serving Whigs',

---

[1] See pp. 34–6.

[2] For the negotiations with the United States over the frontier see p. 239.

wrote *The Times*, '. . . have at the first shot deserted, dishonoured, and dismissed him.' Durham had only been in Canada five months; he had not been able to visit the Maritime Provinces, and although he had done something towards the organization of police and the registration of land titles in Quebec and Montreal, a second outbreak of rebellion in Lower Canada had hampered his efforts. He was still only at the beginning of things and now the government had openly betrayed him. Not unnaturally he resigned and returned to England in the autumn of 1838.

But Durham had not finished. Within a few months of his return he published a Report on Canada—a diagnosis of Canada's ills and a suggested remedy. Some of his ideas—particularly on Public Lands, for which Gibbon Wakefield may have been responsible—were not put into effect; another idea, such as his plan to swamp the French Canadians, so that they might eventually merge with the British, underestimated the resilience of that community. Yet the Durham Report rightly stands in the public imagination as the foundation stone of the British Commonwealth. The future was with the Radical Imperialists, and this Report was the first governmental document which embodied their views.

The Report largely inspired Russell's Canada Act of 1840. This placed Upper and Lower Canada under one government, as Durham had suggested, but for the moment excluded the Maritime Provinces. The Lower House of the new legislature was to consist of forty-two representatives from each province, but, contrary to Durham's plan, the Governor was not bound to choose his ministers from the party with a majority in this House, and the eventual introduction of responsible government was to be a matter for the Governor himself to decide. However, owing to the determination of a number of Governors in the next fifteen years—and particularly to the work of Lord Elgin, Durham's son-in-law—responsible government did very soon become a reality. Elgin's period of rule (1847–54) was not easy. He had to cope with the Canadian reaction to the repeal of the Corn Laws, which left them open to foreign competition, while they were still tied by the remaining restrictions of the Navigation Laws.

This particular problem was straightened out by the repeal of the Navigation Laws in 1849. Another major crisis related directly to the growth of the new form of government. The Canadian House had passed a Rebellion Losses Bill which the British element strongly resented. Elgin was consequently petitioned to use his veto, but he insisted on standing by the decision of the House. The Canadians were to have constitutional government, whether they liked it or not. Thus the British system of responsible government was fairly speedily grafted on to the colony, not through any written document, but through the gradual adoption of certain governmental practices.

Meanwhile, a very different form of colonial development had been taking place in the Pacific. The basis of the settlements in Canada had been a great river and a system of lakes, and the consequent underlying economic unity had brought up the question of unification or federation fairly early in their history. The colonization of Australia, however, was a story of coastal settlements, all looking away from each other and in some cases divided by mountains or desert. Indeed, the rivers of Australia, far from helping to shape the early settlements, remained for some years one of the mysteries that Australian explorers had to solve. The volume of water, draining off the western slopes of the Dividing Range, had suggested at first some great inland sea, and it was not until 1829 that Charles Sturt traced the Murray to its estuary in Encounter Bay.

Not long after the establishment of the first convict settlements, John Macarthur, an officer in the New South Wales Corps, had realized the possibilities of sheep-farming, and in the early decades of the nineteenth century the numbers of free immigrants increased rapidly. In 1823 the Governor was given a nominated Council to advise him; in 1828 this Council was granted the right to veto the Governor's decisions, and in 1842 two-thirds of the seats were thrown open to local election. This led to a series of disputes over the Governor's civil list and the squatters. These last were the natural opponents to Gibbon Wakefield's notion of a 'sufficient' price, which the government rather half-heartedly tried to demand, and although £1 an acre was eventually laid down as a minimum price, a compromise was usually reached in the interest of the existing squatters.

Rapidly the settlements spread and increased in population. Fairly early in the history of New South Wales the tougher criminal element had been transferred to Tasmania, Brisbane to the north, or Norfolk Island in the Pacific. The year 1835 saw the beginnings of what was to become Victoria, and in the following year a landing was made near the mouth of the recently discovered Murray river. Here Adelaide was founded, and in the growth of Southern Australia can be seen the first example of some attempt at planned colonization along the lines suggested by Gibbon Wakefield, although Wakefield himself reckoned that the government selling price of land—twelve shillings an acre—was far too low to allow his scheme to work.

These last two settlements were free of convicts, but the question of transportation was still a live issue in the development of Australia. The squatters who had occupied large tracts of land and wanted cheap labour welcomed the presence of convicts and emancipists. But the crime rate was very high, and an increasing majority of free settlers objected to the continuation of transportation for economic and social reasons. Its abolition in New South Wales was decreed by Parliament in 1840, and then elsewhere, until by 1853 it had been abolished throughout Eastern Australia. In Western Australia, where labour was in short supply and where permission for the introduction of Chinese and Indian coolies had been refused, transportation continued until 1867 mainly to meet the needs of the colony.

In Australia this factor alone had been enough to frustrate the aspirations of the Radical Imperialists. In New Zealand it looked as if they might have a better chance. First sighted by Abel Tasman in 1642, first circumnavigated and charted by Captain Cook in 1769, the two islands remained unclaimed by any European country until 1840. Then a combination of circumstances impelled the British government formally to annex New Zealand. The French were showing a lively interest in the Pacific, and French possession might later represent a threat to Australia. Already for some years missionaries had reported on the lawlessness of pirates, whalers, and escaped convicts, who made use of the shores of New Zealand, and in 1838 Wakefield and his supporters had formed a joint-stock company for its colonization. Unfortunately, although New Zealand escaped the curse of transportation, the presence of about 100,000 Maoris on North Island played havoc with Wakefield's schemes. Agents of the company bought up land from individual natives, but since local custom maintained that land was held by the tribe as a whole, the Maoris afterwards regarded these sales as invalid. The Treaty of Waitangi of 1840 between the Maoris and the Crown, guaranteeing the natives their land in return for submission, appeared to confirm the Maoris' opinion, and the result was a long period of unrest and war between the natives and the new settlers.

The tragedy was that all this while South Island, where there were only about 5,000 Maoris, would have been the perfect area in which to work out the Wakefield experiment. Later two settlements were begun there—Otago, founded in 1848 through the Scottish Presbyterian Church, and Canterbury, founded in 1851 by the Church of England—and here at last one may see the reasonableness of Wakefield's proposals. Both provinces were the result of systematic emigration financed by the sale of land. The Canterbury plan was particularly neat. One thousand five hundred colonists, a quarter of whom were men of some means, were landed on the east coast of South Island, where the land, which they had purchased from the New Zealand company at £3 an acre, was ready for immediate occupation. Wakefield himself reckoned that he had at last come somewhere near success and, in 1853, emigrated to Canterbury, where he spent the rest of his life.

In one other colony at this time the government was confronted with a problem similar to that of Canada. Cape Colony had been captured from the Dutch during the Napoleonic war and was afterwards retained in return for an indemnity of £6 million. The European population, almost entirely of Dutch origin—with a sprinkling of the descendants of French Huguenots —numbered about 26,000, a community of farmers with their focal point at Cape Town. At first, the fact that the colony had changed hands made little difference; in 1819 the British government sent out 5,000 emigrants from the United Kingdom to settle an area to be known as Albany, some 400 miles east of Cape Town, but the purpose of this was simply to establish a frontier settlement between the Europeans and the Bantu tribes to the north-east.

The first serious difficulty was over the emancipation of the slaves. The newly arrived English in Albany had none, but the Dutch colonists had been a slave-owning community since the early settlements of the seventeenth century. By this time they held about 39,000 slaves—Africans or Malays—and the share of compensation to which it was reckoned they were entitled amounted to £1¼ million. But claims had to be made individually in London, and the Dutch-speaking Boer, with no London connections—unlike the West Indian planter—was usually forced to sell his claim to an intermediary for a fraction of its face value.

The anger to which this gave rise, coupled with national and religious antagonism and a general restlessness, soon led to a great migration of about 10,000 Boer farmers, who, between 1836 and 1838, moved north-east, some into Natal on the coast, some over the Orange river, and some still further north over the Vaal river.[1] There were already some British settled at Durban on the coast of Natal, and inland there were large numbers of Zulus under their king Dingaan. The arrival of the Boer trekkers led to war with the Zulus, who were ultimately defeated and moved away. In 1843 the British government declared Natal a British colony, but decided not to annex the territories to the north of the Orange and Vaal rivers, although it was claimed that the Boers living there were, nevertheless, British subjects. A few years later the territory between the Vaal and the Orange rivers was annexed by the British government, but within a short time the expense of various Kaffir wars decided the Colonial Office to cut its losses and to grant independence to the Orange Free State in 1854. Two years earlier, another Boer republic, the Transvaal, had already gained similar terms.

[1] See map, p. 389.

2. *India and the Mutiny*

During the first half of the nineteenth century two distinct tendencies are noticeable in the government of British India. The first was a growing preparedness to accept and to work through the existing structure of local Indian law and society; the second was the introduction of Western culture and technology. Both tendencies sprang from the new notion of trusteeship, but it was inevitable that the one should to some extent conflict with the other.

The first owed much to the activity of a number of very remarkable administrators—Sir Thomas Munro, governor of Madras 1820–27, Mountstuart Elphinstone at Bombay, and Metcalfe at Delhi. In a Minute, written in 1824, Munro outlined his conception of Great Britain's task in India.

> We should look upon India, not as a temporary possession, but as one which is to be maintained permanently, until the natives shall in some future age have abandoned most of their superstitions and prejudices and become sufficiently enlightened to frame a regular government for themselves, and to conduct and preserve it. Whenever such a time shall arrive, it will probably be best for both countries that the British control over India should be gradually withdrawn.

In the meanwhile, these three, among others, made a careful examination of the existing land systems, in order to maintain what was best in them. The study of Indian languages was encouraged and a Chair of Sanskrit was maintained at the Company's College at Poona. The high-water mark of this respect for the native may be seen in the report of the Parliamentary Committee on India in 1833, in which it was stated 'that the interests of the Native Subjects are to be consulted in preference to those of Europeans, whenever the two come in competition; and that therefore the laws ought to be adapted rather to the feelings and habits of the Natives than to those of the Europeans'. And in the realm of government the India Act of 1833 declared that 'no Native of the said Territories, nor any natural-born Subject of His Majesty resident therein, shall, by reason only of his religion, place of birth, descent, colour or any of them be disabled from holding any Place, Office or Employment under the said Company.'

Unfortunately it simply was not sufficient to encourage the existing Indian way of life. India was lacking in any racial or religious unity and so technically backward that a considerable measure of Western influence was essential to her development. Even self-government was a Western idea, and at once raised the question of education. The practice of *suti*—the burning of Hindu widows on the funeral pyres of their husbands—was left untouched for many years, but in 1829 Lord Bentinck, after careful consideration of the possible consequences, ordered its suppression. During Dalhousie's governorship (1848–56) railways, cheap postage, and the electric telegraph were all introduced; the Ganges canal and the Grand Trunk Road were constructed, and an engineering college and village schools were established.

The question of a common language for the purposes of administration presented another aspect of Imperialism. Some sort of *lingua franca* was certainly necessary and no Indian language had a predominant claim. In 1835 Macaulay, who had been appointed a Member of the Supreme Council of India, produced a famous Minute in which his arguments in favour of making English the common language were overwhelmingly powerful, marred only by the arrogance with which they were stated. To teach an Indian language would simply open the door to a knowledge of the literature and science available in that language. It was a question 'whether, when we can patronise sound philosophy and true history, we shall countenance, at the public expense, medical doctrines which would disgrace an English farrier—astronomy which would move laughter in the girls at an English boarding school—history abounding with kings thirty feet high and reigns thirty thousand years long—and geography made up of seas of treacle and seas of butter'.

Westernizing was thus an essential element in the development of India. An English writer of the twentieth century, not usually inclined to praise British Imperialism, has remarked that it is instructive to compare on a modern map of Asia the railway system of India with that of the surrounding countries. But with this westernizing there came a widening gulf between British and Indian. The fact that the British were in so many ways the instructors as well as the rulers of the Indians was bound to put them in a class of their own—particularly in a country whose society was based on caste. The nineteenth-century Victorian administrator was in many ways a more worthy individual than the eighteenth-century merchant, but his sense of moral superiority did not always make him more likable. The new steamships enabled him to come for a short time with his family and then depart. India was no longer a home, but only a posting, and the arrival of the memsahib simply completed the process of insulation from the natives.

The period between 1819 and 1857 was extremely quiet for India south and east of the Sutlej river. The most significant acquisition of all in these years was the result of an entirely peaceful transaction. In 1819 Stamford Raffles, who had fought in the Indies during the Napoleonic war, was able to persuade the East India Company to purchase the uninhabited island of Singapore from the Sultan of Johore, and within four years the volume of trade passing through the newly founded port made it clear that Great Britain had gained possession of what was to be one of the great crossroads of the Far East.

Other gains came through conquest. Frontier disputes around Chittagong led to a short Burmese war, at the end of which, in 1826, the British had taken the most part of the long coastal strip. Rather later, Russian expansion in the direction of Afghanistan awoke British suspicions, and for a while the two European Powers fought a duel similar to that in which Great Britain and France had engaged in the eighteenth century. Kabul and Kandahar were occupied by British forces in 1839, but circumstances forced a retreat from Kabul early in 1842, the army was caught on the move and only one man survived to bring the story of the disaster to Jallalabad. Kabul was taken again by storm that year, but Lord Ellenborough, the new Governor-General, was anxious not to prolong the adventure, and Afghanistan was allowed to remain outside the British sphere of influence. In the following year Sind was forcibly annexed by Sir Charles Napier; 'a very advantageous, useful, humane piece of rascality', he described it— certainly the least justifiable of all the actions of the British in India. Meanwhile, the Punjab was no longer under the firm rule of Ranjit Singh. The Sikhs resented the activity of the British south of the Sutlej, and in the 1840s two wars were fought with them, ending in 1849 with the annexation of the Punjab, which was placed under the rule of John and Henry Lawrence.

All these wars had been fought on the periphery of British India. Soon, however, the long period of peace east of the Sutlej river was to be torn asunder in the most appalling holocaust of the nineteenth century. The Indian Mutiny of 1857, as its name implies, was a rebellion of Indian troops against the Europeans in India. It bore little or no resemblance to a national rising; indeed, the word 'national' could have meant very little in India at this time. It was confined to certain units of the army of Bengal; Indian troops in the Presidencies of Madras and Bombay made no move, and the Punjab, the most recently conquered region of India, did not attempt to join in. The Indian civilian played little part, and there is no evidence of any social or political programme being put forward by the leaders of the mutineers.

The reason that was afterwards given for the outbreak was purely religious. Cartridges for the newly issued Enfield rifle had to be bitten before being inserted, and a rumour went round that the grease for these cartridges was made from the fat of cows and swine. For the Hindu the cow was sacred; for the Moslem the swine was anathema. This grievance—not unentirely unjustified, since the grease was made from beef-fat—momentarily united Hindu and Moslem against the British and certainly played some part in sparking off the Mutiny, but it was by no means the only cause. Discipline in the Bengal army had been weakened by the enlisting of private soldiers of high caste, who looked down upon their Indian officers; and a rumour had recently been circulated that two regiments were likely to be sent by the sea route to relieve the forces in Burma—stationed there after a second war in 1852—and this had also caused alarm since the crossing of water would involve a loss of caste for the Hindu.

There were, however, deeper reasons than these. The governor-generalship of Lord Dalhousie, efficient though it was, had been a classic example of the new imperial conscience at work—rational, fundamentally benevolent, but always a little unimaginative. The railways and Christian missionaries were regarded by conservative Indians as a subtle form of attack on Hindu custom. Brahmin priests still resented the abolition of *suti* and objected to an Act of 1856 which allowed the remarriage of widows. Another aspect of Dalhousie's work added to the discontent. He had instituted a policy of 'lapse', whereby a native state passed under British rule in the event of the ruling family having no heir. This completely ignored the established Indian custom of adoption, and a good many states had 'lapsed' during Dalhousie's governorship, thereby disappointing a number of hopeful princes. In 1856 Oudh had actually been annexed on the grounds of misrule by its king, and it is a significant fact that much of the Bengal army was raised in Oudh. Finally, the Kabul disaster of 1842 had shattered the notion of British invincibility and greatly encouraged the prophecy that British power in India would be ended in 1857, the hundredth anniversary of the battle of Plassey.

The outbreak began on 10 May, 1857, when the sepoys at Meerut mutinied while the British were at church service, and later released a number of Indian troops who had recently been court-martialled and sentenced to imprisonment. In all, three regiments of sepoys marched south on Delhi, called on their comrades to join them, and massacred the European civilians there. The only available troops who might have been able to put a stop to this were under Brigadier Graves outside the city on the Long Ridge that commanded the Kashmir Gate, but these were all sepoys, except for a few British officers, and when one of these regiments was sent in to restore order, they joined the mutineers as soon as they were inside Delhi. For the moment there was nothing that could be done, and in order to save the women

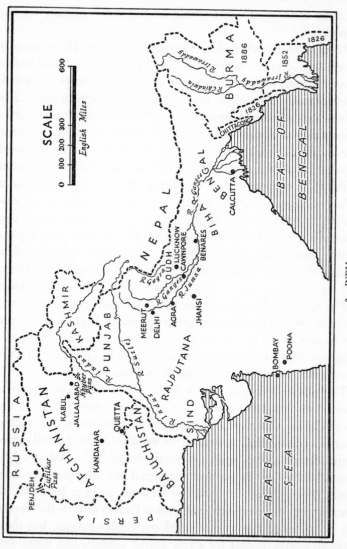

3. INDIA

and children who had escaped out to the Ridge, Graves gave the order for a general dispersal northwards.

At the same time the mutiny was spreading fast among the Indian troops stationed in the great valley of the Ganges, Jumna, and Gogra rivers. Now the real weakness of the British position became apparent. European troops numbered less than 40,000 in comparison with 230,000 Indian soldiers, and at this moment, in the whole of India south and east of the Sutlej, there were only eleven battalions of British infantry; the rest were either in the Punjab or Burma, or had been withdrawn for service in the Crimea. There were simply isolated battalions and depots at places such as Cawnpore, Lucknow, and Agra, and the lines of communication were virtually unguarded. In June Rohilkhand and Jhansi succumbed to their sepoy regiments; and in Cawnpore Sir Hugh Wheeler, with 300 British, 100 loyal Indian troops, and about 400 women and children, was besieged by 3,000 sepoys under the leadership of the Nana Sahib, a discontented prince, who had been deprived of his pension during Dalhousie's governorship.

The fate of the Mutiny was decided by the fact that the British were able to contain the rising. Lord Canning, the Governor-General, who directed operations from Calcutta, had disarmed the sepoy regiments below Benares by the middle of June, and in the Punjab—a crucial region—John Lawrence was able to do the same. Once these two regions were secure it was mainly a question of closing in—on Cawnpore and Lucknow from the east, and on Delhi from the west.

It proved a long, murderous summer. Sir Henry Barnard joined up with the British troops at Meerut and with a force of 3,500 fought his way back to the Ridge against ten times that number of Indians. There they held on until September, repelling innumerable attacks and awaiting the time when they should storm Delhi. This was bound to be a frightful task, since, as one of the British officers described it, the city was 'seven miles in circumference, filled with an immense fanatical Mussulman population, garrisoned by full forty thousand soldiers, armed and disciplined by ourselves, with a hundred and fourteen heavy pieces of artillery mounted on the walls, with the largest magazine of shot, shell and ammunition in the Upper Provinces at their disposal.'

Meanwhile, at Cawnpore, Wheeler had decided to accept the Nana Sahib's offer of a safe conduct, for the sake of the women and children. But as the British put off in boats on the Ganges they were shot down with rifle fire and the survivors imprisoned. Soon, however, Sir Henry Havelock, with a force from Allahabad, was within easy reach of Cawnpore, and on 15 July the Nana Sahib had the remaining prisoners hacked to pieces and their remains thrown down a well. Two days later the British entered Cawnpore. 'Had any Christian bishop', wrote Garnet Wolseley, many years later of what he saw then, 'visited that scene of butchery when I saw it, I verily believe that he would have buckled on his sword.' The reprisals that the British troops exacted during the rest of the Mutiny were as terrible. Neither side seem to have taken many prisoners. Men were burnt to death, crucified, tortured, and hanged, and William Howard Russell, who arrived in India at the beginning of 1858, recorded in his diary his horror at the things that he heard and saw. There can hardly have been another episode in the history of British arms so striking in its bestiality.

After leaving Cawnpore the Nana Sahib had gone on to besiege Lucknow, which held out with 2,000 against 60,000 mutineers. On 15 September Sir Henry Havelock and Sir James Outram, following through from Cawnpore, managed to break in and reinforce the beleaguered garrison, but it was another two months before Sir Colin Campbell, advancing from Calcutta, was able to relieve Lucknow.

Delhi had already fallen. In August a young lean white-faced officer, John Nicholson, had arrived on the Ridge in command of the Lahore Movable Column; he cursed the hesitancy of his senior officers, demanded only that they should attack, and when, in September, the siege train of heavy guns arrived from the Punjab, he had his way. For six nights and seven days the gunners bombarded the Kashmir Gate; on 14 September five columns, amounting to about 5,000 men, flung themselves at the broken walls, and in six hours of fighting lost over a thousand killed and wounded. It was six days before the citadel had fallen and the city was once again in British hands.

The Mutiny was broken, but it took another year to extinguish remaining resistance. There were still many scattered Indian forces, but the most remarkable feature of the fighting throughout the Mutiny was the way in which small bodies of British troops were able time and again to route an enemy that outnumbered them overwhelmingly. The Nana Sahib was never captured; he disappeared into Nepal and was not seen again. His lieutenant, Tantia Topi, avoided capture until April 1859. 'Clemency' Canning ordered the confiscation of landowners' estates in Oudh, but in the main did his best to control the racial hatreds that now seethed throughout the land. The most striking change that came about immediately after the Mutiny was the transference of the territories and properties of the East India Company to the Crown in 1858. In future, the President of the Board of Control was to be Secretary of State for India and the Governor-General was to have the title of Viceroy, but, apart from this, the change was mainly theoretical. The day of John Company had long been over. Its trading privileges had disappeared. The officers whom it was supposed to appoint were actually nominees of the Crown, and since 1853 the Indian Civil Service had been open to public competition.

But if the technical change was small, the psychological consequences of the Mutiny were considerable. From this time on, East and West in British India inhabited different worlds. Reforms and westernizing continued, but the relationship could never be quite the same as it had been in the days of Munro and Elphinstone. The number of European troops in India was increased and the artillery was kept in their hands. British government in India was sufficiently fair and peaceful for the Indians to support the United Kingdom through two world wars in the twentieth century, yet the memory of the Mutiny died hard and lent a certain colour to the whole question of the rights and wrongs of Imperialism. In Cobden's opinion of India, 'its people will prefer to be ruled badly—according to our notions—by its own colour, kith and kin, than submit to the humiliation of being better governed by a succession of transient intruders from the Antipodes'. Whereas Macaulay maintained: 'To have found a great people sunk in the lower depths of slavery and superstition, to have so ruled them as to have made them desirous and capable of all the privileges of citizens would indeed be a title to glory all our own.' The debate still continues, but in the last analysis all argument must be based on one of these two conflicting assumptions.

13

LORD PALMERSTON'S TWO PERIODS OF ADMINISTRATION

1. The first administration, 1855–8

AFTER the Crimean war personality rather than policy remained the decisive factor in English parliamentary history. Lord Derby's Conservatives failed to stand out mainly because their leader seemed utterly uninterested in politics; horses, billiards, and whist were the main topics that his visitors had to discuss with him, and public affairs appeared almost to be taboo. Lord Palmerston himself displayed an eighteenth-century unconcern with matters of domestic legislation. 'Oh, there is really nothing to be done. We cannot go on adding to the Statute book *ad infinitum.*' Both knew that further electoral reform must sooner or later become an issue, but since neither could think of a satisfactory formula that might still avoid universal suffrage, both were perfectly happy to postpone taking a decision.

Palmerston was fortunate in that he had come to power when the worst horrors of the Crimea had already been exposed. He had even survived the period of peace-making—always dangerous ground for any government—and he had by now developed a close friendship with Delane, the editor of *The Times*. Nevertheless, the opposition, although lacking any unity, did include a number of formidable politicians. Disraeli, fuming at Derby's lack of ambition, was longing for another spell of office. Russell, who had had to surrender his place in the Cabinet in July 1855, was another discontented politician. Gladstone, too, was fretting in the wilderness, but whereas Disraeli belonged to a party and was simply hampered by his chief, Gladstone did not yet know where his allegiance lay; a delightfully happy family life at Hawarden, the composition of sermons and the study of

Homer, all provided some consolation, but the satisfaction of political success was still denied him.

John Bright was certainly the greatest of the orators who faced Palmerston. The long attack that he had kept up against the policy of war had eventually led to the break-down of his health and he had had to recuperate abroad. On his return he lost his seat for Manchester, but in 1857 he entered the House again as the member for Birmingham. This change marks an important shift in the centre of active Radicalism in the provincial political scene. The Manchester school had been the focal point in the first half of the century; from now on, the city that was later to elect Joseph Chamberlain as its mayor took the lead. Bright was still unrepentant over his attitude towards the war, and during his first visit to his new constituents made a resounding speech in the Town Hall at Birmingham, denouncing the whole course of British foreign policy since the Glorious Revolution. '. . . this regard for "the liberties of Europe", this care at one time for "the Protestant interests", this excessive love for the "Balance of Power", is neither more nor less than a gigantic system of out-door relief for the aristocracy of Great Britain.'

Before this chequered and highly individualistic opposition Palmerston went on his way with a jaunty optimism. Questions of civil service reform and of cheaper divorce arose. He did not object to them, but the initiative did not come from him. Domestic policy never held the same fascination for him as foreign affairs, and it was events in China that played the most important part in his political career at this time.

The determination of Western merchants to extend their activities in China—contrary to the wishes of the Chinese government—had already led to hostilities earlier in the century. A great market existed for Chinese tea and silks, but the Chinese merchants' main requirement was silver, which commanded a higher value in China than almost anywhere else in the East. This had led to a considerable drain of Indian silver, and an equally accept-able means of exchange had been found in the form of opium, which was cultivated in Bengal. The Chinese government at Pekin had banned its importation, but smuggling increased at an extraordinary rate after 1833, when the East India Company lost its monopoly. In fact, trading conditions were not easy in China. The Chinese government was both suspicious and contemptuous of foreigners and regarded British India as an illustration of the consequences of granting trading privileges. At first, foreign merchants were only allowed to operate through one port—Canton—and even here they might not enter the city, but could only establish their depots outside its walls; nor could they trade on the open market, but only through a single company of Chinese merchants. The Manchu emperors' hold over their dominions was not very firm, however, and local officials at Canton could easily be bribed to allow the importation of opium. By 1837 53% of all Chinese imports consisted of opium, and in 1839 the authorities at Pekin made a determined effort to stamp out this illicit trade. The British surrendered the opium at Canton, but further disputes over the rights of British subjects in Chinese courts led to violence, which in turn brought more demands for compensation, which the Chinese government refused. The outcome was the Opium war. Canton was bombarded, and by the Treaty of Nanking, in 1842, the Chinese agreed that five 'treaty ports', including Shanghai and Canton, should be open to British traders. They were to be free to reside there, and their interests were to be protected by local consuls who would be allowed to negotiate with Chinese officials. Chinese import duties on goods brought in by British merchants were to be limited to 5% and nothing was said about the opium trade. Hong Kong, a barren island at the mouth of the Canton river, was ceded as a military and naval base for the protection of commercial interests. So sure did the British feel of their economic superiority that they had no objection to other European countries enjoying similar privileges, and the Treaty of Nanking thus marks the definite establishment of Western interests in China.

It was doubtful how long restored peace would last. Passive resistance on the part of the Chinese, particularly at Canton, where foreigners were still not allowed into the city, nullified a good deal of the advantage gained, and by 1850 Palmerston was thinking of further governmental intervention. Then, in 1853, an opportunity occurred. The Taiping rebellion against the Imperial Chinese government developed into civil war, and in February 1854 the British government suggested to France that they should persuade the United States to join them in pressing for an extension of commercial privileges in the interior of China. After the fall of Sebastopol there seemed even greater reason, since it was likely that Russia would seek compensation in the Far East for her defeat in the Crimea.

This was the diplomatic position when a couple of incidents in 1856 served to inflame public opinion. A French missionary in the interior was arrested and executed. Later, a sailing-ship, the *Arrow*, flying the British flag, on the strength of the fact that her Chinese owner lived in Hong Kong, was boarded at Canton by Chinese officials and twelve of her crew were arrested. Technically this put the Chinese in the wrong; the British could claim an insult to their flag and a breach of treaty obligations. In fact, local Chinese were making constant use of the protection of the British flag for purposes of smuggling, and the Canton authorities certainly had a case. The British consul at Canton was able to secure the release of the crew of the *Arrow*, but the Chinese refused the demand for an apology. Sir John Bowring, governor of Hong Kong, then reopened the question of trading rights within Canton, and when this came to nothing, Chinese forts on the Canton river were bombarded by a British squadron. The whole problem was obviously a matter for negotiation at a high level, but the uncompromising attitudes of the British Prime Minister and the Chinese Emperor reduced the chances of a settlement. A dispute between the Son of Heaven and Lord 'Pumice-stone' over national prestige was not likely to end in a peaceful solution.

In the Commons a fierce opposition arose towards Palmerston's policy. There had been tender consciences over the 1839-42 Opium war; Peelites, Conservatives, and Radicals all leapt to the attack, and the Commons passed Cobden's vote of censure by a majority of sixteen votes. John Bright, still on holiday in Rome, was delighted at the news of Palmerston's defeat, for here in his opinion was another thoroughly unjustifiable war. But among many of the Radicals a new belligerency was taking the place of the earlier optimistic pacifism. The change is symbolized by Bowring himself, who at one time had been secretary to Jeremy Bentham; and the new view was certainly more consistent than Bright's arguments, since the Chinese war was entirely brought about through unrestricted commercial enterprise and, indeed, far from being wasteful, after it had been won, paid for itself many times over.

Palmerston's immediate reaction to his defeat in the Commons was to ask the Queen to dissolve Parliament, and in the election of 1857 he showed a profound understanding of public opinion by making a simple patriotic appeal to the country. 'He has on his side', Sidney Herbert maintained, 'that which is the strongest element in the mental organisation of all human society, namely the public's national prejudices.' The result was 'a decisive individual triumph to Lord Palmerston', as George Dallas, the American minister in London, put it. About 370 members were returned on whose support Palmerston could to some extent rely.

Lord Elgin was now sent to Hong Kong to negotiate the establishment of some kind of diplomatic mission at Pekin. In the summer of 1857, however, most available troops in the East were needed to deal with the Indian Mutiny, and it was not until much later in the year that any pressure could be brought to bear. After further negotiation had proved fruitless, a combined force of British and French troops was landed outside Canton, and by 30 December the city had been taken. In April 1858 Elgin and the French representative, who by now had been joined by pleni-potentiaries from Russia and the United States, sailed to the mouth of the Peiho river,[1] where, on 20 May, the Taku forts that guarded the approaches were captured. After this the British and French admirals led their force up the river as far as Tientsin, where negotiations were reopened and a treaty was signed on 26 June, arranging for the exchange of diplomatic representatives and throwing open five new cities to British merchants. Meanwhile, the Indian Mutiny [2] had been suppressed, Palmerston having

[1] See map, p. 409.   [2] See pp. 219–24.

refused all outside assistance, maintaining that England must 'win off her own bat'. If a patriotic policy was what the public wanted, Palmerston certainly provided it.

Yet within a year his government had fallen. One underlying factor was a loss of some of his personal ascendancy in the Commons. His sharp dictatorial manner was coming to be resented. Some of his appointments, too, were severely criticized. When Lord Clanricarde was made Lord Privy Seal in December 1857, *The Times*, until now an ally, commented: 'A generation has arisen which requires something more solid in intellect and character than is promised by the previous reputation of the accomplished marquis'. Delane remained on good terms with Palmerston, but in January 1858 Greville noted: 'Delane told me yesterday that he thought they would not remain long in office and that it is time they should go and he ridiculed the idea of its not being practicable to form another government.'

The irony of Palmerston's fall is that for once he failed his public. In January 1858 Napoleon III narrowly escaped an attempt on his life by an Italian revolutionary, Orsini, and when it was discovered that Orsini had been living in London and that his bombs had been made in Birmingham, anglophobia took possession of those in the Emperor's immediate circle. Napoleon regarded their attitude as emotional nonsense, but dared not offend his subjects in their concern for his own safety. Consequently he permitted a fierce protest to be sent to the British government, while at the same time apologizing personally for it to Palmerston. This placed Palmerston in a difficult position. Clearly Napoleon meant no harm, but was the government to act in response to the private apology, which for obvious reasons could not be published, or to the official protest that had stung British national pride? He chose what was theoretically the right course, and decided to co-operate with Napoleon by introducing a Conspiracy Bill which would make foreign refugees plotting such assassinations in England guilty of a felony. This would help Napoleon out of an awkward situation and preserve Anglo-French relations at no cost to Great Britain. The result was fury on the part of the public. Palmerston was jeered at by a mob in

Hyde Park. In the Commons Russell, Graham, and Gladstone all objected to the Bill, and the reputedly pacific Radicals led the attack. 'Truckling to the strong' was the charge laid against Palmerston! On the second reading the Bill was defeated by 234 votes to 215, and two days later the government's decision to resign was announced.

The whole episode is indicative of the growing power of public opinion in the nineteenth century. Over the Chinese affair, in 1857, Palmerston had been at one with the bombastic patriotism of the public and had made no bones about playing upon it. In 1858 he had shown that he was prepared to face defeat in support of a measure that ran counter to those same popular emotions. One must be careful not to make too great a moral issue of the debate; it is probable that Palmerston simply misjudged the strength of the resistance and the outcome was something of a surprise to all sides. Yet the fact remains that his decision was statesmanlike and his opponents had come out with some very odd sentiments in view of their earlier utterances. As during the months before the outbreak of the Crimean war, the force of public opinion had been misguided and inopportune. *Vox populi* is a necessary safeguard against the worst iniquities of unbridled dictatorship; as a decisive factor in the details of diplomacy it can be disastrous.

2. Lord Derby, 1858–9

This time Derby could hardly refuse to form a government. Disraeli became Chancellor of the Exchequer and the Earl of Malmesbury Foreign Secretary, but the most interesting aspect of this Cabinet was the fact that it did not include Gladstone. He was twice approached to join the new Conservative administration, but refused. Personal feeling played a large part in this, for Gladstone would have been loath to serve in the same government as Disraeli. It might have seemed that there was little else to influence him, since, as Gladstone himself said: 'It would be hard to show broad differences of public principle between the government and the bench opposite.' 'I almost went down on my knees to him,' grumbled Disraeli after the failure of the second attempt to win him over. But John Bright had given Gladstone better advice. 'If you remain on our side of the House, you are with the majority,' he wrote to him, 'and no government can be formed without you. You have many friends there . . . and I know nothing that can prevent your being Prime Minister before you approach the age of every other member of the House who has, or can have, any claim to that high office." The mathematics were simple. Gladstone was forty-eight, Palmerston seventy-four, and Russell sixty-six. The groups that supported the two older men would soon need a new leader, and Gladstone's decision to remain in opposition in 1858 can now be seen to have been a crossroads in his career.

The new government's first battle was over the India Bill.[1] This seemed likely at first to be laughed out of the House, but Disraeli was skilful in adopting many of the proposed amendments and the hopes of the Whig–Liberal opposition were disappointed. A Bill was presented for the purification of the Thames, and a law was passed enabling practising Jews to take their seats in the House of Commons. Another row over India arose after a proclamation of Lord Canning's. A two-day adjournment, so that M.P.s might attend the Derby, gave the government time to strengthen its hand, and Derby's constitutionally questionable tactics in threatening to dissolve—only a year after the previous election—coupled with Disraeli's willingness to accept many of the opposition's complaints saved the day. A government with a minority in the Commons could scarcely hope to have a mind of its own.

In one matter Gladstone did cooperate with the government. He agreed to go to the Ionian Islands as Lord High Commissioner Extraordinary to report on a movement among the islanders who were demanding union with Greece. It was an unwise decision, for he accomplished little and his acceptance of an office of profit from the Crown temporarily lost him his seat in the Commons. But the lure of Greece was too much for him and, in any case, his wife had been in poor health and would benefit from the Mediter-

[1] See p. 223.

ranean climate. He drew up a constitution, which the Assembly of Corfu refused to discuss. He was never invited to the mess by the commander of the garrison, and the other British on the islands appeared utterly uninterested in Homer. He returned early in 1859 and was re-elected, unopposed, to his seat for Oxford University.

It was a new turn in foreign affairs that brought Palmerston, Russell, and Gladstone into some definite form of alliance. The 1848 revolutions had ended in failure for the Italian and German nationalists. The period 1859–71 did see the national unification of Italy and Germany, but the creative force was not the liberal parliamentary movements of 1848, but the governmental policy of the kingdoms of Sardinia [1] and Prussia, shaped by two remarkable personalities, Cavour and Bismarck. In Piedmont Cavour was convinced that the expulsion of the Austrians from Italy could be achieved only with the assistance of France. Napoleon was anxious to regain Savoy and Nice, and during conversations at Plombières, in July 1858, a secret bargain was struck between the two men, whereby a confederation of four states under the Presidency of the Pope was to be established. It remained for Cavour to create the circumstances in which Austria would appear the aggressor—a game that Bismarck was to play with great success in the 1860s. A quarrel was provoked, and in 1859 the Austrians made the mistake of presenting Piedmont with an ultimatum. War followed in April, in which Napoleon at once joined his Piedmontese ally. But the French did not fight for long. Two victories over the Austrians at Magenta and Solferino proved costly; the Prussians began to mobilize on the Rhine, and Napoleon grew suspicious of the extent of Cavour's plans. In July 1859 he made a separate peace with the Emperor Francis Joseph at Villafranca, whereby Lombardy, but not Venetia —as originally promised—was granted to Piedmont, and an Italian confederation under the Pope was proposed. This was a disaster for Cavour, but the Italian adventure was not yet over.

In England opinion generally favoured Italian nationalism. Italian refugees had made friends with English literary men and

[1] The capital was Turin and the kingdom will be referred to as Piedmont.

12

politicians, and there was a considerable English colony living in the Italian states. Palmerston and Russell were in agreement over their dislike of the existing governments in most of the states of Italy. Gladstone had spent a holiday in Naples in 1850 and had been appalled at the treatment of political prisoners and the general condition of Neapolitan prisons. On his return he had written to Lord Aberdeen: 'This is the negation of God erected into a system of government', and when it appeared that no effective action could be taken, published his letter as a pamphlet. Derby's government, however, favoured Austria, as did the Court. Malmesbury stated his own view quite simply: 'That Europe should be deluged with blood for the personal ambition of an Italian attorney and a tambour-major, like Cavour and his master, is intolerable.' Thus an issue of some significance had at last arisen in English politics over which opinion was clearly divided.

Derby's government did not survive long after this, but it was a domestic matter that finally brought it down. Disraeli had decided to introduce a Bill for electoral reform. For some time there had been a great majority both inside and outside the House in favour of such a measure in principle. The problem lay in the precise details, and the whole question had degenerated into a game of mental arithmetic, in which each group produced its own answer. Disraeli's scheme was to lower the county occupation franchise to £10, as it stood in the boroughs. Freeholders in the boroughs were to lose their double vote, but a system of 'fancy franchises', as Bright scornfully termed it, was to give the vote to members of the professions and to those with a certain level of savings. Fifteen seats were to be redistributed.

Palmerston had earlier been toying with the idea of something similar to the 'fancy franchises'. He had written that he 'would give much to discover some qualification which would admit some of the best and most intelligent of the working classes'. Both he and Russell, however, joined with the Radicals in demanding an amendment that would lower the borough qualification, and on 31 March, 1859 the government was defeated. A general election followed, but although the Conservatives gained some seats, they still did not have a majority in the House, and on 10 June the government was defeated again, this time on a vote of confidence.

On the following day the Queen asked Lord Granville to form an administration, but when this proved impossible there was only one man to whom she could turn. A new alliance had been in the making during the past few weeks, aided to a large extent by the excitement over Italy. Palmerston and Russell were friends again, and together they negotiated an agreement with the Radicals on the understanding that a new Reform Bill would be introduced lowering the borough franchise, and that Great Britain would remain strictly neutral in the Italian conflict. Palmerston became Prime Minister for the second time, with Russell as Foreign Secretary, Sidney Herbert Secretary for War, and Gladstone Chancellor of the Exchequer. Of the Radicals, Milner Gibson went to the Board of Trade and Charles Villiers became President of the Poor Law Board. It was a new coalition out of which a unified Liberal party was to emerge at last.

3. The second administration, 1859-65

A. FOREIGN AFFAIRS

As Prime Minister, Palmerston continued to interest himself principally in the foreign scene, but although these next few years saw some of the most significant developments in the history of the nineteenth century, Great Britain played a relatively small part in them. Compared with events in Europe and America, the Chinese affair proved relatively straightforward. The Treaty of Tientsin, which Lord Elgin had negotiated in 1858, had not been respected by the Chinese government, and in 1859 British and French envoys were unexpectedly attacked on the Peiho river and had to withdraw with heavy casualties. There was only one possible outcome. The French were determined to act, and Palmerston could not allow them to go in alone. Both governments were well aware of Russian ambitions in the Far East, where the Tsar had already established a diplomatic mission at Pekin, and it was widely believed that the Chinese had received

Russian military aid. 'The barbarian leaders Elgin and Gros have again appeared off our coast,' ran the Chinese Emperor's edict in 1850, and the new Anglo-French expedition soon reached Pekin. One ugly incident marked the bitter antagonism between East and West. A group of British and French officers and correspondents, who had been sent to negotiate under a flag of truce, were captured by the Chinese. Some of them were tortured to death, and the Europeans' angry reprisal was the burning of the Chinese Emperor's Summer Palace to the ground. The treaty of 1858 was now ratified, whereby British and French diplomatic missions were established at Pekin, and when, a little later, trading agreements were made with Japan, a closed country during the previous two hundred years, it was clear that the Far East was well on the way to becoming one more European sphere of influence.

Meanwhile, a new chapter in the Italian adventure had opened. After making peace with the Austrians at Villafranca in 1859, Napoleon had begun to have second thoughts. Piedmont had at least acquired Lombardy, while he had gained nothing. Villafranca had not, in fact, brought things to a halt in Italy. The terms of the peace had included the restoration of the princes who had fled from the duchies immediately to the south of the Po, but here the situation was still unsettled, since the princes did not return and the pro-Piedmontese interests rapidly formed governments to agitate for inclusion within Piedmont. Napoleon hoped that a separate kingdom of Central Italy might be created out of these, but the thought of Savoy and Nice still rankled. He even reopened the question with the Piedmontese Foreign Secretary, Dabormida, but was simply reminded that French promises over Venetia had not been kept. Obviously the possibility of a new bargain was emerging—Savoy and Nice to France in return for the inclusion of the duchies to the south of the Po within Piedmont.

The problem for Piedmont was to prevent intervention in Italy on the part of the great Powers; the problem for Great Britain and France was that neither trusted the other not to make capital out of the Italian situation. Palmerston and Russell had

Legend:

- - - - - Boundary of German Empire 1871
- +++++ Boundary of North German Confederation 1866-1871
- -·-·-· Boundary of German Confederation 1815=66
- ······ Boundary of Kingdom of Italy 1861

SWEDEN AND NORWAY

DENMARK

COPENHAGEN

HELIGOLAND

SCHLESWIG

HOLSTEIN

NETHERLANDS

HANOVER

BELGIUM

PRUSSIA

BERLIN

P R U S S I A

RUSSIA

POLAND

SEDAN

METZ

LORRAINE

KÖNIGGRÄTZ

ALSACE

A U S T R I A N

VIENNA

BUDAPEST

E M P I R E

SWITZERLAND

SAVOY

PIEDMONT

LOMBARDY

VENETIA

NICE

GENOA

TUSCANY

ROME

NAPLES

SARDINIA

KINGDOM OF THE TWO SICILIES

1830

SCALE

0   100   200   300

English Miles

4. CENTRAL EUROPE AND ITALY, 1848–71

no wish to destroy Austria's position in Europe, but both sympathized with the Italian cause and favoured the annexation of the duchies. Victoria and Albert, however, had little liking for Italian aspirations, and a new dispute developed between the Queen and 'those two dreadful old men', her Prime Minister and Foreign Secretary. Russell preached a little sermon to the Queen with the Revolution of 1688 as his text, and, in January 1860, suggested a four-point programme to Napoleon, which included a plebiscite in Central Italy and non-interference by France and Great Britain. Napoleon was agreeable, provided that a similar plebiscite might be held in Savoy and Nice. Palmerston and Russell had no wish for this last, and if Cavour had now sided with Great Britain he might have avoided having to give up Savoy and Nice. But he knew that France was the more effective ally against Austria, and, in March, came to terms with Napoleon, who had grown suspicious of British interest in Cavour. There followed a series of plebiscites which confirmed the inclusion of the central states within Piedmont and the acquisition of Savoy and Nice by France.

The French gains had now brought British suspicions to a head, but it is clear that neither Parliament nor the government was prepared to take warlike action. Then there suddenly opened the most colourful episode in the whole story of Italian unification. In May Garibaldi sailed from Genoa with his redshirts and landed in Sicily to assist the rebels there against their Neapolitan rulers. By July the island was his. Cavour, watching from the north, had refused to give his official support to Garibaldi and, if things went badly, could still disown him. But the greater danger was that the Powers of Europe would intervene and that at a subsequent Congress Cavour's work of the previous year would be undone. The problem was how to hold the ring. He was saved by the general mistrust that existed among the Powers. Austria not unnaturally suspected further French designs. So did Palmerston and Russell, believing that Napoleon was bargaining for Genoa. Napoleon, on the other hand, imagined that the British Cabinet hoped to gain Sicily as a naval base. Thus the great Powers watched one another, each holding back from making the first move that would give the other an excuse to intrude. Meanwhile, in southern Italy the Bourbon King could do little to rally his country against the invader. In August Garibaldi crossed to the mainland, and so slight was the resistance that he covered the last part of his advance on Naples by train. The Powers still held back; even Victor Emmanuel's thrust through the Papal States to head Garibaldi off from marching on Rome did not break the deadlock. On 27 October Russell created a sensation by sending to Hudson, the British minister at Turin, a dispatch in which he openly supported the Italians' demand for self-government. For Cavour this was a moment of joy. Hudson described how 'tears were standing in his eyes. Behind your dispatch he saw the Italy of his dreams, the Italy of his hopes, the Italy of his policy.' The Austrian government did not fail to make the customary reference to British rule in Ireland, but they clearly meant to make no resistance. Plebiscites followed, and by the beginning of 1861 a united Italy had been born, lacking only Venetia and the region about Rome.

The American Civil war broke out within a few months of the meeting of the first Italian Parliament at Turin. Anglo-American relations had been one of the most successful aspects of British diplomacy in the nineteenth century. The sane statesmanlike atmosphere in which the discussions over the Canadian frontier had been undertaken by Castlereagh had resulted in virtual demilitarization of the Great Lakes, and the 49th parallel had been accepted as the boundary line from the Lake of the Woods to the Rocky Mountains. The eastern and western extremities of the frontier had led to greater dissension. It proved difficult, at first, to reach agreement over the line between Maine and New Brunswick. Later, the land to the west of the Rockies, between California and Alaska, known generally as Oregon, became an issue, owing to the number of Canadian and American settlers attracted to that region. The Pacific trade was important, and the British Hudson's Bay Company and American business interests were each anxious for a favourable settlement. For some time negotiations were fruitless. The British Cabinet wanted the line as far south as the Columbia river; American Northern opinion wanted it as far north as 54° 40', and, in 1844, James Polk was partly helped to the Presidency by the cry: 'Fifty-four forty or fight!' Finally, in 1846, Polk took the risk of angering Northern sentiment by agreeing to a compromise, whereby the 49th parallel frontier was to be continued to the Pacific, leaving Canada in possession of Vancouver Island.[1]

The outbreak of the American Civil war in 1861 presented the British government with a different type of problem in its relations with the United States. The election of Abraham Lincoln as President, in November 1860, had prompted seven States of the Deep South at the beginning of 1861 to secede from the Union and to form their own Confederacy under the Presidency of Jefferson Davis. On 12 April, at dawn, the guns of Charleston harbour opened fire on the Federal Fort Sumter; three days later Lincoln issued an appeal for 75,000 volunteers, whereupon four more States left the Union to join the Confederacy. The great conflict that earlier American statesmen had feared had come at last.

British opinion was utterly divided. There was no liking for the slavery that the Southerners hoped to protect. But Lincoln had made it clear that slavery was not the issue. His policy was 'free soil'—simply no extension of slavery outside the existing slave States; he had never been an abolitionist, much as he hated slavery, and even if he had been, it would have been impossible for him to abolish slavery constitutionally throughout the Union. Even after hostilities had begun, he hesitated to proclaim emancipation, for fear of antagonizing those slave States that had not joined the Confederacy. The preservation of the Union was the cause on which Lincoln took his stand.

Thus the emotional impact of *Uncle Tom's Cabin* was not entirely decisive in shaping British reactions to the war. If certain States wished to withdraw from one form of government, why should they be prevented? The Declaration of Independence had said as much. The upper classes naturally preferred the Southern gentleman to the hard-headed Yankee business man. British

[1] See map, p. 367.

shippers saw a chance of capturing Southern carrying trade, which had been in the hands of the Northerners. British manufacturers knew that the Southerners hated tariffs and hoped that the new Confederacy might mean an extension of the area of free trade. It was the British working classes of the industrial regions who most wholeheartedly supported the North, since many had relations who had emigrated to America, settling mostly in the Northern States, where greater opportunities existed. Gradually, however, upper-class opinion also began to swing towards the North, particularly after Lincoln's Proclamation of Emancipation in September 1862—a decisive factor in the hardening of neutral opinion.

The policy that the British government hoped to be able to follow was simple enough. 'For God's sake', said Russell in the Commons, 'let us, if possible, keep out of it.' This required, amongst other things, a careful choice of diplomatic language. A state of belligerency undoubtedly existed, but what the South regarded as war between two independent countries was, in the eyes of the North, simply a widespread rebellion. Seward, Lincoln's Secretary of State, was particularly difficult and, just before the outbreak of hostilities, had suggested fomenting trouble with some European country, possibly Great Britain, as a means of keeping the States united. There were, too, difficulties over the personal feelings of individual members of the British Cabinet. There was a striking example of this in October 1862, when Gladstone, speaking in the Town Hall at Newcastle, placed the government in an embarrassing situation. 'We may be for or against the South. But there is no doubt that Jefferson Davis, and other leaders of the South, have made an Army. They are making, it appears, a Navy. And they have made—what is more than either—they have made a nation.' This was the very thing that Lincoln denied them the right to make. It was perhaps, the most indiscreet and ill-judged comment that Gladstone ever made, and although the government dissociated itself from what he had said, it was hardly surprising that the American minister in London imagined that Great Britain was about to give her active support to the South.

The major difficulties were bound to arise over the command of the sea and British dependence on Southern cotton. The first incident, the *Trent* affair, was largely a question of prestige. Jefferson Davis had dispatched two representatives, James Mason and John Slidell, to London in the autumn of 1861 in order to put the Southern case, but while they were crossing the Atlantic in a British ship, the *Trent*, a Northern sloop, the *San Jacinto*, stopped the *Trent* and took off the two Southerners, who were brought to New York. Feelings on both sides of the Atlantic at once reached fever pitch. Congress asked the President to give the captain of the *San Jacinto* a gold medal. 'Load him with services of plate and swords of the cunningest and costliest art,' said the *New York Times*. British public opinion was outraged. The government decided to give Washington seven days in which to hand over the prisoners with an apology, and arrangements went ahead for reinforcing the garrison in Canada. Fortunately moderating influences were at work. Prince Albert, now on his death-bed, was able to persuade Russell to tone down his dispatch to America, and in Washington Lincoln was persuaded to give way after four hours of argument at a Cabinet meeting on Christmas Day. Mason and Slidell were handed over—without an apology—and proceeded to England, where they actually met with little success.

The second incident was more serious in its implications. The imposition of a naval blockade of the coastline of the Confederate States was an essential part of Northern strategy, and in 1861 a Southern agent in England commissioned the building of two ships which were to be used against this blockade. It was strictly contrary to the Foreign Enlistment Act of 1819 for such ships to be equipped in a British port, but the Northern minister in London, Charles Francis Adams, had considerable difficulty in establishing positive proof of the intention that lay behind the commissioning of these vessels. As a result, no action was taken, and the first of them, the *Florida*, sailed safely from Liverpool in March 1862. The second, known later as the *Alabama*, was not launched until May 1862. By July Adams had further evidence which he thought would force the British courts to detain the ship from sailing, but owing to a number of unforeseen delays the *Alabama* was able to slip out on a trial trip, from which she did not return. For the next two years she played havoc with Northern shipping, and the American government felt justified in presenting the bill to the British. Russell refused to pay, but saw to it that no more armed ships left the British yards to take part in the war at sea. The dispute over reparation dragged on until 1872, when it was decided at Geneva that Great Britain should pay 15 million dollars in compensation to the American government,[1] a sum which American historians have since admitted was excessive.

But disputes over national prestige and the infringement of the laws of neutrality were of slight significance compared with the economic consequences of the Civil war. The Southern States had supplied Great Britain with four-fifths of her raw cotton, and the livelihood of a fifth of the English population was bound up in some way with the cotton industry. The South had always been proudly conscious of their place in world trade. 'England with her millions of people and billions upon billions of pounds sterling,' said Senator Stephens of Georgia in 1857, 'could not survive six months without it.' 'Cotton is king,' boasted Senator Hammond of South Carolina a year later. It was this confidence that caused the Confederacy to hold back in sending the 1861 crop to England before the Northern blockade became effective. Scarcity of raw cotton, they thought, would reveal to England her dependence on the South and encourage her to break the blockade. It would also ensure a high price when the cotton eventually became available.

The plan failed. The 1860 crop had been so heavy that the mills could first of all work off their surplus stocks. It was not until the winter of 1861-2 that destitution faced the workers, as one mill after another came to a standstill, and special measures had to be taken for the organization of parish relief and public works. Other industries, however, particularly shipping, flourished. There was considerable trade with the North, despite the depredations of the *Alabama* and the *Florida*, and few

[1] See p. 289.

business men seriously advocated the breaking of the blockade, which could only result in a naval war with the North. Palmerston was active in urging the development of other sources of raw cotton, and by 1863 supplies from the East began to bring the mills to life again.

The last years of the war saw no new crisis which might force the government to join in the hostilities. On the Continent, however, fresh developments were taking place of far higher significance for the future of Great Britain than any upheaval in the New World. On 24 September, 1862 Bismarck became Prime Minister of Prussia. At first his main task was to manage the recalcitrant Prussian Parliament for his King, but early in 1863 a revolt of the Poles against their Russian rulers brought about a diplomatic situation, in which the chancelleries of Europe had their first glimpse of the remarkable mind that was to create a new destiny for Germany. Bismarck's reaction to the revolt was to dispatch General Alvensleben to St. Petersburg to conclude a convention, whereby Prussian and Russian military authorities would cooperate in suppressing the Poles. This satisfied personal inclinations as well as making a shrewd stroke at the French, since neither Bismarck nor the German liberals had any love for the Polish nationalists. Until now there had existed an *entente* between France and Russia, which the Alvensleben Convention helped to tear asunder. French Radicals and clericals gave vent to noisy indignation at the treatment of the Poles. In Great Britain politicians, the Press, and public opinion all supported them, and on 21 February the French Foreign Minister suggested that Britain and France should present a joint note of protest to Berlin.

It was perfectly natural that the British and French public should enthuse over the idea of Polish nationalism, yet enthusiasm without action was bound to be of little use. The final achievement of Italian unification had been possible only because none of the great Powers had intervened. But in Poland some sort of national independence could be achieved only if the Powers *did* intervene. Both in 1860 and 1863 joint intervention was ruled out through mutual mistrust. It was the old dilemma. Great Britain could not intervene effectively alone; yet if she moved with the French, Napoleon would occupy the Prussian Rhineland. Thus no concerted action was made against the Prussian and Russian governments. Protests and notes filled the air, but the Russians knew that they could safely ignore them, and continued to shoot and deport the troublesome Poles. Even Napoleon's proposal for a Congress in the autumn of 1863 met with no success, mainly because he followed it up with a public statement that in his view the settlement of 1815 was no longer in effect. This frightened off most countries and the British government was provoked to send a curt reminder that 'the provisions of the treaty of 1815 are in full force.'

A similar British policy of threats unsupported by action was to give Bismarck a far greater triumph over Schleswig-Holstein. Technically these two duchies to the south of Jutland were politically independent; the link that existed between them and Denmark was a purely personal one, since the Danish King ruled over them simply in his capacity as their duke. In Holstein the population was predominantly German and the duchy was included within the German Confederation. In Schleswig the population was a mixture of Danes and Germans, and the growing nationalist feeling of the nineteenth century was bound to produce incompatible demands from both sides. Danish policy in this dispute tended towards splitting the duchies, in the hope of incorporating Schleswig within the kingdom. German nationalists maintained that the duchies were indissolubly united. The significance of the German claim was that the Salic Law, ruling out succession through a female line, applied in the duchies, but not in the kingdom of Denmark. Thus it was only a question of waiting for a Danish king to succeed through a female line, when it might be possible to engineer the transfer of the duchies to a German prince.[1]

In January 1848, when Frederick VII succeeded to the Danish throne, it had seemed that their hopes might soon be fulfilled, since Frederick had no male heir. The German nationalists had a German prince to hand, Christian, Duke of Augustenburg, who

[1] See map, p. 237.

claimed that on Frederick's death the duchies should pass to him. Frederick decided that the moment for action had come, and taking his stand on an old Danish claim that the Salic Law did not apply in Schleswig, incorporated Schleswig directly under the Danish Crown. The Powers were far too occupied with their own affairs in 1848 to intervene, and when the Prussians came to the assistance of the forces under Christian of Augustenburg, they succeeded in entering Jutland. Later the Prussians withdrew, and in 1850 the Danes drove the other German troops out of the duchies. By now, however, the Powers were free to consider these new developments, and since, in the main, 1848 had ended in the victory of the old order, their only desire in the Danish question was to restore the *status quo*. This was achieved by the Treaty of London in 1852; the Danish army left Schleswig, and it was agreed that on Frederick's death the succession to the Danish Crown should pass to Christian of Glücksburg, who would rule also as Duke of Schleswig-Holstein, which would remain a separate political entity. The Duke of Augustenburg abandoned his claim in return for financial compensation.

Frederick, however, had not given up the hope of incorporating Schleswig within the kingdom and, in March 1863, he drew up a Patent aimed at putting a wedge between the two duchies. In future, while no law could come into force in Holstein without consent of its Estates, their opposition could not prevent a law passed by the constitutional bodies of Denmark and Schleswig from taking effect. This was, in fact, contrary to the Treaty of London, since the Danes had promised 'not to incorporate Schleswig with the kingdom', and also that no steps 'leading towards that end should be taken'. In November Frederick died, and was succeeded by Christian of Glücksburg, who had to decide whether to continue with his predecessor's policy. Danish public opinion left him no option. The March Patent was ratified, and it remained to be seen how the rest of Europe would react.

In 1852 the restoration of the *status quo* had been achieved by the concerted action of the Powers; if the Danes were to be made to withdraw their scheme, similar action would be needed now.

There was, however, little likelihood of this. France and Russia had fallen out over the Polish rebellion. Austria was already dangerously isolated. Great Britain was still highly suspicious of French designs on the Rhineland. If concerted action was unlikely, what were the other possibilities? One was simple enough. Frederick, Duke of Augustenburg, whose father had renounced his claim to the duchies in 1852, now made a new bid for them. German nationalist sentiment was with him and the German Confederation had already ordered military action in Holstein. There was another more sinister possibility. Prussia wanted to acquire the great port of Kiel, and Bismarck was already hoping to turn the crisis to his own advantage.

Bismarck afterwards regarded the Schleswig-Holstein affair as his diplomatic masterpiece. He took his stand on the principle of legitimacy. He would have nothing to do with the claims of the Duke of Augustenburg, since that would only arouse the suspicions of the Powers that another 1848 was in the making. He sided, not with German nationalism, but with the maintenance of the treaty of 1852, and in January 1864 he signed a treaty with Austria whereby they agreed to act together to ensure the fulfilment of the 1852 agreement. Thus, if he was to have an excuse for occupying the duchies in conjunction with Austria, it was essential that the Danes should persist in their claim. And it was here that he was so remarkably assisted by the failure of British diplomacy.

There were two lines that Palmerston and Russell could have taken. They could have demanded that the Danes should withdraw. This would have kept Great Britain in the right and, if the Danes had agreed, Bismarck would have been a long way from his objective. Or they could have sided with the Danes and at once taken measures to gain a Continental ally, without whom threats would be useless. In fact, they made the worst of both worlds. British public opinion was strongly in favour of Denmark, and in July 1863 Palmerston announced in the Commons: 'We are convinced—I am convinced at least—that if any violent attempt were made to overthrow those rights [of Denmark] and interfere with that independence, those who made the attempt would find in the result that it would not be Denmark alone with which they would have to contend.' *The Times* took up the same cry, and the Danes were sure that they did not stand alone. But one thing was lacking. Great Britain had no ally with whom she could act on behalf of the Danes. Palmerston believed that France would keep Prussia in her place, but after the summary rejection of Napoleon's proposal for a European Congress there seemed no chance of a positive Anglo-French alliance.

No Anglo-Danish treaty was signed. By the end of 1863 the British government was even trying to persuade Denmark to give way, but the Danes would not withdraw their claim. On 1 February, 1864 a combined Austro-Prussian force invaded the duchies and occupied them in under three weeks. Gradually Bismarck's plot unfolded. The invasion had been made ostensibly in defence of the 1852 treaty. But now a state of war existed with Denmark. This, declared Bismarck, meant that, so far as Prussia and Austria were concerned, the treaty was null and void. Frantically the British Cabinet looked for allies. Palmerston's hope that France would never allow this invasion had been disappointed, since Napoleon, conscious of his isolation, was turning towards friendship with Prussia. A conference to settle the whole question without further fighting was held at London in May, but Bismarck, no longer bound by the 1852 agreement, saw to it that none of the proposed solutions were acceptable to the Danes. The conference broke down, as he intended. The war continued, and the Prussian and Austrian forces drove on into Jutland. Last attempts to create an Anglo-French alliance failed, and on 25 June the British Cabinet decided by a narrow majority not to enter into a war alone for the sake of the duchies. In July the Danes signed an armistice, and on 1 August a preliminary peace treaty handed the duchies over to Austria and Prussia.

The weakness of British diplomacy in this crisis is easy to criticize, and home and foreign opinion was quick to do so. Certainly there was little excuse for making threats that could not be carried out, and the Danes might well feel that they had been badly let down. In this lay the fundamental mistake of British policy. There are, however, two points that must be put along-side the general condemnation. First, the diplomatic assessments that had made it impossible for Great Britain to find an ally had not been inaccurate. It was right to mistrust Napoleon; intervention with a French army might well have given him some part of the Rhineland. Russian support might have been obtained, but only in return for allowing Russian warships into the Black Sea. To a British Prime Minister and Foreign Secretary in the 1860s either of these dangers from France or Russia was of greater significance than the question of Schleswig-Holstein, and from a short-term view, at least, Palmerston and Russell were correct in holding back. Second, the Danish policy itself was mistaken. They had put themselves in the wrong; all Bismarck's diplomacy had been based on this. They had refused to withdraw afterwards, al-though they had no firm alliance with any other Power. State-ments in the Press and the House of Commons did not constitute a definite diplomatic agreement, and the Danes had as much oppor-tunity as Bismarck to see that Great Britain would not act without a Continental ally. 'You are not 70 millions, as we are,' the Russian Foreign Minister had warned them in August 1863, but they had taken the risk of acting alone, and in international politics the stakes are always high.

Palmerston died in October 1865, a few months before the out-break of the Austro-Prussian war, which was to shift the focal point of power in Central Europe from Vienna to Berlin. Palmer-ston and Russell had continued to be governed by the assumptions implicit in the settlement of 1815; they had little understanding of the new force whose emergence upset this basic pattern of diplomacy and, as a consequence, Great Britain had no part to play in the process that was to culminate in the creation of the German Empire in 1871.

B. DOMESTIC AFFAIRS

It is Gladstone's work as Chancellor of the Exchequer that dominates the domestic scene during Palmerston's second ad-ministration, and it was evident to many, including Palmerston, that here was a personality who was beginning to stride ahead of his contemporaries. 'Wait till I'm dead,' remarked the Prime Minister. 'If Gladstone gets my place, you'll see some strange things.' William Ewart Gladstone had by this time had nearly thirty years of Parliamentary experience. Chastened and matured by the storms of his own conscience and the vicissitudes of political life, he was at heart unchanged. The intellectual power which he had shown at Oxford was apparent in the extraordinary skill with which he mastered the financial complexity of his Budgets; the moral earnestness which at one time had almost turned him to the Church was still marked in his approach to every political problem. 'He is not frivolous enough for me,' one lady said of him, and the photographs that exist of that long, slightly gaunt face, the deep furrows from the nose to mouth, and the piercing eyes make it possible to understand her complaint.

Gladstone's Budgets from 1860 to 1864 stand as the completion of Sir Robert Peel's work. 'He was a rigid economist! Oh, he was a most rigid economist!' Gladstone had once remarked of his master, and the same could be said of the disciple. His main aims were, as in his Budget of 1853, to destroy the relics of Protection and to abolish the income tax. This could be accomplished only by a reduction of government expenditure. During his earlier period as Chancellor the Crimean war had ruined most of his hopes, and he was determined that this should not happen again. The times did not make it easy for him. Panic over French military power, the American Civil war, and Bismarck's schemes for acquiring Schleswig-Holstein from Denmark, all threatened to take the country into a war which would have wrecked his plans once again, and it was hardly any wonder that there should have been exchanges of long and angry letters between the Chancellor and the Prime Minister.

In 1860 his greatest obstacle was the fear of France. Napoleon had at last gained Savoy and Nice, and his interest in the plans for a Suez Canal and the construction of iron-clad ships only strengthened British suspicions, which had been awoken in 1858 during a visit of the Queen and the Prince Consort to France to attend a naval review at Cherbourg. Gladstone believed that a commercial treaty between the two countries might ease the tension, and Cobden was dispatched to Paris to negotiate this. By this treaty of 1860 import duties on British coal and manufactured goods and on French wines and brandy were reduced, and these readjustments had to find their place in the Budget of that year. In fact, Gladstone went further than the requirements of the treaty demanded, and so reduced the tariffs that there remained only forty-eight articles that were still protected. It was a great triumph for him, marred only by two minor failures. The Chinese war and the demands of the Navy for iron-clads forced him to raise the income tax to tenpence. He failed also to repeal the excise duty on paper. This would have meant a loss of revenue of £1¼ million a year and, in addition to this, the upper classes were horrified at the thought of the emergence of a cheap Press. The Bill did pass the Commons by nine votes, but it was rejected by the House of Lords. Palmerston and the Queen were delighted. Gladstone stormed at such interference with a money Bill, but, except for the Radicals, he gained little support from the government benches. Prime Minister and Chancellor argued bitterly against each other in the Commons, and Derby and Disraeli began to negotiate with Palmerston. For a moment it looked as if political anarchy had returned.

Gladstone, however, had an answer. Aberdeen had once said of him: 'Ah! but he is terrible on the rebound.' In 1861 he introduced an innovation in financial legislation, which has continued until this day. Instead of putting forward a series of separate Bills, as had been the practice in the past, he compressed all the necessary legislation for the Budget of 1861, including the repeal of the paper duties, into a single Bill. The Lords might reject but not amend a Finance Bill, and for the moment Gladstone's innovation achieved its object. It was not until 1909 that the Lords dared to throw out an entire Budget—and then only at heavy cost to themselves.[1]

The removal of duties produced favourable results. National expenditure dropped lower with each year, and Gladstone could use the surplus to make further reductions of tax. In 1863 income tax came down to sevenpence; in the following year he announced

[1] See pp. 417–21.

his hope that it might yet be brought as low as fivepence, and by
1866 he had got it down to fourpence. Such a policy of economy
was bound to bring him into continued conflict with Palmerston,
and it may be asked whether the lowering of taxation was not
gained at too great a price. Many of the necessary sanitary
reforms in the services were held back by the tight-fistedness of
the Treasury—in spite of the lessons of the Crimean war. On the
Continent new military machines were being forged, and although the Admiralty was able to make some headway in the
1860s in developing iron ships with heavier guns, the smallness
of Great Britain's forces was a decisive factor in the violent
changes in the balance of power on the Continent during the next
twenty years.

The Radicals, at least, could be satisfied with the Chancellor's
work. In one respect, however, the government failed them.
Electoral reform played little part in this second administration of
Palmerston's. A Bill had been introduced shortly after he took
office creating a £10 occupation franchise in the counties and a £6
franchise in the boroughs. Palmerston, conscious of his pledge
to the Radicals, hoped that it might succeed, although he felt
that it went too far. Gladstone favoured it, since the new electorate that it envisaged would probably have little interest in
armaments. But its terms only really appealed to the left wing of
the Liberals, and it was almost lost from sight amidst the excitement over Gladstone's 1860 Budget. Eventually it perished
through indifference rather than direct hostility, being withdrawn
by the government in June of that year.

The question made its reappearance in 1864, when a private
member's Bill was introduced in the Commons. During the
second reading Gladstone expressed another of those disturbing
views that punctuated his career at this time. 'I venture to say that
every man who is not presumably incapacitated by some consideration of personal fitness or of political danger, is morally
entitled to come within the pale of the constitution.' Palmerston
was not present on this occasion, but there followed another
angry exchange of letters between them. 'I entirely deny', wrote
the Prime Minister, 'that every sane and not disqualified man has

a moral right to vote.' Afterwards Gladstone modified his remarks, and in any case the Bill was rejected.

But Gladstone's statement had not been a momentary aberration. It pointed significantly to the new direction of his thoughts, and the full consequences were underlined in July 1865, when, at the general election, he lost his seat for Oxford University. It was not only his unguarded reference to electoral reform that brought this about. It had been noticed that he had recently been turning to the leaders of the Nonconformist groups; in March he had criticized the position of the Anglican Church in Ireland, and the introduction of the postal vote made it possible for clerical graduates throughout the country to ensure that William Gladstone should no longer be the man to represent them. Gladstone turned to South Lancashire, and in the Free Trade Hall at Manchester announced to an audience of six thousand: 'At last, my friends, I come amongst you. And I come . . . unmuzzled.' He won the seat, and the general result of the election was a slightly increased majority for the government.

Before the new Parliament assembled, however, the Prime Minister died on 18 October. The individualism of Palmerston has inevitably aroused extreme opinions of him both among contemporaries and historians. He has been accused of arrogant nationalism in foreign policy and of having no policy at all in domestic affairs. Certainly, when the events of the century may be viewed as a whole, there is an enormous gulf between the age of Palmerston and the succeeding decades. Since his day party doctrine has become an accepted feature of English political life, but can he be blamed if he has no place in such a pattern? In many ways he was the last of the eighteenth-century politicians. He had principles, but no doctrine. He had been active in support of many reforms—Catholic emancipation in the face of his own party, Free Trade, Parliamentary reform, and the suppression of the international Slave Trade—always as a consequence of his own feelings. His belief in constitutional Parliamentary government was perfectly genuine; it was in no way inconsistent with a desire to preserve the existing order of society, and there was nothing hypocritical in his dislike of the despotisms of Central and Eastern

Europe. His patriotic utterances may have been bigoted, yet it was these that won him his great support from the public—the most modern note in his career; and in fact there was little that was positively aggressive in his foreign policy, since it was based simply on an awareness of the dangers of Russian or French expansion, and he had no interest in any further territorial acquisitions for Great Britain. Indeed, the most serious criticism that can be made of his government is that it was not aggressive enough over the emergent power of Prussia, and even here Palmerston would have intervened in the Schleswig-Holstein war if he had not been outvoted by his Cabinet.

Thus 1865 points to the approaching end of the mid-century period. Palmerston dead—Gladstone unmuzzled; the moment had almost come for the fulfilment of Palmerston's prediction.

14

THE 1860s

1. The vices and virtues of Victorian England

POLITICAL liberty and social restriction—these are the two characteristics of the Victorian world that particularly struck foreigners who visited England in the middle of the nineteenth century. Political liberty was no innovation; it rested on centuries of historical development, but for refugees from many parts of the Continent, such as Alexander Herzen, who came to England in the 1850s from Tsarist Russia, it was a condition of life that never ceased to astonish. 'Until I came to England', wrote Herzen, 'the appearance of a police officer in a house where I was living always produced an indefinable disagreeable feeling, and I was at once morally on my guard against an enemy. In England a policeman at your door merely adds to your sense of security.' The wider implications of this attitude towards the State were summed up by the *Edinburgh Review* in 1861, when it boasted: 'it is the distinctive feature of this country, a feature of which we are proud, that we conduct our business ourselves and without intervention by the State.'

This atmosphere of liberalism appealed strongly to another foreigner, Hippolyte Taine, who published his *Notes on England* in 1872, although his impressions were formed for the most part during his visit ten years earlier. But Taine, like Herzen, also had criticisms to make. The climate depressed him; the gulf between rich and poor seemed to him greater than in France and, what for an educated Frenchman was the most damning of all, 'le roman, la critique, l'art, la philosophie, la grande curiosité ne subissent pas chez nous les entraves que la religion, la morale et les convenances officielles leur imposent de l'autre côté de la Manche.'

The spirit of which Taine became aware was a late manifestation

of Puritanism in English life of the 1860s—a tyranny of respectability. It is true that some of the features that have been
ascribed to this period had been customary for centuries—the large
families, the awesome position of the father, and the reduction of
the womenfolk to a position of innocuous uselessness. Yet there
is an almost suffocating sobriety about English social life in the
mid-Victorian period that has an atmosphere entirely of its own.
Religious propriety was the standard by which all action was to be
judged; thus, when the directors of the Eastern Counties Railway
wished to run Sunday excursions from London to Cambridge,
the Vice-Chancellor of the University hastened to point out that
'such a proceeding would be as displeasing to Almighty God as it
is to the Vice-Chancellor of the University of Cambridge'.
Volumes of sermons were best sellers; any kind of scandal meant
social death, and when Edward, Prince of Wales, became involved
in a celebrated divorce case in 1870, he was hissed by the crowd
on the race-course at Epsom. Pleasure was wicked; social conformity and hard work were the ideals of everyday life. It was
small wonder that much Victorian painting should descend to the
level of efficiently executed story-telling, that Victorian furniture
should be ugly and uncomfortable, and that Victorian architecture, despite a rich tradition, should produce only a grandiose
over-ornamented uniformity. Even the Victorian novel, vigorous
and colourful as it was, avoided any reminder of Original Sin;
The Hunting of the Snark was the nearest that the Victorian could
ever come to outrageous fantasy, and it is a significant comment
that the Victorian civilization is the only one in the history of the
world to have produced an entire literature for children.

The extraordinary wealth of the Victorian age had by now begun to create a bewildering diversity of classes in society. The
Radical industrialist, always close to his factory workers, was
being succeeded by a new generation of City financiers who dealt
purely in money and whose political sympathies were to move
away from Liberalism and eventually to become an important
element in a revived Tory party. The Limited Liability Acts
brought about a widening gulf between ownership and management, and as the *rentier* class grew, so too did the fashionable

terraces of Kensington and Bayswater and the seaside towns of Bournemouth and Eastbourne. The world of Galsworthy's Forsytes was taking shape. At the other end of the scale the position of the very poor was only slightly and gradually improved by these changes, as Taine noted in his descriptions of great areas of slumland. Between the two extremes, however, the new wealth was everywhere having its effect. The cult of sea-bathing was taken up by thousands, who in earlier decades could never have afforded such holidays, offering opportunities for an army of hotel and boarding-house proprietors and for the shrewd business instinct of Thomas Cook. The professional classes were acquiring a new status; the fortunes of the Baines' family, described by Arnold Bennett in *The Old Wives' Tale*, are a revealing counterpart to the Forsytes at the shop-keeper level in provincial life, and domestic service in the houses of the expanding upper middle class was virtually becoming a profession in itself.

Thus far, the Victorian world might seem to be simply one of complacent and prosperous materialism. But it would be wrong not to stress the genuine moral fervour of the Victorian. In 1859 Samuel Smiles published his book *Self-Help*, and the title is a summing up of the whole age. In many ways the Victorian deserved his success. He had tremendous virtues. He worked hard; he was thrifty; he was honest. He believed in strenuous endeavour even in his relaxations. Within eight years of the forming of the Alpine Club in 1857 nearly eighty peaks and passes of the Alps were conquered by the English amateur on holiday, an achievement crowned by the climbing of the Matterhorn in 1865. The same spirit of toughness, the determination to live hard, and the stress on leadership formed the central theme both at the new public schools and at the older ones, many of which underwent sweeping reforms in this period, due partly to a remarkable generation of headmasters, and partly to a series of Commissions which brought about a general overhaul of school management. Education at these establishments was focused on character rather than intellect. Organized games, not the classroom, exercised the mind of the teaching profession. 'Of course you needn't work, Fitzmilksoppe,' *Punch* portrayed one headmaster saying to a

K

prospective pupil, 'but play you must and shall.' Nor was toughness the only significant feature of the public schools, for, with the
enormous growth of fee-paying pupils, they had become geared
to the social machine, as a process for creating gentlemen out of
the sons of the new rich and the *rentier* and professional classes.

Naturally, much of this moral fervour only strengthened the
Victorians' sense of superiority; but there are too many exceptions, even in Victorian England, for the generalization to be
entirely valid. In many ways the mid-Victorian period was a time
of doubt and uncertainty. At first sight John Ruskin would seem
a typical figure of his generation, a critic who evaluated art almost
entirely in moral terms and whose personal life was a tangle of
inhibitions that eventually destroyed his reason; yet, as early as
1846, he was denouncing the material prosperity of contemporary
England, describing his fears that 'dependence on God may be
forgotten, because the bread is given and the water sure, that
gratitude to him may cease, because his constancy of protection
has taken the semblance of a natural law'; and in 1860, in *Unto
This Last*, he proclaimed that the government had a moral duty to
educate the young, to set up State factories alongside those of
private enterprise, and to provide for the unemployed and the old.

This scheme was indeed a remarkable prophecy, and with it
Ruskin, much as he feared the impersonalizing effects of industrialism, did at least attempt to come to terms with the age in
which he lived. But there were others who could not easily
reconcile themselves to the apparent tendencies of the times. John
Stuart Mill's essay *On Liberty*, published in 1859, and Matthew
Arnold's *Culture and Anarchy*, published ten years later, both point
to profound misgivings. Both were conscious of high ideals that
seemed in danger of being smothered; both feared the age of the
masses. Mill's plea, which is one of the great political writings in
the English language, was for the right of the individual to speak
and act as he wished, even if he stood entirely alone in this.
Arnold, writing two years after the passing of the second Reform
Act, castigated the landed classes ('the Barbarians'), the middle
classes ('the Philistines'), and the masses, finding in all three strong
elements of brutality and materialism. For Arnold and Mill num-

bers did not sanctify, and it is an interesting illustration of the complexity of the Victorian period that two men should write in terms of agonized defence at a time of such widespread optimism.

Even the Bible itself was not safe from the inquiring mind of a Victorian minority. It is true that textual criticism was not prominent in English intellectual life, but this was mainly due to the general lethargy at the Universities during the major part of the century. On the Continent, however, particularly in Germany, Biblical scholars had long been active, and the discovery of the Codex Sinaiticus by Constantine Tischendorf had brought to light a large portion of the Old Testament and the whole of the New, all dating back to the early fourth century. This, coupled with other discoveries since the seventeenth century, made it clear that the Authorized Version, translated from the various sources available to James I's scholars, was in need of revision, and in 1870 a committee was appointed by the Canterbury Convocation to produce a new version, which was ultimately published in 1881.

Textual revision was not entirely acceptable to many who loved the accepted wording of the Bible and who turned a wary eye on the idea of tinkering with Holy Writ, but in itself it was not sufficient to let loose a violent controversy. It was the publications of the scientists in the middle of the nineteenth century that provoked the mighty storm which continued to rage well into the twentieth. Doubts about the story of Adam and Eve in the Garden of Eden in the year 4004 B.C. had already been fairly firmly suggested in certain circles in the eighteenth century. Leibnitz and Laplace had, each in his own field, envisaged a much larger and more gradual process of change in the earth's history and in the development of life upon it. Lamarck and Cuvier had speculated on various forms of evolution of animal life, and at the same time the physicists and chemists were exploring possibilities that would ultimately necessitate a new conception of the universe. But the educated public—and, for that matter, the Universities, whose interests were almost entirely literary—had little interest in such abstractions, and had therefore remained unaware of their implications. It was the new theories of the geologists and the biologists—more easily understandable to the layman and directly challenging the literal truth of Genesis—that at last brought the whole question out into the open.

The first blow was struck by the geologists. The study of fossils had by now made it clear that the earth had been in existence for millions of years and that the process of change had been slow, rather than catastrophic. This second point destroyed the last hope of those who had wished somehow to reconcile the findings of geology with Genesis. The mental anguish to which this incompatibility gave rise is movingly recorded in Edmund Gosse's book *Father and Son*. Gosse's father, a man of extreme Nonconformist views, was also a skilled geologist.

> With great and ever greater distinctiveness, his investigations had shown him that in all departments of organic nature there are visible the evidences of slow modification of forms, of the type developed by the pressure and practice of æons. This conviction had been borne in upon him until it was positively irresistible. Where was his place, then, as a sincere and accurate observer? Manifestly, it was with the pioneers of the new truth, it was with Darwin, Wallace, and Hooker. But did not the second chapter of Genesis say that in six days the heavens and earth were finished, and the host of them, and that on the seventh day God ended his work which he had made?

It seemed an unanswerable dilemma. Gosse did, in fact, attempt an answer: namely, that a catastrophic act of creation would include the creation of evidence which would suggest the presence of life over preceding æons of time, but he convinced neither the public nor himself with this argument.

1859 saw the climax of the assault on established beliefs. In that year Charles Darwin published *The Origin of Species* and followed it up, in 1871, with *The Descent of Man*. The essence of the theory of natural selection was that certain variations were transmitted to offspring and that certain types of life were better fitted to survive than others, according to their environment. Darwin's aim was simply to explain the differentiation of species, but to the Victorian world he seemed to deny not merely Genesis, but also the whole notion of purpose in the process of selection. It was significant that one of the formative influences on Darwin's mind was Malthus' pessimistic philosophy, but while Malthus as a clergyman had pointed to the necessity for moral restraint as the solution to the problem of over-population, Darwin seemed to suggest that the whole process of animal and human development was at the mercy of the law of the jungle.

The Church at once leapt to the attack. Bishop Wilberforce, in a famous debate at Oxford, denounced the theory as atheistic and mocked the whole idea by asking Thomas Henry Huxley, a vigorous supporter of Darwin, whether he was descended from a monkey on his grandfather's or his grandmother's side. The tragedy of the whole controversy was that, as it became more furious, the apparent gulf between science and religion grew wider and both sides took up exaggerated positions of defence. Yet not all scientists were atheists or agnostics—the name coined by Huxley—nor did all Churchmen attack Darwin. Now that the heat has gone out of the debate, it is possible to reflect that religion is concerned with man's purpose in the world and science with an understanding of the relationship between observable phenomena, and that two such aims need not necessarily clash. But coming when they did, it was perhaps inevitable that the new theories of the biologist should cause such a furore. The bitter argument that raged for years reveals the Victorian at his best and his worst. He could be narrow-minded and hypocritical, but whether scientist or layman he could never shirk a conflict, if it seemed that his innermost convictions were challenged. He might be wrong, but he could never remain indifferent, and it is no paradox that these decades should have produced the most outspoken figures of both fervent Churchmanship and militant atheism.

2. The new Trade Unionism

Since the Chartist riots the position of the wage-earner had slowly been transformed. A fundamental reason for this was the astonishing prosperity of the country as a whole. The general improvement in the condition of life was so great that the country could take in its stride a sharply mounting population—nearly 29 million in 1861, 31½ million by 1871. The period after 1850 was a time of rising prices, but wages rose still higher, and although the increase naturally varied from trade to trade, it has been reckoned that in general the average working-class family was about 10% better off by 1870. This improvement is reflected in the number of depositors in various savings banks, particularly in Gladstone's Post Office Savings Bank, opened in 1861.

Another reason for improvement was the gradual extension of the Factory Act of 1850 to other forms of industry. Slowly, through the activity of the Unions and the unwearying campaigns of Lord Shaftesbury, concessions were won—in the bleaching and dyeing industries in 1860, in the lace factories in 1861, and in most kinds of workshop, foundries, blast furnaces, and glass factories in 1867. But it was a long-drawn-out struggle, and since each Act referred only to specific industries, the evils of sweated labour and the employment of children continued in a variety of forms and were still being combated in the twentieth century.

The growth of the Trade Unions is one of the most striking features of this mid-century period, and provides an interesting example of the influence of national character at every level of society. The working-class leaders of this new Unionism had all the Victorian virtues. Hard-working, honest, mostly self-taught, they were determined that their Unions should be recognized as constitutional and essentially respectable organizations. This was a time when theories of international Socialism were being propounded, when Karl Marx was actually living and writing in London; yet the leaders of the English Trade Unions deliberately turned their backs on any violent attempt at social revolution. They eschewed any form of political doctrine, and their attitude towards reform was absolutely consistent with the empirical approach that has characterized the growth of all English institutions. Local Unions were formed to bargain with the employers, Unions in the same trade gradually amalgamated, and the heads of these amalgamations came to confer with one another in times of crisis. The whole process was one of trial and error, resting on the assumption that the basis of society must remain unaltered. It was, perhaps, understandable that Karl Marx should despair of the British working class as incorrigibly bourgeois. In fact, we know today that out of this development the basis of society has been considerably altered, but the general change was not due to a conscious plan and has been mainly incidental to the settlement of particular issues.

The first step was taken in the 1840s and '50s, when groups of skilled workmen in one industry or another began to form their own local Unions, which, through members' subscriptions, soon became sufficiently wealthy to finance sickness benefits, strike pay, and legal assistance when they took their grievances to the courts. The year 1851 was a momentous date in the history of the working-class movement, for in that year most local Unions in the engineering trade—a highly significant class of workman in the Victorian era—agreed to form an Amalgamated Society of Engineers, thereby creating a body of over 11,000 members whose subscriptions gave it an income of £500 a week. The two personalities behind this move, William Newton and William Allan, were convinced that the policy of such a Union should be confined to industrial aims, and that even here the calling of a strike should be adopted only as a last resort. In this they were in agreement with another spokesman of the working class, George Odger, secretary of the Ladies' Shoemakers' Society, who considered that 'strikes in the social world are like wars in the political world; both are crimes unless justified by absolute necessity.'

The new Union of engineers was put to the test almost at once. In November 1851 they presented a demand for an end of systematic overtime and piece-work. The employers decided to retaliate with a form of collective action of their own, and accordingly closed their works. The lock-out lasted for four months, and at the end, despite considerable public sympathy and private donations, the Union funds ran out and the workers were forced to accept the employers' terms, which included the signing of an agreement by every worker that he would promise never to support any Union while he continued at work. The employers had won, but the victory proved to be hollow. The workers claimed that they could not be bound by a promise given under duress, and within three years membership, which had fallen off, had risen to 12,500 and the Union funds amounted to over £35,000.

In 1858 there came another industrial dispute, this time in the London building trade, when the workers demanded a nine-hour day. A strike followed in which both sides found sympathetic allies. Other employers ordered a lock-out of their workers; other Unions gave financial assistance to the builders. The outcome was a compromise, but the lesson to be drawn was obvious. In order to hold out longer than the employers, a Union must be wealthy, and this could be achieved only by a larger membership. The builders consequently decided to follow the lead of the engineers, and in 1860 formed the Amalgamated Society of Carpenters and Joiners, which by 1870 had 10,000 members with 130 branches over the whole country. Their secretary, Robert Applegarth, another of the outstanding personalities produced by the Union movement, was a North-countryman who had left Sheffield for America, worked as a carpenter in New York and Chicago, and then returned to England. Later, in *Who's Who*, he was to describe his principal recreation as 'work, more work, and still more again'—another indication of the way in which the Victorian ethic cut across all class divisions.

Several important developments followed in the 1850s. During the building dispute Applegarth had made the acquaintance of Thomas Hughes, author of *Tom Brown's Schooldays*, and later a member of Parliament. The possibility of an alliance with a section of the middle classes—particularly the Christian Socialists —had already been suggested in the drawings of *Punch*, which at this time was an outspoken champion of the workers, insisting on a clear distinction between the dangerous anarchist and the workman who simply wanted a fair deal. Such support as they gained from the middle classes naturally strengthened the Union leaders' determination that improvements must be won through orthodox channels. Particularly significant was an entirely unofficial group of secretaries whose Unions had their headquarters in London. This group of friends, William Allan, Robert Applegarth, Daniel Guile, secretary of the Iron Founders, and George Odger, has been described as the Junta,[1] and for the next decade they were to be the guiding force in the new Unionism. Official co-operative

---

[1] *History of Trade Unionism*, by S. and B. Webb.

action between all Unions—which, it must be remembered, included only skilled workers—was still far distant, but a hint of it may be found in the Trades Councils established in 1861 in Glasgow, Edinburgh, Sheffield, Liverpool, and London, for these, although essentially regional, did provide an opportunity for the various Unions to consult each other over questions of common policy.

The general tendency towards amalgamation, however, must not obscure the fact that many of the Unions continued to be local and to fight their battles with their employers with a violence of which the Junta could not always approve. The struggle had been particularly fierce in the mines, where a principal grievance had been the fines which were imposed on miners if the weight of a coal-hutch were short, or if it contained too much coal-dust. The miners' leader in this dispute was Alexander Macdonald, a man of extraordinary self-reliance, who had worked in the mines since the age of eight, had studied at evening classes in local schools, and, by the time he was twenty-five, had saved enough to be able to work his way through Glasgow University. Through his leadership an Act of Parliament in 1860 allowed the miners to select a representative of their own to check the weight of the hutches, and in 1863 the newly formed National Miners' Union elected him as their first President.

In the cotton industry a different kind of dispute led to the organization of the Lancashire Cotton Operatives. The length of the working day was an issue common to most industries at this time, but the cotton workers had a particular problem in the complications of piece-work rates. Eventually it was agreed that the workers should be allowed to choose their own officials who might look after their interests in this, and who would be selected through a competitive examination, organized by the Union, since such a post called for considerable skill in mathematics.

These new Unions of the north had little contact with the great amalgamations, whose centres were at London, but in all of them one highly significant tendency may be noted. The coal-miners' check-weighers, the cotton operatives' calculators, the local and general secretaries were all men of intelligence and personality and they formed the nucleus of the body of Trade Union officials who were later to be the leaders and organizers of the working-class movement, as it assumed ever larger proportions.

It could not be forgotten, however, that despite these signs of growing strength and the determination of the leaders that the Unions should be accepted as a perfectly respectable element in an industrial society, the actual legal position of the Unions was very insecure. The repeal of the Combination Acts had given them the right to negotiate with employers over hours of work and rates of payment, but the question of picketing and striking and the legal security of the Unions' funds had been left entirely unsettled. Thus, as workers and employers grew more and more aware of the strength of these new organizations, the task that taxed the wisdom of the Junta was twofold: they had continually to urge restraint on the more hot-headed branches, itching to call a strike, and at the same time they had to convince the upper- and middle-class world that their right to exist could never be called in question. They had to battle on two fronts, and failure on one front would almost certainly involve disaster on the other. In 1866 and 1867 these dangers materialized and the Unions faced the greatest crisis in their history.

It was a series of outrages in Sheffield that at last gave the employers a chance to launch a serious attack. Workers who had refused to join the local Union and others who were behindhand in paying their subscriptions had been subjected to various forms of terrorism. Sometimes a man's tools were removed or broken; in other cases, men had actually been killed, and in 1866 a can of gunpowder was exploded in the house of a workman who had just resigned from the local Saw-Grinders' Union. This last incident caused a considerable outcry, and when the culprit was discovered and confessed to several other outrages, the enemies of the Trade Unions demanded a Royal Commission to examine the whole question. The Junta, too, were outspoken in their condemnation of such outrages, which naturally undermined all their efforts to build up an impression of respectable Unionism. 'By all means, let there be a Commission of Inquiry,' wrote Applegarth, 'and if a searching investigation leads to a discovery of an ulcer in our system, however small it may be, let the knife go to the very core.' He was perfectly sincere in this, but there was no escaping the fact that the findings of the Commission might jeopardize all that had so far been achieved.

Almost at the same time the Unions were faced with a threat from a different quarter. In Bradford the local treasurer of the Boilermakers' Society had embezzled £24 of the Union's funds, and when, in 1867, the case came before the Court of Queen's Bench, the judges confirmed the Bradford magistrates' opinion that Trade Union funds did not come under the protection of the Friendly Societies Act, and added a comment to the effect that, in so far as a Union was in restraint of trade, it was an illegal organization.

Thus, in 1867, the situation looked black for the Unions. Coinciding, as it did, with the turmoil over Parliamentary reform, the workers naturally redoubled their demand for enfranchisement. But at the time the Royal Commission was the more urgent question. Two things saved the Unions from absolute disaster— the skill and obvious integrity of Applegarth, who put the Unions' case; and the support of a few middle-class sympathizers, such as Thomas Hughes and Frederic Harrison, both of whom sat on the Commission. The result was that the Commission produced a somewhat negative report, grudgingly allowing a combination to be free from liability to prosecution, provided that no breach of contract was involved and that there was no systematic refusal to work with any particular person. Picketing, however, without which no strike could hope to be effective, was disallowed. An important feature of the findings was a Minority Report, published by three members of the Commission, including Hughes and Harrison, in which the view was expressed that Trade Union activity should be an offence only if the same activity by a single individual would have contravened established criminal law.

For the moment the situation had been saved, but several questions had still to be settled, and the Minority Report now formed the basis of the Unions' demands. New factors were to transform the whole matter into a question of great political significance. The Reform Act of 1867 enfranchised many of the working classes. The Ballot Act of 1872 meant that they could give their vote without fear of reprisals, and the Unions, lacking a political party of their own, clearly represented a pool of votes for which any politician was bound to make a determined bid. The working classes were about to become a political force in their own right.

3. Ireland after the famine

In Ireland starvation and cholera during the famine had been followed by mass emigration encouraged, to some extent, by the discovery of gold in California. Such a reduction in her population slightly increased the chances of improving the lot of the less than 6 million who remained; yet little or no progress was made. The successive Coercion Acts that had to be passed between 1830 and 1870 point to the utter inability of any English government in those years to find a fundamental solution, and this failure naturally caused Continentals to regard the assertions of English liberalism with a certain ironical amusement. 'They come and tell us', said Mazzini, 'that it is a well ordered state of society in which, for lack of a few potatoes, thousands and even millions are reduced to starvation.'

There was no lack of good intentions. Commissions of Inquiry were constantly being set up, and few governments did not attempt some remedial legislation. But the difficulties were rooted in the whole form of Irish society and economy and could not be overcome by one or two isolated measures. A concerted attack on the Irish landlords would have seemed a general threat to property, and no nineteenth-century Parliament could stomach that. Consequently, in spite of fresh attempts at legislation, the Irish scene after the famine remained as hopeless as ever. 'The war between landlord and tenant has been carried on for eighty years,' wrote Russell in 1847. 'It is evident that this relation which ought to be one of mutual confidence, is one of mutual hostility; nor do I see that they can be left to fight out the battle with any prospect of better result. Murder on one side: ejectment on the other—are as common as ever.'

In 1849 the Encumbered Estates Act enabled insolvent landlords to get rid of their estates, since a very large number had been badly hit by the effects of the famine and were eager to sell. By 1857 the ownership of about a third of the land had changed hands, and most of the 80,000 new proprietors were Irish. It had been the hope of the government that a new class of enterprising landlord, with capital at their disposal, would develop these estates, and thus the whole economic position of Ireland would be improved. But since development could not begin until many of the smallholders had been evicted, the Irish experienced an even greater tyranny at the hands of their own countrymen than they had known before. The new landlords set about their properties with enthusiasm, and in the next few years about 200,000 persons were evicted from their homes.

Irish reactions varied between violence and movements for reform through constitutional channels. In 1848 the 'Young Ireland' party was responsible for an attack on the police—which came to nothing. A little later a Tenant Rights group was formed to negotiate for security of tenure, compensation for improvements on giving up a tenancy, and remission of arrears of rent that had accumulated during the famine. Russell's administration took this up, but got very little way with it, principally because of the anti-Catholic panic.[1] Derby's government of 1852 was prepared to attempt some measure granting tenant rights, but later fell out with the supporters of the movement. No Bill was passed, and shortly afterwards the Tenant Rights party disintegrated. It was not until 1860 that two Acts were passed as a result of Edward Cardwell's efforts as Irish Secretary, but they were so worded as to have virtually no effect on either tenant or landlord. In fact, the only positive piece of legislation concerning Ireland in this period was an Irish Franchise Act, passed in 1850, which had very little to do with the agrarian problem. It was, however, intended as a conciliatory measure and extended the county franchise to the £5 freeholder, although the full force of the reform was reduced by an amendment in the House of Lords which actually raised the qualifying rateable valuation in the boroughs to £12.[2]

[1] See p. 183.   [2] It was lowered to £4 in 1867. See p. 275.

A new period of violence seemed likely after 1858, when a society known as the Fenians was formed in America. At first, however, they accomplished very little, since many of their most likely supporters were absorbed into the Federal army in the American Civil war. At the end of hostilities many returned to Ireland, where, financed by sympathizers in America and led by James Stephens, they planned an armed rebellion. The success of the Italians and the recent rising of the Poles naturally encouraged the idea of resorting to violence, but the plan came to the ears of the authorities, and in September 1865 the leaders were placed under arrest and the Habeas Corpus Act was suspended in Ireland. Stephens, however, managed to escape from prison and reached America, from where he continued his activities. In May 1866 a Fenian raid was made across the border into Canada, but shortly after this Stephens lost his personal ascendancy in the movement.

The scene of action now shifted to England. In February 1867 an attack on Chester was feared and a battalion of Guards was moved into the city. In September a police officer was killed in Manchester during a struggle to rescue two Fenians from a prison van; afterwards the attackers were rounded up and three of them were hanged. In December there was a more spectacular attempt to rescue two Fenians from Clerkenwell Jail by means of blowing up a barrel of gunpowder against the walls of the prison.

Little more was heard of the Fenians after this. They were only a small body of militant conspirators, and since the Roman Catholic Church had strongly disapproved of their activities, they had never gained much support from the Irish peasantry. The Fenian movement was nevertheless significant. The English, on the whole, had wanted to forget Ireland; for the electorate the question had remained remote. But the series of alarms and outrages in English cities made it clear that the Irish could no longer be forgotten, and when William Gladstone determined that his party should find a solution to the problem, the Irish question was to become the very centre of the political scene at Westminster.

4. The passing of the second Reform Act, 1867

On Palmerston's death the Queen turned to Lord Russell, now aged seventy-three, who accepted the premiership. Gladstone was on better terms with the new Prime Minister than he had been with the old and was asked to lead the government in the House of Commons. It was, however, to be a short-lived administration, concerned almost entirely with a new attempt at Parliamentary reform. Nothing could be more typical of this mid-century period than the political history of the three years following Palmerston's death. A measure of reform over which a vast majority of the country was, in principle, in agreement was thrown out by the opposition on the grounds that it was too extreme. Russell was succeeded by Derby and Disraeli, who introduced, not a milder, but a more extreme version of Parliamentary reform, and by the time the opposition had done with it, the Bill had grown even more extreme than many Liberals or Conservatives had envisaged. It became law, but in the following general election of 1868 the electorate, many of whom could vote for the first time as a result of the work of the Conservative government, promptly returned a Liberal majority.

At the time of the Reform Act of 1832 Russell had hoped that the question was settled for good, and this sentiment had won him the nickname of 'Finality Jack'. He had, however, long ago abandoned this view, and in January 1868 he wrote to Gladstone: 'If I bring in, or contribute to bring in a measure, it will be to me a satisfactory close of my political life, whether carried or defeated'. Gladstone had earlier expressed his views on the franchise, and the government accordingly introduced a Representation of the People Bill on 12 March, 1866. It was proposed that the right to vote should be extended in the boroughs to householders paying £7 in rent, and in the counties to householders with or without land paying £14 in rent. It was calculated that, in all, this would increase the electorate by about 400,000 and would include many of the working class. For the moment the government did not broach the question of the redistribution of seats.

The Bill was not a success. The Conservatives opposed it, suspicious of notions of political equality. Lord Cranborne, later
Lord Salisbury, voiced the old argument for a franchise dependent
on a man's stake in the community. 'The wildest dreamer never
suggested that all the shareholders should have a single vote without reference to the number of shares they might hold.' The decisive blow was struck by a section of the Liberals, led by Robert
Lowe. 'Venality, ignorance, and drunkenness' were, he claimed,
the main characteristics of the working class. Despite Gladstone's
reply that they were 'our fellow-subjects, our fellow-Christians,
our own flesh and blood', and John Bright's gibe that the Liberal
rebels had retired to a 'Cave of Adullam'—a Biblical reference
that Abraham Lincoln had made fashionable among politicians a
couple of years earlier—the Liberal revolt was not silenced. An
amendment was introduced whereby the borough vote was to be
based on rateable and not rental value, which would certainly reduce the size of the new electorate, since rates were usually lower
than rent. On 18 June the amendment was carried by eleven
votes, amidst 'shouting, violent flourishing of hats, and other
manifestations,' as Gladstone wrote, 'which I think novel and
inappropriate.'

What was Russell to do? Government defeats had become a part
of the normal pattern of events in the last decade. Russell did not
want to resign and the Queen was convinced that he should not
do so, particularly since war had just broken out between Austria
and Prussia. But Gladstone believed that to hold on to office
would appear discreditable and advised resignation, although later
he thought that a dissolution would have been a wiser course.
Dissolution was considered, but the government Whips persuaded
Russell against it, and so, on 25 June, the Cabinet decided to resign.

Once more the Queen asked Lord Derby to form a government, and for the third time in his life Derby agreed to do so with
a minority in the House of Commons. It might have been supposed that Parliamentary reform was a question best left alone at
this moment. Sudden disorders in the country, however, allowed
the government little choice. Lowe's remarks on the working
classes had aroused bitter feelings, and John Bright, with other

Radicals, had been quick to take advantage of this with a whirl-wind tour of the Midlands and the North. The Trade Unions were facing a crisis in their history and badly needed some sort of representation in the Commons.[1] As early as January 1865 the Reform League had been formed to put forward the working-class demand for manhood suffrage, while in opposition to this a Reform Union had been established at Manchester on behalf of the middle-class demand for household suffrage. To the venom of class war there was added the distress consequent on an econo-mic crisis. The 1865 harvest was bad, cholera had reappeared, and the Limited Liability Act of 1862 had encouraged a wave of spe-culation which was followed in May 1865 by the failure of one of the greatest financial houses in London, Overend and Gurney. This naturally involved the collapse of many other enterprises, and the prospect of unemployment stirred London crowds to make demonstrations. A great gathering marched from Trafalgar Square to Gladstone's house, crying 'Gladstone and Liberty'; and on 23 July, when Hyde Park was closed to a vast meeting sche-duled to take place there, the crowd got out of hand and tore down 1,400 yards of the railings.

These disturbances were local, but they persuaded Derby and Disraeli that they must take up the question of electoral reform. Such a move might offer political advantages. As over Catholic emancipation and the repeal of the Corn Laws, a Conservative government would have a better chance of getting such a Bill through the House of Lords, and in the Commons it would be an agreeable experience to outplay the opposition at their own game—to 'dish the Whigs'. In the outcome it was, of course, a gamble on how the electorate would vote—'a leap in the dark', as Derby described it—but the Prime Minister had backed worse horses in his life. Disraeli, in his early days during the Young England movement, had dreamed of an alliance between the aristocracy and the poorer classes, and however great the risk, the Tories, looking back over the past twenty years, might well feel that they had little to lose.

Once they had made up their minds to introduce a Bill, Derby

[1] See pp. 266-7.

and Disraeli both decided to adopt a bold course. Household suffrage in the boroughs would make a popular cry, and they believed that they could modify the full effects of it by a system of plural voting and 'fancy franchises'. The main difficulty was to reach agreement with the right wing of the Cabinet. Heated negotiations amidst threats of resignation by ministers and personal intervention on the part of the Queen, who had been seriously worried by the Hyde Park incident, resulted in a compromise measure being hurriedly drawn up in time for Disraeli to satisfy the curiosity of the Commons. This Ten Minutes' Bill, as it was called, proposed to extend the franchise to £6 rate-payers in the boroughs and £20 rate-payers in the counties. A majority of the Conservatives, however, preferred Disraeli's original idea, and the government, deciding to act on this, withdrew the Bill. The right wing, Lord Cranborne, Lord Carnarvon, and General Peel, thereupon resigned from the Cabinet, and the new Bill was prepared.

The opposition now took a leaf out of the Conservatives' book. They began to propose amendments that made the Bill still more extreme. It was Disraeli who had to fight the battle in the Commons, and there was probably no moment in his career when he exhibited greater Parliamentary skill. He had put himself in Peel's position in 1846, and if Lord Cranborne had placed himself at the head of the Conservative dissidents in the manner of the young Disraeli, the Bill might never have survived. As it was, by concessions, negotiations, and shrewd tactics in debate, Disraeli avoided disaster.

One complaint of the opposition was that the 'compounders' would be excluded from voting. The compounder was a householder whose rent included the rates which were actually paid by the landlord. This was a highly significant proposal, for to include the compounders would mean another 500,000 working-class voters. Gladstone's great onslaught in their defence was actually defeated, but later Disraeli accepted an amendment making all tenants responsible for paying their rates themselves. Thus, in effect, the compounders were enfranchised through ceasing to be compounders. Other changes followed. Plural voting and 'fancy franchises' disappeared. Then the county franchise came under fire. Disraeli had proposed a £15 rating limit, but when the demand was made for this to be lowered, he gave way again and reduced it to £12. Robert Lowe complained angrily that the Constitution was being auctioned to the highest bidder and it was becoming clear that the Adullamites would have been wiser to have backed Russell's 1866 Bill. As it was, the Conservative Bill survived, and became law on 15 August, 1867.

By the terms of the Act the franchise in the boroughs was extended to all householders who paid rates, provided that they satisfied a one-year residential qualification, and to all lodgers who paid £10 a year in rent. In the counties it was extended to copyholders and leaseholders with property of an annual value of £5 and to the £12 rate-payer. This, however, did not deprive the £50 tenant-at-will of his vote, even if he paid less than £12 in rates.

The government had also undertaken the redistribution of seats. One seat was taken from boroughs of less than 10,000 inhabitants; twenty-five were given to the counties and fifteen to the boroughs. The University of London gained a member, and a third seat was given to Liverpool, Manchester, Birmingham, and Leeds. This last produced a significant amendment in the House of Lords. Electors still normally voted for two members, but the creation of these three-member constituencies might lead to complications, and the Lords ruled that in future no elector should vote for more than two candidates—except in the City of London, where the limit was to be three.

Separate Acts were passed for Scotland and Ireland. Seven seats were transferred from England to Scotland, where the franchise was made similar to the English system. In Ireland the borough franchise was extended to the £4 rate-payers. An amendment was made to the Municipal Corporations Act of 1835 whereby the rate-paying voter's residential qualification was reduced from three years to one, thus bringing the local municipal franchise into line with the Parliamentary franchise.

In many ways the changes brought about in 1867 were greater than in 1832, although the struggle over the first Reform Act had been more dramatic. As with the earlier Act, however, one must beware of exaggerating the extent of the reform. Three factors lessened the full consequences of an increased electorate. First, the voting was still open, so that the newly enfranchised workers in the boroughs were liable to be influenced by their employers. Second, although the property qualification for M.P.s had been abolished in 1858, members received no salary and therefore continued, in the main, to come from the more affluent sections of the community. Third, although the borough electorate far outnumbered that of the counties, the distribution of seats remained such that the large industrial towns of the north still lacked a fair representation in proportion to their population.

Yet against this the consequences of the second Reform Act were enormous. The size of the electorate was almost doubled,[1] and in the boroughs included the more prosperous section of the working class—particularly among the compounders. From this there followed a remarkable transformation of electoral campaigns. Demagogy was to take the place of bribery and 'septennial ale', and the Act of 1867 foreshadowed the great Midlothian speeches of Gladstone and the passionate oratory of Lloyd George. There were many who watched the approach of this new age of the masses with alarm. '. . . what I fear', wrote Walter Bagehot in the introduction to the second edition of his *English Constitution*, 'is that both our political parties will bid for the support of the working man; that both of them will promise to do as he likes, if he will only tell them what it is; that, as he now holds the casting vote in our affairs, both parties will beg and pray him to give that vote to them.'

A further development followed from the Lords' amendment. In the three-member boroughs it now became vitally important to see that votes were not wasted on a candidate who was already certain of victory, and the only way in which this might be achieved was through an efficient local party organization. It was the Liberals in Birmingham who first seized upon this, and once they had taken the first step the Conservatives were bound to follow. From the second Reform Act there was to grow the

---

[1] See Statistics, p. 453.

intricate nation-wide system of local party committees, nursing their voters between elections and mobilizing them when the time came to go to the polls.

This setting of the stage for the new epoch in Parliamentary government coincided with the exit of the two principal political personalities. At Christmas 1867 Lord Russell, now in his mid-seventies, declared his intention of resigning the leadership of the Liberal party; in February 1868 Lord Derby resigned, owing to ill health. It was an appropriate moment. Both men had belonged to the world of the eighteenth-century aristocracy, remote from the spirit of the new times. Thus, within two months of each other Gladstone and Disraeli—both of middle-class origin and of essentially nineteenth-century background—emerged at the head of the two parties whose struggle forms the main theme of political life in the last decades of Victoria's reign.

A general election was bound to follow soon after the Reform Act, and in any case Disraeli could not hope to manage indefinitely a Parliament that had been elected originally in support of Palmerston. It was Gladstone who forced the issue, and the question on which he brought about the government's defeat opens a new chapter in the troubled history of Ireland. In April 1868 he succeeded in passing a resolution in the Commons to the effect that the Anglican Church in Ireland must be disestablished, and Disraeli declared that a dissolution would follow in the autumn, when the new electoral registers had been prepared.

Gladstone's mind had been moving towards a new interest in the Irish question during the previous two or three years. His whole career is a fascinating complex of high moral conviction and good political timing, and the recent Fenian disturbances, coupled with the need to find a new cry for the Liberal party, provided him with a programme in which political expediency was combined with a sincere belief that a final solution must be found to the problem of Ireland.

The election was fought in November. Gladstone stood for South-West Lancashire, and in a series of resounding speeches lashed the Protestant ascendancy in Ireland. He compared it to 'some tall tree of noxious growth . . . but now at last the day has come when, as we hope, the axe has been laid to the root.' South-West Lancashire was too Protestant to accept these sentiments, but although Gladstone himself had to seek refuge in the greater security of Greenwich, the result of the general election was a majority of 112 seats for the Liberals. Symbolically, Gladstone was in the process of cutting down a tree at Hawarden when he received the news that the Queen was going to ask him to form a government. At first he continued to work with his axe and then, turning to his companion, announced with great solemnity: 'My mission is to pacify Ireland'. With those words he was committing himself to a task which he was never to achieve and which was to come near to ruining his party.

IV

THE AGE OF VICTORIAN DEMOCRACY
1868–1901

15

MR. G. AND DIZZY

1. *Gladstone's first administration, 1868–74*

'I ASCEND a steepening path, with a burden ever gathering weight. The Almighty seems to sustain and spare me for some purpose of His own, deeply unworthy as I know myself to be. Glory be to His name.' So wrote Gladstone in his diary on 29 December, 1868. It was now his fifty-ninth birthday and he had been Prime Minister just under a month. His opponents often complained of Gladstone's tendency to confuse his own policy with the will of God, but he may well have felt that this particular moment was to be one of the turning points both in his own career and in the life of the country. During the next five years a legislative programme of vast, far-reaching reforms shattered the old leisurely calm of the mid-century Parliaments. Ireland, the Civil Service, the Army, education, and the Trade Unions were all caught up in the great storm of Gladstone's first administration. Where others had delayed or temporized, Mr. G. and his colleagues cut the Gordian knots one by one. In these years they laid the foundations of the modern state, but the greatness of the ministry eventually involved its own downfall, for the groups interested in reform in the nineteenth century were so diverse and conflicting in their outlook that a reforming government was bound to create many enemies. As one measure succeeded another, Gladstone's majority in the Commons was gradually worn down, and at the general election of 1874 the Liberals had no force left to prevent the Conservatives sweeping into power.

In the Cabinet that he formed in 1868 Gladstone did his best to represent all the various groups that made up the Liberal party. Robert Lowe became Chancellor of the Exchequer, Edward Cardwell Secretary for War, and John Bright President of the

Board of Trade, while Lord Clarendon was made Foreign Secretary despite the objections of the Queen, who was hurt by his reference to her as 'the Missus'. 'Since the dissolution of the Aberdeen Government in 1856', commented *The Times*, 'no Cabinet has included ability so great and so various.'

There could be little surprise over the first measure introduced by the new government. The Prime Minister had stated his intention to pacify Ireland, and on 13 January, 1869 Gladstone noted in his diary at Hawarden: 'Wrote out a paper on the plan of the measure respecting the Irish Church, intended perhaps for the Queen. Worked on Homer. We felled a lime.' The new Bill was launched almost at once, proposing disestablishment and partial disendowment, involving the reduction of Church property to £10 million. The problem was the attitude of the Lords. They had already shown their hostility to the measure, but a speech by Lord Salisbury persuaded them to listen to the voice of the electorate. 'When once we have come to the conclusion from all the circumstances of the case that the House of Commons is at one with the nation, it appears to me that the vocation of this House has passed away, and that it must devolve the responsibility upon the nation, and may fairly accept the conclusion at which the nation has arrived.' The Church party in the Lords behaved with considerable restraint, and the Queen, alarmed at the thought of a constitutional crisis, and acting on Gladstone's advice, told Archbishop Tait that the Bill ought to pass. As a result there was little struggle over disestablishment, but an amendment was introduced whereby the Church saved £13 million of its property, thus losing only a quarter of its revenue.

The Act is an interesting example of the strange position into which Gladstone the statesman had led Gladstone the High Churchman. Gladstone had never yet been to Ireland, and although he was clearly attempting to strike at the root of the problem, instead of applying some temporary remedy, the Irish Church Act was based on a theoretical appreciation of the situation rather than an understanding of immediate practical requirements. 'My Lords,' said Lord Salisbury during the debate, 'it is against the land and not against the Church that the Fenian agitation is really directed. . . . The landlord is a much more complete monument of conquest than the clergyman.' It was to the landlord that Gladstone now intended to turn his attention.

He set about studying the problem with the same scrupulous thoroughness with which he had prepared his Budgets when he had been Chancellor of the Exchequer. For the last three months of 1869 he toiled through the documents until the situation was clear in his mind and a possible solution could be formed. There were two possible lines of approach and the subsequent Bill took both of them into account. Since the tenant's position was insecure, one solution was for him to cease to be a tenant. The government therefore proposed a scheme of loans, whereby the tenant might purchase the land which he rented. It was clear, however, that not many of the Irish would be able to take advantage of this. The only other solution must take the form of restricting the landlord's freedom of action, and here Gladstone knew that he was on difficult ground. How was he to do this without appearing to attack the sacred rights of property? His plan, as he wrote to Cardinal Manning, was 'to prevent the landlord from using the terrible weapon of undue and unjust eviction by so framing the handle that it shall cut his hands with the sharp edge of pecuniary damage'. In future, the tenant was to receive compensation for all improvements that he made to the land and, furthermore, through the extension of the old Ulster tenant-right custom to the whole of Ireland, he was to be compensated for the actual inconvenience of eviction. The last ruling was to apply, even if eviction were due to non-payment of rent, provided that the courts upheld the tenant's claim that the rent had been excessive.

By January 1870 Gladstone had won his Cabinet round to agreement, and the Bill passed the Commons without trouble, since the Conservatives, in the main, were prepared to acquiesce. In the Lords, however, objection was made to the clause that allowed compensation for tenants who had been evicted for non-payment of rent, since Lord Salisbury maintained that no court should have the right to adjudicate on the fairness of a rent. Gladstone was loath to make any change, since he hoped that he had hit upon a method of keeping rents down without positively controlling them, but eventually it was agreed that the courts would order compensation only when it was considered that the rent had been 'exorbitant'—instead of 'excessive', as Gladstone had wanted.

It was no mean achievement for the government to have got the Irish Land Bill through, and for some time Gladstone really believed that he had solved the Irish problem. The Irish were not so sure. The Catholic bishops had approached Gladstone during the negotiations and had urged on him the necessity of establishing fixity of tenure and the certainty of fair rents. Gladstone knew perfectly well that there would be no chance of pursuing such a measure and had no intention of attempting it, but later events proved the bishops to have been right. The interpretation which the Conservative interests in the courts placed on the word 'exorbitant' made it possible for landlords to raise the rents, so that the tenants were unable to pay and were then evicted without compensation. Soon it was not even necessary to raise the rents in order to secure an eviction, since the long agricultural depression, which began later in the 1870s,[1] made it impossible for tenants to pay even the existing rents. Ireland remained unpacified.

The next great measure during this ministry was the Education Act of 1870. Clearly it was time that a British government should concern itself with the problem. Efficient educational systems had already been established on the Continent, and the course of the Austro-Prussian war and the American Civil war had suggested that an educated rank and file were a good investment. In any case, the considerable extension of the franchise in 1867 was a strong argument for establishing something better than the existing haphazard system of elementary education. Any government measure would have to face two problems. The issue of religious teaching had so far forced earlier governments to postpone any general solution and to content themselves with making grants of money to the Anglicans and Nonconformists to assist them in organizing their own voluntary schools. But by now so many of these had developed that they presented a problem in themselves, since any new state system would almost certainly have to

[1] See p. 335.

incorporate the existing Church schools. 'It was impossible for us', said Gladstone later in the Commons, 'to join in the language or adopt the tone which was conscientiously and consistently taken by some members of the House to look upon these voluntary schools having generally a denominational character, as admirable passing expedients, fit, indeed, to be tolerated for a time, deserving all credit on account of the motives which led to their foundation, but wholly unsatisfactory as to their main purpose and therefore to be supplanted by something they think better.'

In February 1870 an Education Bill was introduced by William Forster, vice-president of the committee of the Privy Council for education. In its final form the Act allowed for the continued existence of denominational schools, but in districts where school accommodation was deficient, a locally elected school Board was to be set up with the power to organize schools and to enforce attendance of all children between the ages of five and twelve who were not being educated in any other way. These Boards were to decide locally whether religious instruction was to be given in their schools, but in any event this was not to include the religious doctrine 'distinctive of any particular denomination'. The crux of the matter was financial. Voluntary schools and Board schools were both to receive government grants, but while voluntary schools had otherwise to depend on their endowment, the new Board schools were to be supported also by a local rate. Schooling was not to be free, but a Board might pay the fees for poor children either in the Board schools or in the voluntary schools.

The Act was bound to have political repercussions.[1] The Radical Nonconformists detested the Anglican Church schools, and in Birmingham Joseph Chamberlain had been partly responsible for the founding of the National Educational League demanding free, compulsory, unsectarian education in primary schools. The supporters of religious education had formed the National Education Union in retaliation, and it was against the extremists on both sides that Forster had to fight through his compromise measure. The Nonconformists were particularly furious, since they had

[1] For the educational consequences, see p. 331.

hoped that when government legislation did eventually material-
ize, it would mean the abolition of the Church schools. Forster's
Act angered them in two ways—first, because the Church schools
had been spared, and, second, because Anglicans who gained a
majority in any school Board might be able to use their right to
pay the fees of poor children as a means of drawing on the local
rates to send them to a Church school. Deep sincerity of religious
belief led to bitter disputes at the time of elections to the school
Boards, and the antagonism was so great that the Boards sometimes hindered the growth of educational institutions in order to
spite their rivals.

Further reform added to the government's unpopularity among
the established classes. In 1870 the Civil Service was thrown open
to all who could pass a highly competitive examination. At the
same time Edward Cardwell, Secretary for War, had embarked
upon a series of radical reforms in the Army, utterly transforming
the old organization and abolishing the system of 'purchase'.[1] In
1871 a University Tests Act was passed, whereby all teaching posts
at Oxford and Cambridge were no longer to be an Anglican preserve, but could now be held by men of any religious belief.[2] From
the standpoint of the twentieth century these measures seem
natural and obvious enough, but it is important to stress how revolutionary in implication they were at this time. In the everyday
working of society the nineteenth century was an age of patronage
and amateurism. A position in government service, a College
Fellowship, or a commission in the Army had been considered a
species of property, and there were many who saw the new doctrine of efficiency as an onslaught on the fundamental principles of
society.

At the other end of the social scale the working classes also suffered a disappointment. It had seemed to the London Junta that
the second Reform Act would give them a chance to bargain with
any party in power and to gain the legislation that they needed to
safeguard their funds and their very existence, which had been

---

[1] See p. 327.
[2] Undergraduates at Oxford and Cambridge had already been relieved of religious
tests by the Acts of 1854 and 1856.

threatened in the crisis of the 1860s. The upshot of the Royal
Commission, however, was a measure that virtually ignored the
recommendations of the Minority Report. Legal recognition was
to be granted explicitly to the Unions as friendly and benefit
societies. This certainly safeguarded their funds, but at the same
time the means whereby a Union might effectively enforce a strike
were denied them, since all forms of picketing and coercing other
workers to join them in a strike were defined as criminal offences.
The Union leaders did what they could to resist this, but the most
that their friends in the Commons were able to achieve was to
make this last part of the proposal a separate Act, in the hope that
it might be possible to repeal it later. The Criminal Law Amendment Act was duly passed in 1871, thereby alienating working-
class opinion and creating a new ally for the Conservatives at the
next general election.

At the same time two other incidents in the Commons tended
to increase working-class dissatisfaction. In 1871 the Chancellor
of the Exchequer, Robert Lowe, proposed a tax on matches. This
would have brought in an additional £1 million, badly needed
for the extension of the armed forces, and he tried to laugh off any
objections with a pun: *ex luce lucellum*. When, however, the
match manufacturers complained that they would be put out of
business and their workers in London attempted to march on the
House of Commons, Lowe had to admit that classical scholarship
hardly provided an adequate justification and withdrew the tax,
substituting for it an increase in income tax.

A second measure, which *was* successful, was far more widespread in its effect. This was the Licensing Bill, which, encountering strong opposition in 1871, was then passed in a milder form in
1872. It was understandable that any interference with the public-
houses should be unpopular with those who frequented them, and
the leaders of the liquor industry headed the resistance to the
government proposals. Until this time the Liberals had been able
to rely on the support of most industrial interests, but with this
measure Gladstone did his party immense harm by alienating the
brewers and distillers. Not unnaturally they turned to the Conservatives, who gained enormously from their contributions to

the party funds and from the support of the public-houses, which became active local centres of political influence. Gladstone himself had no doubts, later, over the main cause of his defeat in the election of 1874, and commented in a letter to his brother: 'We have been borne down in a torrent of gin and beer.'

It could be argued that in the sphere of domestic legislation the government had attempted too much. Over foreign affairs the complaint was that it had not done enough. On 15 July, 1870 France declared war on Prussia after a dispute over a Hohenzollern candidature for the throne of Spain. British opinion tended to favour Prussia, on the whole, although the French were thought more likely to win. 'I would lay my last shilling', wrote Delane to William Howard Russell, 'on Casquette against Pumpernickel.' The fear of French gains on the Rhineland was still a prime factor in the British government's attitude towards Continental disputes, and since the smallness of the British Army precluded any possibility of an enforced mediation, neutrality seemed the best policy. On 25 July Bismarck published in *The Times* a draft treaty, drawn up by the French four years earlier, proposing the annexation of Belgium by France, and this had the desired effect of confirming British mistrust of Napoleon III, although Bismarck himself was not considered entirely innocent. 'Six of one and half a dozen of the other,' commented *Punch*. The independence of Belgium was vital to Great Britain, and Gladstone at once asked both Powers for a reaffirmation of the treaty of 1839. Both agreed, Prussia because British neutrality was all that Bismarck wanted, France because she dared not add to her enemies at such a moment.

The astonishing drama of the next few weeks was nothing less than a revolution in the balance of power on the Continent. The Prussian Army was proved in every way to be more highly organized, better armed, and better led than the French. The culmination of the fighting on the eastern front was the defeat and surrender of the French army at Sedan on 2 September. Napoleon III, who had ridden through shell-fire in an attempt to meet death on the battlefield, was taken prisoner and had a last conversation with the Prussian Chancellor who had outplayed him.

By 19 September Paris was encircled and on 14 October the one
remaining French army of 120,000 men, besieged at Metz, surrendered to the enemy.

This shattering collapse of France was at once an opportunity
for others. In September King Victor Emmanuel entered Rome.
At the end of October the Russian Chancellor, Prince Gortchakov,
encouraged by Bismarck, denounced the clauses in the Treaty of
Paris of 1856 neutralizing the Black Sea. This last was a direct
challenge to Gladstone's government, and at once the extent to
which the British and the Turks had been relying on French
support in the Near East was revealed. Lord Granville, Foreign
Secretary since the death of Lord Clarendon, had to handle a
situation in which the use of direct force was almost entirely out of
the question. The result was a compromise in which the British
government could do little more than save face. A conference of
Powers was held at London in January 1871, at which it was
agreed that no Power should have the right to free itself from any
part of a treaty without the consent of all the signatory Powers.
This form of words, however, was immediately followed by a
further agreement that the Black Sea clauses of the Treaty of Paris
should be abrogated. It was a highly significant conference in
many ways. Russia had, in fact, gained what she wanted, but the
agreement on principle was to prove a useful diplomatic weapon
in the Balkan crisis of 1875-8.[1] Prussia, not unnaturally, enjoyed
a commanding position at the conference. British diplomats were
already turning to consider her as a possible friend against further
Russian encroachments, in the place of France, and although Bismarck was not prepared to consider any definite alliance, he did
succeed in establishing agreement that the question of the Prussian
peace settlement with France was not to be a matter for European
negotiation.

The emergence of the German Empire, proclaimed in the Hall
of Mirrors at Versailles, was the result of a remarkable technique
of diplomacy and war. It has become customary to describe Bismarck as a stern militarist, usually portrayed in the steel helmet of
a Prussian war lord. Yet it is important not to confuse 'blood and

[1] See pp. 298-306.

iron' with pure brute force. War was an essential element in his diplomacy, but it was the part that he liked least, since it was here that the outcome was most uncertain, and an unexpected resistance might create diplomatic difficulties that would defeat even his powers. Military victory was not enough; he had to be sure that the Prussian Army could give him victory almost at once, so that he could present Europe with a *fait accompli*. Two factors had enabled him to achieve this object in three short wars—his own diplomacy, which each time had forced his enemy to fight alone, and the efficiency of the Prussian Army. The realization of this second factor had the inevitable consequence that the military and naval estimates of all the great European Powers began to rise sharply after 1870. It was the opening of the period of armed peace.

In Great Britain Gladstone was anxious to keep down the growth of armaments, mainly because of the expense. The naval estimates of 1871 were increased only by £385,826, but the army estimates leapt up by almost £3 million to a total of almost £16 million, and the new situation on the Continent lent impetus to Cardwell's reform of the military machine. British public opinion underwent a considerable change during the Franco-Prussian war, and mistrust of the new Leviathan was strengthened by Germany's acquisition of Alsace and Lorraine. Gladstone and Granville have sometimes been blamed for inaction, but, as over the Schleswig-Holstein issue, the smallness of the British Army put any other policy out of the question, and it seems that they probably made the best of a difficult situation. The public, however, is seldom dispassionate, and the government came in for severe criticism.

It was unfortunate for Gladstone that he had also inherited the squabble over the United States' claims for the losses caused by the *Alabama* during the American Civil war. International arbitration at Geneva found Great Britain responsible and decreed the payment of 15 million dollars to the United States. It was much to Great Britain's credit that she accepted such a ruling but it was perhaps understandable that an electorate that could look back to the days of Palmerston should view the matter differently.

L

In fact, the pendulum was swinging away from the Liberals with increasing momentum. The Irish Land Act had left the tenants unprotected. The disestablishment of the Irish Church and the abolition of the University Tests had annoyed the Anglicans. The end of 'purchase' and the passing of the Licensing Act had both caused consternation among the classes affected. Patriots denounced a foreign policy which they considered had lowered the country's prestige. The Nonconformists had been disappointed by the Education Act, and the Trade Unions looked frankly towards the Conservatives for the repeal of the Criminal Law Amendment Act.

The Liberal government itself had in 1872 created an entirely new factor which was to be of the greatest significance. The passing of the Ballot Act meant that the next election would be the first in which the electorate would vote by secret ballot. It was a great Liberal measure, aimed at ending the violence and corruption that had been rife at elections, and was the natural corollary of the second Reform Act, but it meant, too, that the voters would now act independently of the wishes of their landlords and employers, and thus in the next election political feelings would be reflected more directly than ever before.

It was an opportunity that the Conservatives did not intend to lose. At first, during his time in opposition, Disraeli had occupied himself in writing another novel, *Lothair*. But the lessons of the 1868 election had not been forgotten: in 1870 he placed John Gorst at the head of a Central Conservative Office at Whitehall, and gradually a network of local Associations spread over the whole country. The major problem that confronted Disraeli was the definition of policy, and he never did much more than take refuge in a vague creed of 'popular Toryism'. In his early days in politics he had been much affected by the 'Young England' movement, a romantic conception of an alliance between the aristocracy and the people, and now he attempted to mould a party doctrine which would include 'the improvement of the condition of the people' together with the 'maintenance of institutions' and 'the preservation of the Empire'. There are slight echoes of Cobbett's nostalgia for Old England in this attitude, although precisely what it could mean at this stage in the development of an industrialized society is rather hard to see.

By-elections told increasingly against the government, Disraeli's Conservatives were preparing a great organization for the contest to come, and Gladstone himself was tiring of the whole weary battle of politics. The new agnosticism of the scientists and the decree of Papal Infallibility of 1870 seemed to him to represent a double attack on the Christian religion. 'The welfare of my fellow creatures is more than ever at stake, but not within the walls of Parliament,' he wrote to his sister, and he longed to be free to leap to the defence of his faith. His relations with the Queen also weighed heavily on him at this time. Unlike Disraeli, who delighted her with his charmingly informal letters, Gladstone saw the Queen only as his Sovereign, never as a woman. He hoped at one time to improve the situation in Ireland by sending the Prince of Wales to Dublin as Viceroy. He was concerned, too, over the unpopularity of the Queen, who, since the death of the Prince Consort, had retired from public life, and proposed that, when not in Dublin, the Prince and Princess of Wales should hold Courts in London, deputizing for the Queen. One long memorandum succeeded another, but his schemes came to nothing and did little to make his relations with Victoria any more cordial. 'She must say to General Ponsonby,' she wrote in 1874, 'though he may hardly like to believe it, that she had felt that Mr. Gladstone would have liked to <u>govern</u> HER as Bismarck governs the Emperor. Of course, not to the <u>same</u> extent or in the <u>same</u> manner; but she always felt in his manner an overbearing obstinacy and imperiousness (without being actually wanting in respect as to form) which she never experienced from <u>anyone</u> else, and which she found most disagreeable.'

By 1872 the ministry was a spent force—'a range of exhausted volcanoes', Disraeli called the Treasury Bench. The first downfall came over an Irish University Bill, introduced by Gladstone in February 1873. He proposed a new University at Dublin, where Roman Catholics and Protestants would study on equal terms—a plan which he thought practicable only if controversial subjects such as theology, moral philosophy, and modern history were excluded. He failed to win over the extremists of either side, despite Cardinal Manning's efforts, and on 12 March the Bill was defeated on its second reading in the Commons. On the next day Gladstone announced his intention to resign.

This was a shrewd move, for if Disraeli had agreed to form a government, the Conservatives would have been faced with a minority in the Commons and Gladstone in opposition could have embarrassed them sufficiently during the following six months for the pendulum of popular opinion to have swung back a little in the direction of the Liberals. But Disraeli was far too wily to accept, and for the rest of the year Gladstone was forced to carry on. A series of minor controversies plagued him. Certain irregularities in the administration of the Post Office were revealed and, as a consequence, Robert Lowe moved to the Home Office, while Gladstone took over the duties of Chancellor of the Exchequer himself. This added greatly to his labours and involved him in a rather pointless constitutional dispute over whether assuming this new office necessitated his fighting a by-election.

Finally, in January 1874 he decided that the time had come to dissolve Parliament, basing his hopes for a successful election on a great scheme to abolish the income tax. This could be done only at the expense of the military and naval estimates and naturally involved him in angry arguments with Cardwell and G. J. Goschen, First Lord of the Admiralty. His efforts were fruitless. The result of the first Parliamentary election in Great Britain in which the electors could enjoy the privacy afforded by the Ballot Act was a defeat for the authors of that Act, and Disraeli took office at the head of the first Conservative government to have a majority in the Commons since the break-up in 1846.

2. Disraeli, 1874–80

For Disraeli it must have seemed a weary pilgrimage since the day when the ambitious young novelist had assured Sir Robert Peel that he intended to be Prime Minister. The chance had almost come too late. He was seventy, and throughout the six years of his administration he suffered increasingly from attacks of bronchitis and gout. His wife, on whose devotion he had greatly depended, had died just over a year before. Even now his position as leader of the Conservatives remained a peculiar one, for many of his party still had doubts about him. The Liberal victory of 1868 had suggested a gross miscalculation on his part in bringing in the second Reform Act, and since that day he had hardly been on speaking terms with Lord Salisbury, who was one of the leading Conservatives in the House of Lords.

He succeeded, however, in forming a very promising Cabinet. His greatest achievement lay in winning over Lord Salisbury, who consented to be Secretary for India. Lord Carnarvon, who had resigned from the Cabinet in 1867, took over the Colonial Office; the fifteenth Earl of Derby, son of his old leader, became Foreign Secretary, and Sir Stafford Northcote Chancellor of the Exchequer. Against this government the opposition appeared divided and weak. In addition to this, Gladstone had decided to resign the leadership of the Liberals in the Commons, although he had not yet done with politics and now felt himself free to speak and act without any consideration of the official Liberal policy—to the embarrassment of his successor, Lord Hartington.

But despite what appeared to be a promising opening, Disraeli was hampered by a series of difficulties greater than anything with which his predecessor had had to contend. Gladstone, determined on reform, had simply had to ensure that the more enthusiastic members of his party did not attempt the impossible. Disraeli wished to show that the Conservatives, too, stood for reform, implying that the Liberals had left much undone, but he could not be certain how far his supporters would allow him to go. Indeed, many of them, remembering his speeches while leader of the opposition, might have demanded that he should take reform no further.

Another difficulty was the changing economic position of the country. Such changes are very often due to general circumstances over which a party in power has little control, but it is usually the government that gets the blame or credit for them. Gladstone had been fortunate in that the period 1868–74 had been a time of considerable prosperity. But, as events turned out, this proved to be the eventide of that great day which the Free Traders had imagined would never draw to a close. Continental countries were catching up with British industry; the vast cornlands of Canada and the United States were about to present an unanswerable challenge to the British farmer, and in the last years of Disraeli's ministry the country entered upon the first of the bad depressions which were eventually to drive Great Britain back to a policy of Protection and which contributed more than anything else to the reappearance of the doctrine of Socialism in the working-class movement.

One other difficulty, an unexpected result of the Ballot Act, was the appearance of a new and aggressive Irish party in the House of Commons. An agitation for Irish Home Rule had started in 1870 —a direct continuation of the policy envisaged by O'Connell— and in the election of 1874, in which the Irish voter could enjoy the secret ballot, fifty-nine Home Rulers were returned to Westminster under the leadership of Isaac Butt. It was not long, however, before Butt's gentle patience had aroused the anger of his more extreme followers. One of them, Joseph Ronayne, put forward a suggestion that was to make the next years the rowdiest in the House of Commons. 'The English stop our Bills, why don't we stop their Bills? That's the thing to do. . . . Butt's a fool—too gentlemanly; we're all too gentlemanly.' What followed was a growing tendency on the part of the Home Rulers to intervene in the business of the House, to make long and often irrelevant speeches whose only purpose was obstruction. With practice they developed the filibuster into something of an art, and as the agricultural crisis of the later 1870s re-awoke all the worst aspects of the Irish question, feelings grew more impassioned. It happened that a young Protestant Anglo-Irish landowner, Charles Stewart Parnell, who took his seat as the member for Meath in 1875, witnessed on his first day at Westminster an early experiment in obstruction; by adopting these new tactics he quickly established himself as an adroit politician and in 1878, on Butt's resignation, took over the leadership of the Irish Home Rule party.

The appearance of this new element in Parliamentary debate, coupled with the fact that the government was absorbed in foreign and colonial affairs towards the end of the ministry, explains why most of its measures of domestic reform were passed during the early years. In 1874 Richard Cross, Home Secretary, put through a Licensing Act which modified the Act of 1872. In 1875 the Trade Unions gained their principal object when the Conspiracy and Protection of Property Act replaced the Criminal Law Amendment Act. This had the effect of legalizing picketing and established the long-sought principle that a trade combination might perform any action that was not punishable if performed by a single individual. In the same year an Artisans' Dwellings Act and a Sale of Food and Drugs Act were both passed, and, more famous than either of these, the Public Health Act [1] placed on a national basis most of the local sanitary measures in the municipalities. Quite apart from its practical effects, this last was a great political stroke, since it answered one of the major complaints that the Radicals had made against the Liberal government and won the Home Secretary the friendship of Joseph Chamberlain, the Radical Mayor of Birmingham. In 1876 Lord Sandon's Education Act took Forster's Act a step further by compelling the local Boards to enforce attendance, making provision for financial assistance for parents who were too poor to pay. A Merchant Shipping Act was passed in the same year, to prevent the overloading of merchant ships, mainly due to the outspoken insistence of Samuel Plimsoll, whose bullying of the government in the previous year had caused a great scene in the House and may have helped to convince Parnell of the efficacy of more aggressive Parliamentary tactics.

Thus far, the main difference between Liberal and Conservative administrations seemed to be one of personalities, and one is reminded of Hazlitt's remark at the beginning of the century that Whigs and Tories were like two rival stage-coaches that splashed each other with mud, but went by the same road to the same destination. There were, however, two particular features of Conservative policy that Disraeli tried to make the preserve of his party—the Church of England and the Empire.

Within the Church he was aided by the growing controversy

[1] See p. 329.

over ritualism. The Anglo-Catholic movement had by now become so marked among the lower clergy that the Archbishop of Canterbury, Dr. Tait, was moved to introduce in the House of Lords a private member's Bill which, after amendment by Lord Shaftesbury, Disraeli took up as a government measure. The Public Worship Act was an attempt to restrict what were thought to be Roman Catholic practices in the established Church, a new judgeship being created to adjudicate in these matters; any breach of its regulations made a member of the clergy liable to a charge of contempt of court. The Act had little effect on the growth of ritualism, although several clergymen later suffered sentences of imprisonment. At the time the dispute over the Act hardly coincided with party alignments. Two members of the Cabinet—Lord Salisbury and Gathorne Hardy, Secretary for War—objected to it, while many Liberals supported it, but it was useful to Disraeli, in that it enabled him to demonstrate that his brand of Conservatism was directly linked with the old Toryism that had stood firmly by the established Church.

Over the question of Empire Disraeli established a principle which has remained a permanent characteristic of the Conservative party. Previously there had been no positive pronouncement on colonial policy by any government, and the various gains of territory overseas had been fortuitous—sometimes the result of trade, sometimes of foreign policy. It was Disraeli who seized upon the idea of Imperialism as a positive theme, romantic rather than hard-headed in its general conception. In this lies one of the fundamental differences in policy between Gladstone and Disraeli, for it affected more than the question of overseas possessions. In the crisis in the Balkans and in his later conversion to Home Rule in Ireland, Gladstone showed a growing belief in self-determination, while Disraeli wished as far as possible to preserve the Turkish dominions, made Victoria an Empress, and had no policy at all for Ireland. This divergence of outlook had a marked effect on the history of the last years of Disraeli's administration. It coloured much of his political thinking and it destroyed any idea that Gladstone might have had of retirement.

Disraeli had inherited one small colonial war from his predecessor, for, as the ministries changed over, a series of battles were being fought out in the forests of the interior of the Gold Coast. The outcome was a treaty with the Ashanti which confirmed the British in possession of their protected area. Further results included a promise by King Kofi that human sacrifices would be stopped and a declaration by the British government abolishing slavery on the Gold Coast. In the same year the Fiji Isles in the Pacific were annexed.

Another more spectacular *coup* followed in 1875—the purchase of the Khedive Ismail's shares in the Suez Canal Company. Neither Disraeli nor Palmerston had ever cared greatly for the building of the canal, since it meant that the route to the East would no longer be under British control. It was the French engineer, de Lesseps, who eventually formed the Suez Canal Company, and the canal, which was completed as an entirely French project, was opened in 1869. The Egyptian Khedive, however, who held seven-sixteenths of the shares in the Company, was habitually in financial difficulties. As early as 1870 he had suggested to Lord Granville that the British government should buy up the whole concern, while France was embroiled in war with Prussia. This opportunity was lost, but by 1875 the Khedive was determined to sell his shares and was already in touch with two French groups, when the news that they were on the market reached Disraeli's ear. To forestall the French financiers £4 million were needed at once, and Parliament was not sitting. Lord Derby had doubts; Disraeli had none. The house of Rothschild advanced the £4 million and Disraeli could write to the Queen: 'It is just settled; you have it, Madam.' In fact, the Khedive's shares did not represent a controlling interest, but the government was now at least able to negotiate lower bills for merchant shipping, four-fifths of which was British.

The East figured again in another of Disraeli's strokes. It seemed to him that the British monarchy would make a more direct appeal to the Indians if they could feel that the Sovereign was their own personal ruler, and so Disraeli proposed that Victoria should assume the title of Empress of India. The idea had all the flamboyance of Disraeli's somewhat theatrical nature, and it met with an opposition that was equally typical of the English upper classes, who considered this sort of thing best left to Continentals. Victoria, however, was delighted, and her new title was established by law in 1876.

Eight years before, after the Conservative defeat at the polls, Disraeli had asked the Queen to confer a peerage upon his wife, while he himself remained in the Commons, but by 1876 his health was seriously deteriorating, and in August he moved to the House of Lords after receiving the Earldom of Beaconsfield. Thus it was from the Lords that he had to handle the great crisis that now threatened to shatter the peace of Europe.

In the summer of 1875 Slav peasants under Turkish rule in Hercegovina rose in revolt against the tax collectors after a bad harvest in the previous year. Volunteers from the dependent Principality of Serbia came to their assistance and the fighting spread throughout Bosnia. This was dangerous enough in itself, but in May 1876 the Bulgars also rebelled, whereupon the Turks sent in their Bashi-Bazouks, who proceeded to carry out a series of appalling massacres, in which it was estimated about 12,000 Christians were killed.

With the Balkans aflame none of the great Powers could remain indifferent; yet none of them had any immediate hope of gain from the weakness of Turkey. Gortchakov had summed up the Eastern Question neatly to the British ambassador at St. Petersburg in 1875: 'There were two ways of dealing with the Eastern Question, first a complete reconstruction, or, second, a mere replastering which would keep matters together for another term of years. No one could possibly wish for a complete settlement—everyone must wish to put it off as long as possible.' The problem for Russia was that even in an autocratic state diplomats cannot entirely ignore certain emotional issues, and once the revolts had started Panslav feeling demanded that the Russians should not leave the Balkan Christians unsupported. The problem for Austria was that she dared not allow Turkey to succumb, for, as Gentz had written in 1815, 'the end of the Turkish monarchy could be survived by the Austrian for but a short time'. It was these two conflicting viewpoints that turned the Balkan revolts into a great European crisis.

A possible solution on which it seemed at first that all sides might agree was to present Turkey with proposals for internal reforms. In August 1875 the Powers of Central Europe, Austria, Germany, and Russia, drew up a set of reforms, which came to very little, although Turkey nominally accepted them. In December Andrassy, the Austrian Foreign Minister, drew up another set which the Turks again accepted, but since they did not act upon them, the rebels would not disband. In May 1876 Gortchakov, Andrassy, and Bismarck put forward the Berlin Memorandum which suggested yet another programme of reform, adding a hint of stronger action if this failed. This Memorandum was accepted by France and Italy, but rejected by Great Britain.

The reason for Disraeli's refusal to accept the Memorandum was a mistrust of the motives of the three ministers at Berlin. He suspected them of planning some form of partition and was determined to stand by the established British policy of supporting Turkey. Even the news of the atrocities in Bulgaria did not sway his judgement, mainly because Elliott, the British ambassador at Constantinople, who was extremely pro-Turkish, minimized their extent. For the moment Disraeli preferred to follow an independent line of action and dispatched the British fleet to Besika Bay.

Soon, however, the true picture of the Bulgarian massacres emerged and with it a new political factor on the domestic scene. On 6 September Gladstone published his pamphlet, *The Bulgarian Horrors and the Question of the East*. Within a month about 200,000 copies of this tremendous indictment of Turkish rule had been sold. 'Their Zaptiehs and their Mudirs, their Bimbashis and their Yuzbachis, their Kaimakams and their Pashas, one and all, bag and baggage, shall, I hope, clear out from the province they have desolated and profaned.' Never in all the stormy course of these two men's lives had the hatred between them been so intense. 'That unprincipled maniac,' Disraeli called his great rival in a letter to Derby, 'and with one commanding characteristic—whether preaching, praying, speechifying or scribbling—never a gentle-man.' And in a public address at Aylesbury he remarked that Gladstone was worse than any Bulgarian horror. The unfortunate fact that gained prominence was that the country was divided—Gladstone inviting the Russians to drive the Turks out of Bulgaria, Disraeli threatening Russia with war if she did not cease to give unofficial assistance to the Balkan Christians.

It is possible that this division of opinion in Great Britain may have contributed to a change of front on the part of Tsar Alexander II. In November 1876 he announced that he could no longer remain indifferent to the sufferings of the Balkan Christians. The Panslavs had got their way, and now the problem for Gortchakov was to find some means of enabling Russia to intervene militarily without involving herself in a European war. Two pieces of negotiation made this possible. At the end of 1876 a conference of ambassadors was held at Constantinople, in which Lord Salisbury acted for the British government. While he was there he established good relations with Ignatiev, the Russian ambassador, who convinced him of the reasonableness of the Russian demands for large-scale reforms in Turkey. The conference resulted in agreement over the terms of these reforms, but the Sultan, Abdul Hamid, led on by the Young Ottoman leader, Midhat Pasha, rejected them. In fact, the Turks believed that the pattern of events that had led up to the Crimean war was about to repeat itself, although the existence of a general agreement, in which Great Britain had now joined, should have made it apparent to them that an immediate alliance against Russia was unlikely. The second piece of negotiation led to the Budapest Conventions, completed in the spring of 1877, whereby Austria agreed to remain neutral in the event of a Russo-Turk war, provided that she acquired Bosnia and Hercegovina and that no great Slav state was erected out of the ruin of Turkish territories in Europe. The way ahead now seemed clear and Russia declared war on Turkey on 24 April, 1877.

The course of the war changed everything. The Russian army advanced into the Balkans until, in June, they came up against the fortress of Plevna, which the Turkish commander, Osman

Pasha, was determined to hold. He did hold it until December, when the garrison was finally starved into surrender, and this delay proved fatal for the Tsar. The weary Russian army did not reach Adrianople until 20 January, 1878, and by that time the British public no longer saw the Turks as the perpetrators of the Bulgarian horrors, but as the heroic defenders of Plevna. The threat to Constantinople was obvious and a war fever raged throughout Great Britain.

'We don't want to fight, but by Jingo, if we do,
We've got the men, we've got the ships, we've got the money too.'

Gladstone retained a certain amount of support in the north and among the aristocracy, but the Londoners were with Disraeli, and one witness recorded that 'the ordinary Sunday afternoon diversion of the London rough' was to howl outside Gladstone's house. On 23 January the British fleet was ordered to Constantinople and the government asked for a grant of £6 million for military purposes.

All these circumstances led rapidly to an armistice. The British fleet could have done little more than bombard Constantinople in the event of a Russian occupation, and Great Britain had not been able to find a definite ally with whom to operate—the usual difficulty. Thus the Turks were not encouraged to continue the fight. On the other hand, the Russians, aware that their army had not distinguished itself and was no longer in good shape, were also anxious to terminate hostilities. The war ended, and the next debating point among the Powers was to be the terms of the treaty that the Russians imposed on the Turks.

The Treaty of San Stefano was negotiated by Ignatiev and signed on 3 March, 1878. Russia gained a slice of Armenia and took Bessarabia from Rumania, who was given the Dobruja by way of compensation. Montenegro, Serbia, and Rumania all gained their independence. No mention was made of Austria receiving Bosnia and Hercegovina, originally earmarked as her reward for remaining neutral. The most startling change was the creation of a large autonomous Bulgaria, whose territories were to be bounded by the Danube, the Black Sea, the Aegean Sea, and the Albanian mountains.[1]

From a purely Balkan point of view the idea of a big Bulgaria was not a bad one, but it was put forward without any kind of diplomatic preparation. Gortchakov, who had earlier failed to persuade the Tsar to be content with a little Bulgaria, was furious with Ignatiev and told him to sort out the difficulties himself. This proved impossible. Andrassy would not accept the big Bulgaria, claiming that it was a breach of the Budapest Conventions. Disraeli was determined to stand firm, and carried his Cabinet with him in calling up the reserves and ordering a large contingent of Indian troops to Malta. Derby, who until now had hoped to hold him in check, resigned from the Foreign Office and was replaced by Lord Salisbury. This change certainly pleased the Queen, who had been strongly in favour of the Turks, and enabled Disraeli to present a much firmer front to the Russians.

Salisbury's first action was to draft a Circular Note to the Powers, setting out a reasoned argument against the Treaty of San Stefano, objecting to the attempt to create a vast Russian puppet state, and invoking the agreement of 1871 [2] that no territorial readjustment could be made without consultation with all the Powers.

The reaction to this Note really pointed to the way in which the crisis would end. Russia did not feel equal to embarking on a war in which Great Britain and Austria would probably be allies. A further blow was the realization that Bismarck did not intend to be drawn in as Russia's ally. The friendship between Russia and Prussia had been long established, but Bismarck's earlier policy of aggrandisement at the expense of Austria and France made it essential for him to avoid a situation in which either of those Powers might find allies and, in a general conflagration, regain something of their position in Europe. Now Russia was disappointed in her hopes of support from her one friend and was forced to negotiate. A further weakness for Russia was revealed in the fact that Austria's sole concern was to preserve the *status quo* in the Balkans, and there was consequently no price that

---

[1] See map, p. 305.   [2] See p. 288.

Russia could offer her in compensation for the creation of a big Bulgaria. The Russians accordingly agreed to a Congress at Berlin, and it looked as if Disraeli could call the tune.

Many of the issues were settled beforehand by a series of secret conventions which Great Britain signed with Russia, Austria, and Turkey. In the first of these Russia agreed to give up her dream of a big Bulgaria, and the last was a British guarantee of Turkish possessions in Asia in return for the island of Cyprus. Later, the British government was momentarily embarrassed by the publication of the Russian treaty in *The Globe*, who got hold of it through one of the copying clerks employed at the Foreign Office, but the incident had little effect on the Congress, which opened at Berlin in the middle of June.

For a month Berlin was the scene of great banquets, concerts, and Royal audiences, and Disraeli loved every minute of it. 'What are you thinking of?' the Princess Radziwill asked him at a reception given at the Austrian embassy. 'I am not thinking,' he answered, 'I am enjoying myself.' The Congress itself, at which the British delegation consisted of the Prime Minister, his Foreign Secretary, and Odo Russell, the British ambassador, was held in the Radziwill Palace, and at the first session Disraeli had been determined to address the gathering in French, until dissuaded from this by his colleagues, who felt that enough confusion existed already. Despite the preliminary treaties, the Russians were able to create a good many difficulties and at one point, when they appeared resolute over refusing to allow Turkey to put troops into Eastern Roumelia, a territory invented at the Congress to the south of the small Bulgaria that Russia had accepted, Disraeli delivered his own little ultimatum by ordering a special train for Calais, by which his mission would leave the Congress at once. His firmness had results, since Bismarck hastily persuaded the Russians to give way. For Disraeli the whole Congress was the climax of his career, and with his own personal success he took his country to a new peak of prestige in Europe. At Dover on his return he leant from the carriage window and assured the crowd: 'Gentlemen, we bring you peace, and, I think I may say, peace with honour.' The cheers that greeted him here and at London only confirmed the comment that Bismarck had already made: 'Der alte Jude, das ist der Mann!'

By the terms of the agreement reached at Berlin, the Russians kept Bessarabia and Batum on the Black Sea. Big Bulgaria was sub-divided into three areas by two frontiers running roughly east–west. To the south of the Danube a small Christian principality of Bulgaria was established under Russian organization. Below this, Eastern Roumelia was to be a Turkish province under a Christian governor. The southernmost territory, locally known as Macedonia, was to remain under Turkish rule. Austria was to occupy Bosnia and Hercegovina and to garrison the Sanjak of Novibazar, separating Serbia and Montenegro. The British gained an agreement which for all practical purposes allowed them to send a fleet through the Straits into the Black Sea whenever they wished. With this was coupled a scheme for posting British military consuls in Armenia, where they were to superintend the fortifying of the northern frontiers of Turkey-in-Asia.

No Congress could have solved the Eastern Question, but the agreements did at least carry out fairly effectively the replastering of which Gortchakov had spoken three years before. The whole crisis had involved a series of setbacks for Russia. The war itself had shown that the Turkish army was not to be entirely discounted; the settlement at Berlin had been a defeat for Panslavism and had shown that the British were still dominant in the eastern Mediterranean. The new Straits settlement, Cyprus, and the dispatch of military consuls to Armenia all pointed to a positive policy in the Near East for bolstering up Turkey against Russia. Austria had been on the winning side, but there had actually been little for her to win, and the occupation of Bosnia and Hercegovina really only served to demonstrate the rickety political state of Turkey whom she was bent on preserving. The most significant aspect of the crisis lay in Bismarck's change of front. The Russians felt themselves badly let down and Alexander II described the Congress as a European coalition against Russia led by Bismarck. From now on Austria occupied first place in Bismarck's scheme of things and this foreshadowed the close alliance of the Central Powers and the gradual cooling of relations between

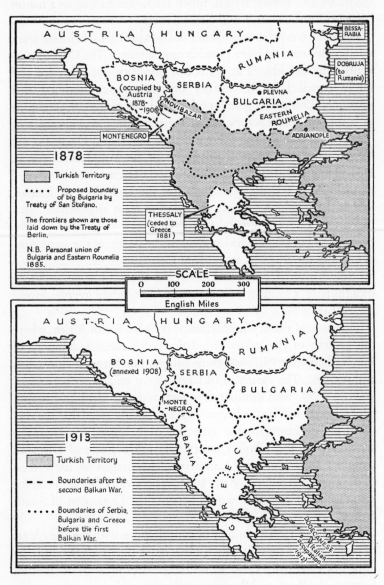

5. THE BALKANS, 1878–1913

Germany and Russia, which, much later, was to lead to alliances between Russia, France, and Great Britain.

Disraeli's reception in England did not prevent Gladstone from assailing his rival at every possible opportunity. The Cyprus convention he denounced as 'an act of duplicity not surpassed and rarely equalled in the history of nations'—an outburst that prompted Disraeli to give his celebrated description of Gladstone as 'a sophisticated rhetorician, inebriated with the exuberance of his own verbosity'. But there is little doubt that if Disraeli could have fought an election at this moment, he would have won it. He had just accepted the Garter from the Queen, who had wanted to make him a Duke—although not the Dukedom of Jericho, which the Gladstone family regarded as most appropriate, provided that he were dispatched there as soon as possible. In the eyes of the country he had preserved the peace, at the same time as keeping the Russians away from Constantinople. But this was no time for an election, and when the moment came, eighteen months later, a number of subsequent disasters had overshadowed the glories of 1878.

The scene of the first misfortune was laid in South Africa, where the growth of the white population with the development of mining had led to an increasing antagonism between Europeans and natives. The existence of large native armies, such as Cetewayo's Zulus, who numbered 40,000, added to the likelihood of general war, and it was becoming increasingly clear that the day of *ad hoc* decisions on the spot was over. Some statesmanlike settlement of the whole country was called for, and Disraeli's Colonial Secretary, Lord Carnarvon, encouraged by the success of the Canadian federation in 1867,[1] was convinced of the need for a similar federation that would become the Dominion of South Africa.

In 1875 and 1876 a number of consultations with the Presidents of the two Boer republics took place in South Africa and in London, but eventually came to nothing. An outbreak of fighting between the Boers and the Bantu tribes persuaded Carnarvon that delay would be fatal and, as a preliminary measure, he drafted a

[1] See p. 368.

Parliamentary Bill that would permit the formation of a federation. Simultaneously he sent Sir Theophilus Shepstone out to South Africa to negotiate with the Transvaal and to annex the republic, if the inhabitants were willing. In the spring of 1877 Sir Bartle Frere was appointed Governor of the Cape, but on his arrival he learnt that Shepstone had already proclaimed the annexation of the Transvaal. Carnarvon had made the mistake of dividing his authority in South Africa. It was soon clear that Shepstone had rushed the whole thing through too quickly, and in jeopardizing the chances of getting the Transvaal Boers to acquiesce had added considerably to the difficulties that faced the new Governor, although for the moment the Boers made no resistance owing to the presence of the Zulus.

A boundary settlement between the Transvaal and the Zulus was urgently needed, and Frere managed to negotiate an extremely fair-minded agreement with Cetewayo, which went a long way to meet the Zulus' claims. At the same time, however, he stipulated that the Zulu army must be disbanded and a British resident be allowed into their territory. The Zulus, feeling that this would mean death for their form of society and way of life, rejected the terms, and at the end of 1878 Disraeli and his Cabinet found that they had a colonial war on their hands.

This was bad enough, but there was worse to follow. Ten days after Lord Chelmsford had marched his forces into Zululand, a Zulu army fell upon his camp at Isandhlwana and carried out a wholesale massacre. The British public first heard the news on 11 February, 1879, and opinion which had been so enthusiastically in favour of the government the previous summer now became highly critical. Fortunately the situation soon improved. Natal, endangered by the defeat, was saved by the defence of Rorke's Drift and in July the Zulu army was smashed at the battle of Ulundi. There followed the capture and deportation of Cetewayo and the splitting up of Zululand into eight principalities.

Long before all this Lord Carnarvon had resigned from the government, together with Lord Derby, over Disraeli's Balkan policy. He sincerely believed that federation had been successfully achieved, but time was to prove him wrong. As it was, the opposition had gained considerable ammunition. The war was stigmatized as unjust and expensive, and although Frere had acted on his own responsibility, Disraeli got the blame for it. The annexation of the Transvaal was another charge that Gladstone laid against the government, and here the Boers, now freed from the Zulu menace, saw the possibility of a future ally.

The other trouble spot, Afghanistan, was more closely related to European politics. Afghanistan, and Baluchistan to the south of it, formed a couple of buffer states between Russian Turkestan and British India. Naturally each Power was anxious to prevent Shere Ali, the Amir of Afghanistan, from falling under the influence of the other. In 1876 Lord Lytton, the son of the novelist, was appointed Viceroy of India, and in the December of that year a treaty was concluded with Baluchistan allowing British troops to be stationed at Quetta, just on the southern border of Afghanistan. In July 1878, however, immediately after the Congress of Berlin, the Russians, in return for financing the Amir's military preparations, were allowed to establish a mission at Kabul under General Stoletov. Lord Lytton at once demanded similar facilities, and when his mission was refused permission to enter the country, British armed forces invaded Afghanistan at three separate points. Shere Ali fled to Russian Turkestan and the British set up his son Yakub Khan in succession to him. The Treaty of Gandamak was signed in May 1879, establishing a British minister at Kabul and giving the British full control over Afghan foreign policy. This at first seemed like success, but disaster soon followed. On 3 September the Afghans in Kabul rose in revolt. The entire British mission was massacred and serious fighting continued in the south of Afghanistan during the following year.

Isandhlwana and Kabul proved to be two mortal blows for Disraeli. In a sense he was just a little ahead of his time, for the British public had not yet warmed to the policy of Imperialism. The country was in the throes of economic depression, and the lack of any policy for Ireland caused the Irish Home Rule party to redouble their efforts at obstruction in the Commons. It was at this moment that Gladstone chose to carry out a whirlwind campaign of rhetoric against the government, in preparation for the next election. For a fortnight he 'stumped' Midlothian in an ecstasy of moral indignation at the iniquities of Imperialism. He poured invective on a ministry that had annexed Cyprus and the Transvaal, made war on the Zulus, interfered in Turkey-in-Asia, and was now engaged in war against the Afghans. 'Remember the rights of the savage. Remember that the happiness of his humble home, remember that the sanctity of life in the hill villages of Afghanistan, among the winter snows, is as inviolable in the eyes of Almighty God as can be your own!' Such a political campaign was a remarkable innovation and, needless to say, Queen Victoria was horrified. 'The Colossus of Words', *Punch* called him, and there was little doubt that, despite his resignation, Gladstone was still the real leader of the Liberal party.

In February 1880, after the Conservatives had won an un-expected victory at a by-election at Southwark, Disraeli judged that the moment had come to dissolve. He was confronted by the most formidable organization that had yet developed in the history of British party politics. At Birmingham, Schnadhorst, the secretary of the Liberal Association, and Joseph Chamberlain were the driving force behind a great nation-wide propaganda campaign for further social reform, and had been responsible for much of the support that Gladstone had gained in the north during the Balkan crisis. In these years the Radicals came near to captur-ing the Liberal party, and in the election of 1880 they left the Conservatives little hope of victory. The Liberals won a majority of 135 seats over their opponents, while the Irish Home Rulers consolidated their position as a third party with sixty-one seats. Disraeli resigned. The Queen, in despair, turned to Lord Harting-ton and Lord Granville, the official Liberal leaders in the Com-mons and the Lords, but the second Midlothian campaign, with which Gladstone had won his seat in this election, pointed to only one man. The electorate had chosen their own Prime Minister.

3. Gladstone's second administration, 1880-5

Gladstone certainly had no doubts about the rightness of this decision. 'Looking calmly on this course of experience,' he wrote,

'I do believe that the Almighty has employed me for His purposes in a manner larger or more special than before . . .' But the tragedy of this second administration of Gladstone's was that in spite of their leader's renewed vigour the Liberals lacked a definite policy, largely owing to the continued threat of a split between Whigs and Radicals. Gladstone, well aware of the Whigs' growing dislike of Radical demagogy, gave them the majority of places in his new Cabinet; only two Radicals were included—John Bright and Joseph Chamberlain. But the Radicals would never allow him to forget that he owed his electoral victory mainly to them, and watched him with growing suspicion.

Disraeli still led the Conservatives in the Lords, but his health was failing fast and on 19 April, 1881 he died, thus presenting Gladstone with the task of proposing a national memorial in Westminster to his bitter opponent—a task which he performed with typical skill and magnanimity. But although Disraeli was dead, the duel between the two men did not end. Throughout this turbulent ministry Gladstone was haunted by the ghost of the late Conservative Prime Minister, for Disraeli had left a legacy of Imperialism that Gladstone might curse but could never escape. As a result, the issues that arose were too seldom of his own choosing. During his first administration there had been difficulties enough, but these had been the consequences of a dynamic domestic policy. This time the difficulties imposed themselves from outside, forcing the government to find solutions as it went.

In the Commons two new personalities faced him—Parnell, now with a sizeable party behind him, and Lord Randolph Churchill, who headed a small 'ginger' group within the Conservatives. The vitality of the Churchill group was demonstrated at once in what began as a small incident at the very beginning of the administration. Charles Bradlaugh, Radical M.P. for Northampton, maintaining that as an atheist he could not take the Parliamentary oath, offered to make an affirmation of allegiance. When a committee of the House voted against an affirmation, Bradlaugh agreed to take the oath, but the younger members of the opposition now saw a chance to exploit the religious issue. They could rally many of the Nonconformist M.P.s and all the

Irish with the cry of 'Bradlaugh and Blasphemy', and during the whole of the administration the wretched struggle went on to keep Bradlaugh from taking his seat. Three times he was re-elected by his constituency and on one occasion he was ejected from the House by ten policemen. Gladstone, whose Church-manship could never be doubted, asked the House to exercise tolerance. Indeed, if the Speaker had acted with greater vigour at the beginning, the incident would never have developed in this way, but it was not until 1886 that a new Speaker summarily withdrew the whole question as being outside the House's province.

Apart from the Bradlaugh incident Gladstone's first months were taken up with the problem of rounding off Disraeli's foreign and colonial policies, with which he had so strongly disagreed. The Turks were forced to hand over to Montenegro and Greece certain territories that had been specified in the Treaty of Berlin. Disraeli's military consuls in Asia Minor were withdrawn, although Great Britain did not give back Cyprus to Turkey. Gladstone wanted to give it to Greece, but was eventually persuaded against this by Lord Granville. In Afghanistan, where fighting was still going on, General Roberts' troops carried out a remarkable march from Kabul to the relief of the besieged British forces at Kandahar, but the decision was finally taken by the government to evacuate the whole country, and a nephew of Shere Ali, Abdurrahman, was set up as Amir on the understanding that he would allow British control of his foreign policy in return for a subsidy.

Over Turkey and Afghanistan it had been possible for Gladstone to take a line consistent with his great pronouncements during the Midlothian campaign. The question of the Transvaal was not so straightforward. The Boers hoped for the restoration of their independence. The Radicals expected the recall of Sir Bartle Frere. Neither happened. Gladstone hoped that some sort of federation might be achieved out of the existing situation, and Frere was far too knowledgeable to be dispensed with at a moment like this. In the summer of 1880 an attempt at federation failed owing to the obstinacy of the Boers, and after this Frere was recalled. The Transvaal was still not given back its independence, and, as it turned out, these were the last months when Gladstone might have restored it with dignity. In December the Boers took to arms; in January 1881, under Piet Joubert, they repulsed Sir George Colley's troops at Laing's Nek, and a month later, on 27 February, destroyed his forces on Majuba Hill. In Great Britain the news roused a fresh wave of 'jingoism', but Gladstone refused to be moved by it. He believed that he was being drawn into a colonial war, contrary to all his principles, and in any case the situation was an unhealthy one, since he could not be sure that the Cape Dutch would not join in and the war become more widespread. The only thing to do was to swallow national pride and to make terms. On 2 August, 1881 the Convention of Pretoria restored independence to the Transvaal, leaving Great Britain responsible for its foreign relations. Such a concession was in perfect accord with the sentiments that Gladstone had expressed in opposition, but it would have looked better if he could have made it a year earlier.

His worst difficulties arose over the very question that he had sworn to solve—Ireland. In the last years of Disraeli's administration the growing agricultural depression had swept away what little Gladstone's Land Act of 1870 had achieved. As increasing numbers of Irish tenants were unable to pay their rents, evictions mounted, until, in 1880 alone, the figure was well over 10,000. A new despair took hold of the Irish and they turned once more to violence. In 1879 a Land League was formed by Michael Davitt to gain Home Rule and security for tenants, and in the following year Parnell agreed to become its President. This alliance between the Land League and Parnell's Home Rulers, whose position at Westminster had been strengthened in the 1880 election, presented the government with a challenge greater than anything since O'Connell's battle for Catholic emancipation. When a half-hearted measure for compensating evicted tenants was thrown out by the Lords in 1880, fury blazed up in Ireland. Ricks were set on fire, cattle were maimed, and men were dragged out of their houses and assaulted. Parnell was prepared to condone anything short of murder and one of his suggestions was a policy of 'boycott', so named after the first person against whom it was tried. Captain Boycott had taken over a farm from an evicted tenant and suddenly found that no one—servants, labourers, shopkeepers—would have anything to do with him. As Parnell said, it was as if he were a leper of old, and the scheme was found to be so effective that it was soon put widely into use.

To Gladstone only one course seemed now possible—another Irish Land Bill. He set to work on it, but at once came under great pressure from Forster, Chief Secretary for Ireland, and Lord Cowper, the Lord Lieutenant, who insisted that, in the meantime, a new Coercion Act was essential to deal with the disorders. Gladstone agreed reluctantly, and in the course of the debate over this Bill in the Commons the Home Rulers showed the power of their tactics of obstruction by prolonging one sitting for forty-one hours; even then the Speaker had to close the debate on his own responsibility. Eventually it took an amendment of the rules of procedure to get the Coercion Bill through. Gladstone rapidly followed it up with his Land Bill. This has been summed up as the three F's—fixity of tenure, fair rents, and free sale for Irish tenants. Rent tribunals were to be set up and the tenant was to be free from the fear of eviction as long as he paid the rent that the tribunal established. An amendment prevented the rent being raised against improvements carried out by the tenant. It was the kind of measure that Gladstone had believed impossible in 1870, and even now it took up fifty-eight sittings of the Commons while Gladstone fought through clause after clause. The Queen helped him to prevent the Lords from destroying the Bill and on 22 August, 1881 it became law. Lower rents would mean the lowering of the price of land and thus the way was paved for tenants later to be able to buy their farms—aided by government purchase schemes. With this Act Gladstone struck at one of the fundamental causes of Irish misery, and although he never lived to see the pacification of Ireland for which he hoped, he had made possible the eventual emergence of a land-owning peasantry, on which a new life for Ireland could be based.

The tragedy was that the measure had come too late. The passing of the Act seemed only to prove the efficacy of a policy of terrorism. Parnell and his nationalists actually opposed the Bill in the Commons. They had two reasons for this. One was that no provision had been made for the numerous tenants who owed arrears of rent; the other was to preserve their group as an extremist party who might force the tribunals to put the rents as low as possible. Gladstone's patience was at an end. In a public speech at Leeds, in October, he warned Parnell that if the Irish outrages did not cease, 'the resources of civilisation are not yet exhausted'. By this he meant jail. In reply Parnell called Gladstone 'this masquerading knight errant, this pretending champion of the rights of every nation except those of the Irish nation'. This was open defiance, and on 13 October, under the new Coercion Act, Parnell was arrested and imprisoned at Kilmainham.

As might have been foreseen, this did little good. The Land League proclaimed a rent strike, and a new wave of violence and crime burst upon the Irish countryside. Accordingly, in April 1882, negotiations were reopened through Joseph Chamberlain and Captain O'Shea, an Irish Liberal M.P. Parnell had his own reasons for wishing to come to terms. He was afraid that during his absence he might lose his control over the nationalists in Ireland. There was also a more personal reason that was later to ruin his career. In 1880 he had made the acquaintance of Mrs. O'Shea, who was living apart from her husband. The two had fallen in love at first sight, and for Parnell, aloof and isolated in the bitterness of the political struggle, this was the lasting relationship of his life. Katherine O'Shea had been looking after an aged aunt, on whom her whole family depended, and it had been agreed that in order to save the old lady's feelings they would make no attempt to gain a divorce until after her death. In February 1882 Mrs. O'Shea gave birth to a daughter by Parnell. The child died, and in the circumstances it was natural that he should wish to be able to see the mother. In April he was allowed out of prison, ostensibly to visit his sister in Paris, and it was while he was with Mrs. O'Shea that her husband was able to bring Parnell into touch with Chamberlain and Gladstone. Agreement was reached over an Arrears Bill, which the government promised to introduce, whereby tenants' arrears would be paid off out of some public fund, and as a result of the Kilmainham Treaty, as it was called, Parnell and two other Irish leaders were released.

Once again Gladstone might hope that pacification had been achieved. Once again tragedy followed. On the conclusion of the treaty Lord Cowper, the Viceroy, and W. E. Forster, Chief Secretary, resigned and were replaced by Lord Spencer and Lord Frederick Cavendish. On the evening of 6 May Cavendish and Mr. Burke, the under-secretary, were walking in the Phoenix Park in Dublin when they were attacked and stabbed to death with knives. The assailants belonged to a group known as the Invincibles, who had sworn to kill Burke, and there followed an appalling period of murder throughout the summer in Ireland, as the Invincibles struck again and again. It was only after the passing of a new Coercion Act that they were finally arrested; five of the Phoenix Park murderers were hanged, after two of the others had turned Queen's evidence, one of whom attempted to get away to Natal afterwards, but was shot by another of the band while on board ship.

It seems clear that Parnell had had nothing to do with the Phoenix Park outrage. He was much shaken by it and believed that it was an attempt to ruin his work. For the next few years he aimed at appeasement, and the combination of the Land Act and the Kilmainham Treaty made it possible for the government to enjoy a lull in Irish affairs. It had been an ugly period. Obstruction and violence had culminated in the imprisonment of M.P.s and the murder of high government officials. Parnell himself carried a revolver with him when he sat in the Commons, a symbol of the times, and it was understandable that Gladstone should have fears for the future of Parliamentary government and should be thinking once again of the possibility of retirement.

Meanwhile, still unable to shake off the legacy of Disraeli, he had become involved in a somewhat unpleasant piece of Imperialism of his own. It was France and Great Britain who made the principal gains along the southern shore of the Mediterranean, but during the last few years North Africa had become a theatre of European diplomacy, and it was typical of Bismarck's skill that he should be able to turn these interests to his own account. In 1878 he had suggested to the French that they should set about annexing Tunis, since this might possibly take their minds off Alsace-Lorraine. 'I want to turn your eyes away from Metz and Strasbourg by helping you to find satisfaction elsewhere.' It might also have the effect of annoying Italy, whom, later, Bismarck was to include in a Triple Alliance with Germany and Austria.[1] Similarly, he had suggested that Great Britain should take Egypt in return for Russian control of Constantinople, since this would certainly stimulate ill-feelings between France and Great Britain. Bismarck himself wanted nothing from North Africa, and he was therefore in an excellent position to set the cat among the pigeons.

Disraeli and Salisbury had had the sense to keep clear of Egypt. Cyprus and the 1878 Straits agreement with the Turks had given them all that they needed to maintain British interests in the eastern Mediterranean. The weakness, however, lay in the financial instability of the Khedive Ismail. In 1876 he had announced virtual bankruptcy—with a total debt of about £90 million—and an Anglo-French dual control had been set up over Egyptian financial affairs. This was followed by the deposition of Ismail, who was succeeded by his son Tewfik. Then, during the first two years of Gladstone's ministry, a new factor appeared on the scene in Cairo—a nationalist movement under Colonel Arabi Pasha, who voiced a growing hatred for Turkish overlords and European intruders, and throughout 1881 the position of the Khedive Tewfik became considerably weakened. To France, anxious to safeguard the interests of her shareholders, and to Great Britain, concerned for the canal itself, it was becoming clear that the very existence of the canal implied some form of Anglo-French occupation of Egypt. Negotiations, which included an unsuccessful plan to call in the Turks, continued throughout the early months of 1882, while Arabi's movement grew increasingly aggressive. As a precautionary measure, in May, the French and British fleets were dispatched to Alexandria. On 11 June Egyptian nationalists massacred fifty Europeans and, amongst others, wounded the British consul. By the end of the month Arabi was

[1] See p. 353.

fortifying Alexandria and the Powers had to decide on what action they should take.

At this point the two countries followed separate courses. The French Prime Minister, Freycinet, had at last agreed to an Anglo-French force occupying the Canal Zone, but he was defeated in the French Chamber. France in this period remained obsessed with the thought of another German attack and would not risk military ventures so far afield. On 11 July the French admiral outside Alexandria steamed away, while Admiral Seymour remained behind to destroy the Alexandria forts in a ten and a half hours' bombardment.

This was Gladstone in a new role. He had had to decide whether interference was justified and whether Great Britain could make that interference alone. The state of Egyptian finances and the rise of Arabi Pasha left him no doubts. 'We should not discharge our duty', he said in the Commons eleven days after the bombardment, 'if we did not endeavour to convert the present interior state of Egypt from anarchy and conflict to peace and order.' One man he could not convince. John Bright, the old Quaker, resigned from the Cabinet, commenting that Gladstone's action was 'worse than anything perpetrated by Dizzy'. Gladstone respected him for this—'splendid old fellow, such a grand moral tone'—but stood unswerving by his decision. Sir Garnet Wolseley was sent out with an army to Egypt, and after routing the Egyptian forces at Tel-el-Kebir on 13 September, occupied Cairo.

The speed and efficiency of the whole operation was a testimony to the remarkable change brought about by Cardwell during Gladstone's first ministry, but the neatness of the military aspect was not matched by the political arrangement that followed. The capture of Egypt had come about without any pre-conceived plan and the British government could never quite make up its mind what to do with it. Gladstone and succeeding Prime Ministers were continually promising to withdraw, yet the very factor that had brought them in—control of the canal—prevented them from leaving. There was no official connection, but Sir Evelyn Baring, later Lord Cromer, returned to Egypt, where he had been finance member of the Viceroy's council, and for the next twenty years looked after the interests of the shareholders as British agent and Consul-general. The European repercussions were as Bismarck had foreseen. French pride was hurt; Russia had had to watch the British make far greater gains than anything that she had made in 1878. Such a position naturally threw Great Britain willy-nilly towards Germany. When Baring wrote to Lord Rosebery, Foreign Secretary, in 1886, 'Berlin and not Cairo is the real centre of Egyptian affairs', he put in a nutshell the immediate significance of Gladstone's intervention in Egypt.

Meanwhile, at home, the Radical section of the Liberals was growing impatient. Excitements overseas and the turbulence of the Irish nationalists had considerably lessened the flow of measures of domestic reform. Certainly there had been some. Chamberlain was able to pilot through a Seamen's Wages Act and a Grain Cargoes Act. Flogging in the Army and Navy was abolished in 1881. The Married Women's Property Act was passed in 1882 and the same year produced the Settled Land Act, which allowed the sale of settled land from the great hereditary estates. Most significant of all was the Corrupt Practices Act of 1883, which defined precisely the amount of money that could be spent on each electoral campaign, ruled out every form of bribery and undue influence, and even laid down the number of conveyances that could be used for bringing voters to the polls. The Act went a great way towards clearing up various forms of electoral corruption, and elections are still governed by its rules to this day.

But all this was little enough for the Radicals. The speeches of Joseph Chamberlain pointed more and more to out-and-out democracy, mobilizing all the violence of class warfare. In one furious attack on Lord Salisbury he stigmatized the whole class to which he belonged—'who toil not neither do they spin'. In a country just recovering from a depression, where the new message of Socialism was already finding ready hearers among the working classes, these bold sentiments set Chamberlain apart as the man of a new age, reaping the harvest sown by mid-century Liberalism. It was this Radical agitation, together with the realization of existing anomalies, that persuaded Gladstone's Cabinet that the time had come for a new electoral reform.

A Bill was accordingly introduced early in 1884, but after passing the Commons, was held up by the Lords who demanded that a Redistribution Bill should be passed first. In fact, they believed that this might be the simplest way of killing the whole thing, and throughout the summer Chamberlain and John Morley did their best to leave the people in no doubt over this. The Lords had been careful to avoid crucial issues during the last few decades, but now the Radicals seized their opportunity. 'The Peers against the People', 'Mend them or end them' were the cries which the populace took up, and this agitation played some part in forcing an agreement between leading Conservatives and Liberals.

Two Acts were passed. The effect of the Franchise Act [1] was simply to extend household suffrage to the counties, while the Irish system was made uniform with that in England. Throughout the United Kingdom the county electorate rose from 1,200,000 to just under 3,500,000, while the total electorate now reached 5,700,000. The Radicals were not entirely satisfied, since the ancient right franchises, involving the continuation of plural voting, still lingered on and the vote was not given to women. In the main, however, the Act of 1884 completed a process that had begun in 1832, and apart from the question of female suffrage, which was to lead to a long battle later on, all that still remained to be done was largely a matter of tidying up minor peculiarities.

The redistribution measures also brought the electoral scene to something close to what we know today. Boroughs of less than 15,000 inhabitants lost both members; others of less than 50,000 lost one member, and in all 142 seats became available for redistribution among the more heavily populated regions. Another striking change was the end of the old two-member system. Except for twenty-three boroughs of between 50,000 and 165,000 inhabitants, Scottish Universities, and Oxford and Cambridge, the whole country was now divided into single member constituencies, and one unforeseen consequence of this was to stop the Liberals' tactics of running two candidates, one Whig and one Radical, in each electoral contest.

This very considerable measure of reform might have done

[1] See Statistics, p. 453.

something to add to the popularity of the Liberal government, had it not been followed almost at once by the most spectacular disaster of the whole administration. This was the incident of General Gordon's death at Khartoum. The Sudan, the great territory to the south of Egypt, had been under Egyptian rule so appallingly inefficient and corrupt that a local leader, proclaiming himself the Mahdi, had succeeded in rousing the whole country in revolt. The Khedive, determined to suppress the Mahdi, had sent an army commanded by a British officer, Hicks Pasha, but this force was utterly destroyed by the Mahdi in November 1883, and Gladstone was at once made aware by the Queen and public opinion in general that Hicks' defeat was a blow to British prestige which could not be ignored.

The Prime Minister was extremely reluctant to act, since he was deeply involved in the Reform Bill and in any case was determined to avoid any more adventures in Africa. In Cairo, Sir Evelyn Baring was doubtful whether any British officer should be sent to the Sudan. Public opinion, however, was all in favour of action and clamoured for General Charles Gordon to be entrusted with the task. Gordon was a typical Victorian Evangelical, a fearless Bible-reading soldier and something of a public hero. He had already performed distinguished service in China and in the Sudan, where his astonishing, almost mystical power of persuasion over native peoples certainly suggested that he alone might be able to handle the present difficulty. Unfortunately, Gordon, a man of considerable self-will, had already stated that he believed the Mahdi could be effectively resisted, and both Gladstone and Baring had serious doubts about his appointment. By the middle of January 1884, however, Gladstone agreed that Gordon should be sent.

This at once raised the question of what instructions Gordon should be given and here the lack of any positive decision on the part of the government was to play a great part in the tragic events that followed. Gladstone wished him to do no more than visit Suakim on the coast of the Red Sea, from where he would report on the position. His function was to be no more than advisory. Baring wanted him to be granted executive powers that would authorize him to organize the evacuation of the Sudan by Egyptian troops, and in this he seems to have been supported by a section of the Cabinet—Granville, Hartington, Dilke, and the Earl of Northbrook. This was highly significant, since Gladstone was away from London at Hawarden at the time and left the actual negotiations to them.

On 18 January, 1884 Gordon visited the War Office, and it is clear from his own letters that he believed that the instructions which he received there from the four ministers were to organize the withdrawal of Egyptian forces from the Sudan. The official written instructions stressed his advisory capacity, but allowed him executive powers 'as may be communicated to you by Sir E. Baring'. On the other hand, Hartington's report to Gladstone suggested that Gordon's role was not much more than that of an observer. The whole question of Gordon's instructions remains blurred and incoherent, and this partly explains why afterwards Gladstone and Gordon each considered that he was being let down by the other.

At Cairo Gordon was given two *firmans* from the Khedive, in agreement with Baring, appointing him Governor-General and authorizing him to evacuate the Sudan and to establish a government there. On this Gordon set out for Khartoum. Baring reported to the Cabinet on Gordon's mission, but by now the government had had second thoughts and reproved Baring for extending Gordon's powers. Gordon, too, was later blamed by the authorities for going beyond his instructions; yet it seems certain that he had kept within both the verbal and written orders that he had received in London. In any case, the government hardly seemed to know its own mind, for, on 12 February, Gladstone announced in the Commons that Gordon was to evacuate the Sudan and to reorganize its government, while a week later Hartington declared that the British government was not in any way responsible for what might happen in the Sudan and that Gordon was purely the agent of the Egyptian Khedive.

Meanwhile, Gordon had reached Khartoum, where his presence at once rallied the dispirited inhabitants. From now on the factor of uncertain communications was to add confusion to an already complex situation. Gordon asked for troops to keep open the

M

Nile route out of the Sudan; he asked for permission to set up an erstwhile slave-trader, Zebehr Pasha, as governor on his own departure, since he believed him to be the only local leader who could cope with the present difficulties. Baring strongly supported Gordon on these points, but both requests were refused. In another telegram Gordon warned the government that if Egypt was to be quiet, the Mahdi would have to be smashed, and although the wording suggests that Gordon was giving no more than forceful advice, there was a frenzy of alarm in the government at home, where it was imagined that Gordon was going to take the law into his own hands. There were other telegrams, referring to local fighting, as the Mahdi's troops closed in; in one Gordon stressed the need to retain 3,000 black troops in the Sudan to assist the succeeding government—Sudanese troops, he meant; Egyptian troops, the government inferred. And so the misunderstandings multiplied, until on 12 March the Mahdi's troops had laid siege to Khartoum and on 28 May the fall of Berber made any further evacuation or escape impossible.

What was Gladstone to do? In the thick of his Reform Bill negotiations, he still shirked the idea of another colonial intervention. In the Commons he stated that such an attack on the Mahdi would be 'a war of conquest against a people struggling to be free', but Gladstone's earlier attack on Egypt made the argument a weak one, and W. E. Forster went so far as to accuse the Prime Minister of self-deception. At last, in August, he had to give way. The Commons were asked for a grant of £300,000 to finance a relief expedition, and in October a force of 10,000 men was ready to advance up the Nile from Cairo under Lord Wolseley. It took them three months to fight their way along the 850 miles of the river, and when an advanced detachment came within reach of Khartoum on 28 January, 1885, they were met by the news that the town had fallen to the Mahdi two days before and that Gordon was dead.

In England a wild hysteria of anger and despair took hold of the country. In Downing Street Gladstone had to suffer the hisses of the crowd. G.O.M.—Grand Old Man—had become M.O.G. —Murderer of Gordon. The Queen sent a telegram to the Prime

Minister blaming him for the delay in sending out an expeditionary force, and gave orders that this telegram was not to be
sent in cypher, so that all officials through whom it passed might
read their Sovereign's disapproval of her Prime Minister.

The controversy over the rights and wrongs of the Gordon incident has gone on ever since. For many years the official defence
of the government was that Gordon was simply an officer who
had disobeyed his orders and was therefore responsible for his own
death. In fact, he seems to have been a victim of a governmental
muddle. Gladstone had not given a firm lead; the Cabinet, as a
whole, had never been agreed on a definite policy, and the man
on the spot, after being given vague discretionary powers, was left
with inadequate support. In situations such as these the serving
officer may often be the only man who can act in time, yet any
action that he does take may afterwards be disowned by his
government. It would be unfair to underestimate the difficulties
of the politicians. They hardly knew what they were going to do
about Egypt and had no wish to add to their commitments; they
did not believe that the Mahdi represented a threat to British interests in the Suez Canal; they were hampered by the emotional
force of uninformed public opinion. But when all that is granted,
there is no escaping the fact that, once the situation had developed,
the dispatching of a relief force was unavoidable, if only for political reasons. The delay in ordering it was undoubtedly responsible
for Gordon's death, and here Gladstone must be blamed.

Gordon's death had seriously embarrassed the government, but
it did not create a new Sudanese policy. Events elsewhere made it
possible for the government to turn away from the Sudan since
on 30 March, 1885 the Russians had attacked the Afghans at
Penjdeh on the northern frontier of Afghanistan. To the Russians
the fact that the British were enmeshed in the Sudan affair had
suggested that this was a suitable moment. In fact, Gladstone
almost welcomed the attack. The British Press represented Penjdeh as the gateway to India, and Gladstone hastened to put himself
on the side of public opinion. On 27 April he asked the Commons
for a Vote of Credit of £11 million and announced that the force
now in the Sudan would be used to meet the new threat. These

forces could hardly fight two wars simultaneously, and Gladstone was thus able to extricate himself from further commitment in the Sudan at the same time as his resolute action persuaded the Russians to negotiate. A final settlement in Afghanistan was concluded by the succeeding ministry, whereby Russia obtained Penjdeh, while the Zufilkar Pass on the Persian border was given to Afghanistan.[1]

The days of this turbulent second ministry of Gladstone were numbered and the circumstances of its fall are an indication of the confusion of political alignments at this time. Within the Cabinet Joseph Chamberlain had been growing increasingly critical of the lack of social legislation which was the major concern of the Radical group. 'Radical Joe', the Nonconformist Free Trader, the self-made business man of Birmingham, who in three years as Mayor had completely transformed the face of his city, was by now a leading figure in the House of Commons. In the early summer of 1885 disputes within the Cabinet came to a head over his scheme to provide a system of local self-government in Ireland. He had Gladstone's support, but when the Cabinet rejected the scheme, the Prime Minister was not prepared to press the matter any further. Shortly after this Chamberlain and Sir Charles Dilke resigned, although this does not seem to have been final.

As it turned out, Gladstone was able to escape the task of reconstructing his Cabinet. Negotiations had not gone entirely smoothly between Chamberlain and Parnell, mainly because O'Shea had been their intermediary, and Parnell now began to look elsewhere for an ally. Among the Conservative opposition Lord Randolph Churchill, who at the age of thirty-six seemed destined for a great political career, had vigorously opposed coercive measures against the Irish, and for the moment Parnell decided to throw in his lot with the opposition, although he had made no positive treaty with Lord Randolph. The outcome was that on 8 June Gladstone's government was defeated on an opposition amendment to the Budget. On the next day Gladstone resigned, and the Conservatives were faced with the problem of forming a coherent government of their own.

[1] See map, p. 220.

16

THE GROWTH OF THE COLLECTIVE STATE

THE passions with which debates in the House of Commons were charged during the 1870s and 1880s cannot be entirely explained by the personal bitterness of the dispute between Gladstone and Disraeli. It was a period in which totally new political and social issues were emerging, and these questions were to mean a fundamental realignment of forces, foreshadowing the scene with which we are familiar today.

The original teaching of Jeremy Bentham had been based primarily on two ideas—liberty for the individual and a greater efficiency in the administrative machinery of the state. During the first half of the century the demands of the Radicals had been mainly centred on the removal of governmental restrictions, and administrative reform had been prompted by a desire for the rationalizing of an antiquated system, rather than egalitarianism. Even the Factory Acts, running counter to the prevailing mood of *laissez faire*, as they did, suggest nothing more positive than a slight curb on the activity of the industrialists.

With the growth of democracy, however, a new conception of the state began to appear. It had ceased to be an ogre holding down the mass of the population in the interests of an out-moded society of landowners. *Laissez faire* had created an ogre of its own in a prosperous middle class whose wealth and political power were derived from the labour of a great industrial proletariat to whom this vaunted liberty of the individual meant only liberty for others to grow rich out of their efforts. A gradual realization of this, aided by the extension of the Parliamentary franchise, now becomes noticeable in a new form of Radicalism which turned back to a conception of the state as an omnipotent paternal authority, and throughout the last decades of the nineteenth century the old notion of unrestricted individualism was to be increasingly challenged by the new idea that the greatest freedom for *every* individual was possible only within the framework of the collective state.

The change to this new conception was only gradual, and certainly the social reforms carried through by Gladstone and Disraeli were never seen by either of them as part of a greater pattern. But the new issue loomed ever larger on the Parliamentary scene as Joseph Chamberlain and Lord Randolph Churchill each struggled to capture the working-class vote for his party. The most striking aspects of the change in these years, however, were to be seen outside Parliament, and here the question was not collectivism itself, but the method by which it might be attained. There seemed to be two possibilities. One was the way exemplified by the extraordinary extension of national and municipal enterprise. This was the hope of benevolent liberalism, headed by sections of the middle classes, applying the methods of private enterprise to social problems. The other lay in the doctrine of Socialism, which now reappeared for the first time since the 1830s, scorning the aspirations of liberal humanitarianism as a capitalist delusion. It is the growing struggle between these two viewpoints that lies behind the history of the last decades of the century.

1. The quest for efficiency: Whitehall and local government

Efficiency in government had always been the cry of the Radicals, and the reorganization of the administrative departments in 1870 was a natural consequence of the growing complexity of government demanding the greater expertness of the trained professional. The Civil Service, which Bagehot, writing in 1867, actually left unmentioned in his essay, *The English Constitution*, had remained small and its personnel had owed their position almost entirely to patronage. In 1853 a Commission on the Civil Service had proposed that the senior posts should be filled by university graduates through some form of examination, but this suggestion had at once aroused the old argument against 'clever devils', and although the scheme was put into operation to some extent, the door was still left open to patronage. It was not until 1870 that Gladstone established the system which has lasted, in a modified form, to this day, based on three grades, clerical, executive, and administrative, the last of these being recruited by competitive examination from the Universities. 'The tendency of the measure', commented Sir Charles Trevelyan, 'will, I am confident, be decidedly aristocratic, but it will be so in a good sense by securing for the public service those who are, in a true sense, worthy.' The measure led to the development of a highly efficient Civil Service, and one of its indirect consequences was to stimulate the Universities of Oxford and Cambridge to overhaul much of their teaching and examination system. College Fellowships were no longer to be a form of property, only remotely connected with education. Patronage and amateurism were fading fast, and the evidence lies in the rise of families of a new intellectual middle class in the upper reaches of the Universities and the Civil Service.

One of the more spectacular administrative reforms carried out during Gladstone's first government was that of the Army. The Crimean war had revealed a good many of its deficiencies, but although a certain number of minor reforms had been introduced, the calibre of the armies involved in the Continental wars of 1866 and 1870 made it clear that a radical transformation of the British Army was needed if Great Britain was to have any significance at all as a military power. It was Edward Cardwell, Secretary for War, who brought about that transformation. At first he dealt with a number of preliminary details; troops were withdrawn from the colonies, flogging in peace-time was abolished, and by Order in Council the Commander-in-chief of the Army was subordinated to the Secretary for War, although given more direct control over all military forces in the country. The root of the problem, however, lay in the system of purchase and the existing organization of the regiments.

Purchase was more than a system; it rested on a fundamental conception of society. An officer's rank in the Army was his property, to be bought and sold in the same way as the goodwill of a business or a doctor's practice. The first assault on this citadel was made through Parliament. A Bill for abolition, offering generous compensation for the existing holders of commissions, was passed in the Commons. When, however, the Lords decided to shelve the Bill indefinitely, Cardwell had his answer ready. It was argued that an officer's commission was not fundamentally a Parliamentary matter, since it was the Sovereign alone who granted commissions, and accordingly the government now simply stated that purchase was abolished by royal warrant. Senior officers and Conservatives argued furiously that this was an abuse of the royal prerogative, but the government stood firm and simply allowed officers time to reflect on the fact that abolition by royal warrant would mean no compensation whatsoever. They had been out-manoeuvred. The Lords made haste to reopen the debate on the original Bill and passed it without further difficulty, thereby enabling the selection and promotion of officers in the Army to be based, in future, on merit. Even the military had been powerless to stem the tide that was overtaking the civil servants and the University dons.

The other changes were mainly administrative. The old regiments of the line had by now little connection with any particular part of the country and many of their battalions were under strength. Cardwell divided the whole of Great Britain and Ireland into sixty-nine districts, each with its own county regiment consisting of two 'linked' battalions, one at home and one overseas, the regimental depot also forming the local centre for the county militia. Existing line regiments were dovetailed into this new system and there was a delicate grafting of regimental histories and battle honours. For the troops themselves the old system of twelve years' service was changed to six years with the colours and six in the reserve—a method suggested by the excellence of the Prussian Army. Cardwell attempted, with less success, to organize the artillery on a local basis, similar to the new infantry system; with the cavalry he could do very little, owing to the strongly entrenched social position of the officers, although he increased the total strength from 8,762 to 10,422 men. He tried also to improve the equipping of the new Army, but although he was successful in introducing a breech-loading Martini-Henry rifle for the infantry, he failed to make any impression on the officers of the artillery, who actually chose to return to muzzle-loading cannon.

It is easy to summarize this achievement; the struggle that it involved against the opposition of the most conservative body in the world completely exhausted Cardwell, and after 1874 he retired from public life with a peerage. He had, in fact, virtually recreated the Army; its strength in the United Kingdom had risen by twenty-five battalions and 156 field guns; the reserves for foreign service had been increased from 3,545 to 35,905 men, and despite the absence of any general staff and the continued presence of the Duke of Cambridge as Commander-in-chief, the prestige of this new force put a weapon in the hands of British Foreign Secretaries in the 1880s and '90s that they had never had before.

These reforms of the Civil Service and the Army were mainly a matter for Whitehall itself. A much more revolutionary tendency towards collectivism is illustrated by the question of public health, since this was bound to involve measures affecting every district of the country and inevitably helped to bring about a fundamental revision of the whole relationship of local government to the central authority. Indeed, until the last decades of the century there had been virtually no relationship at all. Except for the boards of Poor Law guardians, local government consisted of a remarkable confusion of uncoordinated bodies—municipal corporations and improvement commissioners in the towns, parish councils and Justices of the Peace in the counties.[1]

Edwin Chadwick's scheme for a Public Health service had been effectively crushed in the 1850s, but in 1868 one of Disraeli's last acts as Prime Minister had been to appoint a Royal Sanitary Commission, which, in 1871, recommended the setting up of local boards of health under the supervision of a central authority. Acts of Parliament followed in 1871 and 1872, whereby the activities of the Poor Law Board, the medical department of the Privy Council, and the local government section of the Home Office were all placed under a Local Government Board with a salaried President. The scope for such a department was almost limitless,

---

[1] See pp. 28–9.

for the condition of the poor and the maintenance of public health in the large towns opened up questions of slum clearance, the planning of parks, and the provision of main drainage, gas, and pure drinking water. But the Local Government Board, dominated by the Poor Law element whose main function was to save money rather than to spend it, made little of this. Enormous changes did take place in the larger cities, but the driving force came almost entirely from the municipal corporations.

In Birmingham Joseph Chamberlain, Mayor from 1873 to 1876, carried through tremendous clearance schemes and in his own words Birmingham was 'parked, paved, assized, marketed, Gas-and-Watered, and *improved*—all as the result of three years' active work'. Many other cities of the north were carrying through similar development plans—a main street and a new town hall at Manchester, improved docks and vast slum clearance at Liverpool, and schemes for electricity, gas, water, and trams everywhere in evidence. In London the Metropolitan Board of Works undertook the rehousing of 28,352 people. Two Acts of 1875—a Housing Act and the Public Health Act—empowered local authorities to carry through much of this work, and one has only to compare the achievement of this period with Edwin Chadwick's forlorn struggle a few years earlier to realize what a fantastic change had overcome the whole conception of governmental activity.

A further step towards collectivism was taken in 1888 with the passing of the County Councils Act. This was a natural step from the third Reform Act of 1884, which had extended the Parliamentary franchise to householders in the counties. The Act brought to an end the rule of the Justices of the Peace, and in its place established sixty-two county councils, elective bodies responsible for the local administration of urban and rural districts. Only boroughs of over 50,000 inhabitants, to be known as county boroughs, were excluded from this system, and while judicial and licensing functions remained the responsibility of the magistrates, the police were placed under the control of the Standing Joint Committee of Quarter Sessions and the County Council. The size of London naturally created a special problem, which was answered by making it a county of its own, subdivided into twenty-eight Metropolitan Boroughs, while allowing the City a considerable degree of autonomy within the general framework.

These striking changes were typical of English history—fundamentally revolutionary in their implications, yet constantly compromising with certain features of the old order, never part of an over-all plan or doctrine. In the same way, the enormous growth of educational institutions after 1870 was mainly the result of local activity, only very loosely supervised by the central authority, which simply tidied up a little after the developments had taken place. The new elementary schools were at first concerned simply with the problem of illiteracy, but once the three R's had been mastered, many of them began to experiment with more senior forms, where no outside authority imposed any curriculum. This soon became something close to a kind of secondary education, and many Boards began to organize courses in drawing and elementary science, so that some of their brighter pupils might win grants to new institutions such as the science and art departments at South Kensington. These last were by no means the only new ventures in further education. In Wales and the north of England a whole variety of colleges were making their appearance, several of them to become provincial universities. In 1889 the Technical Instruction Act made the new County Councils the local authority for technical education, and in the same year Parliament agreed to a state grant in support of the new colleges. Parallel with this was a great movement for the education of women, with the gradual development of schools and colleges for girls, culminating in a long siege of the Universities, where, it was demanded, they should have the right to study.

Direct action by the government had so far been limited to a few isolated Acts. In 1876 all parents were made responsible for seeing that their children received instruction in reading, writing, and arithmetic; in 1890 the system of 'payment by results' was replaced by grants dependent on average attendance, and in 1891 all elementary education was made free.[1] Clearly this was hardly enough. The rapid haphazard growth of these establishments was

[1] See p. 348.

in danger of creating an educational anarchy through an utter lack of coordination between the authorities responsible for the various institutions, and in 1894 the Bryce Commission made recommendations for a stream-lining of the existing situation by fitting them into the new structure of local government. It was not, however, until 1902 that Robert Morant, who was among those who had served on the Commission, was able to carry through many of these suggestions in the great Education Act of that year.[1]

2. New technical advances

The movement towards a greater personal efficiency and administrative tidiness was accompanied by a whole welter of new technical improvements and inventions that were to add enormously to the collectivizing of social life. First, the background of domestic comfort that it made possible inevitably brought with it a general standardization, the natural concomitant of mass-production. Second, much of this technical achievement involved the creation of many public services which meant new interests and responsibilities for the government, either national or local, and these responsibilities in turn involved greater powers of supervision. Third, the natural extension of this principle, combined with ever-increasing technical means, was to place in the hands of any government, whether democratic or despotic, a degree of control over the whole community undreamed of in any earlier period of the world's history.

The use of electricity for facilitating swift communication had already been realized earlier in the century. In 1851 an electric cable connected England with France and the year 1866 saw the first permanent one laid across the Atlantic. In the United States, in 1876, Edison demonstrated the first telephone, and before the end of the century Marconi had established wireless communication across the Channel. In industry electricity was to have an even greater effect. The invention of the dynamo meant that electric power could be created from some other form of energy and future factories need no longer be tied to the region of the coal

[1] See p. 399.

mines—just as, a hundred years before, the development of steam power had enabled them to move away from the river-sides. In 1882 the first generating station was operating in New York, soon to be followed by the formation of electric light companies in London and many of the provincial cities. This was only the beginning. Electric trams followed and, later, electric trains, although these last were developed more widely on the Continent than in Great Britain, where their use was at first restricted to an underground suburban service for London.

The dynamo, however, could not create its own energy, and the supply of electric current was ultimately dependent upon steam engines. The significance of the invention of the internal-combustion engine was that it overcame this difficulty. The earliest engines were fed on gas, but modifications later allowed the use of liquid fuel, creating incidentally a new trade in paraffin, and eventually leading to the production of the Diesel engine in 1895. In 1887 Gottfried Daimler brought out the first motor car, and the later development of petrol at last put men within reach of the centuries-old dream of human flight. In 1903 the Wright brothers made their first successful flight in a propeller-driven aeroplane, and in July 1909 Louis Blériot flew from France across the Channel, landing safely above the cliffs of Dover. England's moat had been bridged at last.

At the same time the world was moving from the iron to the steel age.[1] In 1856 Sir Henry Bessemer had discovered the process that bears his name, and the production of steel, lighter, stronger, more flexible, and cheaper to make, brought about a minor revolution in industry in America and Western Europe. At first ore that contained only a small proportion of phosphorous could be used, and since this could be found mostly in Sweden and Spain, the British industrialist, who could ship it direct to the coalfields on the north-east and north-west coasts of England and in South Wales, had a great advantage over his counterpart in France and Germany, where coalfields lay inland. It was a British discovery that robbed him of this lead, when, in 1879, a young London chemist, Gilchrist Thomas, was able to demonstrate a process

[1] See Statistics, p. 454.

whereby phosphoric ores might be used in the manufacture of
steel. There was no lack of these ores on the Continent, and a
tremendous German steel industry soon grew up, which was to
mean both a great reinforcement of her military power and a
challenge to British industrial supremacy.

These three—electricity, internal combustion, and steel—were
basic elements in the new technical age. It would be impossible to
enumerate all the other varieties of invention and discovery whose
cumulative effect was to revolutionize everyday life: the fruits of
chemical research—the manufacture of synthetic dyes, margarine,
soap, and new drugs; medical research leading to a better understanding of malaria, cholera, and tuberculosis, and the development of antiseptic methods in hospitals; a mass of new office
equipment—the typewriter, the adding machine, the cash register, and the dictaphone; larger and faster steel ships, which, by the
1880s, could cross the Atlantic in less than six days, canning and
refrigeration, by means of which the produce of the ends of the
earth could be brought to the dinner table; and in the arts of war
bigger shells, heavier naval armour, the sea mine, the torpedo, the
submarine, and poison gas. The list is endless, and one invention
following upon another only confirmed the average Victorian in
his belief that all was for the best in this unprecedented age of
progress.

3. The reappearance of Socialism

A widening bureaucratic control and enormously increased
technical power—both these were essential factors in the growth
of the collective state. Neither of them, however, necessarily con-
tradicted the prevailing doctrine of individualism; indeed, despite
the impressive title of 'municipal socialism' that was later given to
the sweeping changes that had taken place in the cities, the bulk of
all this achievement had been the work of free enterprise. One
further development in this period, however—the reappearance
of Socialism—soon revealed the staggering collective power of
the working classes, a power which was to challenge the whole
basis of unrestricted private enterprise.

Throughout the middle years of the nineteenth century most classes had enjoyed some sort of prosperity. It had been a time of gradually rising prices with wages mounting rather higher, and the peak of this prosperity coincided almost exactly with Gladstone's first administration. From 1874 until the end of the century, however, the country entered upon a long period of falling prices. The principal reason for this was the increase in competition from other countries—Continental industry and American agriculture—to which Great Britain's policy of Free Trade left her wide open, and while the threat to industry was only gradually felt, the effect on British farming was catastrophic. The drop in rates of interest and agricultural rents, which followed from this, mainly affected the capital-holding class; wages did not fall in proportion and their purchasing power was considerably increased. What did hit the working classes was unemployment during the three serious slumps of 1879, 1886, and 1894. After 1896 prices began to rise and the problem took another form, since three great booms in 1900, 1907, and 1913, although highly satisfactory for the capital-owners, recreated for the wage-earners all the old difficulties of a rising cost of living.

The widespread unemployment during the slumps and the diminished purchasing power of wages during the boom years were problems to which the heirs of mid-Victorian Trade Unionism had no satisfactory answer. They had always accepted the existing social and economic framework and had claimed no more than the right of skilled workers to negotiate a fair wage and to organize their own systems of insurance. Every reform that should have brought about prosperity and happiness for the whole country had been gained—the Parliamentary franchise, Free Trade, Factory Acts, and established Trade Unions—and yet, despite all this, prosperity seemed to be at the mercy of the unpredictable fluctuations of trade.

The attraction of Socialism, which had already been an active political force on the Continent for some decades, was that it claimed to have an answer. The struggle between the capitalists and the proletariat was simply a further stage in the class war on which Marx's theory of history was based, but the essential feature of Socialist teaching, which seemed particularly relevant at this time, was that capitalism was inevitably doomed, since an un-planned economy must constantly swing between boom and slump, ultimately creating the circumstances in which the indus-trial proletariat would rise and overthrow their masters. Thus the Socialist lecturer and writer, who became extremely active among the Unions in the 1880s, could point to the slump of 1879 not as a piece of bad luck, but as a symptom of a basically unsound sys-tem, which would undoubtedly recur. It did recur; and the Unions found a new growing element in their ranks, demanding a general policy of nationalization, whereby the economy of the country might be planned and controlled.

Throughout the 1880s this battle between the old order and the new was fought out in the Unions. The old Unionists advocated peasant proprietorship, the system whereby every agricultural labourer should become a small landowner; the Socialists con-demned this as a means of creating a society of tiny capitalists and demanded the nationalization of land. The old Unionists were content with a system of a sliding scale for wages, negotiated with the employers; the Socialists demanded an assured standard of living. The old Unionists defended their own schemes of insur-ance against unemployment and sickness; the Socialists claimed that it was the duty of the state to give every man employment and to provide for him when he was sick. The old Unionists pre-ferred to work in conjunction with the Liberals; the Socialists demanded a political organization of their own.

The Socialists really began to get a grip after the second slump, and a new stage in the working-class movement was reached when the leaders began to organize the unskilled workers. Open-air meetings in London were growing continually larger and on 13 November, 1887—'Bloody Sunday'—a pitched battle took place in Trafalgar Square between the police and the crowd. The area eventually had to be cleared by Life Guards, and although the troops did not open fire, two of the crowd died from their in-juries and over a hundred became casualties. The greatest com-motion came two years later with the London Dock strike of 1889. The dockers, mostly classed as unskilled workers, were organized by Ben Tillett, assisted by Tom Mann and John Burns, both members of the Amalgamated Society of Engineers, in a demand for a standard rate of sixpence an hour. Public feeling was very much on their side and John Burns' speeches on Tower Hill captured more and more newspaper space; £18,000 was raised in voluntary subscriptions and another £30,000 was telegraphed by the Unions in Australia, so that strike pay could be organized and other workers bribed not to take the strikers' places. At the end of a month the dockers got their sixpence.

The London Dock strike was something more than a manifestation of working-class unrest. Its significance lay in the fact that it represented the first successful attempt to mobilize the forces of unskilled labour. It had been local; its demands had not been startling, but to men of imagination it gave a glimpse of the enormous reservoir of power that lay in the total labour force of Great Britain, and it marks the opening of a new phase in the working-class movement, of which succeeding governments were soon to be made aware.

17

THE HOME RULE QUESTION

1. The first attempt at Home Rule

A. LORD SALISBURY'S FIRST ADMINISTRATION, 1885-6

THE fall of Gladstone's government in 1885 could hardly have been less welcome to the Conservative party. 'The prospect before us is very serious,' wrote Lord Salisbury to Lord Cranbrook two days afterwards; 'the vote on Monday night was anything but a subject for congratulation.' The new electoral rolls were not yet ready, so that there could be no general election until the autumn, and the Conservatives were presented with the task that Disraeli had wisely refused in 1873—that of forming a caretaker government with a minority in the House of Commons.

There were other difficulties that made the moment particularly inopportune. Since Disraeli's death the question of the leadership of the Conservatives had never been finally settled. Sir Stafford Northcote firmly believed that if a government were formed, the premiership must be his, but his leadership of the opposition in the Commons during Gladstone's administration had been undistinguished and had created the impression that, while he did not entirely approve of the forceful tactics of Lord Randolph Churchill's 'ginger group', he was really unable to control them. It was for Lord Salisbury that the Royal Summons eventually came, and he left at once by the night mail for Balmoral. The problem of the Cabinet, however, still had to be solved. The rapid rise of Churchill as a political personality of striking brilliance made it essential that he should be included and Salisbury told the Queen that he proposed giving him the India Office. But Churchill would not serve under Northcote as leader in the Commons and the ministerial crisis was only ended several

338

days later after Northcote had been raised to the peerage, as Earl of Iddesleigh. He was made First Lord of the Treasury and Sir Michael Hicks Beach became the government's leader in the Commons. Salisbury himself took over the Foreign Office, where there was plenty to occupy him in new difficulties that had arisen in Bulgaria.[1]

It was the Irish Home Rule question that played the dominating part in the very complicated negotiations which ensued during the next twelve months. The reason for this was that both Liberals and Conservatives were facing a crisis within their own organizations. In each party a new extremist wing under a dynamic leader had developed. Chamberlain's Radicals had for long pointed to a possible split in the Liberals, and now Lord Randolph Churchill's group, with its cry of 'Tory Democracy', presented a similar threat to the Conservatives. Each was playing for votes. Each was regarded with some alarm by the right-wing element of his own party. To the official leaders it was becoming clear that some new policy was required that would restore unity and perhaps steal the thunder of these break-away groups. The Irish vote was an obvious prize, and Parnell had only to remain in touch with both sides, watching eagerly for the highest bidder.

As soon as the Conservatives were in power, they embarked on a new course of action in Ireland. The policy of coercion was brought to an end. Lord Carnarvon, the new Lord Lieutenant, made a series of journeys throughout the country, and it was apparent that he was hoping to find some way of increasing Ireland's political control over her own affairs. Among Parnell's aims had been the development of a land-owning peasantry, and Lord Ashbourne's Act duly introduced a scheme for state-assisted land purchase. Carnarvon also had a secret conversation with Parnell at a house in Mayfair—secret, because the Irish question was a very delicate matter—and reported on it to Lord Salisbury, afterwards, at Hatfield House. The Conservatives had not so far committed themselves over Home Rule, but they were clearly prepared to go further than any Conservative government had gone before.

[1] See p. 354.

At the same time, in this summer of 1885, there occurred one of the most momentous political decisions in the nineteenth century —equal in significance to Peel's conversion to repeal. Gladstone became converted to Home Rule. It is impossible to tell how long his mind may have been moving in this direction, but a number of factors helped to convince him at this particular moment. The sudden end of the policy of coercion by the Salisbury government showed that English policy in Ireland could never be consistent while it rested on the whims of Westminster. By now high government officials at Dublin had come to the same conclusion. Another contributory factory was a yachting trip that Gladstone made to Norway that year, when he was deeply impressed by what he saw of a simple people enjoying a democratic way of life. Possibly, too, the new political scene may have helped to bring him round, for a Cabinet that included Carnarvon and Churchill, both friendly towards the Irish, may have suggested to him that the Conservatives were about 'to dish the Whigs'.

But whatever the reasons for his conversion, he was sure that for the time being he could say nothing. He could hardly relish the prospect of having to win his own party over to his new views. And even if he succeeded and then attempted to wreck the present government, form a new administration, and introduce a Home Rule Bill, what would be its fate in the House of Lords? He knew that Parnell was in communication with the Conservatives and it looked as if they might attempt a similar measure. In that case, Gladstone might be able to bring at least a section of the Liberals to cooperate with the government and the pattern of 1829, 1846, and 1867 would be repeated. In any case, to speak out now, on the eve of the autumn election, would only seem like a political move to win Parnell over to the Liberals. 'It is right I should say', he wrote to Mrs. O'Shea on 8 August, 'that in any counter-bidding of any sort against Lord Randolph Churchill I, for one, cannot enter.'

In contrast to Gladstone, Chamberlain had no doubts over announcing his own policy to the world and, in September, embarked upon a prodigious electoral campaign—a great drum-roll of social reforms in education, rural conditions, and local government. One feature of this 'unauthorized programme'—aimed at the new county electorate—was the creation of a class of small land-owning farmers, and Conservatives and right-wing Liberals looked on aghast at the antics of this new 'Jack Cade', as Iddesleigh called him. But Chamberlain knew what he was doing, for if the party had not become divided, peasant proprietorship might have captured for the Liberals many of the votes that in a few years' time were to go towards the building of a Labour party.

It was in this generally confusing situation that Parnell had soon to make a decision. In addition to the Irish constituencies there were a great many Irish among the electorate in England. Should he tell these followers to vote for the Conservatives or the Liberals? He could not know of Gladstone's change of mind, but in the past Gladstone had done more for Ireland than any other English statesman. On the other hand, Gladstone had refused to commit himself, and Chamberlain was strongly opposed to Home Rule. As for the Conservatives, Parnell realized that Lord Salisbury might hold back for fear of Churchill running away with the party, but at least Churchill and Carnarvon did favour the Irish. There was, too, the fact that the Conservatives seemed the weaker of the two parties and were therefore more likely to be dependent upon the Irish vote in the House. With these considerations in view, two days before the election Parnell told his supporters in England to vote Conservative.

At first it looked as if he had made the right choice. The Liberals came back with a majority of eighty-six over the Conservatives. This was mainly due to Chamberlain, since while several of the large cities rejected Gladstone, the county electorate, attracted by the 'unauthorized programme', flocked to the Liberal side. But the Liberal majority was exactly balanced by Parnell's party, for in Ireland the Home Rulers had been overwhelmingly successful and returned to Westminster with precisely eighty-six seats. This meant that, provided the Conservatives were prepared to work with Parnell, they could at least resist the Liberals, without actually commanding a majority, but if Parnell withdrew his support, the Liberals could defeat the government whenever they wished. For a moment the Home Rulers had achieved the position of power desired by any third party in a Parliamentary assembly, and Gladstone certainly assumed that the Conservative government would continue on the basis of an alliance with Parnell.

It was at this point that a totally new development altered the whole situation. Gladstone's son, Herbert, who acted as his secretary, naturally knew of his father's change of mind over Home Rule, and on 15 December, while in London, disclosed this information to a number of editors. By 17 December the news was in the headlines and the task of persuading the Liberal party could be postponed no longer. The excitement everywhere was intense. The Conservatives could hardly outbid Gladstone on this and their policy at once reverted to the defence of the Union against Irish terrorists. Carnarvon and his Chief Secretary, Sir W. Hart Dyke, resigned and the Conservative–Parnellite alliance was obviously at an end. On 26 January, 1886 the government announced its intention of introducing a new Coercion Bill, and that same night Home Rulers and Liberals combined to defeat the government over the absence of any mention in the Queen's speech of measures for the benefit of the English agricultural labourer. On the next day Lord Salisbury resigned and two days later Gladstone was asked by the Queen to form a new administration.

It is easy to imagine an undercurrent of political bargaining during this extremely involved period of negotiation. Lord Salisbury could be accused of jettisoning the Parnellites since they no longer served his purpose. Still more easily, Gladstone could be charged with accepting Home Rule in order to regain office with a working majority in the Commons. Neither of these accusations holds water. Once Gladstone's conversion had been announced, Salisbury had had little choice but to rally the anti-Home Rule element. The peculiar circumstances of Gladstone's change of mind leave his actions open to a variety of interpretations, but the fact remains that his new views on the Irish question were purely his own personal decision and he must have realized the extent of opposition that he would have to meet in his own party. 'I am prepared to go forward without anybody,' he told Sir William Harcourt. This was hardly the attitude of a man who had just brought off a political *coup*. For Parnell the situation had simply turned upside down. He had made the wrong choice, after all, and through his election campaign he had actually added between twenty-five and forty seats to the Conservatives, the very party that would do its utmost to prevent Home Rule.

B. GLADSTONE'S THIRD ADMINISTRATION, 1886

The success of a Home Rule Bill now depended upon Gladstone's handling of his own party. With some he succeeded. Lord Spencer, Lord Rosebery, Lord Kimberley, Lord Ripon, and Sir William Harcourt all agreed to follow their chief. The Whig element, under Lord Hartington, seceded, and once they were lost, Gladstone should have done his best to keep the Radicals with him. It was here that he made his greatest mistake. It would not have been impossible for him to have converted Joseph Chamberlain into a firm ally. With Hartington gone, the eventual succession to the party leadership would have been his, and by this time Chamberlain, despite his demogogic utterances, was clearly beginning to enjoy the social round of success. But it was precisely this worldliness that turned Gladstone against him. He could not bring himself into close touch with a man whom he regarded as a cold-blooded careerist, and although Chamberlain was prepared to serve in his Cabinet, Gladstone disappointed him by only making him President of the Local Government Board. Within a couple of months, while the Bill was still under discussion in the Cabinet, Chamberlain and Sir George Trevelyan had resigned, and when the Bill came before the Commons, it was Chamberlain's attacks that did more than anything else to bring about its defeat.

On 8 April Gladstone introduced the Home Rule Bill. It proposed that an Irish Parliament and executive should be set up in Dublin. The new Irish government would control all its own affairs except matters affecting war and peace, the defence forces, foreign and colonial relations, trade, customs and excise, and coinage. One fifteenth of the Budget requirements for the whole of the United Kingdom was to be found by Ireland; the rest of Ireland's revenue was to be at her own disposal. In order to protect the interests of the Protestant minority, the Irish legislature, while remaining a single chamber, was to be divided into two 'orders', each with a suspensory veto. The Irish government would appoint its own judges, but the judicial committee of the Privy Council would act as a supreme court of appeal as well as adjudicator in any constitutional dispute. At the same time as the Home Rule Bill, a Land Purchase Bill was launched providing for the buying out of the landlords by means of an enormous loan.

The battle over Home Rule began with the second reading and for sixteen days the Commons were torn with dissension. Moderate elements everywhere were in a state of alarm. If Gladstone could change his views on Ireland, where next would he begin to meddle? The recent years of violence in Ireland and the long campaign of obstruction by the Irish M.P.s had hardened the minds of many. To them it seemed that Gladstone was surrendering once again, as, they maintained, he had surrendered in the Transvaal and in the Sudan. The predicament of the Irish Protestants in Ulster was an obvious issue. 'Ulster will fight,' said Lord Randolph Churchill, 'and Ulster will be right.' Then the question of Irish representation at Westminster was taken up. Surely Irish M.P.s must be able to take part in debates on Irish customs and excise. Gladstone, who had wished to exclude Irish M.P.s from Westminster, where they might be able to bring pressure to bear on matters that did not concern Ireland, wavered on this. At last, on 7 June, he made his last appeal. 'Ireland stands at your bar, expectant, hopeful, almost suppliant . . . she asks a blessed oblivion of the past, and in that oblivion our interest is deeper than even hers.' The House divided at one o'clock in the morning and the Bill was thrown out by 343 votes to 313. Gladstone's first attempt at Home Rule for Ireland had failed.

He would not yet admit defeat. The next step must be an appeal to the electorate; the Queen was asked to dissolve Parliament and the election was fought out during the last weeks of June 1886. Gladstone was indefatigable. 'An old man in a hurry' Lord Salisbury had called him during the arguments over Home Rule, but his age appeared to mean nothing. He was seventy-six, yet he swept through the northern towns with one long speech after another. Glasgow, Manchester, Liverpool, he harangued them all. 'I went in bitterness, in the heat of my spirit, but the hand of the Lord was upon me.' It was all in vain. The recent outrages in Ireland had made the country even more opposed to Home Rule than the House of Commons had been. Three hundred and sixteen Conservatives and seventy-eight seceding Liberal Unionists were returned to make a total of 394 against 191 Gladstonian Liberals and eighty-five Irish Nationalists. 'Well, Herbert, dear old boy,' said Gladstone to his son, 'we *have* had a drubbing, and no mistake.' His resignation followed at once and Lord Salisbury formed a new Conservative administration.

2. *Lord Salisbury's second administration, 1886–92*

There are obvious points of similarity between Gladstone's change of mind over Home Rule and Peel's decision to repeal the Corn Laws. In each case a party had become utterly divided over a decision taken by its leader without reference to the constituents. The parallel, however, is a fairly superficial one and the consequences for the Liberals proved ultimately to be far more disastrous than the setback suffered by the Conservatives in 1846. The question over which the Peelites and the Protectionists had split had ceased very shortly afterwards to be an issue. The Parliamentary scene in the 1850s and 1860s became a tangle of personalities, and since no new third party emerged during that time, Disraeli had ultimately been able to reorganize the Conservatives. But after Gladstone's conversion to Home Rule, Ireland remained a very real issue, and so the split hardened. This by itself was not disastrous. The Liberals, after a shaky administration from 1892 to 1895, were to return to power in 1906 with one of their greatest electoral triumphs. But the damage that had been done lay deeper. The Liberal Unionists who had seceded from the Liberal party over Home Rule included many, such as Chamberlain's Radicals, who, had they remained in the party, might have harnessed the new forces rising in the working-class movement. As it was, these Liberals turned to the Conservatives and by 1895 had contrived to form a Unionist party out of their coalition. Thus the way was clear for the Socialists to set about

capturing the working-class vote for a new third party—Labour
—a factor which had no counterpart in the 1850s and 1860s.

The new Conservative administration in 1886 depended upon
the careful handling of clearly defined political groups. The
Gladstonian Liberals and the Parnellites would remain in a
minority, provided that the seventy-eight Liberal Unionists did
not rejoin them. It was this situation that prompted Lord
Salisbury, first of all, to offer the position of Prime Minister to
Lord Hartington, who, however, declined it. The Cabinet that
Salisbury now selected included Lord Iddesleigh as Foreign Secre-
tary, Sir Michael Hicks Beach as Chief Secretary for Ireland, and
W. H. Smith at the War Office. Lord Randolph Churchill, at
the age of thirty-seven, became the youngest Chancellor of the
Exchequer and leader of the House of Commons since William
Pitt.

The Conservatives, however, were by no means free themselves
from the fear of a split. The bulk of their party, coupled with
the Whig element among their new allies, looked for a policy
which would really be conservative, and in this they could
have every confidence in their Prime Minister. The presence
of Lord Randolph Churchill, brilliant, impulsive, and determined to construct a new party platform out of Tory Democracy,
naturally made them uneasy, fears that were not eased by a speech
of his at Dartford on 2 October. Here, before a vast audience, he
outlined a far-reaching programme including a thorough investigation of the situation in Ireland, a reform of Parliamentary
procedure, alterations in the law of tithe, and a scheme whereby
the agricultural labourer might acquire his own plot of land; he
dealt, also, with foreign affairs, demanding liberty for the Balkan
peoples. It was a startling list of projects, daring the wrath of the
right-wing Conservatives in an attempt to outdo the Radicalism
of Joseph Chamberlain, and for a moment it looked as if the
Tories, in bringing about the defeat of 'an old man in a hurry',
had delivered themselves into the hands of a much younger one.

The trouble came to a head almost at once in the Cabinet, followed by the fall of Lord Randolph Churchill, perhaps the most
remarkable eclipse of a political personality in the whole century.

One of the promises that he had made at Dartford had been a reduction of taxation. This he now embodied in his Budget proposals which came up before the Cabinet in December. He intended to increase death duties and house duties and to make a saving in government expenditure of over £8 million through reductions of the Army and Navy estimates. This would enable him to balance his Budget and would give him enough in hand to lower income tax from 8*d*. to 5*d*., to reduce duties on tea and tobacco, and to make a considerable local government grant. Even after this there would still be a surplus of £730,000. This was Tory Democracy in action—reforms and lower taxation at home at the expense of the armed forces.

The crisis came quickly. W. H. Smith refused to accept the cuts for the War Office and Lord Randolph would not compromise. 'You will shortly have to decide', he wrote to Lord Salisbury on 15 December, 'whose services you will retain—those of your War Minister or those of your Chancellor of Exchequer.' Lord Salisbury had no wish to take such a direct decision, but when he refused to overrule Smith, Churchill accepted this as his decision and announced his resignation both to the Prime Minister and in *The Times*.

This step, which in fact proved to be the end of his career, has been the occasion of countless arguments. It is true that his Budget was almost a statement of principle, but it was not absolutely vital that the saving which he wished to make should come from the services. It seems that he could have gained most of what he wanted by some other kind of economy. It has been suggested that in resigning he was attempting to repeat his tactics of 1884, when his resignation from the chair of the Council of the National Union of Conservative Associations was followed at once by his reinstatement. Yet it is hard to believe that, if this had really been his aim, such a skilful Parliamentarian would have made the mistake of resigning at a moment when Parliament was not sitting and when no one could know the course of Cabinet discussion. As his son, Sir Winston Churchill, has pointed out in his biography, a more unscrupulous man would have waited until he could embarrass his own government in the Commons. Perhaps the answer lies mainly in his temperament. He was at odds with many of the Cabinet over foreign policy and Ireland, and for one of his impatient nature the struggle over the Budget was the last straw. But whatever the reasons for his fall may have been, it was final. G. J. Goschen, a Liberal Unionist, took his place as Chancellor of the Exchequer; Lord Salisbury's nephew, A. J. Balfour, took over as Irish Secretary from Hicks Beach, whose eyesight was failing; W. H. Smith made good as the new leader in the Commons. It was an illustration of the old truth that no man is ever entirely indispensable. Lord Randolph never regained office and only a few years later he was stricken with a rare disease that was to cut his life short at the age of forty-five.

The Conservative administration, which ran its full course until the election of 1892, lacked the startling boldness of the great period of the Gladstone–Disraeli duel, yet in a quiet way it did achieve a great deal. In his Budget Goschen was able to introduce many of the economies that Churchill had wanted, including his most important measure, the conversion of the National Debt, thereby bringing about a saving in interest, and by 1888 the income tax had been reduced to 6d. In this year, also, a local government Act brought about a fundamental reform of local administration, establishing the system of County Councils, which, with certain modifications, has continued until today.[1] In 1891 fees in all elementary schools were abolished. This was a perfectly comprehensible measure of reform, but there was also a political motive. Lord Salisbury was sure that when the Liberals regained power they would simply make the Board schools free. This would have utterly undermined the position of the Church schools, and the Conservatives' only chance of saving them was to get their blow in first by making all elementary schools free. In the same year a Factory Act made eleven the minimum age for the employment of children and extended the 1850 Act to include women employed in every kind of factory. The Tithes Act, which transferred payment from the occupier to the owner of the land, put the tax in a new guise and thereby ended much of the resentment that it had caused in the country districts.

[1] See p. 330.

All this, however, was achieved against a background of growing turbulence. A second great economic depression at the end of the 1880s pointed clearly to the fact that Free Trade and administrative reforms were hardly sufficient to ensure a happy and stable society. The growing wealth of the upper and middle classes only served to accentuate the gap between the Two Nations and the depressions had reawakened the anger of the working classes, adding enormously to the power of the Socialist movement. 'Bloody Sunday' in Trafalgar Square and the London Dock strike [1] were both indications that the country was entering on a new period of social stress, and, as in the early decades of the century, no government had much idea of what the remedy might be.

Violence also faced the government in Ireland. In the autumn of 1886 Parnell, despairing of Home Rule for the moment, but hoping to secure some relief for tenants in the grip of the agricultural depression, made certain proposals that might have eased their lot. Things took their usual wretched course. The government rejected the idea; five months later the Cowper Commission made very similar suggestions which the government embodied in a Bill in 1887. But the damage had been done. On the rejection of Parnell's proposals a new scheme had been hit upon in Ireland—the 'plan of campaign', which demanded that the tenants of each landlord should combine to take collective action against him. Theoretically this meant the refusal to pay exorbitant rents and the voluntary support of any tenant who was evicted as a consequence. In fact, it meant a reopening of the old war by which Ireland had been torn so long. Parnell recognized this and deplored the return of cattle-maiming and moonlighting, which could only antagonize the English electorate, but he was powerless to stop such die-hards as William O'Brien and John Dillon, who, in September 1887, involved their followers in a riot with the police at Mitchelstown. This proved to be an unhappy year, for the incident of 'Bloody Sunday' in Trafalgar Square occurred a couple of months later.

The next stages in the story of Ireland's struggle are bound up

[1] See p. 336.

very closely with Parnell's own life. The first incident, which at first looked like being fatal, ultimately turned out extremely well for him. As with most matters concerning Parnell, it has a certain note of melodrama. In April 1887 *The Times* published a facsimile of a letter apparently written and signed by Parnell, dated 15 May, 1882. The writer fully condoned the Phoenix Park murders— 'Burke got no more than his deserts'. Parnell at once denounced the letter in the Commons as a forgery, but although the letter was obviously highly damaging politically, he took no further action, mainly because he doubted whether he would obtain justice in an English court of law. One of his followers, however, F. A. O'Donnell, who was mentioned in a series of articles entitled 'Parnellism and Crime' appearing in *The Times*, decided to sue the newspaper for libel. In the course of the hearing the defendants produced more letters which were supposed to have been written by Parnell, and it was obvious that Parnell would have to take some action in his own defence. He demanded a select committee of the House of Commons, but instead the government set up a special commission of three judges to examine the whole affair.

The result ultimately was a complete vindication for Parnell. *The Times* had published the original letter in all good faith, after having submitted it to a handwriting expert. But, in fact, all the letters, unknown to them, were forgeries, the work of a Richard Pigott, an Irish journalist, who had sold them to an intermediary. Lines of inquiry were mercilessly followed up; in February 1889 Pigott was called to give evidence and betrayed himself over certain types of spelling mistake. Immediately afterwards he fled the country and sent by post a full confession to *The Times*. He had, however, been charged with perjury, and when the police traced him in Madrid, he shot himself. Parnell was cleared and the costs of the whole inquiry—£250,000—were awarded against *The Times*. It was a moment of triumph for Parnell; the public, excited and intrigued by the unmasking of the Pigott forgeries, saw him in a new light, and if Gladstone could have fought an election over Home Rule at this time, he might have had some chance of winning it.

Yet within twelve months Parnell's career was over and his

name only an encumbrance to his party. This tragedy for Ireland came about through Parnell's relationship with Katherine O'Shea. The aunt whom they did not wish to hurt by divorce proceedings did not die until 1889, at the age of ninety-seven. O'Shea, who had been living apart from his wife before she met Parnell, was well aware of the liaison which had been kept a secret from the world for nine years, and knowing that the scandal which it could cause would mean political death for Parnell, had been able to put pressure on Parnell to advance his own career. When the aunt died, leaving £144,000 to her niece, O'Shea saw a further opportunity for profit and offered to allow his wife to divorce him in return for £20,000. The will, however, was contested by other members of the family and neither Mrs. O'Shea nor Parnell could produce such a sum. O'Shea carried out the threat with which he had been blackmailing Parnell and instituted proceedings for divorce, citing Parnell as co-respondent. In this sordid struggle the strength of personal feelings put all the cards in O'Shea's hands. Parnell and Mrs. O'Shea, longing to be free to marry, made no defence and on 17 November, 1890 a decree nisi was granted to O'Shea. The facts, as O'Shea had chosen to present them, were now public, and this could mean only one thing in Victorian England. Divorce was disgrace. Only four years before, Sir Charles Dilke's political career had been abruptly terminated after he had been cited as co-respondent in a divorce case. What hope, then, had Parnell of surviving this blow?

Parnell did not see it like that. He did not regard himself as English; he had no wish to attend Queen Victoria's Court, and there was no question of his becoming a minister. Accordingly, when the National League at Dublin gave him support, he decided not to resign the leadership of the party. But he well knew that the success of his hopes for Ireland depended upon more than the Irish vote, and here there was no escape. At Sheffield the National Liberal Federation, among whom the English Nonconformists were strongly represented, made it clear to their chiefs that they could not work in any sort of alliance with the Irish party unless they changed their leader, and Gladstone, informed of this feeling, wrote a letter to John Morley for Parnell to see, saying that unless the Irish did change their leader, he himself would resign the leadership of the Liberal party.

Parnell, who did not see Gladstone's letter until he had heard that the Irish party had just re-elected him, flatly refused to resign, and on this Gladstone published his letter in the Press. It is a striking indication of Parnell's ascendancy over the Irish that, despite the disapproval of the bishops, Ireland did not immediately desert him. It was in the Irish Parliamentary party at Westminster that the first serious assault was launched on his position, when the anti-Parnellite group demanded his deposition as their chairman. Heated argument in Committee Room 15 at the beginning of December led to a split in which the Parnellites were in a minority. In 1891 Parnell was determined to fight on, but by now the full effect of Liberal opinion, the Irish clergy, and the division in his own Parliamentary party began to tell against him. Even a man of Parnell's standing ultimately could not ignore the significance of the parish priest in an Irish election, and an overwhelming defeat at a by-election held immediately afterwards in Kilkenny brought home the truth. Still he struggled on, refusing to accept the inevitable, until, in September 1891, only four months after his marriage to Katherine O'Shea, he caught a chill addressing a meeting in the rain and died shortly afterwards at Brighton.

Melodrama had stalked Parnell's life until the end. From the moment when he had seen that the passing of the Ballot Act in 1872 might make possible the realization of O'Connell's great hope of an Irish Parliament, his struggle had led him on through a succession of bizarre episodes. The sad tangle of his private life was in keeping with his political career, and there is a strange sense of fatality in his final undoing. The tragedy was not only Parnell's; it was also Ireland's, for his refusal to resign wrecked his cause. Common sense and moderation obviously demanded his resignation, but these were not the qualities that had won the Irish party its position in the 1880s. Two great emotions had possessed the soul of this remarkable man. A passionate determination for Ireland's freedom had made him stop at nothing, and his love for Katherine O'Shea caused him to put in jeopardy and finally to destroy all that he had achieved. In character he was consistent to the end, and in the *dénouement* the sense of inescapable doom lends a touch of classical tragedy to the story of his life.

Meanwhile, on the Continent, the Berlin Congress of 1878 had been followed by the making of a series of alliances. Behind much of this lay the extraordinary mind of Bismarck, seeking to establish a system whereby the achievement of his earlier years might be preserved. His underlying fear remained the possible outbreak of hostilities between Russia and Austria over the Balkans, and part of the significance of the Congress had been that Bismarck had been unable to keep both governments equally in play.[1] He had chosen the Austrian side, and this friendship was cemented a year later by the Dual Alliance of 1879 between Germany and Austria, whereby the two Powers agreed to defend each other against Russian attack and to preserve a benevolent neutrality in the event of either of them being involved in a war with any other Power. Although this might seem a definite commitment for Germany, Bismarck hoped to use the Dual Alliance to restrain Austrian chauvinism. The treaty was fraught with great dangers. It might, in fact, encourage Austria to become bolder; it might alarm Russia and drive her towards a treaty with France, whom Bismarck was determined to keep isolated; it could involve Germany in Balkan questions which were directly no concern of hers. Everything rested on which of the two gained the initiative within the alliance. While Bismarck held the reins this was fairly clear, but after Bismarck's dismissal there was a growing tendency for German diplomacy to be harnessed to Austrian requirements, and this was ultimately to be one of the principal factors in the outbreak of world war in 1914.[2]

Two other agreements followed. The first, the *Dreikaiserbund* —Germany, Austria, and Russia—was created in June 1881, a general pact of neutrality, aimed mainly at improving relations between Russia and Austria. The second, the Triple Alliance, was the result mainly of the French occupation of Tunis, in 1881, which had robbed Italy of a prospective colony. Bismarck had encouraged the French to make this move, partly to keep France

[1] See p. 304. [2] See p. 431.

N

happy,[1] partly to cause antagonism between her and Italy, and the fruits of his efforts were an alliance whereby Germany and Austria agreed to help Italy against French attack. The treaty also guaranteed general assistance in the event of any one of the signatories becoming involved in a war with two Powers. These last two agreements, the one envisaging Russia as a friend, the other seeing her as a possible opponent, are a typical example of Bismarck's policy of insuring and reinsuring, but they did in themselves involve Germany in new risks. Germany's two main partners were the most restive elements in the European scene—Italy, hungry for African colonies; Austria, aiming at an economic expansion through the Balkans, a policy reinforced by two secret treaties—with Serbia in 1881, and with Rumania in 1883.

The juggling which this growing complex of treaties involved was well illustrated by the Bulgarian crisis of 1885-7. The trouble started in 1885, when Eastern Roumelia, that meaningless area to the south of Bulgaria invented by the diplomats at the Congress of Berlin, announced its determination to unite with Bulgaria. This was precisely what the Russians had wanted in 1878, but by now the attitude of the Powers had changed. Alexander of Battenberg, who had become Prince of Bulgaria as a Russian nominee, had shown himself too vigorous and independent to make his country the satellite state that Russia had originally intended, and the Tsar accordingly demanded the maintenance of the 1878 settlement. But the British attitude had also altered. Lord Salisbury had at first wished to defend Disraeli's settlement, but was eventually persuaded against this by the pressure of public opinion which favoured the Balkan Christians, and by the advice of the British ambassador at Constantinople. Fighting had already broken out in the Balkans, since Serbia, after demanding compensation from Bulgaria, went to war and was badly defeated by the Bulgarians. The Powers now intervened and in April 1886 it was agreed that there should be a personal union of Bulgaria and Eastern Roumelia.

But the trouble was not yet over. The Russian objection to an enlarged Bulgaria had been based, not on frontiers, but on the

[1] See p. 316.

activity of Alexander of Battenberg in Bulgaria. In August 1886 Alexander was kidnapped by Russian agents and forced to abdicate. The Bulgarians, however, were determined to find another anti-Russian prince and the Powers began to prepare for trouble. Bismarck was able to make use of the war scare to secure a co-operative Reichstag from the elections early in 1887, and in March gained an increase in the German Army. In June he followed this up with a secret Reinsurance Treaty with Russia, which just kept within the letter of his other engagements, hoping thereby to quieten Russian alarm. At the same time Lord Salisbury, feeling that a new grouping of the Powers was in the making and not wishing France to take advantage of this to the detriment of Great Britain, concluded a Mediterranean agreement with Italy in February 1887, a vague promise of mutual support in that region. A little later a treaty with Austria followed, thus ensuring the *status quo* in the Mediterranean.

In July the Bulgarians elected Ferdinand of Coburg as their prince, and since this was contrary to Russia's wishes, Great Britain, Italy, and Austria strengthened their position with a second Mediterranean agreement in December. Russia, in fact, had no wish to become involved in a Balkan war and had been reassured by her treaty with Germany. It was Austria who was the more warlike of the two. The German and Austrian military staffs were keen to embark on a preventive war with Russia, but nothing could have been further from Bismarck's intentions, and in February 1888 he published the text of the Dual Alliance of 1879. This ended the likelihood of war, for the Alliance only promised German aid to Austria in the event of a Russian attack. Thus it was now public knowledge that Austria would fight alone, if she attacked Russia; and the Russians were confirmed in their intention to leave well alone. Face was saved by the Russians asking the Sultan to declare Ferdinand's election illegal, and when the Sultan had done so, the new solution was quietly accepted by everyone and Ferdinand settled down to enjoy his new principality.

The crisis illustrated both the extraordinary diplomatic skill of Bismarck and the increasingly difficult position that his policy

created for him. German alliance with Austria, German friendship with Russia, continued isolation for France—how long could
he continue to maintain all three conditions? It is fascinating to
speculate on what Bismarck might have done, if he had not been
dismissed by the young Emperor William II in 1890. Certainly no
one else could manage such a situation for long, and within a year
or two of his departure France and Russia had moved together,
first to create an *entente*, then to form a firm alliance in January
1894.

The significance of this Franco-Russian alliance was immense.
It drew Germany and Austria closer together; it raised the German
spectre of war on two fronts and caused the German general staff
to draw up a plan of attack that was to become a political factor
in itself.[1] For Great Britain the alliance of her two most likely
opponents meant an alarming change in the balance of naval
power in the Mediterranean. French neutrality was essential before the British fleet could ever be sent through the Dardanelles to
Constantinople, and since that neutrality was now ruled out, the
British government came to see Egypt—where they had never
meant to remain—as the key to the continuance of their power in
the eastern Mediterranean. Already in the 1880s there had been a
growing awareness in Great Britain of the weakness of her Navy
—the mainstay of her security—and in 1889 the war scare of the
previous year had led to the passing of a Naval Defence Act that
provided for a considerable increase in the size and quality of the
Navy. The Franco-Russian alliance only added to these fears and
prompted the experts to think continually in terms of the 'two-
Power standard' whereby the British Navy must remain stronger
than the combined fleets of the two Powers who came closest to
her in naval strength.

In England the time for the next general election was approaching, and with it the need for the Liberals to consider their tactics.
They might hope to gain a little from the swing of the pendulum,
but it was clear that their general appeal would have to be a wide
one. Home Rule had robbed them of much of their right wing,

[1] See p. 432.

while the more extreme Liberals were beginning to toy with Socialism. In October 1891 Gladstone put forward the 'Newcastle programme' in a speech designed to win back many of these discordant elements. Home Rule and disestablishment of the Church in Scotland and Wales should please the voters outside England. Employers' liability for accidents suffered by workers was designed to attract the Trade Unionists, while constitutional changes, such as the abolition of the plural franchise, triennial Parliaments, and a vague reference to the payment of members of the House of Commons, were to appeal generally to Radical sentiment. The weakness of the plan was that it tried to please too many people—the fate of any party struggling against disintegration—and the likelihood of a Liberal reunion was made even fainter, when, shortly before the election, Joseph Chamberlain took over the leadership of the Liberal Unionists in the Commons.[1]

The election of July 1892 was in one way a grievous disappointment for Gladstone. The Liberals gained only an infinitesimal majority over the Conservatives—273 seats against 269—and although this did at least mean that he could form a government, it was hardly possible to speak in terms of a mandate from the country. Eighty-one Irish Home Rulers were Gladstone's only safeguard against forty-six Liberal Unionists, but when Salisbury's Cabinet failed to obtain a vote of confidence after Parliament had reassembled, Gladstone seized what was clearly his last opportunity and accepted the Queen's invitation to form a government.

3. The second attempt at Home Rule. Gladstone and Rosebery, 1892–5

On 15 August Gladstone kissed hands at Osborne. He was, by now, approaching his eighty-third birthday, still a man of prodigious mental power, despite failing eyesight and hearing, and determined to bring in his solution to the Irish problem. At the dinner-table at Osborne, seated at some distance from the Queen,

---

[1] The previous leader, Lord Hartington, moved to the House of Lords as eighth Duke of Devonshire on his father's death in 1891.

he talked endlessly of Home Rule. 'He always will,' remarked the Queen afterwards. In fact, whatever Gladstone's views had been, a Liberal government at this moment could hardly have evaded the issue, entirely dependent as they were on the Irish vote.

The core of Gladstone's new Cabinet was as in 1886—Harcourt, Chancellor of the Exchequer; John Morley, Irish Secretary; Rosebery, Foreign Secretary; and Campbell-Bannerman, Secretary for War. The most significant newcomer was Herbert Asquith, who was given the Home Office. A Cabinet committee soon set to work on drafting a new Home Rule Bill, which received its first reading on 13 February, 1893. In many ways it resembled the 1886 Bill. The question of Ulster was still ignored, and the Irish legislature was to have no control over the Army, Navy, customs, trade, and foreign relations. The major point of difference lay in the proposal that eighty Irish members should sit at Westminster, where they might speak and vote on all matters that concerned Ireland; similarly, representative Irish peers would sit in the House of Lords.

Tension in the almost equally divided Commons was already mounting when Asquith introduced, between the first and second reading of the Irish Bill, a preparatory measure for the disestablishment of the Anglican Church in Wales. The Queen turned on her Prime Minister with fury; the opposition hurled charges of the basest form of political bargaining at the government bench. 'On behalf of the Irish policy nothing must be spared,' cried Lord Randolph Churchill, now very close to his death, '—not even the Established Church in Wales. Votes! Votes! Votes!' But the anger fomented by the prospect of disestablishment was as nothing compared with that unleashed by the debates over the Irish Bill.

The struggle raged throughout the whole length of the summer of 1893. For a man of eighty-three it was an extraordinary performance. He was 'like a great white eagle at once fierce and splendid', wrote Winston Churchill, who witnessed the second reading. During the sixty-three sittings, while the House was in Committee, he spoke again and again, tirelessly warding off amendments. At one moment Chamberlain, in the middle of a great onslaught on Gladstone, was interrupted by a cry of 'Judas'

from the Irish members, and for a few minutes there was actually
a riot on the floor of the House. At last, at the beginning of
September, the Bill passed its third reading and was sent up to the
House of Lords, where a week later it was rejected by an over-
whelming majority. The next move now lay with the Prime
Minister.

Gladstone never had any doubts over what that move should
have been. To the end of his life he maintained that the government ought to have asked the Queen for a dissolution and in the
ensuing election have demanded a mandate from the country for
a revision of the powers of the House of Lords. In this he was
anticipating by seventeen years the tremendous campaign on
which the next Liberal administration was to embark. The justification for such a fundamental change in the Constitution
would have been that the Lords were simply using their power of
veto on behalf of the Conservative party. This was certainly not
an empty charge. In 1894 a Parish Councils Bill was radically
amended by the Lords, and an Employers' Liability Bill made virtually useless, and the contrast between these tactics and the Lords'
acquiescence in the measures of the previous Conservative government made it plain that this was a conscious policy.

But Gladstone could not shift his Cabinet. To them the chances
of an electoral victory on so radical a measure seemed too slight,
and Gladstone allowed himself to be overruled. He hoped that
further obstruction by the House of Lords might exasperate
them into changing their minds, but in January 1894, when, on
holiday at Biarritz, he thought that the moment had come, a
telegraph message from the Cabinet quickly disillusioned him.

Thus it was apparent that Gladstone would never see the accom-
plishment of the last great aim of his life. It was perhaps his acceptance of that fact which, more than anything, persuaded him finally
to retire from politics. His failing eyesight and hearing gave him a
perfectly good excuse, but it was another issue over which he found
himself once again in disagreement with his Cabinet, that convinced
him that there was no longer any case for continuing in office.

Before the end of 1893 the opposition had already raised the
question of a further expansion of the Navy. The fears awoken by

military and naval preparations by France and Russia had not been entirely quietened by the Naval Defence Act of 1889 and the Cabinet, strongly supported by public opinion, were certain that a new programme for the construction of more battleships must be authorized at once. Gladstone deplored what he called a 'monstrous scheme of the Admirals'. The dead were with him, he said, 'Peel, Cobden, Bright, Aberdeen!' And the irony of this last dispute is that Gladstone, whose policies had become increasingly venturesome and forward-looking as he had grown older, was now for once looking backward. He could not shed that belief of the earlier Liberals that armaments were wasteful and unnecessary. He believed passionately in the Concert of Europe and could not accept this later phase in European relations, the armed peace, which Bismarck's tactics had made inevitable.

On 1 March, 1894 he announced to his Cabinet his decision to resign. That afternoon in his last speech in the Commons he attacked the activities of the House of Lords, predicting a restriction of their powers, and on the next day, after finishing a translation in verse of five of Horace's love odes, he went to Windsor to tender his resignation. Here a short remote conversation with the Queen brought the greatest political career of the nineteenth century to an end.

It would be presumptuous to attempt to sum up William Ewart Gladstone in a single paragraph, for the facets of that extraordinary personality defy any neat conclusion. He was a giant, a rock, as much a part of the nineteenth century as Victoria herself, and his strength and failings are those of the age. He was capable of self-deception; he could sound sanctimonious, not merely keeping the ace of trumps up his sleeve, as a friend put it, but maintaining that Almighty God had put it there. It seems remarkable that so able a man with so great a respect for the monarchy could have remained on such bad terms with the Queen. He had little interest in foreign affairs, hated imperialism, and beyond a certain point regarded social reform with suspicion.

Where, then, does his greatness lie? Not so much in particular issues as in the underlying governing principle. It became the fashion in the emancipated period of the 1920s to mock the high-mindedness of Victorian England; it was only later in the twentieth century that men, chastened by their own experiences, learnt that they had been wrong to laugh. A totalitarian epoch may look back on Mr. Gladstone with a new respect. He believed in the individual; he believed that the responsibility of government lay in service to God, and if at times he had to take many devious turns, he, above all men, knew that, with the highest ideals in the world, politics remains the art of the possible. But if an action seemed right and necessary, he would perform it, even though he might break his party, as he did over Home Rule. In this he was the natural heir to Robert Peel.

He believed in Free Trade and in democracy. Loathing war, he believed in the Concert of Europe. It is easy to argue that Free Trade eventually involved its own downfall,[1] that democracy unleashed an unreasoning Imperialist spirit, and that to ignore the arms race after 1871 was unrealistic. Disraeli in many ways seems the more effective personality of the two, but as time lends a sense of perspective to their work, so the greater stature of Gladstone becomes apparent. The foundation of modern government was laid during his first great administration. Colonialism, in which he had little interest, is almost a thing of the past, and the mother country now prides herself as much on the skill with which she sheds her possessions as she did earlier on their acquisition. Ireland has achieved more than Home Rule, although only after bloodshed and bitterness that might have been avoided if Gladstone could have had his way. Free Trade, it is true, was doomed, yet there still sounds an echo of its ideals in the Europe of the mid-twentieth century, groping towards a removal of tariff barriers, and although the scope of international alignment has changed beyond all recognition, the notion of a Concert of Powers remains the most realistic aspect of twentieth-century aspirations. It took the fear of atomic war to convince the democracies of the political soundness of Mr. Gladstone's moral principles.

The Queen chose to exercise her prerogative in selecting Gladstone's successor without consulting him. Sir William Harcourt

[1] See p. 176.

seemed the natural choice, but he had made himself extremely unpopular with the Cabinet and neither the Queen nor Gladstone
considered him suitable. If Gladstone had been asked, he would
have proposed Lord Spencer. In fact, Victoria chose Lord Rosebery. He appeared to have all the gifts—youth, wealth, popularity, eloquence; he was even lucky, winning the Derby two
years in succession during his premiership, but one thing he lacked
—experience of the House of Commons and of the complicated
tactics of party management.

During the fifteen months that his government survived it was
able to accomplish very little. Measure after measure passed the
Commons only to be thrown out by the Lords, and although it
was the government's hope that eventually the Lords would exasperate the electorate into giving greater support to the Liberals,
they were to be disappointed in this, since public opinion tended
to interpret the whole situation as a proof of the government's
weakness. The Lords' policy was certainly dangerous and there
was much truth in the Liberals' complaint that they were shame-
fully abusing their position as a second Chamber. There was,
however, just one loop-hole of defence for their action. In the
debate on the Irish Church Disestablishment Bill in 1869 Salisbury
had declared that when 'the House of Commons is at one with
the nation', the Lords were not justified in rejecting a measure.
But this was precisely what Rosebery's Liberals could not claim.
The Commons were almost equally divided, and the Cabinet's
refusal to dissolve and to appeal to the electorate seemed a tacit
acknowledgement of the fact that they did not have the country
with them.

Ultimately, in 1911, the Lords were to pay the price for their
rashness. But at the moment the most significant development in
the political field concerned neither the Conservatives nor the
Liberals. 1893 was a year of great industrial unrest. A demand by
the owners for a 10% reduction in wages in the coalfields of the
English federated area—all those south of the Tweed, excluding
Durham, Northumberland, and South Wales—led to a great
lock-out. In the past strikes had been local, aimed primarily at
bringing pressure to bear on individual employers. Now the

miners' leaders embarked on a more ambitious policy, to hold the whole community to ransom by cutting off supplies throughout the country. Such a plan, however, meant considerable cooperation between the Unions and at this time actually led to war among the workers themselves, when the miners of Ebbw Vale decided to resist the hauliers who attempted to shut down the mines in South Wales which had not been concerned in the original dispute. This resistance spoiled the hopes for a general stoppage, but in the Midlands there was serious rioting and on one occasion at Featherstone, when the police had lost control of the situation, troops had to be ordered out and two miners were killed when they opened fire. Eventually Gladstone, who at first had not wished to involve the government in the dispute, had to devise some form of mediation, and in November Lord Rosebery, presiding over a conference, was able to reach a compromise which brought the dispute to an end for a time.

These events of 1893 were to have an important effect upon the working-class electorate. Until now Trade Unionists had hoped to rely upon contact with Conservative or Liberal M.P.s. The Liberals had seemed to offer greater prospects, but the Featherstone incident did much to undermine the chances of further Liberal and Trade Union collaboration, and for long afterwards Asquith, the Home Secretary, was decried as a murderer. This new development accorded well with the plans of the Socialists, who believed that it was essential to wean the Trade Unions from their alliance with the Liberals. In 1892 Keir Hardie, one of the leaders of this movement, had been elected to a seat in the House of Commons and in 1893 he took the chair at a conference which finally set up the Independent Labour Party.

At a governmental level the Rosebery administration was a relatively quiet one. Harcourt's 1894 Budget introduced death duties on all forms of estate, an innovation of striking social significance which might, at first sight, seem a piece of purely party legislation, but which has never since been relinquished as a means of revenue by succeeding Conservative governments. Abroad, two developments were to be of profound significance in foreign relations. In August 1894 a war broke out between China and Japan, in which

Japanese forces were victorious in Korea and the Liao-Tung peninsula, and captured Port Arthur.[1] By the treaty of peace in 1895 China gave up all these, as well as Formosa, but diplomatic intervention on the part of Germany, Russia, and France forced Japan to give back the Liao-Tung peninsula and Port Arthur. China in return allowed the Russian Trans-Siberian railway to make an invaluable short cut through Manchuria to Vladivostok. In 1894 there was also trouble in Turkey. A series of massacres of Armenians had been carried out by the Turks, and Great Britain, France, and Russia did their best to bring the slaughter to a halt, but were by no means entirely successful. In contrast, Germany made the most capital out of the situation by giving Turkey full support over the massacres, thus greatly improving her own diplomatic position at Constantinople.

On 21 June, 1895 Campbell-Bannerman was censured by the Commons for not having provided the Army with sufficient cordite, a new smokeless explosive. On the next day the Cabinet decided to resign. Lord Salisbury at once formed a Conservative government and in July a general election gave the new Prime Minister a majority of 152 seats, including seventy-one Liberal Unionists, who were now prepared to act entirely alongside the Conservatives.

[1] See map, p. 409.

18

THE IMPERIAL THEME

BRITISH Imperialism as an expression of Victorian patriotism developed comparatively late in the nineteenth century. In one respect this was simply a direct continuation of the work of the Radical Imperialists, as the new lands, colonized predominantly by British emigrants, moved towards federation and the attainment of Dominion status. A totally different aspect of Imperial development was presented by the opening up of Africa, for, as the interior of the Dark Continent was explored in the middle of the nineteenth century, the European Powers had to come to agreement over their spheres of influence and to cope with new problems of governing primitive peoples.

It would be hard to imagine two more different types of colony. Yet the future Dominions and the new African possessions had one thing in common. They were part of a development in the history of the world that heralded the opening of a new age. It has been observed how in Great Britain and on the Continent the growth of new roads, railways, and the electric telegraph had brought with it revolutionary social and economic changes. The period from 1860 to the end of the century now saw the same process at work throughout the vast land masses outside Europe. The Union-Pacific and Canadian-Pacific railways in North America and the Trans-Siberian railway to Vladivostok opened the way to the settlement of lands that sheer distance had previously made impossible. The search for raw materials took Europeans into the heart of Africa and the study of tropical diseases made it possible for them to stay there. The produce of all this new territory, the invention of refrigeration, the development of large fast steamships, and the shortening of sea routes through the Suez and, later, the Panama Canal were together to have as cataclysmic an effect on the world scene as the opening of new trade routes at the end of the fifteenth century. The laying of telegraph cable across the ocean bed was in itself like a shrinking of the whole earth's circumference.

During the rest of the century the concentration of technical knowledge in Europe and the under-population of the lands outside Europe put them at the mercy of European intruders. But the pattern of technical development bringing in its wake revolutionary social and economic consequences was to be repeated. This very intrusion carried with it the seeds of the ultimate dwindling of European predominance in the world, and, in the same way as the roots of nineteenth-century England stretch far back into the eighteenth century, so the world picture of the mid-twentieth century had already begun to be sketched in the reign of Queen Victoria.

1. The development of Dominion status

In Canada the twenty years following the passing of Russell's 1840 Act had revealed both the wisdom and the flaws in Lord Durham's report. Responsible government had developed apace, but in the united Province of Canada the French element had remained unsubmerged, contrary to Durham's hopes, and the continuing Anglo-French discord appeared to present a growing danger to the future of Canada, particularly in view of the westward expansion of her neighbour south of the 49th parallel.

The need to find a solution to this problem eventually led to the final stage in the constitutional development of the Canadian provinces. In the 1860s ideas were at work for a return to the old division of Upper and Lower Canada for local government, while retaining some sort of union for national purposes. The discussion of such a scheme coincided with the growth of similar ideas in the Maritime Provinces of Nova Scotia and New Brunswick. Here technical development was helping to break down the earlier isolation and plans were on foot for a railway line linking the Maritime Provinces with one another and with the area of the

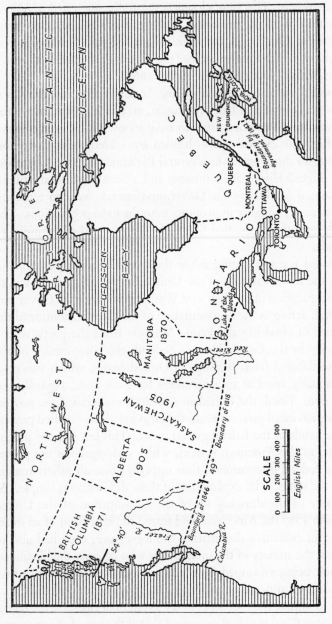

6. CANADA AND THE UNITED STATES BORDER

St. Lawrence. This new closeness naturally suggested a general federation of all the provinces in the east of Canada, and after a meeting at Quebec in October 1864 a federal constitution was drawn up, which finally received the British Parliament's approval in the British North America Act of 1867.

The Province of Canada on the St. Lawrence and the Great Lakes was divided in half once again, and each region, as well as the Maritime Provinces, was to have its own local government, in which the executive was headed by a Lieutenant-Governor. At Ottawa there was to be a central Parliament of two Chambers —an elected House of Commons and a Senate where members, nominated for life by the Governor-General, were to represent the provinces roughly in proportion to the local populations. The whole area thus federated was to be known as the Dominion of Canada.

Several features distinguished the new Canadian government from the federal system of the United States. First, there was to be no separation of powers, as at Washington, since the Governor-General, acting as the representative of the Crown, continued the practice of choosing the Prime Minister from the party with a majority in the Lower House. Second, the composition of the Senate differed from that of the United States, which was constitutionally fixed at two members for each State, regardless of their size. Third, the Canadian constitution specified the powers of the provincial governments, thus leaving all unspecified powers in the hands of the federal government. This last was the precise reverse of the American system, which only specifies the power of the federal government, thus implying that all others remain with the states. The explanation of these differences is simple. At the time of the drawing up of the Constitution of the United States in 1787 the Americans had feared the repetition of an over-powerful executive dominating the legislature; they had also to quieten the anxiety of the small States who foresaw the likelihood of their being swamped by the larger ones. In contrast to this, British constitutional development by 1867 encouraged the Canadians to imitate the mother country's system of rule, and the recent American Civil war had suggested that if the new federation was to survive, the power of the central government must be stronger than that in the United States.

The presence of their American neighbour continued to influence the development of the new Dominion. In 1867 the United States had purchased Alaska from Russia. The Canadians had been conscious of American territorial ambitions ever since the unsuccessful attempt to bring them into the War of Independence and were now more than ever aware of the threat to the lands that lay virtually uninhabited west of Ontario. These lands were held by the Hudson's Bay Company by licence from the Crown and the Company had positively discouraged settlement, since this would have interfered with fur trapping. In 1869, however, the Canadian government successfully petitioned the Crown for the acquisition of this territory and the Company was bought out of most of its holdings for £300,000. Except for a small rising of settlers by Red River, who feared that their own interests might be badly affected by the exchange, the transaction was fairly simply accomplished. In the following year Manitoba, a new province next to Ontario, joined the federation. British Columbia, whose population had increased enormously since the discovery of gold on the Frazer river, was a particularly significant addition in 1871, for it implied the building of a trans-continental railway line, and after the completion of the Canadian-Pacific in 1885 the organization and settlement of the Prairie Provinces of Saskatchewan and Alberta was bound to follow in the course of time.

Meanwhile, in Australia the six separate colonies had been thriving. In the 1850s and 1860s the discovery of gold, particularly at Ballarat in Victoria, naturally led to a sharp rise in the population. The governments had at first viewed these discoveries with some apprehension. 'Put it away, Mr. Clarke, or we shall all have our throats cut,' said the Governor of New South Wales to the clergyman who was among the first to report a find of gold. The presence of hardened criminals among the transported convicts was certainly not ideal in a country anticipating all the excitement of a gold rush, but although there was one serious outbreak of violence at Ballarat in 1854, the general disorders were remarkably small. The discovery of gold also gave rise to a fear that prices would soar and bring ruin for the sheep farmers. Naturally, prices did rise considerably, but inflation is not necessarily disastrous in a new community in which every man has his way to make, and in fact the sheep-farmers benefited from a generally increased purchasing power.

Federation came comparatively late in the history of Australia, since geographical factors tended to divide the colonies. There were no great Powers nearby who might frighten them into uniting, and they were thus free to enjoy local squabbles amongst themselves. In the last decades of the century, however, these conditions were changing. An influx of cheap Chinese labour presented a threat to the Australian wage-earner. The growing colonial rivalry among the European Powers in the Pacific was gradually undermining the security that their earlier isolation had given the Australian settlers, and the German annexation of the north coast of New Guinea in 1884 had made them particularly aware of these new developments. It was clear that there would soon have to be a common policy over defence and immigration and this could only be achieved through some sort of federation.

As early as 1868 Sir Henry Parkes, Prime Minister of New South Wales, had favoured the idea, but it was not until the 1890s, when Australia was in the throes of a great depression, that he was able to make much headway with it. One referendum rejected the proposal, but a second, in 1899, accepted it, and by 1900 a detailed constitution for a central government had been drawn up. Only Western Australia wished to remain outside, but was finally persuaded to join by Joseph Chamberlain. The Australian Commonwealth Act was passed without incident by the British Parliament. 'Whatever is good for Australia', said Chamberlain in his introductory speech in the House of Commons, 'is good for the whole British Empire. Therefore, we all of us—independently altogether of party, whether at home or in any other portion of the Empire—rejoice at this proposal.'

The new federal government was to have its centre at Canberra, a new city, to be built at a spot roughly equidistant from the major cities of eastern Australia. The general pattern of the constitution was not unlike the Canadian, but in certain respects it came closer to that of the United States. It was the powers of the central government, not the individual governments, that were defined. The Upper House, the Senate, representing the one-time colonies, was to consist of six members from each state and was to be an elected body. Thus, in accordance with their own wishes, the six Crown colonies had now become the Commonwealth of Australia, responsible for their own government and linked to the mother country only by the personal tie of the Crown, represented by a Governor-General at Canberra.

New Zealand had resisted all suggestions that she should join in the Australian system. On the other hand, federation within New Zealand had come much earlier than in Australia. In 1853 Sir George Grey, the Governor, had organized a central two-chamber government at Wellington, while each of the six provinces managed its own affairs through elected councils. Three years later responsible government was granted to New Zealand, and in 1875 an Act turned local government into something close to the existing system in England today. From then on New Zealand continued as a self-governing unitary state, and although she was recognized as a Dominion in 1907, this was no more than a change of title. She had already long enjoyed the rights of Dominion status.

2. The partition of Africa

For the European Africa had remained virtually an unknown continent until the middle of the nineteenth century. In the north a Moslem culture had been established for well over a thousand years; of the central regions almost nothing was known and the colonial Powers of earlier centuries had done little more than to establish one or two remote trading stations on the coast. The incursions that European Powers began to make along the north coast of Africa in the nineteenth century were mainly a slight extension of their Continental policies. France's conquest of Algeria gave her greater control of the Mediterranean opposite her own coastline: her interest in Egypt since the time of Napoleon

was due to the fact that its possession would command the
overland route to India, and her conquest of Tunis in 1881 was no
more than compensation for her losses in the Franco-Prussian war.

The partitioning of the interior of Central Africa, however, is a
much more complicated story, hardly motivated by the European
political scene, although naturally influenced by it. Here Imperialism became an aim in itself. A variety of ambitions led to
the exploration of the tropical regions—purely scientific interests,
a humanitarian desire to stamp out the activities of the Arab slave-
traders, missionary zeal, and the search for new sources of raw
materials. Very early in the century Mungo Park had traced the
course of the Niger; two German missionaries had later discovered
Mounts Kilimanjaro and Kenya, and German explorers were active in the Cameroons. In the 1850s and 1860s Dr. Livingstone
had mapped the Zambesi, the Congo, and Lake Nyasa; and Lakes
Victoria, Albert, and Tanganyika were identified by Burton,
Speke, and Baker.

It has been customary to speak of the 'scramble for Africa', as
the potentiality of these regions was grasped by European governments. The phrase is not inappropriate, yet it must be put to the
credit of nineteenth-century diplomacy that, despite the keen
rivalry in marking out spheres of influence, almost the whole of
this vast continent was partitioned amongst the Powers without
resort to armed force. The first international agreement over
Africa was the result of a conference held at Berlin in 1884-5.
The basin of the Congo, which was rich in rubber, was perhaps
the greatest prize, and this was accordingly guaranteed inter-
nationally under the suzerainty of the King of the Belgians. Germany received the Cameroons, Togoland, and, further south, a
section of South-West Africa. Great Britain gained the lower
basin of the Niger, while France was granted a vaguely defined
area north-west of the Congo.

The second general agreement over further partition took the
form of a series of treaties between Great Britain and the other
Powers in 1890. By this time the issues had become rather more
strategic; with greater exploration and settlement the question of
the precise establishment of interior frontiers had grown more

acute, particularly since the unclaimed areas inland were dwindling and a skilfully chosen boundary line might prevent further expansion on the part of a rival Power. The obvious aim was to establish a belt of territory across the continent, and thus the later period of negotiation became a struggle for the centre square in an international game of noughts and crosses. The treaty of 1890 with Portugal enlarged the area of the existing Portuguese possessions of Angola and Mozambique in return for the recognition of Mashonaland and Nyasaland as a British sphere of influence. The agreement with Germany established Kenya and Uganda as British areas, while the island of Zanzibar was to be a British protectorate. This was a considerable concession on Germany's part, gained by the granting of Heligoland by Great Britain to Germany. At the same time French suspicions were quietened by a more exact definition of the boundaries of West Africa and the acquisition of Madagascar.

As in earlier periods of colonial history, the first stages of settlement in the British zones in Africa were undertaken by private companies. Of these the most famous is the British South Africa Company under Cecil Rhodes, but in addition to this there were two others that did a great deal towards the opening up of the eastern and western regions of Africa. In 1886 the Royal Niger Company was formed, mainly through the enterprise of Sir George Goldie, who wished to prevent the infiltration of French business interests. The normal method of development was by private treaties with the chiefs of local native tribes. This system was considerably extended after 1899, when the government took over Northern and Southern Nigeria. In the north Colonel (later Lord) Lugard based his administration on the recognition of the local Moslem emirs; they continued to administer their own justice and were left to collect their own taxes, half of which were to be paid into a central fund for the development of the country. Throughout Lugard's work there is an echo of the ideas of British administrators in India in the first half of the century, such as Munroe and Elphinstone, and the relationship with the emirs came close to the control exercised over the Indian princes, who had been left a considerable degree of independence within their own states.

On the other side of the continent the British East Africa Company was formed in 1888, operating in the regions that later became Kenya and Uganda. The leading figure in this was Sir William Mackenzie, who was concerned with stopping German infiltration from Tanganyika. The same method was adopted as in West Africa—the making of private treaties with local chieftains—for much of which the explorer William Stanley was responsible. Financially, however, the enterprise did not flourish, and in 1893 the British government established a protectorate over Uganda, and two years later, somewhat reluctantly, took over the whole of East Africa from the Company.

The history of South Africa during these years is inevitably different, since parts of it had already long been settled by the Boers and the British. Here the rivalry was between two resident communities and a period of territorial and economic expansion eventually brought about the first major clash in the settlement of South Africa.

The Boers laid claim westwards to Stellaland, Goschen, and Bechuanaland; in the east they began to move into Zululand—a highly significant region, since the Transvaal was anxious to find an outlet to the sea. It was this last that the British government was determined to stop, and in 1885 Zululand was annexed to the Crown. Finally in 1894 Pondoland, the sole remaining coastal region, to the south of Natal, was declared to be within the British sphere of influence. The westward thrust into Bechuanaland did not lead to the sea, but, had the Boers made good their hold on it, this would have brought their western borders up to German South-West Africa and further British expansion northwards from the Cape would have been cut off. Accordingly, in 1885, the British government annexed Southern Bechuanaland and declared a protectorate over the rest of the area.

Newly discovered mineral wealth added a further element to the growing antagonism. In 1870 diamonds were found at Kimberley. This was at a point east of the Orange Free State, but the frontiers were so ill-defined that both sides might well have laid claim to it. The Governor of Natal, hardly an unbiased judge, when asked to arbitrate ruled that Kimberley lay outside the

Boer republic, and the British later paid the Boers £90,000 in compensation for a somewhat disputable decision.

Of far greater political significance was the discovery of gold in the very centre of the Transvaal in 1886. The inevitable gold rush brought a whole host of foreigners to Johannesburg, the mining centre in the Witwatersrand, but although the history of California and Ballarat had shown that a country might expect many advantages from this new industry, the peculiar position of the Boers forced them to watch these developments with some trepidation. They were a small pastoral community, intensely jealous of their language, customs, and religion, and the sudden advent of so many foreigners, actually outnumbering them, confronted them with the threat that they might cease to remain masters of their own country. It was consequently understandable that Paul Kruger, President of the Transvaal, should follow a policy that was as discouraging as possible to the Uitlanders, as the foreigners were called. They were heavily taxed, but were allowed no civic rights either in the government of the Transvaal or in the city of Johannesburg, which virtually owed its existence to them. Government revenue rose from £154,000 in 1886 to £4 million in 1898, yet none of this was used to give the heavily populated Rand a decent system of drainage or water supply. Thus there were grievances on both sides. Relations grew steadily worse during the thirteen years between the discovery of gold and the outbreak of the Boer war, and before long Kruger was using the new wealth of the Transvaal to buy armaments from Germany, an activity strictly contrary to the Convention of Pretoria of 1881.

The Uitlander problem was not a specifically British matter, but it inevitably became part of a bigger quarrel, as the British extended their own area of settlement. This was mainly due to the imagination of a remarkable personality. Cecil Rhodes, the son of an English clergyman, had come out to South Africa when still in his teens for the sake of his health. Within a very few years he had made a fortune out of the diamond mines at Kimberley, came back to England to study at Oxford, and then returned to the Cape, where he entered Parliament in 1881. The annexation of

Bechuanaland in 1885 was largely the result of his efforts, and within a few years he was already sending out agents to explore the economic possibilities of the land north of the Limpopo river, the northern frontier of the Transvaal. As soon as they had returned with favourable reports, he formed the British South Africa Company in 1889 and within a couple of years had established outposts at Salisbury and Victoria in what later became Southern Rhodesia. At first local treaties were made with the Matabeles who, under their king Lobengula, were the dominant native people in the region. In a short time, however, relations had broken down and there followed a short war with the Matabeles which ended in their defeat, the capture of Bulawayo, and the flight and death of Lobengula.

The presence of the British to their north completed the encirclement of the Boer Republics, and this naturally led to a heightening of their fears. Rhodes' dream was that one day an unbroken line of British territories in Africa would stretch from Cairo to the Cape, linked by a great railway, and as a first step in this process he outlined a scheme for a customs and railway union throughout the regions south of the Zambesi. The Boers, however, saw this as one more plan to smother them, resisted it strongly and concentrated on building their own line from Pretoria to the port of Laurenco Marquez in Portuguese East Africa. Nor was there entire agreement among the British, since the government of Natal was equally interested in a line from Johannesburg to Durban. The Cape line was eventually constructed northwards to the east of the Boer republics as far as Bulawayo. Thus the rivalry continued, containing all the elements that were later to lead to the tragedy of the Boer war.

The history of Africa in these last decades of the nineteenth century points to a remarkable transformation of the general attitude in Great Britain towards overseas expansion. Colonies were no longer a nuisance or even the concern of a tiny group of government officials. They had become matters of political significance and of public pride. The growth of Imperialism among all classes in Great Britain was a profound psychological change, reflected in the writings of the time and best summed up in the title of Sir John Seeley's lectures, *The Expansion of England*. The late Victorians saw Imperial rule not simply as a peculiar right of the British, but as a moral duty. In his play *The Man of Destiny* Bernard Shaw seized upon this point with delight. 'Every Englishman is born with a certain miraculous power that makes him master of the world. When he wants a thing, he never tells himself that he wants it. He waits patiently until there comes into his mind, no one knows how, a burning conviction that it is his moral and religious duty to conquer those who possess the thing he wants. Then he becomes irresistible.' Shaw put this speech into the mouth of Napoleon, but it was to an English audience of 1896 that he addressed it.

In fact, it was government rather than conquest that captured the popular imagination, fired by Rudyard Kipling's stories of India and the Near East. The public schools turned out the sons of rising middle classes as Christians and gentlemen, whose duty it was to guard and to govern this Empire. They were not likely to make good empire-builders; that called for the kind of qualities that had enabled Rhodes to make a fortune out of the Kimberley diamond mines in his early twenties, but because they could never lose, under any circumstances, the fundamental assumptions of moral superiority on which their whole lives were based, they tended to make good pro-consuls. The work of Dr. Arnold was bearing greater fruit than he could ever have imagined.

19

THE CLOSING YEARS OF QUEEN VICTORIA

1. Lord Salisbury's last administration, 1895–1902. The Boer war

OLD age did not have the same startling effect on Lord Salisbury as it did on Gladstone, but despite the Prime Minister's natural quietism, this last administration of Salisbury was to be eventful. It was a coalition government,[1] and owing to the number of distinguished and experienced politicians among the Liberal Unionists, a strong element of erstwhile Liberals found their way into the Conservative Cabinet. The Duke of Devonshire became Lord President of the Council. Joseph Chamberlain refused the Chancellorship of the Exchequer, since he was determined to make imperial development the major theme of the new government, and therefore chose the Colonial Office. Goschen accepted the Admiralty and Lord Lansdowne became Secretary for War. The Prime Minister himself took over the Foreign Office.

For those who thought back to the days of 'Radical Joe' it must have seemed odd to see him serving under a Conservative Prime Minister. In fact, it was Joseph Chamberlain who dominated the governmental scene in these years, but since his main interests now lay elsewhere, the government brought in rather less social legislation than might otherwise have been expected. The major measure was the Workmen's Compensation Act of 1897, which made the employer directly responsible for any injury suffered by a workman in an industry. Other measures included an Agricultural Rates Act and a Coal Mines Act, but the question of an old age pension scheme got no further than being considered by two successive committees.

[1] The alliance between Conservatives and Liberal Unionists lasted from 1895 until 1922 and their official collective title was 'Unionist'.

The fact that the most important events during the Salisbury administration were mainly in the colonial field was not simply due to the dynamic force of Joseph Chamberlain. Since 1894 Europe had become divided into two camps—the Triple and the Franco-Russian Alliance—and for a while it was Asia and Africa that offered the Powers greater room for manoeuvre. There were opportunities in the Far East, where useful pickings were to be had at the expense of China. For some ten years Russian diplomacy, encouraged by the plans for the Trans-Siberian railway, was almost entirely focused on possible gains in this region. The weakness of Turkey-in-Asia led to a growing German interest in a great railway scheme from Berlin to Baghdad, while in Africa the successful carving up of the continent into spheres of influence was followed by a more tense period as the colonizing powers negotiated over the precise details of the frontiers in the interior.

Naturally these colonial complications all had a bearing on the European scene, but they did not immediately suggest that there might be anything dangerous for Great Britain in her continued isolation. 'British policy', said Lord Salisbury on one occasion, 'is to drift lazily down stream, occasionally putting out a boat-hook to avoid a collision.' Two factors explain the general acceptance of this view. The sense of Empire was a matter of pride and confidence for the new electorate and Chamberlain was completely in tune with public opinion when he announced his intention to build up the colonies, the 'undeveloped estates'. Great schemes for the development of the West Indies and the Gold Coast were introduced; scientific research was carried out with a view to a greater realization of their economic potentiality; and the Colonial Service became professionalized. But while the Empire was a symbol of public confidence, the key to British security remained the Navy. Just as Great Britain could play little effective part in Continental diplomacy without having a land Power as an ally, so in all matters that rested on control of the sea routes she was the one Power that could entirely dispense with allies.

Thus her main fear in the 1890s was never directly her own isolation, but rather any possible threat to her naval supremacy. Once that supremacy was effectively challenged, isolation could not long survive. In fact, questions of naval power were to be a source of growing anxiety during these years. In the first place, technical inventions such as the torpedo and, later, the submarine seemed likely to revolutionize sea warfare; the small ship would be able to attack the big ship, and Powers that lacked a large navy might, by a sudden 'knock-out blow', be able to cripple the striking force on which British security rested. From this time on the authorities could never entirely lose this fear and the opening chapters of Sir Winston Churchill's *World Crisis* show clearly how great it had grown by 1914. In the second place, new political alignments affected the issue; Great Britain's most likely naval rivals had been France and Russia, and now their alliance of 1894 had caused considerable alarm over the consequent weakening of British predominance in the Mediterranean. Thus little is needed to explain the later anger and horror excited by the German policy of building a fleet which might compete with the British. Germany had already shown herself to be a past master of the 'knock-out blow' on land, and the conclusion to be drawn was obvious.

At the beginning of the Salisbury administration, however, two incidents seemed to suggest that Great Britain could still well dispense with Continental allies. The first arose over a boundary dispute of long standing between British Guiana and Venezuela. In 1895 Richard Olney, Secretary of State during the Presidency of Grover Cleveland in the United States, suddenly provoked a crisis by accusing Great Britain of violating the Monroe doctrine and demanding that she should submit the matter to arbitration. It was not a good argument. The Monroe doctrine had explicitly recognized existing European colonies in the New World, such as British Guiana, and had nothing to do with a boundary dispute. In any case, the Monroe doctrine was not recognized as part of international law and it would be rash for the Americans to quarrel with the one Power on whose naval strength they depended for the doctrine to have any significance at all. When Lord Salisbury's reply pointed out the fallacies in the Olney note, the President, hotly supported by Congress, was roused to announce his intention to impose his own arbitration, even if it meant war with Great Britain. 'Waal, Salisbury, Sir,' *Punch* depicted Cleveland as saying, 'whether you like it or not, We propose to arbitrate this matter Ourselves and, in that event, We shall abide by Our Own decision.' It was a crisis which Salisbury was admirably suited to handle. He did nothing. And as time passed, tempers cooled. The British public had not the slightest wish to go to war; nor had the Americans, as they realized when they had had time to think about it. The whole thing was too silly. Notes continued to be exchanged—Salisbury's at a fairly leisurely pace—and eventually, in 1899, after an Anglo-American commission had been set up, the boundary was established almost exactly along the line originally claimed by the British government.

The second incident, in South Africa, was rather more serious and took place when the Olney crisis was at its noisiest. By 1895 the exasperation of the Uitlanders at Johannesburg, outnumbering the whole of the Boer population in the Transvaal by more than two to one and paying about nine-tenths of the taxes, had reached the point of rebellion. Both Chamberlain and Rhodes were aware of the plan and reckoned that once the situation had got out of hand they would have a good case for intervening. Rhodes, however, meant to make sure and had posted Dr. Jameson in command of a force of mounted police in Bechuanaland just outside the Transvaal frontier, from where he was to make a dash for Johannesburg. But the Uitlander rising, planned for December 1895, failed to take place, owing to disagreement over whether they were to put themselves under British rule. There was now no possible reason for Jameson to move, but he was determined to press on, to force the Uitlanders' hand, and on 29 December he invaded the Transvaal with 450 mounted police.

The raid was an utter fiasco from the beginning. Jameson's party was intercepted some forty miles from Johannesburg and, on 1 January, 1896, surrendered to Kruger's Commandos. As soon as he had any suspicion of the raid, Chamberlain sent strong orders forbidding the operation and officially repudiated the whole attack. Kruger kept himself strictly in the right by handing over Dr. Jameson and his companions, who were sent home to London for trial; the Uitlander conspirators were rounded up and four condemned to death, although Chamberlain was eventually able to intercede on their behalf.

The whole episode had momentous consequences. Rhodes, deeply involved as he was, resigned the premiership of the Cape; the Dutch in the rest of South Africa, who previously had not been particularly sympathetic towards the Transvaal, now rallied to Kruger, convinced that the whole thing had been a British plot. Indeed, there were many people in Great Britain who believed that Chamberlain had known not merely of the Uitlander conspiracy—which he admitted—but also of the plan of the raid, although a select committee of the House of Commons acquitted him of this last charge. The most significant event was the German Emperor's famous telegram to Kruger, on 3 January, in which he congratulated him on restoring order 'without appealing for the help of friendly Powers'. This was not simply a whim of William II's. It was a carefully considered act designed to bring home to the British the realization of their dangerous isolation. In fact, it had the worst possible consequences. The British government at once fell back on their Navy and sent out a flying squadron to ensure that there could be no intervention of any Continental Power. British public opinion was greatly incensed, seeing Germany as a serious antagonist for the first time, and the German public became convinced that the flying squadron pointed to Germany's need for a strong navy.

The raid had given Chamberlain's enemies a chance to brand him as an Imperialist adventurer. In the following year, during the Queen's Diamond Jubilee, he was able to give expression to the more constructive aspect of his ideas on the Empire. At the Colonial Conference of 1897 he strongly urged his scheme of Imperial federation, but from the political point of view and from that of military and naval defence the scheme encountered opposition from the colonies. Those that had achieved or were in the process of achieving self-government had no wish to surrender part of their independence to a federal body. Over defence there was inevitably a divergence of views between the mother country, concerned with the requirements of world strategy, and the individual colonies concerned with their own local defence. Nor

was there agreement in the economic sphere. Chamberlain hoped
for an Imperial customs union—along the lines of the German
Zollverein—but the colonies had no wish to end the duties whereby they protected their own industry against the products of the
mother country. What they would have liked was a system of
Imperial Preference. In fact, either system would involve some
modification of Free Trade—particularly with regard to foodstuffs, which formed the major part of the Dominions' exports to
Great Britain—and when Chamberlain returned later to the idea
of Protection, the consequences were to be momentous.[1]

The year 1897 also saw some important developments in Imperial aspirations among the Continental Powers. Russia's acquisition of a twenty-five year lease of Port Arthur,[2] which was to be
linked with the Trans-Siberian railway by a branch line, convinced
the German government that they, too, must compete in this
region, and the murder of two German missionaries in Shantung
in August 1897 offered a convenient excuse for bringing pressure
to bear on the Chinese government, with the result that Germany
gained a ninety-nine year lease of the harbour of Kiao-chau. This
naturally provoked protests from Great Britain and France. Salisbury hoped mainly to preserve the Chinese empire, and would
have done nothing but for pressure from his Cabinet and public
opinion. Any attempt to force Russia to give up Port Arthur
seemed too dangerous in view of the Franco-Russian alliance, but
Chamberlain demanded that the situation simply could not be
ignored and Salisbury reluctantly agreed to accept compensation
in the form of a lease of Wei-hai-wei. 'It will not be useful and it
will be expensive; but as a matter of pure sentiment we shall have
to do it.' At the same time France received Kwang-Chau-wan in
southern China.

Meanwhile, events in Europe had given Germany an oppor-
tunity for improving her position. A war had broken out between
Greece and Turkey through a Greek attempt to take possession of
Crete, and in the fighting on the mainland Turkish forces suc-
ceeded in defeating the Greek army and occupied the plain of
Thessaly. The alteration of any frontier in this part of the world

---

[1] See p. 401.   [2] See map, p. 409.

was bound to concern the Powers, but nothing could have been more illustrative of the disharmony that existed in the so-called Concert of Europe. Russia naturally opposed any concession to Turkey. British public opinion, inflamed by the massacre of the Armenians,[1] sided with Gladstone, who in some of his last public utterances continued to scourge the Turks. Salisbury himself had no great love for Turkey and in the House of Lords complained bitterly that in 1854 'we put all our money on the wrong horse'. But in the era of the armed peace, when the colonial scramble was at its height, he felt that he must hold out for the *status quo*. And so Crete remained under Turkish rule and the Turks withdrew from Thessaly.

In all this the Germans had strongly supported Turkey, and the result of this friendship was a concession for a German railway to be built from the Sea of Marmora to the Persian Gulf. The German government maintained that the plan for a Berlin–Baghdad railway was of only commercial significance, but it was obvious that such an economic expansion through the Near and Middle East would be bound to have considerable political repercussions. Indeed, the only significance that it ever did have in the pre-war period was political, since the line itself had not been completed by 1914. Russia was the Power that objected strongly to the scheme, forseeing the possible strengthening of Turkey. For the same reason Great Britain had no objection to it and was glad to see German interests diverted away from Africa. France was even more enthusiastic and offered to put up 40% of the capital.

Still more striking than Great Britain's acceptance of this new German enterprise was the attempt on the part of the British government in 1898 to make a positive treaty of alliance with Germany. The author of the plan was Chamberlain, his motive the fear of Russian advance in the Far East, where there were large British commercial interests. A long period of bargaining ensued, but although Chamberlain was persistent, very little came of it. This was not due to any deep-rooted antagonism on the part of Germany. Great Britain simply wanted an ally against Russia, but

[1] See p. 364.

William II pointed out, 'Chamberlain must not forget that in East Prussia I have one Prussian army corps against three Russian armies and nine cavalry divisions,' and Germany had no intention of going to war with Russia for the purpose of driving her out of China. One local agreement did emerge from all the wrangling. Chamberlain was greatly concerned to get possession of the Delagoa Bay railway, the Boers' only link with the outside world through Portuguese East Africa, and saw a way of doing so by offering a loan to the Portuguese government, which was financially embarrassed. Germany thought at first of resisting this, but when she could get no support from Russia or France, an agreement was signed in August 1898, whereby Germany agreed to give up all further interest in the Transvaal.

One other reason why no Anglo-German alliance was achieved was that the German government was determined by now to build a navy, and an alliance with Great Britain would have made that impossible. The German admirals were naturally keen on the idea and had no great difficulty in winning over William II. Germany had colonies, she had interests in the Far East; therefore she must have a strong navy. The desire for prestige lay behind every point in the argument, and an older and wiser generation saw the folly of it. Bismarck, now in disgruntled retirement, considered the whole plan as irrelevant to the main stream of German policy. 'Germany should keep within her frontiers.' And Gladstone, observing the German battleships when he attended the opening of the Kiel Canal, commented: 'This means war!' But nothing could dissuade William II or his admirals, and in 1898 and 1900 two German Navy Laws were passed which provided the means whereby Germany would ultimately rank as a great sea Power. For the German Emperor the future lay on the water, and it was natural that the British should view that future with the gravest apprehension. They had good reason, as is revealed by William himself, when, at the beginning of the Boer war, he wrote to Bülow: 'I am not in a position to go beyond the strictest neutrality, and I must first get for myself a fleet. In twenty years' time, when the fleet is ready, I can use another language.'

Meanwhile, the major crisis in European relations was over

o

British and French aims in North Africa. The British scheme for a chain of territories from the Cape to Cairo inevitably clashed with a similar French plan for a trans-continental belt running from West Africa to the Indian Ocean. The central area in this dispute was the upper waters of the Nile, as yet unoccupied by either side. In March 1896 the Italians suffered an overwhelming defeat at Adowa at the hands of the Abyssinians, from whom the French hoped for cooperation, and the British government decided that the moment had come for the effective conquest of the Sudan. Shortly afterwards, Kitchener, in command of a nominally Egyptian army, set out southwards, and on 2 September, 1898 the conquest of the dervishes under their Khalifa was completed at the battle of Omdurman.

The race had been very close. Within a few days news reached Kitchener at Khartoum that a small French force had been encountered to the south at Fashoda. This was a party under Captain Marchand, who had just made an epic journey through the heart of Africa from the west in a bid to cut off the British from further expansion southwards. Kitchener at once went to Fashoda, and a conversation took place between the two commanders, remarkable for its restraint and good sense. Both the French and the Egyptian flags were hoisted, and the next move was left to the diplomats.

The problem for the French was that there was very little that diplomacy could achieve. 'We are the stronger,' Kitchener had remarked to Marchand during their conversation, and, indeed, Marchand was so far from his base that he was dependent upon British aid for further supplies and the French government could only communicate effectively with him by means of the British–Egyptian telegraph service along the Nile. Salisbury simply claimed the Sudan by right of conquest, and although the French might logically ask why they did not have to deal with the Egyptian government rather than the British, they looked in vain for support from other European Powers, and had eventually to accept the situation. In March 1899 the two governments agreed upon a dividing line between the basins of the Nile and the Congo, and as a final piece of tact the name of Fashoda was changed to

Kodok so that further mention of the place might not awaken unpleasant memories.

In another part of Africa tact could play little part. Since the Jameson raid relations between the Transvaal Boers and the Uitlanders had grown worse, and the overwhelming victory enjoyed by Kruger in the Transvaal presidential election in February 1898 enabled him to add greatly to his own powers as President. The incident that finally led to the outbreak of war was the killing of an English workman, Tom Edgar, by a Boer policeman. The Uitlanders declared that it was murder, but a jury of Boers acquitted the policeman of a charge of manslaughter and he was actually commended by the judge. This at once provoked a mammoth petition of over 21,000 signatures to the Crown by British subjects in the Transvaal. It was presented in March 1899, but it was not until May that the government decided to take it up, and throughout the summer there followed a series of negotiations which broke down at every stage and which culminated in the long-dreaded outbreak of hostilities in October 1899.

The tragedy of the whole story is that there were strong moderating influences on both sides. Recent publications have shown that Chamberlain tried hard to find a peaceful solution, contrary to the charge of war-mongering that was later laid against him. The leaders of the Cape Dutch were anxious to avoid war, and in the Transvaal itself the State Attorney, a young man of twenty-nine, Jan Christiaan Smuts, put forward proposals that might well have saved the situation. If the right men had been in the key positions, there would have been no war. But the two men on whom everything hinged were of a very different calibre —each of them, in his own way, obstinate and uncompromising— Sir Alfred Milner, the High Commissioner, who was convinced that only strong measures would hold Kruger back, and Kruger, whose actions during this period of negotiation did much to justify Milner's suspicions.

As usual, there was something to be said for each side. The Uitlanders' petition had put the British government in an awkward position. If they accepted it, war might result. If they rejected it, they would place a very serious strain on the loyalty of their own subjects in the whole of South Africa. As against this, the Boers were not unreasonable to mistrust the rampant Imperialism of Great Britain in the 1890s; a small community, fearful of losing their identity, they firmly believed that Joseph Chamberlain had been at the back of the Jameson raid, and the recent victory at Omdurman had so enflamed the enthusiastic Imperialism of the British public that the Boers may well have imagined that direct conflict could not be postponed any longer.

The war, which broke out in the autumn of 1899, began with a series of victories for the Boers. This is not difficult to explain. The Orange Free State joined the Transvaal on 27 September, and this gave the Boers a total force of 50,000 mounted infantry; interior lines, high morale, mobility, and a good knowledge of the country all combined to offer them a great initial advantage over the 14,750 regular British troops stationed in South Africa. Only time was against them, and their major hope was to strike such a blow before reinforcements could arrive by sea that the British government would be prepared to reopen negotiations. The first clashes quickly led to the bottling up of British forces at Ladysmith in Natal and at Kimberley and Mafeking on the railway line running up east of the republics from Cape Town to Bulawayo. So far, so good. The mistake that they made now was to settle down to long sieges of these three towns. Ladysmith particularly concerned them, since they were anxious to press on into Natal and to capture Durban. This need for a port was political and economic; it had little bearing on the military situation, which demanded a rapid sweep through Cape Colony, but the sweep was never made and the precious early months of campaigning were squandered on siege warfare.

The Boers' only hope that the British would be unable to bring in reinforcements lay in Europe, but although public opinion on the Continent was strongly in favour of the Boers, the governments were less ready to commit themselves. Germany, from whom Kruger expected much, took advantage of the situation to force Great Britain to abandon her interests in Samoa. Then later, in 1900, the outbreak of the Boxer rising in China against all western elements caused the Powers to combine in sending out

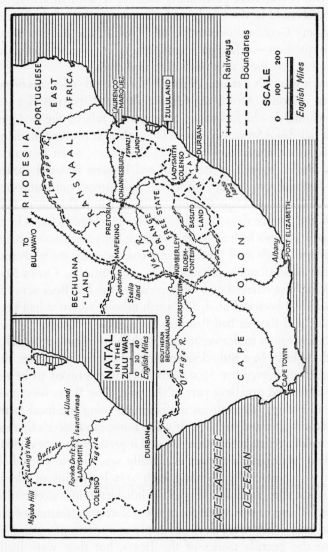

7. SOUTH AFRICA IN THE BOER WAR

an international force. The Germans, whose minister at Pekin had been murdered, were particularly anxious to send an army, but since this could be done only with the cooperation of the British Navy, any German intervention on behalf of the Boers was out of the question—as Kruger learnt, when he came to Europe in December 1900 on a vain mission to find allies.

Thus it was only a matter of time before the tide of events began to turn in South Africa. At first, while Sir Redvers Buller was Commander-in-chief, various attempts to relieve the besieged towns failed—at Stormberg on 10 December, at Magersfontein on 11 December, and at Colenso on 15 December, when Botha defeated Buller himself. After this Lord Roberts replaced Buller, and, forming one army out of all his forces, outmanoevred General Cronje in Cape Colony, relieved Kimberley on 15 February, and twelve days later forced Cronje to surrender. On 28 February Buller's fifth attempt to relieve Ladysmith was successful. From March until June, Roberts continued his main advance through Bloemfontein, Johannesburg, and Pretoria. On 17 May Mafeking was relieved and by September the last Boer army in the field had been defeated, all British prisoners-of-war had been released, and Kruger had fled into Portuguese territory.

Kitchener now took over to deal with the mopping up of what was thought to be a little desultory guerilla activity. In fact, this period from September 1900 until May 1902 proved to be the most bitter and gruelling part of the war. The Boers fought on in small groups, wearing no uniform and using the local farmsteads for shelter and support. It was a European Power's first experience of a resistance movement, and it presented a very difficult problem. Kitchener's answer eventually was to clear the whole country systematically, holding each area by means of blockhouses and wire, and rounding up the inhabitants in concentration camps. These camps were the most unfortunate feature of the whole war. They were devised simply as a means of putting an end to the guerilla tactics of the Boers, but they were badly managed, disease broke out, and in fourteen months over 20,000 died.

The first use of such camps was often pointed out by Germans in the 1930s, when criticism was made of the Nazi concentration camps. They were, however, hardly parallel. The Boer camps were a war-time innovation, designed to deal with a problem caused by the fact that the Boers had adopted methods which were not in accordance with the customs of war at that time; they never had any political purpose and they were certainly never intended as a means of extermination. They were simply an inefficient method of internment and in the circumstances it is hard to know what else the authorities could have done. Boer wounded were reasonably treated and from a civilized standpoint the British policy may be favourably compared with the German treatment of resistance movements in the second World War. When independent witnesses brought back accounts of the conditions in the camps, the government was furiously assailed inside and outside Parliament for employing what Campbell-Bannerman called 'methods of barbarism', and it was due to this outcry that Chamberlain took over the administration of the camps, after which conditions improved.

Another aspect of the war which the Continent is inclined to forget is the remarkable humanity of the peace terms. A treaty was finally signed at Vereeniging in 1902. The two republics were annexed, but while English was to be the official language, Afrikaans was to be allowed in schools and the law courts. A civil administration was to be established with the promise of eventual self-government, and Great Britain made a grant of £3 million to the Boers to assist them in rebuilding their farms. It has often been said that Great Britain wins a war, but loses the peace. In this case she won both, and although it was a little early to expect Boers and British to fall into each others' arms, the mildness of the terms was a useful beginning to reconciliation and was eventually to make possible a permanent settlement in 1906.[1]

The war had taken its toll of the British. Nearly 6,000 troops had been killed in action and a further 16,000 had died of disease. In money it had cost over £222 million. Most telling of all, British self-confidence had suffered a serious blow; the early defeats and the long-drawn-out guerilla war had chastened the

[1] See p. 414.

public, and the general hysteria on the news of the relief of Mafeking was the outburst of a nation that had suffered a severe
psychological shock.

Division at home over the war never presented Lord Salisbury's government with any serious crisis. The Liberals were split
over the question. The Liberal Imperialists under Lord Rosebery
were in favour of the war; the pro-Boers included John Morley
and a young Welsh nationalist, Lloyd George, whose Celtic fire
marked him out as a new personality on the political scene, but
they could do little against the government. Chamberlain was
mainly responsible for the decision for a general election in October 1900—known as the Khaki election, since the moment was
chosen when the war was almost certain to ensure a victory for
the government. The election made virtually no difference to the
situation in the Commons. Far more significant in this year was
the creation of the Labour Representation Committee, with
J. Ramsay MacDonald as its secretary, a new body which was to
aim directly at increasing the number of Labour M.P.s in Parliament and in whose support the Unions consented to raise a levy.

2. Fin de siècle

It has been said [1] that the 1890s were a battleground of two
types of culture, the *Yellow Book* and the Yellow Press, and it
could be added that the war is still being waged between the
descendants of the original protagonists. The *Yellow Book*, a
literary periodical, did not appear until 1894, but the 'decadence'
in English art and writing was simply an expression of a later stage
of the Romantic movement. Its devotees were obsessed with the
notion of exploring every form of sensual experience, in the hope
of communicating momentarily what they learnt through some
form of art. 'It was the strangest book he had ever read,' runs a
paragraph from Oscar Wilde's *Picture of Dorian Gray*, published
in 1891. 'It seemed to him that in exquisite raiment, and to the
delicate sound of flutes, the sins of the world were passing in dumb

---

[1] Holbrook Jackson: *The Eighteen-Nineties.*

show before him. Things that he had dimly dreamed of were suddenly made real to him. Things of which he had never dreamed were gradually revealed.' The respectability of Victorian England had made the progress of such a movement considerably slower than on the Continent, but contact through Baudelaire and Swinburne, George Moore and the French Impressionists, had enabled it to set its own stamp on the England of the 1890s.

The movement took a variety of forms. It meant an intense concentration on the intrinsic beauty of a sentence or a paragraph. It led to the cultivation of the 'purple patch', the gentle careful prose of Walter Pater. Precious young men became sufficiently recognizable in social life for Gilbert and Sullivan to poke fun at them in Patience:

> If you walk down Piccadilly
> With a poppy or a lilly
> In your mediaeval hand . . .

There developed an engrossing interest in the wildly exotic experiences of the artists of Paris, as suggested in George du Maurier's Trilby. The long slender figure of Aubrey Beardsley, portrayed in Walter Sickert's painting of him, his short career of unparalleled brilliance, and his death from consumption at the age of twenty-five were together almost a personification of the Romantic type. His pen drawings for Malory's Morte d'Arthur, the Yellow Book, Wilde's Salome, and his own uncompleted romance, Under the Hill, revealed a fantastic imagination in all the elaborate detail and delicate convolutions of the weird scenes that he devised. A more robust aspect of the decadents was represented by the American James Whistler, a dapper, fiery little man, who had a tongue like a rapier, a fact best illustrated, perhaps, by the title that he gave to a published collection of his letters and writings, The Gentle Art of Making Enemies. Whistler was the plaintiff in one of the most famous trials of the century, when he took Ruskin to court for calling his picture of Old Battersea Bridge a pot of paint flung in the public's face. He won his case and was awarded as damages the contemptuous sum of a farthing—which he wore ever afterwards on his watch-chain. Another side of the movement appears in the urbane, sophisticated essays and caricatures of Max Beerbohm—'the incomparable Max', as Bernard Shaw called him. It is, perhaps, Oscar Wilde who, in his plays, his wit, and the tragedy of his private life, stands most completely for this remarkable *fin de siècle*. 'I wish that I had said that,' he commented once, when a remark of Whistler's had pleased him. 'You will, Oscar,' replied Whistler, 'you will.' But the anecdote is unfair, for Wilde's brilliance was peculiarly his own.

The 'new woman' was a further element in the revolt against Victorian England. In 1889 Ibsen's play *The Doll's House* was first performed in England, and the slam of the door as Nora left her husband at the end of the last act echoed in the minds of thousands of young women. The right to drink and smoke in public, to wear bloomers, to ride a bicycle, all these demands were only a step towards the cry for the right to vote—a great rebellion against the world of Soames Forsyte, whom Galsworthy depicted as a Man of Property even in his marital relations.

In William Morris one has a link between the movement in the arts and a new approach to social problems. Morris was the apostle of beauty in everyday things—in the design of furniture, wall-papers, household goods, and printing. He stood out for the importance of craftsmanship in an age that was daily succumbing to the factory. Like Ruskin, he came to feel that a society which allowed such an enormous gulf between rich and poor was fundamentally unhealthy, and because only a healthy society would produce good art, he championed the working-class movement which might undo the harmful consequences of the Industrial Revolution.

Morris' Socialism was essentially emotional. It was the Fabians who were able to suggest a more practical solution which might act as an alternative to revolutionary Socialism. As the name of their society suggested, they believed in gradualism; Socialism, in the form of the nationalization of land, would slowly be achieved, and the Socialist state would come in, not overnight with fire and sword, but on a gentle, irresistible tide. The Fabians gained a fame out of all proportion to their size, owing to the writings of such members as Sidney and Beatrice Webb and Bernard Shaw.

They represent that aspect of English social reform that is constantly emerging in the nineteenth century—the desire for change and re-adjustment within the existing framework; there are obviously many points of difference in origin and outlook between the Evangelical humanitarians, the Trade Union leaders of the 1860s, and the Fabians, yet one thing they shared: they combined a passionate desire to improve the lot of the individual with a deep-rooted respect for the constitution, the law, and a stable society.

Thus far, these facets of the *fin de siècle* concerned a minority. The other side of the 1890s is the age of the masses, the noisy, merry world of the music-hall 'Palace of Varieties' and the Victorian public-house. This was a populace whose emotions could now be touched on a nation-wide scale through the development of the popular Press. Alfred Harmsworth, later Lord Northcliffe, was the pioneer of this new technique, whereby news reports were sub-edited into an easily readable form with great concentration on the personal appeal, 'the human angle'. Harmsworth was a man of extraordinary energy with a genius for sensing the way to the widest possible market, and through his successive ventures, *Answers*, *Tit Bits*, the *Evening News*, and the *Daily Mail*, he carried through what was indeed a minor revolution. This was not simply the fruit of the Education Act of 1870, as has sometimes been suggested; there had been a popular Press throughout the century and a reasonable level of literacy had existed before 1870. Harmsworth's success was due to his genius for organization, aided by a prosperity that had by now affected a large proportion of working-class families. The masses were an easy public to satisfy. They were intensely patriotic, far more Imperialist than their rulers, full of an optimistic confidence that British supremacy was part of the order of things. The Golden and Diamond Jubilees of 1887 and 1897 marked the height of this exuberance, before the Boer war introduced a note of doubt. The rousing words of 'The Soldiers of the Queen' were the theme of the last decade of Victorian England, and for the moment the plea for humility that runs through Kipling's 'Recessional' went unheeded.

The soldiers of the Queen! What must the little old lady have thought that summer of 1897, as she rode in her gilded carriage to St. Paul's Cathedral through the cheering crowds, escorted by troops from every corner of the Empire? Did her mind run back to the night when a girl of eighteen had been awoken to be told that she was Queen of England, the England of Chartism, the England of Wellington, Melbourne, and Peel, a time when men of middle age could well remember the Napoleonic war? There had been bad periods in the Queen's relations with her people. They had never accepted her beloved Albert. They had resented the seclusion into which she had retired after his death. But now, as with another great Queen who had ruled three centuries earlier, her years conquered everything. She had become the symbol of an age, and it was not inappropriate that her death should coincide with the war that first shook the confidence of her people. She lived on just long enough to see the turn of the tide in South Africa, but her health began to fail in the summer of 1900 and she died on 22 January, 1901. That date does not mark any stage in the development of the new social and political scene that had been emerging since the 1880s, yet for the bulk of the population, who could not remember any other sovereign, that day must have seemed like the closing of an era.

V

PRELUDE TO THE TWENTIETH CENTURY
1902–14

20

THE CONSERVATIVE DECLINE, 1902–5

1. Balfour's home administration

H. G. WELLS once observed that the death of Queen Victoria was like the lifting of a paper-weight in a draughty room. Certainly the new notions of the aesthetes, feminists, Fabians, and scientists had sent a chilly current of air through the staid calm of Victorian drawing-rooms, and there were many who believed that the accession of Edward VII would turn the draughts into a whirlwind. In fact, Edward's wild oats belonged to an earlier epoch. He was approaching sixty years of age and it was a mellow monarch who now ascended the throne. But Edward had certainly not lost the art of enjoyment and during his reign he delighted in the passing show of the *beau monde* at Ascot, Henley, and Cowes. The wealthiest society in the world had at last ceased to be ashamed to display its opulence, and aristocracy and new rich created a scene of extraordinary brilliance, presided over by a King whose name now stands for the whole of that glittering decade. To those who looked back to it with nostalgia after the holocaust of the first World War, Edwardian England seemed like some splendid sunset, a time of limitless security, peace, and pleasure.

Security, however, lay only on the surface. The ultimate crash of this world in 1914 was not a sudden catastrophe, consequent on the assassination of an Austrian archduke at Sarajevo. New social forces and growing discord had already begun to undermine it long before that date, and the effect of the first World War was simply to accelerate the changes with dramatic suddenness. It did not entirely create them.

In July 1902 Lord Salisbury, who was by now well over seventy, resigned from office and was succeeded by his nephew, Arthur

Balfour. Hicks Beach, a politician of considerable Parliamentary experience, had no wish to become Prime Minister; Joseph Chamberlain had recently been injured in a cab accident; and the Duke of Devonshire was a Liberal Unionist. Urbane, detached, seeming in his personality to sum up all the charm and sense of security of Edwardian England, Balfour took over at a time when the future of the Conservatives hung in the balance. After Lord Salisbury's long reign certain questions could no longer be postponed. Two issues arose almost at once—a new Education Act and the possibility of a return to a policy of Protection—and although other questions were to play a part in the Conservative defeat at the general election of 1906, it was these two that caused them the greatest harm in enabling the Liberals to close their ranks.

The real author of the Education Act of 1902 was Robert Morant, at the Board of Education. He was a strong supporter of secondary education, but he had no love for the local Boards through which many institutions of higher education had recently developed.[1] In 1899, during a dispute between a school Board and the L.C.C., Morant was instrumental in bringing about a test case in which the judges ruled that school Boards had no right to maintain these new day and evening schools for further training. Once this had been established, the way seemed clear for new legislation and the Education Bill, introduced first in 1901, and then modified in 1902, embodied Morant's plan whereby all state schools might be incorporated within the new pattern of local government. The school Boards were to be abolished. All secondary and technical education was to be under the county and county borough councils. A similar arrangement in general was made for the elementary schools, except that certain of the larger non-county boroughs and urban districts were to retain control through their own councils. The crux of the question was, as usual, the position of the Church schools. The new scheme meant that these were now to be maintained out of the rates, although they would still enjoy a certain degree of independence, since the local authority was to select only one-third of the school managers, who would retain the right to appoint the teachers.

[1] See p. 331.

In rationalizing a chaotic situation, one of Morant's aims had been to get education out of the hands of the squabbling school Boards, but in the debates in the Commons the religious issue was inescapable. Anglicans and Roman Catholics supported the Bill, since it saved them from the acute financial embarrassment which had threatened their schools. The Nonconformists objected to it for precisely the same reason. They had looked forward keenly to the impending bankruptcy of the Church schools, and now they saw them about to be saved by support from local taxation. In Wales, where the only Anglicans in a district were very often the parson and the schoolmaster, there was a furious outcry. Lloyd George, who had already made himself violently unpopular over his attitude towards the Boer war, led the attack on the Bill in the Commons, and as he flayed the government proposals with Celtic fervour, stood out clearly as a future leader of the Liberals. The Bill became an Act by the end of 1902, but the struggle did not end there. Lloyd George advised the Welsh County Councils to do all that they could to find ways of legally circumventing the Act, and Carmarthen actually refused to administer the Act at all. The government retaliated with the Defaulting Authorities Act of 1904—known locally as the Welsh Coercion Act—whereby deficiencies in payment to the voluntary schools were to be made up out of the financial grant to the local authority. English Free Churches joined with Welsh County Councils in defiance of this last Act, and the revolt was still at its height when the Conservative government fell.

The anger of the Nonconformists was the first stage in the restoration of Liberal unity. During the same period, however, an even greater issue had arisen which challenged the very basis of Liberal thought. The Colonial Secretary, Joseph Chamberlain, decided that the moment had come to renounce Free Trade. The idea had already occurred to him in the 1890s, but it was during the Colonial Conference of 1902 that he realized that he could evade the question no longer. The Budget of 1902 had imposed a shilling duty on corn—simply as one means of covering the cost of the war—and when the colonial premiers maintained that Free Trade within the Empire was not practicable, but expressed the .

hope that the mother country might favour some system of Imperial Preference, Chamberlain at once began to consider the possibility of remitting the shilling duty on corn from the Empire. Such a remission would have been purely symbolic. The whole duty did not bring in more than £2 million, but to remit the duty within the Empire, while retaining it on foreign-grown corn, would imply the regulation of trade through tariffs. This would be to fly in the face of the last fifty years of the nineteenth century, and the Cabinet, not unnaturally, became divided; there, for the moment, the question rested.

Chamberlain now made a trip to South Africa, during which the idea matured in his mind. On his return he was back in his old role of *enfant terrible*. On 1 May, 1903 he addressed a meeting at Birmingham, proclaiming that duties on imported foodstuffs would have to be restored, alongside a system of Imperial Preference, for the sake of consolidating the Empire. On the very same day, in London, Balfour announced his intention of repealing the shilling duty on corn. It was clear that all unity within the government had been lost, and it says much for Balfour's skill that he managed to ward off the immediate disintegration of his Cabinet. He worked furiously to puzzle out some sort of compromise measure—turning 'his fence into a pedestal', but in September he could temporize no longer within the Cabinet. Chamberlain offered to resign; Ritchie, Chancellor of the Exchequer, and Lord Balfour of Burleigh were virtually dismissed; Lord George Hamilton and the Duke of Devonshire resigned on the following day, whereupon Balfour accepted Chamberlain's resignation. The Duke was persuaded to stay for a while, but resigned a second time three weeks later.

Balfour was clearly moving in the direction of some moderate form of Protection, and his handling of the problem of a fundamental change of policy showed that he had learnt much from the Liberal split over Home Rule in 1886. A Prime Minister may change his mind; he may rearrange his Cabinet. But the main difficulty lies in convincing his party of the need for the change. Both Peel in 1846 and Gladstone in 1886 had failed to do this, and the result had been political disaster. Balfour's tactics were summed up by the Liberal Campbell-Bannerman, when it was learnt that Chamberlain's son Austen had replaced Ritchie as Chancellor of the Exchequer: 'This plan of Joe outside and Arthur inside working in cooperation with "our Mr. Austen" in charge of the counting-house is too bare-faced for anything.' At least it was a brave attempt—Joseph Chamberlain, free from governmental responsibility, to convert the electorate, Balfour to play for time in the Commons and perhaps to win round the waverers.

Chamberlain certainly went ahead with his contribution. A Tariff Reform League was organized and the new apostle of Protection stumped the country with a series of speeches in which the original plan of Protection for the sake of the Empire was soon lost in the demand for Protection for its own sake. 'Agriculture, the greatest of all trades and industries, has been practically destroyed. . . . Sugar has gone, silk has gone, iron is threatened, wool is threatened, the turn of cotton will come. At the present moment these industries and the working men who depend on them are like sheep in a field.' A 10% duty on foreign manufactured goods was the remedy that he proposed. But the great blow that he struck for the new Conservative policy had the very reverse effect to what he had hoped. On the anvil of Chamberlain's oratory the Liberals were hammered into a unity that they had lacked for nearly twenty years. Gladstone, as leader of the Liberals, had broken his party over Home Rule; it was the Conservatives whose own change of front now brought the Liberals together again. And in each crisis it was the voice of Joseph Chamberlain that was decisive.

Thus education and Protection wrought the destruction of Conservative power. The issues could perhaps have been avoided, yet it is certain from the standpoint of today that both were highly relevant and it is to the government's credit that they did not take refuge in the greater safety of inaction. Another matter, less significant politically, but of tremendous importance for the future, marks a more positive achievement of the Balfour administration. In 1903 an Irish Land Purchase Act was passed. This was the work of George Wyndham, the Irish Secretary, and by its provisions Ireland was to be rapidly transformed from a land of tenants to one of peasant proprietors. Landlords and tenants were to agree upon a price of sale; the landlord was to be paid in stock floated on government credit, and the tenant purchasing his holding would pay an extremely low rate of interest, the total debt to be cleared in sixty-eight and a half years. From the passing of this Bill the social problem that had bedevilled relations with Ireland was solved. But the political question remained and was yet to play an unhappy part in the history of the next few years.

The Balfour administration was also responsible for reforms carried out in the Army and Navy. The Boer war had revealed a good many deficiencies in organization and led to the abolition of the post of Commander-in-chief, whose place was taken by an Army Council, although nothing was done yet about forming a general staff. Far more striking changes took place in the Navy. This was due to the growing awareness of German naval rivalry, and was mainly the work of two important personalities, Sir John Fisher, First Sea Lord, and the Earl of Cawdor, First Lord of the Admiralty. Two major features of their work were directed to meet the German challenge. First, the fleet was to be redistributed. In the past the far-distant sea routes to India and the East had been mainly endangered by France, and the policy of giving them strong naval protection had now been rendered obsolete by the new *entente*.[1] The major forces were now to be drawn closer to Europe, organized in three fleets based at Malta, Gibraltar, and the home ports. Second, plans were made for building a new all-big-gun battleship—the *Dreadnought*—together with the *Invincible* class of battle-cruiser. The main reason for this decision was that the range of torpedoes had by now greatly increased, and if a battleship was to remain out of their reach, the only guns that it could use effectively would have to be big ones. It was hoped that this new fleet would give Great Britain such an enormous lead that Germany would give up the competition, but only two months after the launching of the first Dreadnought the German government authorized the widening of the Kiel Canal, without which German ships of a similar size could not pass through to

[1] See p. 408.

command the Baltic as well as the north-west coast of Germany. Far from ceasing, the race had become more stern.

Ireland and service reform had had no repercussions at a party level. Public-houses, however, were quite another matter, and here the government could not hope to be so fortunate. The Licensing Act of 1904 attempted to settle a dispute which had arisen over the withdrawal of licences from brewers and publicans. Ever since Gladstone's government had incurred considerable disfavour through requiring the licensing of public houses, a struggle had developed over whether the licensing bench had the right to refuse the renewal of a licence at the end of a year, if there was no evidence of misconduct. Some authorities had refused renewal simply because they wished to reduce the number of public-houses in the district, and in the eyes of the publicans and the brewery shareholders it was time for their alliance with the Conservatives to play a part in the dispute. The Act of 1904 outlined a scheme of compensation in the case of licences surrendered simply on grounds of policy, this compensation being drawn from a fund raised by the liquor trade itself. It was in many ways a fair and sensible compromise, but gave little satisfaction to the Liberal Nonconformists, who regarded any public-house as a place of sin.

Drink, Church schools, Protection—each was an affront that was to pull the Liberals back into fighting shape, and before the 1906 election two additional questions were to contribute to the Conservative defeat. The first lent itself perfectly to all the confused thought that attends a general election. In South Africa the mine-owners on the Rand, running short of Kaffir labour, had persuaded the British government to consent to the employment of Chinese coolies. The living conditions in the great compounds in which they were kept were utterly primitive and before long represented the lower level to which humanity can sink. This policy aroused a general animosity. Australia, New Zealand, and Canada objected to the precedent of importing Asiatic labour. The working classes in Great Britain referred to it as 'Chinese slavery', resenting the implied degradation of labour. The Liberals seized their chance and during the election set up great pictures of Chinamen. This, according to one observer, had the curious effect of stimulating a general hatred of the Chinese, which by an interesting psychological process was then transferred to Mr. Balfour.[1]

The second factor was the position of the Unions at this time. After a strike of the railwaymen of the Taff Vale Railway Company in South Wales in 1900, the Company had proceeded to sue the Amalgamated Society of Railway Servants for the actual financial loss that it suffered as a result of the strike. Mr. Justice Farwell had decided in favour of the Company and the A.S.R.S. was faced with a bill of £32,000 for damages and costs—a decision that was upheld by the House of Lords. Until the Taff Vale case Union leaders had believed that the legislation of 1871 and 1875 had left them free of such a liability, and since this interpretation by the judge would mean eventual ruin for any Union that called a strike, the Unions naturally pressed for new legislation. The Balfour government did not seem keen to act, but at last set up a Royal Commission. However, since no Trade Unionist was allowed to sit on this, the Unions refused to give evidence before it and, in fact, the Commission's report did not appear until after the defeat of the Conservatives at the polls. Meanwhile, the threat presented by the Taff Vale decision had caused a tremendous leap in the number of supporters of the Labour Representation Committee—from 356,000 to 861,000 in a single year—and in 1902 and 1903 three Labour candidates, including Arthur Henderson, won seats at by-elections. Labour representation in the Commons, however, remained very small, and working-class opinion was moving fast towards a temporary alliance with the Liberals, who might give them the legislation that they desired.

By the autumn of 1905 Balfour had been left in no doubt by both the extreme Protectionists of his own party and the opposition that there was considerable dissatisfaction with his government. At first he ignored all protests and then during the Christmas recess decided to play his last card. He tendered his resignation to the King. It was the same stratagem as Gladstone had used against Disraeli in 1873, and there were Liberals who

[1] Graham Wallas: *Human Nature in Politics.*

advised Campbell-Bannerman to refuse office, as Disraeli had done. But Campbell-Bannerman judged rightly that the chance was not to be lost, agreed to a government and staked his chances on an immediate election in January 1906.

2. The end of isolation

In the meanwhile, a revolution had taken place in British foreign policy. Great Britain, having for so long held aloof from general schemes of European alliance, now allowed herself to be drawn into one of the two systems that dominated the diplomatic scene. Despite the German Emperor's determination to build a navy, it was not immediate fear of German rivalry that motivated this fundamental change. The country with whom war had always seemed most likely was Russia, and at the turn of the century the Far East, rather than the Balkans, had become the centre of international tension. Russian expansion in this area,[1] with her lease of the open-water harbour of Port Arthur and her ambitious railway schemes, had been watched with growing concern, and although the Boxer rising of the Chinese against Western intrusion had been put down by an international force,[2] it had not escaped notice that Russia had made the most capital out of the situation by consolidating her influence in Chinese Manchuria.

Thus at the beginning of the twentieth century Great Britain, concerned for her commercial interests in Chinese waters, still hoped to find an ally with whom she might make a limited agreement, whereby Russian expansion might be checked in the Far East. France at this time was still sulking after Fashoda; Germany seemed the other possibility. This, as it turned out afterwards, was one of the most significant moments in world history, and it was considered, after the first World War, by both German and British historians that this second failure to establish an Anglo-German alliance had a profound effect upon the course of later events. Great Britain and Germany had recently collaborated over action taken against Venezuela for the collection of debts,

[1] See map, p. 409.   [2] See p. 388.

and during 1901 both Lord Lansdowne, Salisbury's successor at the Foreign Office,[1] and Joseph Chamberlain approached Germany in the hope of a definite alliance. There had been indignation in England at the time of William II's telegram to Kruger, but Germany had left the Boers alone during the war, and British public opinion would not have reacted against an Anglo-German alliance against Russia.

All proposals, however, came to nothing. The German government fully anticipated war between Russia and Great Britain and shaped its policy accordingly. 'It is in our interest to keep our hands free,' wrote Holstein, the head of the political department of the German Foreign Office, 'so that His Majesty will be able to claim appropriate compensation not only for eventual support, but even for remaining neutral.' Germany would make a treaty only if Great Britain would join the Triple Alliance of Germany, Austria, and Italy, and the British government sheered away rapidly from committing itself to one of the two sides on the Continent.

A direct negotiation with Russia failed, and at length the British turned to the only Power who had a real and immediate interest in checking Russia in the Far East. The treaty with Japan, which was published at once, was signed in January 1902. In return for the guarantee of her interests in China and the Pacific, Great Britain recognized the Japanese right to Korea and promised that, in the event of another Power joining Russia in any Russo-Japanese war, she would come to the assistance of Japan.

It seemed at first that this arrangement had answered Great Britain's needs without actually dragging her into the Continental network. The Anglo-Japanese treaty, however, was to have many important repercussions. The German reaction to it was an increased confidence in the belief that Great Britain was soon bound to be involved in war with Russia, and the French, who drew precisely the same conclusion, became seriously alarmed, since the Franco-Russian treaty of 1894 might very well bring them into war on Russia's side against Great Britain. Despite the intermittent animosity between the two countries, war with the British

[1] Lord Salisbury gave up the post of Foreign Secretary in December 1900.

was the last thing that the French wanted, and it was out of the desire to avert this danger that French politicians now turned to consider the possibilities of an Anglo-French *entente*.

The *entente*, which was finally achieved in 1904, was something more than a series of political agreements; it was a sentimental reconciliation between the two countries, considerably assisted by Edward VII's famous official visit to Paris in May 1903, and all the more remarkable since the French Press had been particularly anti-British during the Boer war. Such a friendship was not inconsistent with the Anglo-Japanese treaty, since it made French participation in any Russo-Japanese war much less likely. The major difficulty had lain in reaching agreement over North Africa, and the final outcome was a mutual understanding that Egypt and the Sudan should remain a British sphere of influence, while Morocco, in which there were already certain British interests, should come purely within the French sphere.

All these agreements, however, were still far from amounting to a positive alliance. It was a series of events following the *entente* that really cemented Anglo-French friendship and finally brought Great Britain out of her isolation. In February 1904 the long-anticipated war between Russia and Japan broke out, when Japan suddenly attacked Port Arthur. Germany at once imagined that this would lead to an Anglo-Russian war, and the German government opened negotiations for an alliance with Russia. The situation became particularly tense in October, when the Russian Baltic fleet, on its way to Japan, opened fire on British fishing-vessels off the Dogger Bank in the North Sea. France, however, desperately anxious to avoid the spreading of a war in which she would have to choose between her Russian alliance and her friendship with Great Britain, hastened to mediate, and the Russian government, not wishing to add to its enemies, apologized and agreed to submit the matter to international arbitration.

The war in the Far East proved to be disastrous for Russia. In March 1905 Mukden was lost to the Japanese army advancing from Port Arthur, and in May the Russian fleet, which had sailed half-way round the world in order to come to grips with the enemy, was utterly destroyed by the Japanese in the Straits of

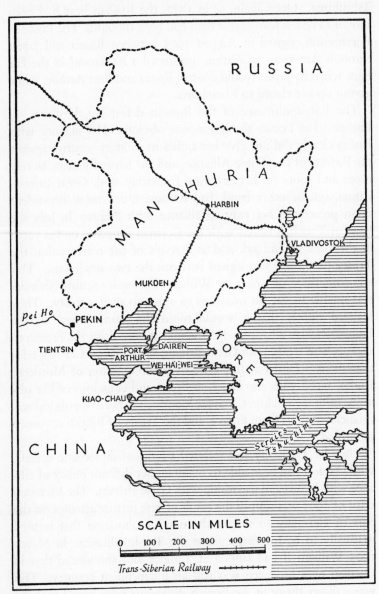

SCALE IN MILES

0   100   200   300   400   500

Trans-Siberian Railway ┼┼┼┼┼┼┼

8. THE FAR EAST

Tshushima. Once again, as in 1877, the Russian bear had been shown to be less formidable than had been thought. The Peace of Portsmouth, signed in August 1905 between Russia and Japan through American mediation, produced a settlement in the Far East, whereby Japan would control Korea and Port Arthur, while giving up her claims to Manchuria.

The full significance of the Russian defeat lay, however, in Europe. For France the lesson was obvious. Her alliance with Russia clearly did not give her sufficient military security against the Powers of the Triple Alliance, and she naturally came to rely more and more on her growing friendship with Great Britain. Russia, on the other hand, had become much more dependent upon preserving her existing alliance with France. In July the Russian Tsar had talked with the German Emperor on his yacht in the Gulf of Finland, and as a result of the conversation the Treaty of Björkö was signed between the two sovereigns. This was something of a *coup* for William, but on his return Nicholas was unable to get his ministers to agree to such a treaty. They realized rightly that it would mean the abandonment of the Franco-Russian alliance, which would at once drive the French to make a firm treaty with Great Britain, since Franco-German relations were strained at this time over the question of Morocco. Russia, faced with revolution at home and conscious of her obvious military weakness, was far too much in need of political and financial support from France, and the Treaty of Björkö remained unratified.

Thus far, Germany had suffered a series of diplomatic defeats, while France had been able to maintain her difficult policy of alliance with Russia and friendship with Great Britain. The Morocco crisis of 1905 was simply the result of one further attempt on the part of Germany to shatter the new combination that seemed gradually to be forming against the Triple Alliance. In March 1905 William II had landed at Tangier and announced that in German eyes Morocco was still an independent country. This was a direct thrust at the French diplomats who hoped that the Anglo-French *entente* had solved the main part of the problem of establishing French influence there. The German aim was an international conference at which they hoped to demonstrate the general unreliability of France's allies, and in June 1905 the French government agreed to confer, whereupon Delcassé, the Foreign Minister, resigned. In January 1906 all the Powers, including the smaller ones'who had an interest in Moroccan trade, met together at Algeçiras. The French demanded control of the Moroccan bank and police; the Germans demanded Moroccan independence. After six weeks of argument a general vote showed that Germany was supported only by Austria and Morocco. Russia clung to France, and the British feared that if the French came to terms with the Germans it might mean the concession of Agadir as an Atlantic port for Germany. Germany's gamble had failed, and Italy's defection from the side of Germany had even revealed a chink in the armour of the Triple Alliance.

Algeçiras forms a landmark in the diplomatic history of Europe at this time. Even by 1906 Great Britain's serious commitments consisted only of her Japanese treaty and her limited agreements with France. Yet common political needs are the operative factor in European alignments; formal alliances simply follow as a consequence and seldom last longer than the needs that prompted them. The new needs that had become apparent during the period of the Russo-Japanese war and Algeçiras established the fact that British isolation was by now almost a dead letter. No alliance yet bound Great Britain to the Continental system, but she was already inextricably involved in the diplomatic tangle that was eventually to culminate in the first World War.

21

THE TRIUMPH AND TRAGEDY OF
LIBERALISM, 1906–14

1. The struggle with the House of Lords

FEW Cabinets have been so outstanding as the one that Sir
Henry Campbell-Bannerman was able to form on Balfour's
resignation. Herbert Asquith as Chancellor of the Exchequer, Sir Edward Grey at the Foreign Office, John Morley as
Secretary for India, David Lloyd George as President of the Board
of Trade, Winston Churchill[1] as Under-Secretary for the Colonies
—the names run on like a peal of triumph for resurgent Liberalism. The Prime Minister is today perhaps the least remembered of
the whole group. He was not a great speaker and had not shone
in opposition, but his powers of patience and endurance and his
kindly wisdom had brought his party to accept him since the
day when he had become their leader in succession to Lord Rosebery at the end of 1898. In 1906 he had only just over two years
to live, but in that time as Prime Minister he transformed a
Cabinet of brilliant individuals into an efficient working team.

The quality of the Liberal Cabinet was matched by the victory
that their party won in the general election of January 1906.
Chinese labour and the alarm created by much of Balfour's legislation played havoc with Conservative chances, and when the
House of Commons reassembled the Liberals occupied 377 seats—
a figure which gave them a strong majority over any combination
of groups in opposition. The Conservatives had dropped to 157,
of whom 109 were supporters of Joseph Chamberlain. The Irish
nationalists under John Redmond held 83. More noticeable than
any of these was the startling increase in Labour seats. Until now
working class hopes had been limited to establishing one or two
spokesmen in the House of Commons, but the 1906 election

---

[1] He entered the Cabinet in 1908 as President of the Board of Trade.

brought them 53 seats and with that they had become a Parliamentary party.

At this moment of triumph for the Liberal party chance removed the one man who might have seriously embarrassed them in the Commons. Joseph Chamberlain was still at the height of his powers and was clearly ready to fight a great duel with the government. Then suddenly, on 11 July, when Birmingham was still celebrating the seventieth birthday of its hero, paralysis struck him down and left him a helpless invalid. His end was typical of his career. Of all politicians in the last decades of the nineteenth century he had been the closest in touch with the new spirit of the age, yet, apart from his work as Mayor of Birmingham and his reshaping of the Colonial Service, his positive achievement had been remarkably small for a man of such possibilities. It was the Home Rule question that wrecked his career; but for that he would almost certainly have succeeded Gladstone as leader of the Liberals, and with Radical Joe as Prime Minister, the whole story of English politics before the first World War might have been very different.

In the Commons of 1906 the Conservatives had no hope of resisting any government legislation, and Lord Lansdowne and Balfour, the leaders in the two Houses, now decided to use the absolute veto of the House of Lords to block Liberal legislation. It was not a new scheme, for the shaky Liberal government of 1892–5 had been undermined by similar tactics. In 1906, however, it was a dangerous and scarcely justifiable policy. The Lords had always been a very right wing body in political outlook, but Lord Salisbury, during the first Gladstone administration, had made it clear that as a revising Chamber—'a bulwark against revolution', as Bagehot called them—they still could not ignore the wishes of the electorate when those wishes had been clearly expressed. Balfour's plan was nothing more than to harness the Lords to the Conservative party and to confront the Liberal government with a permanent Conservative majority in the Upper House, at a time when the Liberals had just received an undeniable mandate from the electorate, a policy that was to culminate in a constitutional crisis as momentous as the great struggle over the Reform Act of 1832.

At first, however, the Liberals were able to carry through a good deal of legislation—some of a non-party nature, and some mainly benefiting the working classes, whom the Conservatives were anxious not to offend. The question of Chinese labour was dealt with at once. No more coolies were to be brought into the Rand and as existing contracts expired, those already there were returned to their own country. Over the question of the Boers Campbell-Bannerman was personally responsible for an extremely far-sighted and typically Liberal settlement—the granting of complete self-government to the Transvaal and, a little later, to the Orange Free State. In the Transvaal a general election gave the premiership to Botha who, together with his colleague Smuts, responded generously to this spirit of reconciliation, and within a few years the work of a handful of enlightened men had produced the Dominion of South Africa. It is a striking fact not merely that South Africa voluntarily sprang to the assistance of the mother country in two world wars, but that the Prime Ministers of the Union during each of these wars, Botha and Smuts, were Boers themselves.

These early years of the Liberal administration saw also the passing of a mass of social legislation. A fairly moderate Bill was put forward to relieve the Unions of the danger in which the Taff Vale decision had placed them. The Labour section of the House, however, were dissatisfied with this, and introduced a private member's Bill which was eventually adopted by the government. The Trades Disputes Bill of 1906 relieved the Unions of all actions for tort and was passed by both Houses without great difficulty. During the same period Lloyd George at the Board of Trade launched a series of Acts that established him as one of the most Radical members of the government. He was responsible for the Merchant Shipping Act which improved conditions for sailors, the Patents Act of 1907 which gave greater protection to British inventors, and the first Census of Production taken in Great Britain. In 1908 he set up the Port of London Authority, to restore order out of the chaos of innumerable dock companies. At the same time free meals and medical service were established in the schools and a Trade Boards Act was passed for the purpose of suppressing 'sweated' labour. In 1908 a non-contributory scheme of old age pensions was drawn up granting a pension of five shillings a week for all who had reached the age of seventy, not a handsome sum, but five Edwardian shillings would at least ensure that old people might live with their families without loss of self-respect.

All this was consistent with the policy of the Liberals. The expansion of the armed forces was less palatable, but the international scene seemed to leave them little option. Bismarck was supposed to have said on one occasion that if a British army ever made a landing on the Continent, he would have it arrested by the police, but the end of isolation made it necessary to see that the police would at least have some difficulty in doing this. A certain number of reforms in the Army had already been undertaken during the Conservative administration, and now, under R. B. Haldane at the War Office, the whole aspect of the British Army underwent a profound transformation. A general staff of seventy-two officers was created in September 1906. An Expeditionary Force of six infantry divisions and one cavalry division was organized, and since the whole of this force was liable to be dispatched overseas in time of war, the military defence of the United Kingdom was to be entrusted to a Territorial Army of part-time volunteers, consisting of 14 divisions and 14 mounted brigades. In 1909 the Officers' Training Corps was moulded out of the various military training wings at the public schools.

These military changes were largely a matter of organization and cost little. A strengthening of the Navy, however, could only mean the building of more ships, and here the Liberals dug their toes in. The Cawdor–Fisher plan was dropped. In 1906 the building programme fell from four ships to three, and in 1907 from three to two. At once von Tirpitz saw his chance to catch up, and in 1906 the German programme rose to three ships and between 1907 and 1909 four more were laid down for each year. This was too much even for the Liberals, and in 1909 R. McKenna, First Lord of the Admiralty, asked for permission to lay down six with the intention of a further six in each of the two succeeding years. This demand led to fierce debates in the Cabinet and the Commons, but in the words of Sir Winston Churchill, who at the time believed that four would be sufficient, 'the Admiralty had demanded six ships; the economists offered four; and we finally compromised on eight'. The ultimate total of eighteen new Dreadnoughts remained unchanged.

How was this new expense to be met? Until now the social legislation that the Liberals had passed had not presented them with any major financial problems. Consistent with the principle of Free Trade, Asquith's Budgets had slightly reduced some of the remaining duties; there had been one or two adjustments in income tax, and death duties had been increased. The bulk of the cost of the social reforms had been borne by a substantial reduction in the Army and Navy estimates, but now the new naval policy meant either heavier taxation or a halt in social legislation. This was the problem that faced Lloyd George, who had become Chancellor after Asquith had taken over as Prime Minister on Campbell-Bannerman's death in 1908.

In fact, Lloyd George set about his 1909 Budget with relish. Dreadnoughts there might have to be, but they were not to stand in the way of the main stream of Liberal policy. Labour Exchanges were to be opened; a board was to be set up for the improvement of roads, necessitated by the increase in automobile traffic, in addition to a Development Commission whose aim would be to develop country life and natural resources. Child allowances in the assessment of income tax were to be introduced. To pay for all this, there could be no escape from further taxation. Death duties, as well as duties on tobacco and spirits, were raised. Income tax was put up from one shilling to one shilling and twopence, and supertax was imposed for the first time. But the most startling innovation was the Land Values duties—a tax of 20% on the unearned increment of land value, whenever an estate changed hands. This last was a direct blow at the landed classes, all the more obnoxious since it involved an immediate survey of all land. It was a People's Budget with a vengeance.

Although the implications of the Budget as a weapon in the

class war might be alarming, its demands could hardly be called crippling. Yet the Conservatives decided to leap to the attack, fully supported by all the fulminations of the Harmsworth press. Nothing could have pleased Lloyd George more. He counter-attacked in a series of speeches throughout the country that recalled the violence of the 1880s, when Joseph Chamberlain had been in the heyday of his Radicalism. The difference was that Lloyd George was not fighting his battle as a free lance; some of his colleagues were admittedly a little worried, but he knew that he had Asquith's support, and on 4 November, 1909 the Budget passed the Commons by 379 votes to 149. It was then that the Lords took the final step in their fatal policy of alliance with Balfour's Conservatives. The Budget came before them as a matter of course and on its second reading they rejected it outright.

This rejection came as the culmination of the policy of obstruction which they had pursued since the beginning of the Liberal administration. In 1906 they had thrown out an Education Bill and a Plural Voting Bill. In 1907 two Lands Bills for Scotland had suffered a similar fate. In reply to this Campbell-Bannerman had carried a resolution in the Commons, stating that 'in order to give effect to the will of the people as expressed by their elected representatives, the power of the other House to alter or reject Bills passed by this House must be so restricted by law as to secure that within the limits of a single Parliament the final decision of the Commons should prevail'. But the Lords had paid no heed to the warning and in 1908 a Licensing Bill, passed in the Commons, had been rejected. Asquith had made it plain in a speech at the National Liberal Club at the end of 1908 that the veto of the House of Lords was 'the dominating issue, because in the long run it overshadows and absorbs every other'. And now the Lords had taken the ultimate step. Financial legislation had been the preserve of the Commons for over two hundred and fifty years and the rejection of their Budget meant that there could be no further postponement of a major constitutional crisis.

Asquith at once took up the challenge, passed a resolution in the Commons to the effect that the Lords' action was unconstitutional,

P

dissolved the House, and, in January 1910 fought a general election. The issues were the Budget, the principle of Free Trade, and the future of the House of Lords; the result was a Liberal victory, but only by a narrow margin. 40 Labour M.P.s and 82 Irish nationalists held the balance, and Asquith was now faced with the magnitude of the task that he had set himself. The Irish under Redmond at once seized the opportunity to extract a promise of Home Rule in return for their support. There was, too, uncertainty over the precise nature of the reform to be imposed on the House of Lords. Conservatives and a number of the Lords were prepared to consider reforms based on a more democratic composition of the House. This was a shrewd plan, since it would have been much harder, at a later date, to justify any curtailing of the Upper House's right of veto, if its composition were based on merit rather than birth. Most of the Liberals, smarting from the experience of the last four years, simply wished to end the power of absolute veto that the Lords enjoyed, but the Cabinet was not entirely united over this. A further question was the attitude of the King. Only a large creation of peers, in the last resort, could get such a measure through the Lords, and Edward VII had told Asquith privately that he would consent to a creation only after a *second* general election had been held.

Over the actual terms of the new legislation Asquith felt his way carefully in the Commons with a series of resolutions which were then drawn up in the form of a Bill, ending the power of absolute veto by the Lords. This passed the Commons in April 1910 and was sent up to the Lords. At the same time the Budget was passed and was accepted by the Lords without comment. The greater issue was now the Parliament Bill. What would the Lords do about it? As the nation waited, the whole struggle was brought to an unexpected halt, when, on 6 May, Edward VII was suddenly struck down by an attack of heart asthma and died within a few hours.

His son, who ascended the throne as King George V, now had to begin his reign when a constitutional controversy was at its height, one in which he would soon be called upon to play a decisive part. During the period of mourning there was a lull, but after the funeral King George, hoping for an amicable settlement, called a conference of the leading politicians of both parties. The Constitutional Conference lasted for five months and eventually broke down. The Conservatives looked for a loop-hole in classifying future Bills so that those which were considered to be 'constitutional' should be subject to a national referendum, but the Liberals, knowing that Home Rule would come within this category and realizing their dependence on the Irish vote in the Commons, would have none of it.

The question now was whether King George would consider himself bound by his father's promise. The new King gave his consent, but stipulated that, in addition to a second election, the Lords must be given a chance to express their views on the Parliament Bill. The Lords, however, took refuge in Lord Rosebery's scheme for a change in their composition, and in November Asquith decided on a second election.

The result of the election of December 1910 was almost exactly the same as in the previous January. The excitement in the country was intense, for it was clear that general opinion on the issue was constant and King George was convinced that he was right to hold back no longer. In February 1911 the Parliament Bill was introduced once again in the Commons. On 15 May it passed its third reading and was sent up to the Lords. There was a short pause during the Coronation in June, but on 6 July the Lords returned it to the Commons with a mass of amendments which, amongst other things, would still have made Irish Home Rule dependent upon a referendum.

The struggle had reached its last stage. It remained to be seen whether the Lords would actually force the King to create peers, or whether the threat alone would be enough. Peers who had never attended a debate before in their lives, the 'backwoodsmen', were rounded up and throughout the long hot days of a blazing July the fury of the battle reached fever pitch in both Houses. In the Commons Asquith was howled down by an opposition livid with rage, but on 8 August the Lords' amendments were rejected outright and the decision could be postponed no longer. In the Lords, Lord Selborne put the case for the Die Hards, 'the

Ditchers', who were prepared to face a mammoth creation of peers rather than consent to the Bill. 'The question is, shall we perish in the dark, slain by our own hand, or in the light, killed by our enemies?' At Buckingham Palace King George awaited the answer. At last the peers voted; Contents 131; Non-contents 114. The Ditchers had lost, the Parliament Bill was through and King George was spared from having to create two hundred and fifty peers of the realm.

The terms of the Act can be summarized very simply. Any money Bill, defined as such by the Speaker of the House of Commons, should become law one month after it had been sent to the Lords. Any other Bill—except one extending the maximum duration of a Parliament—should become law despite rejection by the Lords, provided that it had passed the Commons in three successive sessions and that two years had elapsed between the date of the second reading of its first passing and the date of its passing in the third session. Finally, the duration of Parliament was to be reduced from seven to five years.

Thus, although the Lords retained the power to delay a Bill—and, indeed, to nullify it during the last two years of the life of a Parliament—the ascendancy of the House of Commons had been finally stated in black and white. At any time after this, if the Commons so decreed, the Lords would not even be able to resist their own extinction. Yet although this was the work of a Liberal administration, it was to play a considerable part in the later eclipse of the Liberals. The House of Lords outlived the party that had undermined it. For the Irish the Parliament Act meant Home Rule; for Labour it meant that, in future, victory in the House of Commons was all that they would need. The expedient of alliance with one of the two major parties now seemed less attractive; a greater goal lay in sight and the furore of strikes and class war that burst upon the government in the last years before the war was ample evidence of a new social and political force that sooner or later meant to pass its own legislation. Before this glimpse of the Leviathan of organized labour, determined on a policy of Socialism, moderate elements drew back; to them the Conservative party seemed a greater bulwark of defence than the Liberals.

The whole of the English politics was about to undergo a tremendous simplification. In a society utterly transformed by the stress of world war a great gulf was to divide Socialist from non-Socialist and in that simple division of views the Liberal party was to have no place.

2. The rising storm: industrial unrest, Suffragettes and Ulster

1911 should have been a great year of triumph for the Liberals. The barriers were down. Provided that they could keep the Irish with them, they were secure in the House of Commons until 1915 and any Bill that Asquith's government chose to put forward during the next eighteen months was bound to reach the Statute book, even if the Lords imposed a delay of two years. In fact, the Liberals were not slow to take their opportunity. A Shops' Act introduced a weekly half-holiday. A Scottish Small Landholders Act, a Coal Mines Act, and the National Insurance Act were all passed, together with a resolution for the payment of members of the House of Commons.

Payment of members had had some sort of place in the Liberal programme during the previous twenty years, but the question had been brought to a head by the recent Osborne judgement [1] that forbade the financing of the Labour party out of Trade Union funds. The resolution that was passed simply established a salary of £400 for every member of the House of Commons. The National Insurance Act was prompted by rising unemployment in 1908 and 1909 and laid down two separate schemes of insurance against unemployment and illness, financed by contributions from the workers, the employers, and the state.

These two measures had a marked effect upon the relations of Liberals, non-Socialist Trade Unionists, and Socialists. Naturally the Conservatives rose in fury at the National Insurance Bill; the licking of insurance stamps was decried as a monstrous piece of governmental tyranny imposed upon employers, and the workers were exhorted to refuse payment of contributions. What is more

---

[1] The case owed its name to the secretary of the Walthamstow branch of the Amalgamated Society of Railway Servants, W. V. Osborne, who, in 1907, had successfully sued for an injunction against the levying of such compulsory contributions.

significant is that the Act also displeased a certain section of the working class. The Socialist element in the Unions objected to the fact that the scheme was contributory, since in their view it was the duty of the community to provide employment. There was much more here than a simple desire to get a better bargain. The Liberal Insurance scheme was no more than a refinement of the nineteenth-century doctrine of self-help—with the encouragement of a benevolent state—and was naturally abhorrent to the Socialists, who wished to use the prevailing discontent to bring about a fundamental change in the economic basis of society. Many of the Unions, however, were glad to see the state relieving them of some of their financial burden, and as a consequence Labour M.P.s were divided during the debate on the Bill in the Commons.

On the other hand, the payment of M.P.s had not entirely set right the damage done by the Osborne judgement, since there were many other political expenses that the Unions incurred over and above the support of their own M.P.s. For the next two years the Labour party demanded legislation, but Asquith, knowing that Labour could depend only on the Liberals, hung back and eventually introduced a compromise measure in 1913, whereby Unions might organize a separate political fund to which their members should not be forced to subscribe. This struggle had the effect of weakening the Liberal–Labour alliance and caused Socialists and non-Socialist Trade Unionists to draw closer together again.

If on the political front there was division and uncertainty, it was the extremists who dominated the industrial scene. Prices were rising, wages had not moved, and from the middle of 1910 the country was partially paralysed by a wave of gigantic strikes. An unhealthy atmosphere of violence seemed to have affected every class. The Conservatives and the peers had shown how they were prepared to stretch the Constitution until it almost cracked. The Suffragettes [1] had embarked upon a new campaign of public disturbance in their campaign for votes for women. And now a new movement in militant working class action had appeared.

[1] See p. 424.

Syndicalism, which had developed first in France, held that the Trade Union was the true basis of democracy. It was a natural extension of the same principle that had already been grasped in the 1890s, whereby a strike was no longer simply a weapon to be used against individual employers, but was the means whereby the whole society could be brought to heel.

Trouble began with a four-day railway strike in the area of Newcastle. In September 1910 a dispute produced a general lock-out that involved 120,000 cotton-workers. In November a local coal strike in the Rhondda and Aberdare valleys led to rioting that eventually forced the chief constable of Glamorgan to call for troops. The infection was spreading, and the blazing heat of the summer of 1911 that had helped to increase the anger of the House of Lords had its effect also on the industrial world. A strike of seamen and firemen in June was followed in July by a strike of dockers in the Port of London. In the north similar dock strikes resulted in violent rioting, and on 15 August the troops opened fire and two men were killed. On the same day the Amalgamated Society of Railway Servants called their men out and the government was faced with a general stoppage of railway traffic throughout most of the north of England. Once again troops were used and in the rioting at Llanelly they had to open fire. The winter brought no relief. In December 126,000 weavers were involved in a lock-out. In March 1912 850,000 coal miners struck, but eventually agreed to return after the government had promised to bring in a Bill whereby a minimum wage could be negotiated. In May the dock workers in the Port of London struck again, but this was mainly due to the incitement of extremists and by the end of July the men had agreed to return to work.

For the moment there was a lull. The government had worked ceaselessly, sponsoring councils of arbitration between workers and employers—principally through the efforts of Lloyd George and George Askwith, an official at the Board of Trade. The working class movement had become a question of state, and there were many among both the Liberals and the older Trade Unionists who watched these revolutionary developments with deep misgivings. The leaders of the movement had learnt something of the power at their disposal. Yet the 1910–12 strikes had been sporadic and utterly uncoordinated; a strike in one industry had very often created unemployment in another. It was this realization that now caused the leaders to think in terms of what was later known as 'the Triple Alliance'—an alliance of miners, railwaymen, and transport workers who could present their individual demands in unison and threaten a simultaneous strike in all three industries. It was one more step in the process of amalgamation, and the further it went, the greater grew the possibilities of power that it offered.

The government's struggle with industrial unrest had been carried out against a background of a totally different kind of revolutionary violence. Mrs. Pankhurst and her two daughters Sylvia and Christabel had grown impatient at the government's indifference to their campaign for votes for women and resolved to attract greater attention to their demands. At first they made windows the object of their attack and soon, day by day, Whitehall, Downing Street, banks, and London clubs resounded with the noise of breaking glass. Later, sterner methods were adopted. Houses, schools, and a railway station were set on fire. Pictures in public galleries were slashed, bombs were exploded, and burning rags were dropped through the slits of letter boxes. Arrests naturally followed, but the women in prison went on hunger strike; they were forcibly fed, but often suffered so much harm in their struggles to resist the feeding tube that they were released for fear that they might die. In 1913 the Suffragettes found their first martyr when Miss Emily Davison, after having laid a wreath before Joan of Arc's statue, flung herself to her death under the hoofs of the King's horse at the Derby. The whole movement was something more than a political agitation. It was a psychological revolt, a state of war declared on the whole Victorian world of men.

There seemed to be no respite for the well-meaning Liberal government. They had kept trade free; they had carried through an enormous programme of social reform and had removed one of the major constitutional obstacles to further reforms; they had even attempted to reduce naval armaments. And yet none of the old principles seemed to answer. The clouds on the Continent had grown darker so that they had had to redouble the naval building programme, and now the whole country was in the grip of a series of violent disorders. It was all profoundly disturbing and still new trials lay ahead of them. Ireland was about to play her traditional part on the English political scene.

In April 1912 the Home Rule Bill which Asquith had promised the Irish nationalists was introduced in the House of Commons. The terms of this Bill involved a modification of that of 1893. Fifty-two Irish members were to continue to sit at Westminster, since the Imperial Parliament was to remain the supreme governing body. But for all purposes of internal government the whole of Ireland was to be under a representative government of her own. It was a moderate experimental measure and the temper of Ireland, now quietened by the development of a class of small land-owning farmers, suggested that it might well mean the ultimate solution to the Irish problem.

Unfortunately a new difficulty had by now emerged. There had always been antagonism between Catholics and Orangemen in the past, but the growth of local government during the past few years, and particularly the prosperity of Belfast, had done much to increase the inhabitants' awareness of the gulf between Protestant Ulster and the rest of Ireland. Thus the whole idea of Home Rule was abhorrent to the Ulstermen, for it would condemn them to becoming a small Protestant minority at the mercy of an Irish government. In February 1910 Sir Edward Carson, an Irish barrister, accepted the leadership of the Ulster party, and during the next two years, as the time approached for John Redmond in the Commons to demand his pound of flesh from Asquith, plans were announced whereby, as soon as Home Rule was passed, Ulster would secede and set up its own provisional government. In January 1912 the Ulster party went so far as to obtain permission from the magistrates for the drilling of volunteers.

At this point the question took a new political turn. The Conservatives, now deprived of their last stronghold, the House of Lords, clutched at a straw. Ulster and the Conservative party formed an alliance—already long ago suggested by Lord Randolph

Churchill in 1886. On 26 January, 1912 Bonar Law, who had succeeded Balfour as leader of the Conservatives, announced at a public meeting in the Albert Hall: 'we who represent the Unionist Party in England and Scotland have supported, and we mean to support to the end, the loyal minority [in Ireland],' and in April Carson and Bonar Law were among those who took the salute at a great review of 80,000 Ulster Volunteers at Belfast. The Conservatives were coming dangerously close to fostering rebellion.

Asquith was not prepared to take any immediate decision over Ulster or its private army. He preferred to 'wait and see', and since the House of Lords intended to hold up the Home Rule Bill for as long as their newly defined powers allowed, there followed two years of suspense during which feelings in Ulster and Ireland grew steadily more heated. Various forms of compromise were debated in the Commons, but came to nothing. In Ireland a wave of strikes between 1912 and 1914 led to the formation of a private army of Irish nationalists which was not disbanded and was clearly intended for use against the Ulster Volunteers. After this the government imposed an embargo on the importation of arms, but it did not escape the notice of the Irish that this measure only followed the formation of their own army and not that of the Ulster Volunteers. While the two armies glowered at each other, a compromise was eventually arranged between the Parliamentary parties in March 1914, whereby separate counties in Ulster might vote themselves out of Home Rule for a period of six years. But the decisive area where agreement had to be reached seemed to be no longer at Westminster. The Ulstermen certainly would not accept this compromise; nor would the Irish nationalists, regardless of what Redmond might negotiate at Westminster. 'Ulster is Ireland's', stated one of their newspapers, 'and shall remain Ireland's.'

By now it was clear that the government was approaching a very ugly dilemma. If Home Rule were to be suspended, Redmond's support of the Liberals would be withdrawn at a time when the government's position had already been considerably weakened, and there would be the likelihood of open war with the Irish nationalists. On the other hand, if Home Rule went through, Ulster would fight and units of the British Army in Ireland would have the exceedingly unpleasant task of operating against their own countrymen in order to force them to live under Irish rule. It was this second difficulty that the Conservatives were now committed to exploiting, and, if taken to its logical conclusion, their policy was tantamount to supporting an Ulster rebellion against legislation passed constitutionally at Westminster. They were even prepared to suggest that the Army should refuse to obey its orders; and already at the end of 1913 Bonar Law, speaking at Dublin, had made a pointed reference to James II in 1688: 'There was no civil war. Why? Because his own army refused to fight for him.'

Asquith could certainly be criticized for his inaction during the last two years, but now it looked as though the government was prepared to enforce its will. The Atlantic fleet was dispatched from Spain to the Isle of Arran, and the Secretary for War, Colonel J. Seely, ordered Major-General Sir Arthur Paget, the Commander-in-chief in Ireland, to concentrate his troops in Ulster. There now followed a very odd incident known as the mutiny at the Curragh, the large Army barracks outside Dublin. Paget came to London in order to gain a very remarkable concession from the War Office. Officers who were Ulstermen were to be allowed to 'disappear' for a short time from Ireland; other officers who had reasons of conscience for not carrying out their duty should say so and would be dismissed from the service. On Paget's return to Dublin he put this to his officers and later in the day telegraphed to the War Office that 57 out of 70 officers of the 3rd Cavalry Brigade preferred to accept dismissal.

Asquith now rose to the challenge. He was quite clear in his own mind that no officer could be dismissed simply because he might object to orders that the government might issue in the future. In an Army order he stated that no officer had the right to bargain for any guarantee about orders that might be issued to him at some later date. He hoped to persuade the officers concerned to withdraw their resignations, but their spokesman, General Gough, still held out for an assurance that they would not have to fight the Ulstermen. Scandal, however, became unavoidable when Colonel Seely, supported by the chief of staff, Sir John French, and the adjutant-general, Sir Spencer Ewart, gave on their own responsibility a written guarantee that the Army would not be used to crush resistance in Ulster. Asquith could not compromise with this situation, and Seely, French, and Ewart all resigned. Asquith took over the War Office himself. 'The Army will hear nothing of politics from me,' he said, 'and in return I expect to hear nothing of politics from the Army.'

Probably it will never be known how far the Curragh mutiny was a deliberate attempt on the part of Conservative officers to force the government's hand over the question of Ulster. Both France and Germany drew their own conclusions about the state of the British Army, and Sir Henry Wilson, who had been involved in the incident himself, hurried over to Paris to reassure the French military authorities.

In Ireland the question of Ulster was mounting to a climax. On 24 April the Ulster volunteers carried out a successful gun-running operation which brought them 30,000 rifles and 3 million rounds of ammunition. This news brought a sharp increase in the recruiting rate of the Irish nationalist army. On 26 May the Home Rule Bill had the third reading of its third passage through the Commons. In June the March amendments which satisfied neither side were sent to the Lords. Further negotiations broke down. Redmond would not accept a general plebiscite throughout Ulster, and Ulster herself proclaimed her own provisional constitution.

Ireland was now poised on the verge of civil war and King George, who had been assailed with pleas for intervention on his part, but who could see no decision that would be free of party implications, made a desperate attempt to find a settlement by summoning the Buckingham Palace conference, attended by the leaders of all sides. It lasted four days and came to nothing. A couple of days later an incident in Dublin led to bloodshed. The Irish nationalists had organized a gun-running expedition of their own, and when government troops were sent out to prevent it, the crowd attacked them with stones. The troops opened fire in

Bachelor's Walk and three civilians were killed and thirty-eight wounded.

Then, at the last minute, the whole situation was completely transformed when there sounded a new note in state affairs. On 24 July the Cabinet had reached the end of a discussion on the break-down of the Buckingham Palace conference, when Sir Edward Grey read out to the ministers the ultimatum which Austria had just presented to Serbia. In the words of Winston Churchill, 'the parishes of Fermanagh and Tyrone faded back into the mists and squalls of Ireland, and a strange light began immediately, but by perceptible gradations, to fall and grow upon the map of Europe.'

As with the Cabinet, so it was with the nation. The German invasion of Belgium revealed a greater issue than anything on the domestic scene and all the tumult within was suddenly stilled. The Irish party in the Commons accepted an indefinite postponement of Home Rule. 'We offer to the government of the day,' said John Redmond in the Commons, 'that they may take their troops away, and that, if it is allowed us, in comradeship with our brethren in the North, we will ourselves defend the coasts of our country.' The great strike of miners, railwaymen, and transport workers, anticipated for the autumn of 1914, never happened. The women ceased to set fire to houses and to chain themselves to railings and turned instead to making bandages and pouring cups of tea for soldiers. The war which earlier Liberals had believed their doctrine would make impossible had at last brought the government its release.

THE APPROACH OF WORLD WAR, 1906–14

FEW years in history have been the subject of such controversy as those that preceded the outbreak of the first World War. When it ended, the politicians of the West sought to prove German war guilt in order to justify the policy of reparations imposed by the Treaty of Versailles; the Germans, convinced of the injustice of that policy, sought to prove that all governments had been powerless in the grip of historic forces. Socialists pointed darkly to the machinations of capitalists; pacifists blamed the growth of vast armies and navies. All these views contain an element of truth, yet not one of them gives the single decisive cause of the war, simply because there was none.

An economic explanation has exercised a certain attraction, for once two sides have come to grips it is very tempting to oversimplify the economic rivalry which is perpetual between nations and to explain the outbreak of hostilities in terms of markets and raw materials. Russia's desire to prevent the development of a German economic empire in the Balkans, the growing significance of the Middle East, the clash between British and German business interests—all these were factors that had a considerable bearing on the political scene, but it would be wrong to regard them as decisive simply because they happen to fit in with the events of 1914. Economic competition is too complex for diplomatic alignments to run entirely in accord with it. In the Middle East, for example, it was Russian designs—and not the Berlin–Baghdad railway—that presented the greatest threat to Great Britain, and as late as the spring of 1914 the Anglo-Iranian Oil Company, on which the Admiralty depended for its new policy of using oil-fuel ships, actually came to an agreement with German interests with an eye to keeping out competitors from Russia

and the United States. If the long-anticipated war between Great
Britain and Russia had ever broken out, it would not have been
hard to find an economic explanation for it. The disadvantage of
economic history is that it can explain almost anything. In fact,
none of these stresses alone need necessarily have led to hostilities
—any more than did the partition of Africa, which by all the rules
should have plunged the whole of Europe into war.

What of the political factors? Obviously it is right to look far
beyond the murder of an Austrian archduke and his wife at Sarajevo in June 1914 for the causes of the war. The focal point, however, remains in the Balkans, since war would not have broken
out in 1914 if Austria had not decided to use the assassination as an
excuse for striking down Serbia. On the other hand, the Austrians
could argue that the emergence of Serbia had presented the Habsburg monarchy with the supreme crisis of its existence. After
1905 Russia's defeat by Japan had turned her attention back to the
Near East, where she saw danger in the expansion of German and
Austrian economic interests, and by 1913 the Balkan states—particularly Serbia—were developing fast as political and military
entities of their own. Thus for Austria, Serbia, supported by
Russia, represented a greater threat than ever before. Turkey,
hammered by Italy in 1911 and by the Balkan states themselves in
1912–13, seemed to be finally on the point of dissolution, and the
Austrians, mindful of Gentz's[1] prediction nearly a hundred years
before, feared that the Habsburg Empire might not long survive
Turkey, and resolved to take the bull by the horns and to act
against Serbia while there was still time.

But Austria's plans, which she knew must result in war with
Russia, could never have taken the form that they did if she had
not known that Germany would support her. This German subservience to Austria was due to her inability to find another ally.
It has already been seen how Germany had tried unsuccessfully to
break up the Franco-Russian alliance in the hope of winning over
Russia.[2] If, however, at the beginning of the century she had
allied herself with Great Britain, she would have regained the
diplomatic initiative in her dealings with Austria, and certainly

[1] See p. 298.   [2] See pp. 408–10.

such a treaty with Great Britain should not have been impossible, since there was less likelihood of a territorial dispute between these two countries than between almost any of the Powers. It was here that the folly of William II sowed the seeds of later disaster. By his pointless—and ultimately untrustworthy—support of Kruger and, more particularly, by his insistence on building a large navy, he created a barrier of active mistrust and hostility where there had been little before; thus the chance of an Anglo-German alliance was lost and Germany, lacking other allies, became tied to the demands of Vienna.

How far was the armaments race a factor in itself? All countries had been arming for years, but a prolonged armed peace is not an impossibility, and it was the demands of strategy rather than the manufacture of guns and ships that were immediately relevant to the events of 1914.

Ever since the Franco-Russian alliance of 1894 German generals had envisaged a war on two fronts, and in order to meet this problem the German chief of staff of that time, von Schlieffen, had outlined a scheme which was later to govern all German military thought. France could mobilize more quickly than Russia; therefore, France must be knocked out at once in a lightning campaign, after which the bulk of the German army could be disengaged to march eastwards against Russia. His plan for the rapid defeat of France was based on a gigantic 'right hook' smashing its way through Belgium across the plains of north-east France on to Paris, and preparations for such an assault were made to the last detail, including the building of large railway stations, whose purpose could only be military, close to the Belgian frontier.

The essence of the whole plan was speed, and the drawback to this from the diplomatic point of view was that in any crisis Germany would have to move first in order to get her blow in. As has been seen, German foreign policy was already fatally tied to Austria; before long, it was also to surrender itself to the requirements of the German general staff. This is not to suggest that the German generals deliberately planned the war of 1914-18, although they were certainly responsible for some of the final moves. All general staffs are a professional *élite* whose task is to ensure that they may win the next war. The fault lay rather in the whole framework of German government in which a military staff could gain a preponderance over the diplomats and politicians.

The Schlieffen plan had long been known to the French military authorities, who planned to contain the German thrust, while making their own attack through Alsace-Lorraine. Anglo-French military conversations had started immediately after Algeçiras in 1906, and although they were not in any way binding for either Great Britain or France, an exchange of ideas with the French general staff naturally involved a closer cooperation between the two countries. It has sometimes been suggested that if a firm military alliance had been announced between Great Britain and France, it might have warded off a European war, but this argument ignores the fact that such an alliance would only have strengthened the German claim that they were being encircled and would hardly have frightened off the German general staff, who had a poor opinion of British military power.

These are the economic, political, and military factors that have to be borne in mind when studying the recurrent crises that culminated in war in 1914. In 1906 Germany had just suffered a diplomatic defeat at the conference of Algeçiras, and this was followed by a further disappointment for her when, in 1907, the British and Russian governments succeeded in easing the tension between their two countries by means of a purely local agreement over spheres of influence in Central Asia. Russia gave up direct contact with Afghanistan, both sides agreed to leave Tibet alone, and Persia was theoretically divided into three zones, the northernmost and southernmost to be respectively Russian and British spheres of interest, with a neutral belt in between. The *entente* was not inconsistent with the Anglo-Japanese treaty, since Russia had already, in the same year, come to terms with Japan over the sharing of Manchuria.

For the moment this Anglo-Russian *rapprochement* was hardly a threat to the Central European Powers, although they obviously disliked it. Grey had made it clear that he was not thinking in terms of a Triple *entente* with Russia and France, and the agreement

had made no reference to European affairs, although in his conversations with Izvolski, the Russian Foreign Minister, Grey had
hinted that Great Britain might not object later to the opening of
the Bosphorus and the Dardanelles to Russian warships. Persia
was the crux, and even here it was not long before Russian intrigue at Teheran, the capital, which was situated within their
sphere, began to injure the new Anglo-Russian friendship. In
fact, Campbell-Bannerman's government had some difficulty in
persuading its supporters to stomach an *entente* with a country that
a year before had crushed a short-lived experiment in constitutional rule. At the same time Haldane's visit to Germany in 1906
suggested an improvement in Anglo-German relations for the
moment.

In 1908 a crisis over Bosnia put the new alignments to the test.
The crisis was provoked by the Austrian government, where there
had recently been two important changes. Conrad von Hötzen-
dorf had become chief of the general staff and Count Aehrenthal
Foreign Minister. Both were convinced of the growing danger
from Serbia, who might appeal to the national sentiment of the
Slavs under Magyar rule in Hungary, and when, in July 1908, a
Young Turk revolution took place in Constantinople, Conrad
reckoned that the time was ripe to strike a blow at Serbia. What
he had in mind was the official annexation of Bosnia and Hercegovina, technically still Turkish, although occupied by Habsburg
troops ever since 1878. This would not involve any addition to
the internal problems of government of the Habsburg monarchy,
but would be a disappointment for the Serbs, who had hoped one
day to annex the provinces. The Austrians, noting Germany's
isolation at Algeçiras, reckoned that they could rely upon her to
support them. In this they were right, for Germany remained
harnessed to Austrian policy until 1914.

The main problem was Russia, to whom Serbia would certainly
turn. In September 1908, however, Aehrenthal found that the
Russians were prepared to acquiesce in the annexation of Bosnia,
provided that they could negotiate the opening of the Straits.
This was good enough for Aehrenthal, and while Izvolski was
still on a tour of the capitals of Europe to gain agreement over the

Straits, the Austrians suddenly announced the annexation of Bosnia and Hercegovina. At once this caused a sensation throughout the Continent. The Turks were furious; so were the Serbs who demanded support from Russia, on whose attitude everything now rested. Izvolski considered that he had been tricked by Aehrenthal, since he had gained nothing in his negotiations over the Straits with the British, who were annoyed at Russian intrigues in Persia. In response to the Serbs he demanded a conference, but Austria, sure of Germany's support, had no intention of submitting to this, and for some months Europe seemed to be on the verge of war.

Peace was saved by the fact that while the Austro-German alliance held firm, the opposing alliance of France and Russia did not. 'The moment Russia mobilizes,' Moltke, chief of the German general staff had written to Conrad, 'Germany also will mobilize, and will unquestionably mobilize her whole army.' On the other hand, the French, whose doubts about the strength of the *entente* with Great Britain were increased by the news of Edward VII's visit to Berlin, refused to be drawn in on the side of Russia. It then only needed the presentation of what was virtually an ultimatum from Germany at St. Petersburg and the Russian government, quite unready to wage war single-handed, decided to ignore any further Serbian appeals and agreed to the annexation. The Turks also accepted the situation in return for a money payment and the Austrian evacuation of the Sanjak of Novibazar—this last through the mediation of Sir Edward Grey.

The effect of this diplomatic triumph for the Central Powers was to be seen in public opinion as well as in the chancelleries of Europe. 1909 was the year of renewed naval rearmament in Great Britain and the demand for the building of new Dreadnoughts became something more than a Cabinet matter; it was taken up by the music halls in the cry: 'we want eight and we won't wait!' Various attempts were made after this to slow down the armaments race between Germany and Great Britain, but the Germans always tried to extract a promise of benevolent neutrality in the event of Germany's going to war with another Power and this Great Britain would not accept. 'An *entente* with

Germany', wrote Grey, '. . . would serve to establish German hegemony in Europe and would not last long after it had served that purpose.'

The next crisis was over Agadir in 1911. A rebellion against the Sultan in Morocco had caused the French to march their troops into Fez, the capital, and Germany, convinced that the French absorption of the whole area was imminent, demanded compensation and, as a demonstration of her interest in the matter, sent a warship, the *Panther*, to Agadir. On 3 July Grey told the German ambassador that the British Cabinet could not be indifferent to 'any new arrangements' in this area, but for over a fortnight there was no answer from the German government. During this time, however, negotiations were continuing between France and Germany, and the British Cabinet became concerned lest France might be forced into making concessions to Germany in Africa. Asquith's difficulty was that he had to keep the Radical element in his government with him. Consequently, the decision of Lloyd George, the leading Radical in the Cabinet, that Great Britain could not stand aside at this moment was of the utmost importance. When, on 21 July, the Chancellor of the Exchequer expressed these views in a public speech given at a Mansion House dinner, there were repercussions throughout Europe. A colonial dispute between France and Germany had been transformed into a direct crisis in Anglo-German relations. 'So now', wrote Winston Churchill, 'the Admiralty wireless whispers through the ether to the tall masts of ships, and captains pace their decks absorbed in thought.' In August the tension was so great that Lloyd George was even able to negotiate an end to the great railway strike in view of the imminence of war. Then in the autumn Germany agreed to a French protectorate over Morocco in return for obtaining two pieces of territory in the French Congo, and it seemed that war had been averted.

But from this time on Europe knew no peace. French expansion in Morocco and the weakness of Turkey, demonstrated in the Bosnian crisis, stimulated the Italian government in September 1911 to make a bid for Tripoli. The weakness of the Young Turk government in this Turco-Italian war led to a revolt of the

Moslems in Albania, and this was at once seen by the Balkan states as a chance to extract more Balkan territory from Turkey. In March 1912, Bulgaria had signed a treaty of alliance with Serbia. Over this they had Russian approval, since the recent Turco-Italian war had made it clear to Russia that Turkey was no longer strong enough to hold the Straits, and fear of the Central Powers' ambitions to the east made it essential for Russia to find a substitute who at the same time might not rank as a great Power. In May they were joined by Greece and Montenegro and on 18 October, 1912 war broke out with Turkey. The four Balkan allies struck out over their frontiers and within a month had overrun most Turkish territory in Europe; the Ottoman army fell back on Constantinople, leaving Adrianople to be besieged by the Bulgarians.

These victories for the Balkan states meant nothing less than a fundamental transformation of the Eastern Question. Until now it had been accepted that only attack by one of the great Powers could cause the Sick Man of Europe to die, and since each Power had seen the maintenance of Turkey as a bulwark against the expansion of the others, they had all felt it to be cheaper to keep him alive. But now at last the Sick Man was really dying— through no direct action of theirs—and it was clear that the day of 'replastering', as Gortchakov had called it, was over.

How were the Powers to deal with this new problem? Even before the outbreak of the war they had had serious forebodings. On 10 October, 1912 Austria and Russia had presented a joint note to the Balkan allies, warning them that they would not tolerate any modification of the *status quo*. Now, however, things had gone too far. Russia was concerned over the fate of Constantinople, fearing absolute victory for the Bulgarians. 'The occupation of Constantinople' wrote Sazanov, 'could compel the appearance of our whole Black Sea fleet before the Turkish capital.' Germany saw the emergence of new Powers in the Balkans as a direct obstacle to her plans for economic expansion towards Baghdad. Austria feared the growth of Serbia on her frontiers. Great Britain was alarmed at the prospect of a war into which France might be dragged by her Russian ally and which would unleash the Schlieffen plan with its consequent threat to the Channel ports.

On 3 December, 1912 the Balkan states signed an armistice with Turkey and there followed a conference at London, where the Powers attempted to sort out the new situation. It was in many ways a successful meeting. Berchtold, the new Austrian Chancellor, was determined to prevent Serbia from gaining Albanian territory, which would have given her a port on the Adriatic, and accordingly demanded the establishment of Albania as an independent nation state. Grey supported this Austrian demand even over many points of detail about the frontier, and the new state was established by the Treaty of London in May 1913. Grey's hope had been that he might show the pacific intentions of the *entente* Powers; in fact, he only encouraged the belief among German politicians that they might yet detach Great Britain from her friends.

It was not long, however, before this arrangement among the Powers had led to the outbreak of a second Balkan war. The Serbs, by way of compensation for the loss of Albania, insisted on retaining parts of Macedonia which were supposed to have been Bulgaria's share of the spoil. Bulgaria, confident of her own military prowess, declared war on Greece and Serbia, and at once encountered disaster. Rumania joined her two opponents and marched in from the north, and the Treaty of Bucharest in August 1913 stripped Bulgaria of almost all her gains; the Turks were even able to take advantage of this second war to recapture Adrianople.

The Treaty of Bucharest set the scene which, in a year's time, was to explode in world war. The key to the situation was the new position of Serbia as a political and military power in the Balkans. The dilemma which had haunted Austrian foreign policy for so long could be avoided no longer. She dared not allow the continual growth of such a Power which, with the connivance of Russia, would act as a focal point for all the Slav minorities within the Habsburg Empire; and yet any further absorption of Balkan territory was out of the question. Diplomacy had reached an impasse and from this time Berchtold, strongly influenced by Conrad, the chief of staff, thought purely in terms of war.

From this decision everything else followed. As early as August 1913 they suggested secretly to Germany and Italy that the time had come for a joint attack on Serbia, but owing to Italy's refusal the plan was dropped. If the Austrians could not count on Italy, however, Germany was certainly with them. In October 1913 William II told Berchtold: 'you can be certain I stand behind you and am ready to draw the sword whenever your action makes it necessary . . . whatever comes from Vienna is for me a command.' In both capitals there was a firm belief that the situation in the Balkans could now only mean war with Russia. 'General von Moltke expressed the opinion', wrote Conrad of their meeting at Carlsbad in May 1914, 'that every delay meant a lessening of our chances; it was impossible to compete with Russia in numbers.' This subservience of German policy to Austrian requirements, coupled with the need to have the advantage in time in order to carry out the Schlieffen plan, governed all decisions in this last fateful period. In January 1913 increases in German armed forces had already added £50 million to the German budget—a sum which may be compared with the extra £15 million for which Lloyd George had asked in 1909. In March 1913 Winston Churchill, now First Lord of the Admiralty, had proposed 'a naval holiday' during which neither side would build battleships, but received no answer. The widening of the Kiel Canal was proceeding with speed, and throughout 1914 German firms were calling in all debts to them from abroad.

The tension mounted. In August 1913 France extended her period of military service to three years. In Great Britain measures were taken for the defence of the new naval bases at Cromarty and Scapa Flow. Russia, too, was planning a considerable extension of her armed forces, alarmed by the fact that the Turks had given the command of both Constantinople and the Turkish army to a German general, Liman von Sanders. The reactions of the *entente* Powers, however, remained defensive. Neither Great Britain nor Russia had any wish for war with Germany. They clung simply to the *status quo*; but the tragedy of the situation was that the *status quo* no longer offered security for Austria and her German partner.

On 28 June, 1914 the Austrian archduke Francis Ferdinand and his wife were assassinated at Sarajevo by a Bosnian Serb. Berchtold at once decided to use this as an excuse to smash Serbia, and Bethmann Hollweg, the German Chancellor, gave him the promise of full support from Germany. On 23 July an absolutely overwhelming ultimatum was presented to Serbia. The Serbs agreed to almost every point, but Austria was relentless and on 28 July declared war. Grey at once attempted mediation, and by now both William II and Bethmann Hollweg were advocating caution. But the requirements of the German general staff cut across these second thoughts. 'Moltke says the situation is critical,' the Austrian military attaché at Berlin wired to Vienna, 'unless Austria mobilizes against Russia. Refuse England's new peace offer. . . . Germany unconditionally with you.' On the same day—30 July—Russia mobilized and on 31 July Germany did so also. On 1 August Germany declared war on Russia and, two days later, on France, after the French had refused to give a guarantee of neutrality.

In Great Britain Grey and Asquith were held back by the need to keep their government together. Grey was certain that he could not allow a German victory on the Continent, yet the *entente* did not bind Great Britain to assist France in war and there was no treaty at all with Serbia. Public opinion in Great Britain was almost indifferent to the Balkans—'to Hell with Serbia', one newspaper headline had run—and a British Cabinet that had taken their country to war at this moment would certainly not have survived. So far they had simply rejected another German bid for British neutrality, and on 2 August they warned Germany that they could not allow a German naval attack on France in the Channel. It was the German invasion of Belgium that was decisive for Great Britain. The German government knew that Great Britain was pledged to defend Belgian neutrality, as the British attitude had been made perfectly clear at the beginning of the Franco-Prussian war. It has been suggested that if Grey had spoken out earlier, the disaster could still have been avoided. In fact, it would have made no difference at all. The German general staff did not care whether Great Britain joined France or not; their only concern was to carry out the Schlieffen plan as rapidly as possible and thus the violation of Belgian neutrality was inevitable. That violation solved Asquith's problem for him. Despite the resignations of Lord Morley and John Burns from the Cabinet, the official leaders of the other parties in the Commons gave their support to a policy of intervention, and on 4 August, 1914 Great Britain entered the European war at the side of France and Russia.

In this way the long peace of the nineteenth century came to a close. The *entente* Powers, fighting what was primarily a defensive war, certainly had grounds for pointing to the chauvinism of their enemies. All countries had been prepared for war, but only one of them had consciously and deliberately embarked upon a policy of war—Austria. German diplomacy throughout had been muddled, weakened by William II's determination to have a navy, which had put friendship with Great Britain out of reach and had made her dependent upon Austria. This weakness, together with the technical requirements of military strategy, had deprived her of the diplomatic initiative which it had always been Bismarck's skill to retain. In these respects the Central Powers bore a greater burden of responsibility than their opponents.

One miscalculation, however, was shared by all the Powers and must be mentioned, since it is relevant to the final decisions of the summer of 1914. Not one Power seriously anticipated a long war. In this they were misled by the memory of Bismarck's achievements and the short duration of the two Balkan wars. But in 1914 the diplomatic prelude had been too chaotic, too many great Powers had become involved and the military forces were too evenly matched for any speedy outcome. The machine-gun, the most recent development in military armament, dominated the battlefield and lent itself ideally to defence. The Germans aiming at Paris were halted on the Marne and driven back; the Russian thrust through East Prussia was smashed at Tannenberg, and the armies of the great Powers settled down to digging themselves in. The failure of the diplomats had been followed by the failure of the generals and the whole Continent was now condemned to the misery of a four years' deadlock.

CONCLUSION

IT is never difficult to find reasons for breaking down any date which has come too easily to be accepted as the beginning or the end of an era. In English history 1066, 1485, 1714, 1815 have all been attacked, and it is possible to bring the same criticism to bear on 1914. The new social and political scene of the 1920s was not purely and simply the consequence of the first World War and many of the characteristics of the post-war years were already noticeable even before the turn of the century—the challenge to Great Britain's economic position that must eventually render the policy of Free Trade untenable, the new collectivism in government, Socialism in the Unions, the formation of the Labour party, and the gradual break-down of Victorian sobriety and self-confidence.

Yet there remains a stronger case for 1914 as a dividing line in history than almost any other year. Looking back over a period of time, the historian has to try to single out the main threads of development, but the men who lived through those years cannot always have been aware of their meaning. Certainly the Edwardians were conscious of vast forces of change, but they saw them as superimposed upon an earlier pattern of life which still seemed fundamental. The significance of the first World War is not merely that it completed the destruction of the pattern; it made that destruction apparent to every man alive at the time.

On the Continent the break was even more dramatic and obvious than in Great Britain. A war that culminated in the collapse of the social and political structure of three empires created one of the biggest breaks in the continuity of history. In the past the men who have emerged after some great cataclysm—Napoleon or Cromwell—have usually had a recognizable, albeit obscure, position in the world before their rise to fame. But the men of destiny of the post-war years were of a kind utterly set apart from the preceding period. In 1914 Adolf Hitler had just spent four years in the doss-houses of Habsburg Vienna; Lenin, Trotsky and Stalin had lived for years in the anonymity of secret conspiracy; Benito Mussolini, the most respectable—and, later, the least significant of them—was a young Marxist newspaper editor. They were not merely below the surface; they were of a different world, representatives of a new violence utterly alien to European civilization of the nineteenth century. 'You know that I cannot love Bismarck,' said a Danish historian to a German during the second World War, 'but now I recognize that he belonged to our world.' From a Dane, to whom Bismarck meant the annexation of Schleswig-Holstein, there could be no more profound comment.

It would be pedantic to attempt to put a precise date to this change. 1914 marks the break-down of the existing diplomatic system, 1918 the collapse of Central European society. Perhaps 1917 is the most pregnant date, the year of the Bolshevik revolution in Russia and the entry of America into the war. But the change was not simply political or social. A new atmosphere had swept away the assumptions that had remained unquestioned in the previous century and here Great Britain was as much affected as any Continental country. The long months of appalling conditions in the Flanders mud, punctuated by periods of mass slaughter, were experienced not only by professionals, but by civilians who had become soldiers for the duration. The emotional shock of that experience seared the minds of a whole generation. Whatever their political views, the British officers and men who fought in the trenches, all of them volunteers during the first part of the war, had grown up in an atmosphere of hazy liberalism, believing that life was fundamentally good and reasonable, that prosperity and optimism were the natural condition of mankind. A single day, among many, may be taken as a symbol of that brutal disenchantment. On 1 July, 1916 the battle of the Somme opened with an assault by the British Army on a front of six miles and in the fighting of the first day, during which 60,000 British troops were killed, wounded, or taken prisoner, the flower of a generation nurtured on the peaceful achievement of the nineteenth century was mown down by lines of well placed machine-guns. It would not be entirely fanciful to suggest that from this date the twentieth century had begun.

Appendix i

ROYAL GENEALOGICAL TABLE

N.B.—The family tree has been very much simplified. The dates beneath the Sovereigns refer to their reigns.

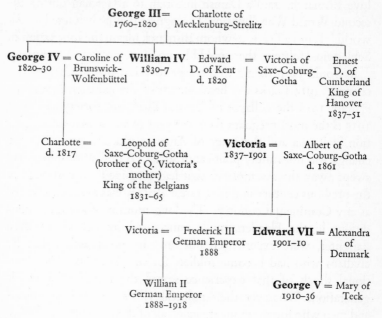

George III= Charlotte of
1760–1820　　Mecklenburg-Strelitz

George IV = Caroline of　**William IV**　Edward　=　Victoria of　Ernest
1820–30　　Brunswick-　1830–7　D. of Kent　Saxe-Coburg-　D. of
　　　　　Wolfenbüttel　　　d. 1820　　Gotha　Cumberland
　　　　　　　　　　　　　　　　　　King of
　　　　　　　　　　　　　　　　　　Hanover
　　　　　　　　　　　　　　　　　　1837–51

Charlotte =　Leopold of　**Victoria** =　Albert of
d. 1817　Saxe-Coburg-Gotha　1837–1901　Saxe-Coburg-Gotha
　　　　(brother of Q. Victoria's　　　　d. 1861
　　　　mother)
　　　　King of the Belgians
　　　　1831–65

Victoria =　Frederick III　**Edward VII** = Alexandra
　　　　German Emperor　1901–10　of
　　　　1888　　　　　Denmark

William II　　　　　**George V** = Mary of
German Emperor　　　1910–36　Teck
1888–1918

444

MINISTRIES, 1815–1914

Ministry formed	Prime Minister	Chancellor of Exchequer	Home Secretary	Foreign Secretary
June 1812	Lord Liverpool	N. Vansittart F. J. Robinson, 1823	Viscount Sidmouth Robert Peel, 1822	Viscount Castlereagh George Canning, 1822
April 1827	George Canning	George Canning	W. Sturges Browne Marquis of Lansdowne (July)	Viscount Dudley
Sept. 1827	Viscount Goderich	J. C. Herries	Marquis of Lansdowne	Earl of Dudley
Jan. 1828	Duke of Wellington	H. Goulburn	Robert Peel	Earl of Dudley Earl of Aberdeen (June)
Nov. 1830	Earl Grey	Viscount Althorp	Viscount Melbourne	Viscount Palmerston
July 1834	Viscount Melbourne	Viscount Althorp	Viscount Duncannon	Viscount Palmerston
Dec. 1834	Sir Robert Peel	Sir Robert Peel	H. Goulburn	Duke of Wellington
April 1835	Viscount Melbourne	T. Spring Rice Sir F. T. Baring, 1839	Lord John Russell Marquis of Normanby, 1839	Viscount Palmerston
Sept. 1841	Sir Robert Peel	H. Goulburn	Sir James Graham	Earl of Aberdeen
July 1846	Lord John Russell	Sir C. Wood	Sir G. Grey	Viscount Palmerston Earl Granville, 1851
Feb. 1852	Earl of Derby	B. Disraeli	S. H. Walpole	Earl of Malmesbury
Dec. 1852	Earl of Aberdeen	W. E. Gladstone	Viscount Palmerston	Lord John Russell Earl of Clarendon, 1853
Feb. 1855	Viscount Palmerston	W. E. Gladstone Sir G. C. Lewis (Feb.)	Sir G. Grey	Earl of Clarendon
Feb. 1858	Earl of Derby	B. Disraeli	S. H. Walpole T. H. Sotheron-Estcourt, 1859	Earl of Malmesbury

Q

MINISTRIES, 1815–1914—*Continued*

Ministry formed	Prime Minister	Chancellor of Exchequer	Home Secretary	Foreign Secretary
June 1859	Viscount Palmerston	W. E. Gladstone	Sir G. C. Lewis Sir G. Grey	Lord John Russell
Oct. 1865	Earl Russell	W. E. Gladstone	Sir G. Grey	Earl of Clarendon
June 1866	Earl of Derby	B. Disraeli	S. H. Walpole Gathorne Hardy, 1867	Lord Stanley
Feb. 1868	B. Disraeli	G. Ward Hunt	Gathorne Hardy	Lord Stanley
Dec. 1868	W. E. Gladstone	Robert Lowe W. E. Gladstone, 1873	H. A. Bruce	Earl of Clarendon Earl Granville, 1870
Feb. 1874	B. Disraeli	Sir Stafford Northcote	R. A. Cross	Earl of Derby (son) Marquis of Salisbury, 1878
April 1880	W. E. Gladstone	W. E. Gladstone H. C. E. Childers, 1882	Sir William Harcourt	Earl Granville
June 1885	Marquis of Salisbury	Sir Michael Hicks Beach	Sir R. A. Cross	Marquis of Salisbury
Feb. 1886	W. E. Gladstone	Sir William Harcourt	H. C. E. Childers	Earl of Rosebery
Aug. 1886	Marquis of Salisbury	Lord Randolph Churchill G. J. Goschen, 1887	Henry Matthews	Earl of Iddesleigh Marquis of Salisbury, 1887
Aug. 1892	W. E. Gladstone	Sir William Harcourt	H. H. Asquith	Earl of Rosebery
Mar. 1894	Earl of Rosebery	Lord Tweedmouth	H. H. Asquith	Earl of Kimberley
June 1895	Marquis of Salisbury	Sir Michael Hicks Beach	Sir Matthew Ridley C. T. Ritchie, 1900	Marquis of Salisbury Marquis of Lansdowne, 1900
July 1902	A. J. Balfour	C. T. Ritchie Austen Chamberlain, 1903	A. Akers-Douglas	Marquis of Lansdowne
Dec. 1905	Sir Henry Campbell-Bannerman	H. H. Asquith	Herbert Gladstone	Sir Edward Grey

APPENDIX 3

DATES OF GENERAL ELECTIONS

Aug. 1818	July 1847	Nov. 1885
April 1820	July 1852	July 1886
July 1826	Mar. 1857	July 1892
July 1830	April 1859	July 1895
April 1831	July 1865	Oct. 1900
Dec. 1832	Nov. 1868	Jan. 1906
Jan. 1835	Feb. 1874	Jan. 1910
July 1837	April 1880	Dec. 1910
June 1841		

By the Septennial Act of 1717 the life of a Parliament could not exceed seven years. The Parliament Act of 1911 reduced this maximum period to five years. An election was normally held at the beginning of every Sovereign's reign, but this practice was not continued after the accession of Victoria.

APPENDIX 4

SPEAKERS IN THE HOUSE OF COMMONS

1802   Charles Abbot (Lord Colchester).
1817   Charles M. Sutton (Viscount Canterbury).
1835   James Abercromby (Lord Dunfermline).
1839   Charles Shaw-Lefevre (Viscount Eversley).
1857   J. Evelyn Denison (Viscount Ossington).
1872   Sir H. W. B. Brand (Viscount Hampden).
1884   Arthur Wellesley Peel (Viscount Peel).
1895   William Court Gully (Viscount Selby).
1905   James W. Lowther (Viscount Ullswater).

APPENDIX 5

IMPORTANT EVENTS ABROAD, 1815–1914

1814–15   Congress of Vienna.
1819–20   Revolutions in Spain, Portugal, Sicily and Germany.
1830   The fall of Charles X and the establishment of the July monarchy in
          France.
1830–1   Revolution in Belgium.
          Unsuccessful revolts in Italy.
1848   The year of revolutions.
          Establishment of the Second Republic in France.
1849   Fall of the Roman Republic.
1851   *Coup d'état* of Louis Napoleon in France.
1852   Establishment of the Second Empire in France.
1854–6   Crimean war.
1859   French assistance to Piedmont in the war against Austria.
1860   Garibaldi's march through Southern Italy.
1861   Unification of Italy except for Rome and Venetia.
          Emancipation of the serfs in Russia.
1861–5   American Civil war.
1864   Schleswig-Holstein war.
1866   Austro-Prussian war.
1867   Establishment of the North German Confederation.
          Establishment of the Dual Monarchy of Austria-Hungary.
1870–1   Franco-Prussian war.
1871   Proclamation of the German Empire.
          Paris Commune.
1875   Establishment of the Third Republic in France.
1877–8   Russo-Turkish war.
1878   Congress of Berlin.
1879   Dual Alliance between Germany and Austria.
1890   Bismarck dismissed by William II.
1894   Franco-Russian alliance.
1904–5   Russo-Japanese war.
1904   Anglo-French *entente*.
1905   First Morocco crisis. Conference of Algeçiras.
1907   Anglo-Russian entente.
1908   Crisis over the Austrian annexation of Bosnia.
1911   Second Morocco crisis. Agadir.
          Turko-Italian war.
1912–13   Turko-Balkan war.
1913   Second Balkan war against Bulgaria.
1914   Outbreak of the first World War.

STATISTICS

A. POPULATION OF THE UNITED KINGDOM

Source: *'Commerce and Industry': Vol. 2. Tables of Statistics*, ed. by W. Page (1919)

	England and Wales	Scotland	Ireland	Total
1811	10,164,256	1,805,864	5,937,856	17,907,976
1821	12,000,236	2,091,521	6,801,827	20,893,584
1831	13,896,797	2,364,386	7,767,401	24,028,584
1841	15,914,148	2,620,184	8,196,597	26,730,929
1851	17,927,609	2,888,742	6,574,278	27,390,629
1861	20,066,224	3,062,294	5,798,967	28,927,485
1871	22,712,266	3,360,018	5,412,377	31,484,661
1881	25,974,439	3,735,573	5,174,836	34,884,848
1891	29,002,525	4,025,647	4,704,750	37,732,922
1901	32,527,843	4,472,103	4,458,775	41,458,721
1911	36,070,492	4,760,904	4,390,219	45,221,615

B. Population of the Colonies

Source: Page, op. cit.

Figures given in thousands

	Canada	South Africa		New Zealand
		Cape	Natal	
1850	2,375	285	121	27
1861	3,206	267	153	99
1871	3,688	583	290	256
1881	4,325	721	403	490
1891	4,833	1,527	544	627
1901	5,371	2,410 [1]	1,109 [2]	773
1911	7,207	2,565	1,194	1,008

[1] After the annexation of Pondoland and British Bechuanaland.
[2] After the annexation of Zululand. See p. 374.

AUSTRALIA

	N.S.W.	Queensland	S. Australia	Tasmania	Victoria	W. Australia
1850	266	29	63	—	76	6
1861	358	35	127	90	542	16
1871	504	120	185	102	732	25
1881	751	214	280	116	862	30
1891	1,124	394	320	147	1,140	50
1901	1,355	498	363	172	1,201	184
1911	1,648	606	412	191	1,316	282

C. Emigration from the United Kingdom

Source: Page, op. cit.

Figures given in thousands.

1815	2	1840	91	1865	210	1890	218
1816	13	1841	118	1866	205	1891	219
1817	21	1842	128	1867	157	1892	210
1818	28	1843	57	1868	138	1893	209
1819	35	1844	71	1869	186	1894	156
1820	26	1845	94	1870	203	1895	185
1821	19	1846	130	1871	193	1896	162
1822	21	1847	258	1872	210	1897	146
1823	17	1848	248	1873	228	1898	141
1824	15	1849	299	1874	197	1899	146
1825	15	1850	281	1875	141	1900	169
1826	21	1851	336	1876	109	1901	172
1827	28	1852	369	1877	95	1902	206
1828	26	1853	330	1878	113	1903	260
1829	31	1854	323	1879	164	1904	271
1830	57	1855	177	1880	228	1905	262
1831	83	1856	177	1881	243	1906	325
1832	103	1857	213	1882	279	1907	396
1833	63	1858	114	1883	320	1908	263
1834	76	1859	120	1884	242	1909	289
1835	44	1860	128	1885	208	1910	398
1836	75	1861	92	1886	233	1911	455
1837	72	1862	121	1887	281	1912	468
1838	33	1863	224	1888	280	1913	470
1839	62	1864	209	1889	254	1914	293

D. Distribution of Seats in the House of Commons

N.B. University seats are included with the boroughs.

Minor rearrangements made between Reform Acts are not shown on this table.

The details of redistribution are given in:

N. Gash: *Politics in the Age of Peel.*

C. Seymour: *Electoral Reform in England and Wales.*

		Before 1832		1832		1867		1885	
England:	County	80		144		172		234	
	Borough	409		327		291		231	
		—	489	—	471	—	463	—	465
Wales:	County	12		15		15		19	
	Borough	12		14		15		11	
		—	24	—	29	—	30	—	30
Scotland:	County	30		30		33		40	
	Borough	15		23		27		32	
		—	45	—	53	—	60	—	72
Ireland:	County	64		64		64		85	
	Borough	36		41		41		18	
		—	100	—	105	—	105	—	103
Total seats			658		658		658		670
Total County seats		186		253		284		378	
Total Borough seats		472		405		374		292	

E. Registered Electorate

Source: Sessional Papers of the House of Commons.
Figures for 1832 are taken from N. Gash, op. cit.

N.B.—After 1832 an elector had to be on the register in order to exercise his right. These registers were not always correct; some electors failed to register; others registered twice and there were many plural voters, but the registered electorate is the nearest that one can get to the figures for the potential electorate enfranchised by succeeding Reform Acts.

		England	Wales	Scotland	Ireland	Total U.K.
1830 *	County	247,000		2,500	19,000†	268,500
	Borough	188,000		1,500	20,000	209,500
		435,000		4,000	39,000	478,000
1832	County	345,000	26,000	33,000	61,000	465,000
	Borough	275,000	11,000	31,000	32,000	349,000
		620,000	37,000	64,000	93,000	814,000
1866	County	501,979	40,654	49,979	172,010‡	764,622
	Borough	499,668	14,358	55,515	25,000‡	594,541
		1,001,647	55,012	105,494	197,010	1,359,163
1868	County	720,435	60,744	76,077	177,460	1,034,716
	Borough	1,158,412	51,589	163,779	47,293	1,421,073
		1,878,847	112,333	239,856	224,753	2,455,789
1883	County	897,043	69,678	99,652	165,997	1,232,370
	Borough	1,582,366	69,366	210,789	58,021	1,920,542
		2,479,409	139,044	310,441	224,018	3,152,912
1886	County	2,362,220	174,360	325,529	631,649	3,493,758
	Borough	1,784,827	69,853	248,829	110,264	2,213,773
		4,147,047	244,213	574,358	741,913	5,707,531

* Figures before 1832 are only approximate, since no registers were kept.
† After the Act of 1829 had reduced the franchise to the £10 freeholder.
‡ These marked changes are due to the Irish Franchise Act of 1850. See p. 269.

F. Textile Factories

Source: W. Page, op. cit.

	Total No. of factories	Power looms	Persons employed
1835	3,156	116,776	354,684
1850	4,330	298,916	596,082
1861	6,378	490,866	775,534
1870	6,807	610,004	907,230
1885	7,465	773,704	1,034,261
1896	9,891		1,077,687
1898	10,767		1,036,570

G. Coal, Pig-Iron, and Steel

Source: W. Page, op. cit.
(output in thousands of tons)

	Coal	Pig-Iron		Steel
1854	64,666	3,070		
1860	80,043	3,827		
1870	110,431	5,964		227
1880	146,819	7,749		1,321
1890	181,614	7,904		3,637
		British ores	Foreign ores	
1900	225,181	4,667	4,293	4,901
1910	264,433	4,976	5,036	6,374
1914	265,664	4,786	4,138	7,835

H. Corn and Livestock

Source: W. Page, op. cit.

Acreage of corn crops in the United Kingdom (in thousands)

	All crops	Wheat
1866	11,494	3,698
1869	12,000	3,982
1870	11,755	3,774
1880	10,672	3,066
1890	9,574	2,483
1900	8,708	1,901
1910	8,371	1,858
1914	8,217	1,906

Livestock (in thousands)

	Cattle	Sheep
1867	8,731	33,818
1870	9,235	32,787
1874	10,281	34,838
1876–82	9,800 *	
1883	10,098	28,348
1890	10,789	31,667
1900	11,455	31,055
1910	11,765	31,165
1914	12,185	27,964

* Average.

I. Prices of Wheat and Bread

Source: W. Page, op. cit.

	Wheat (per quarter), annual average		Bread (per 4 lbs.)
	s.	d.	d.
1815	65	7	10·3
1817	96	11	14·3
1822	44	7	8·3
1831	66	4	10·4
1835	39	4	7·0
1839	70	8	10·0
1845	50	10	7·5
1850	40	3	6·8
1854	72	5	10·5
1860	53	3	8·8
1870	46	11	8·0
1880	44	4	7·0
1890	31	11	6·0
1900	26	11	5·2
1910	31	8	5·9

J. Trade Union Membership

Source: G. Slater, *Growth of Modern England* (1932)

Membership, in thousands, of Unions represented at the T.U.C.

1866	110	1873	509	1880	381	1887	561
1867	155	1874	594	1881	—	1888	568
1868	50	1875	414	1882	404	1889	687
1869	250	1876	455	1883	467	1890	1,593
1870	—	1877	565	1884	488	1891	1,094
1871	289	1878	486	1885	500	1892	1,155
1872	270	1879	412	1886	515		

Number of Trade Unions and Members

	Unions	Members (in thousands)		Unions	Members (in thousands)
1892	1,233	1,576	1903	1,285	1,994
1893	1,279	1,559	1904	1,256	1,967
1894	1,314	1,530	1905	1,244	1,997
1895	1,340	1,504	1906	1,282	2,210
1896	1,358	1,608	1907	1,283	2,513
1897	1,353	1,731	1908	1,269	2,485
1898	1,326	1,752	1909	1,260	2,477
1899	1,325	1,911	1910	1,269	2,565
1900	1,323	2,022	1911	1,200	3,139
1901	1,322	2,025	1912	1,252	3,416
1902	1,297	2,013	1913	1,269	4,135
			1914	1,260	4,145

FURTHER READING

I. ORIGINAL SOURCES

The whole period is rich in original sources and the lists that follow simply include some of the more easily available publications with which the student ought to make acquaintance as early as possible.

A. OFFICIAL DOCUMENTS.

The Law and Working of the Constitution, Vol. II, 1784–1914, ed. by W C. Costin and J. S. Watson.

English Historical Documents (Gen. ed. D. C. Douglas), Vols. XI, XII, (1) & (2).

Hansard's Parliamentary Debates.

The Annual Register (a yearly summary of the main events of the year).

Foundations of British Foreign Policy, 1792–1902, ed. by H. Temperley and L. M Penson.

Selected Speeches and Documents on British Colonial Policy, ed. by A. R. Keith (excluding India).

The Making of British India, 1756–1858, ed. by Ramsay Muir.

B. PERSONAL DOCUMENTS.

The Letters of Queen Victoria.

The Greville Memoirs.

> Charles Cavendish Fulke Greville, grandson of the third Duke of Portland, was Clerk-in-Ordinary to the Privy Council, 1821–59. His diary runs from 1814 to 1860.

The Croker Papers, ed. by L. J. Jennings.

> John Wilson Croker was Secretary of the Admiralty (1809–30).

The Creevey Papers, ed. by Sir H. Maxwell.

> Thomas Creevey (1768–1838), a Whig M.P., was a social and political commentator whose letters and memoranda only came to light in 1903.

Life and Letters of Lord Macaulay, ed. by G. O. Trevelyan (1800–59).

C. Contemporary Writing (Non-fiction).

The Letters of Sydney Smith, ed. by N. C. Smith.
Sydney Smith: *Peter Plymley's Letters.*
W. Hazlitt: *The Spirit of the Age* (1825).
W. Cobbett: *Rural Rides* (1830).
T. Carlyle: *Past and Present* (1843).
H. Mayhew: *London Labour and the London Poor* (1851).
S. Smiles: *Self-Help* (1859).
J. S. Mill: *On Liberty* (1859).
J. Ruskin: *Unto This Last* (1860).
J. S. Mill: *Representative Government* (1861).
J. H. Newman: *Apologia pro Vitâ Sua* (1864).
W. Bagehot: *The English Constitution* (1867).
M. Arnold: *Culture and Anarchy* (1869).
H. Taine: *Notes sur l'Angleterre* (1872).
J. S. Mill: *Autobiography* (1873).
E. Gosse: *Father and Son* (1907).
B. Webb: *My Apprenticeship* (1926).
W. S. Churchill: *My Early Life* (1930).
H. G. Wells: *Experiment in Autobiography* (1934).

D. Contemporary Fiction.

T. L. Peacock: *Headlong Hall.*
Mrs Gaskell: *Cranford.*
    North and South.
B. Disraeli: *Coningsby.*
    Sybil.
A. Trollope: *The Barsetshire Novels.*
    Phineas Finn.
C. Kingsley: *Yeast.*
    Alton Locke.
C. Dickens: *Pickwick Papers.*
    Oliver Twist.
    Bleak House.
G. Eliot: *Middlemarch.*
    Adam Bede.
    Silas Marner.
R. S. Surtees: *Jorrock's Jaunts and Jollities.*
J. Galsworthy: *The Forsyte Saga.*

A. Bennett: *The Old Wives' Tale.*
T. Hardy: *The Mayor of Casterbridge.*
H. G. Wells: *Kipps.*
R. Kipling: *Plain Tales from the Hills.*
W. S. Gilbert: *The Bab Ballads.*

E. MISCELLANEOUS.

Ackermann's *Microcosm of London* (Pelican).
Punch cartoons.
Museums: Victoria and Albert, and Science Museums.
      London Museum in Kensington Palace.
      Osborne House (Queen Victoria's residence on the Isle of Wight).
      Apsley House (The Duke of Wellington's London house).
      The Public Record Office has a permanent exhibition of documents.
Pictures: National Portrait Gallery (including several pictures of the House of Commons before the 1834 fire).
      Hogarth's Election series may be seen in Sir John Soane's house in Lincoln's Inn Fields.
      The state apartments at Kensington Palace, Apsley House and Kew Palace contain a number of interesting portraits.

II. SECONDARY SOURCES

Serious secondary works are legion, probably outnumbering those of any other period of history; full bibliographies are to be found in some of the larger general histories, and I have simply included a few books which may be useful in following up some of the themes touched on in this book.

GENERAL:

R. C. K. Ensor: *England, 1870–1914.*
E. Halévy: *History of the English People in the Nineteenth Century.*
B. Russell: *Freedom and Organization, 1814–1914.*
G. Slater: *The Growth of Modern England.*
E. L. Woodward: *The Age of Reform, 1815–70.*

CONSTITUTIONAL AND POLITICAL:

G. Dangerfield: *The Strange Death of Liberal England.*
H. W. C. Davis: *The Age of Grey and Peel.*
A. V. Dicey: *Law and Public Opinion in England.*
F. W. Maitland: *Constitutional History of England.*
M. Ostrogorski: *Democracy and the Organization of Political Parties.*
E. and A. Porritt: *The Unreformed House of Commons.*
C. Seymour: *Electoral Reform in England and Wales.*

BIOGRAPHIES:

B. M. Allen: *Sir Robert Morant.*
H. C. F. Bell: *Life of Palmerston.*
A. Briggs: *Victorian People.*
Lord David Cecil: *Lord M.*
Lady Gwendolen Cecil: *Life of Robert, Marquess of Salisbury.*
G. Kitson Clark: *Peel and the Conservative Party.*
W. S. Churchill: *Lord Randolph Churchill.*
G. D. H. Cole: *Chartist Portraits.*
Sir E. Cook: *Delane of the Times.*
B. E. C. Dugdale: *Arthur James Balfour.*
S. E. Finer: *Life and Times of Sir Edwin Chadwick.*
J. L. Garvin: *Life of Joseph Chamberlain.* (Concluding volume by
    J. Amery.)
P. Magnus: *Gladstone.*
W. F. Monypenny and G. E. Buckle: *Life of Disraeli.*
J. Morley: *Life of Richard Cobden.*
Lord Newton: *Lord Lansdowne.*
C. O'Brien: *Parnell and his Party.*
J. A. Spender: *Sir Henry Campbell-Bannerman.*
J. A. Spender and C. Asquith: *Life of Lord Oxford and Asquith.*
G. M. Trevelyan: *Life of John Bright.*
                Lord Grey of the Reform Bill.
G. Wallas: *Life of Francis Place.*
C. Woodham Smith: *Florence Nightingale.*

FOREIGN POLICY:

Cambridge History of British Foreign Policy.
A. F. Pribram: *England and the International Policy of the Great
    Powers, 1871–1914.*
R. W. Seton Watson: *Britain in Europe, 1789–1914.*

A. J. P. Taylor: *Struggle for Mastery in Europe, 1848–1918.*
H. W. V. Temperley: *The Foreign Policy of Canning, 1822–27.*
                                 England and the Near East: The Crimea.
C. K. Webster: *The Foreign Policy of Castlereagh, 1815–22.*

SOCIAL AND ECONOMIC:

T. S. Ashton: *The Industrial Revolution.*
J. H. Clapham: *Economic History of Modern Britain.*
Sir K. Clark: *The Gothic Revival.*
C. R. Fay: *Great Britain from Adam Smith to the Present Day.*
             The Corn Laws and Social England.
W. Gaunt: *The Aesthetic Adventure.*
J. L. and B. Hammond: *The Age of the Chartists.*
                 The Rise of Modern Industry.
L. C. A. Knowles: *Industrial and Commercial Revolutions in Great Britain.*
H. M. Lynd: *England in the 1880s.*
S. and B. Webb: *History of Trade Unionism.*
B. Willey: *Nineteenth-Century Studies.*
C. Woodham Smith: *The Reason Why.*
G. M. Young: *Victorian England.*
           (ed.) *Early Victorian England.*

IMPERIAL:

Lord Elton: *Gordon of Khartoum.*
E. A. Walker: *The British Empire.*
B. Williams: *Cecil Rhodes.*
J. A. Williamson: *Short History of British Expansion.*

INDEX

Principal references are given in heavier type. Treaties and Acts of Parliament are listed together alphabetically. Dates after rulers refer to their reigns, and ranks attained after 1914 are omitted.